MIKE MEYERS' CERTIFICATION
Passport ★

CompTIA Security+ ™
Certification Third Edition
Exam SYO-301

T. J. SAMUELLE

New York • Chicago • San Francisco
Lisbon • London • Madrid • Mexico City
Milan • New Delhi • San Juan
Seoul • Singapore • Sydney • Toronto

Cataloging-in-Publication Data is on file with the Library of Congress

McGraw-Hill books are available at special quantity discounts to use as premiums and sales promotions, or for use in corporate training programs. To contact a representative, please e-mail us at bulksales@mcgraw-hill.com.

Mike Meyers' CompTIA Security+™ Certification Passport, Third Edition (Exam SY0-301)

34567890 QFR QFR 1098765432

ISBN: Book p/n 978-0-07-177035-4 and CD p/n 978-0-07-177036-1
of set 978-0-07-177038-5

MHID: Book p/n 0-07-177035-6 and CD p/n 0-07-177036-4
of set 0-07-177038-0

Sponsoring Editor Meghan Riley	**Copy Editor** Robert Campbell	**Illustration** Apollo Publishing Service
Editorial Supervisor Jody McKenzie	**Proofreader** Nancy Bell	**Art Director, Cover** Jeff Weeks
Project Editor Rachel Gunn	**Indexer** Jack Lewis	**Cover Series Design** Ted Holladay
Acquisitions Coordinator Stephanie Evans	**Production Supervisor** Jim Kussow	
Technical Editor Chris Crayton	**Composition** Apollo Publishing Service	

Contents

Check-In   xxi

I Organizational Security   1

1 Organizational Security and Compliance   3

Objective 1.01 Explain Risk-Related Concepts **5**

Risk Control Types   5
    Management   5
    Technical   6
    Operational   6

Risk Assessment   6
    Asset Identification   7
    Risk Analysis   8
    Risk Likelihood and Impact   9
    Solutions and Countermeasures   10

Risk Management Options   11

False Positives and Negatives   12

Use Organizational Policies to Reduce Risk   13
    Security Policies   13
    Network Security Policies   15
    Human Resources Policies   20

Objective 1.02 Carry Out Appropriate Risk Mitigation
Strategies **22**

Change Management Policy   23

Incident Management and Response Policy   23

Perform Routine Audits   24

User Rights and Permissions Reviews   24

Data Loss Prevention and Regulatory Compliance   25

CHECKPOINT 26
REVIEW QUESTIONS 27
REVIEW ANSWERS 29

2   Security Training and Incident Response 31

Objective 2.01 Explain the Importance of Security-Related
Awareness and Training. 32
Accessing Policy Documentation 33
Awareness Training 34
    Threat Awareness 34
Data and Documentation Policies 35
    Standards and Guidelines 35
    Data Retention Policy 38
    Hardware Disposal and Data Destruction Policy 38
    IT Documentation 39
Best Practices for User Habits 40
    Password Policy 40
    Clean Desk Policy 41
    Personally Owned Devices 41
    Workstation Locking and Access Tailgating 42
    Instant Messaging 42
    P2P Applications 43
    Social Media 43
Objective 2.02 Analyze and Differentiate among Types
of Social Engineering Attacks 44
Phishing 45
Whaling 46
Shoulder Surfing 46
Tailgating 47
Pharming 48
Spim 48
Vishing 48
E-Mail Spam 49
E-Mail Hoaxes 49
Objective 2.03 Execute Appropriate Incident Response
Procedures. 50
First Responders 51
Damage and Loss Control 51
Forensics 52
    Collection and Preservation of Evidence 52

Escalation Policy 56
Reporting and Disclosure 56
CHECKPOINT 58
REVIEW QUESTIONS 58
REVIEW ANSWERS 61

3 Business Continuity and Disaster Recovery 63

    Objective 3.01   **Compare and Contrast Aspects of Business**
    Continuity **65**
    Recovery Plans 65
        Disaster Recovery Team 66
        Risk Analysis 66
        Business Impact Analysis 67
        Types of Disasters 67
        Disaster Recovery and Contingency Plans 69
        Documentation 70
        Testing 71
    Objective 3.02   **Execute Disaster Recovery Plans**
    and Procedures **71**
    High Availability and Redundancy Planning 72
        Service Levels 72
        Reliability Factors 73
        Spare Equipment Redundancy 74
        Alternative Site Redundancy 77
    Fault Tolerance 78
        Hard Drives 79
        Power Supplies 80
        Network Interface Cards 81
        CPU 81
        Uninterruptible Power Supply 81
    Backups 81
        Planning 82
        Backup Hardware 83
        Backup Types 83
        Media Rotation and Retention 85
        Backup Documentation 85
        Restoration 86
        Offsite Storage 86
        Online Backup 87

Objective 3.03 Exemplify the Concepts of Confidentiality,
Integrity, and Availability (CIA) 88
Objective 3.04 Explain the Impact and Proper Use
of Environmental Controls 89
  Facility Construction Issues 89
      Location Planning 89
      Facility Construction 90
      Computer Room Construction 90
  Environmental Issues 91
      Temperature 91
      Humidity 92
      Ventilation 92
      Monitoring 92
      Electrical Power 93
  Cable Shielding 94
      Coaxial 95
      Twisted Pair 95
      Fiber-Optic 96
      Wireless Networks and Cells 96
  Fire Suppression 96
      Water 97
      Chemical-Based Fire Suppression 98
  CHECKPOINT 98
  REVIEW QUESTIONS 99
  REVIEW ANSWERS 101

II Cryptography 103

4 Cryptography and Encryption Basics 105
  Objective 4.01 Summarize General Cryptography Concepts ... 107
  Information Assurance 107
      Confidentiality 107
      Integrity 107
      Authentication 107
      Nonrepudiation 108
  Algorithms 108
      Symmetric Keys 110
      Asymmetric Keys 111

Steganography   113
Digital Signatures   113
Basic Hashing Concepts   114
Message Digest Hashing   115
    Message Digest 4 (MD4)   115
    Message Digest 5 (MD5)   115
Secure Hash Algorithm (SHA)   115
RIPEMD   116
HMAC   116

Objective 4.02 **Use and Apply Appropriate Cryptographic Tools
and Products** **117**
Symmetric Encryption Algorithms   117
    DES and 3DES   117
    AES   118
    Blowfish   118
    Twofish   118
    IDEA   118
    RC4   119
Asymmetric Encryption Algorithms   119
    RSA   119
    Elliptic Curve Cryptosystems   119
    Diffie-Hellman   119
    DSA (Digital Signature Algorithm)   120
One-Time Pad   120
Quantum Cryptography   120
Implementing Encryption Protocols   121
Wireless Encryption   121
    Wireless Encryption Protocol   121
    WPA and WPA2 Security   121
Pretty Good Privacy (PGP)   122
GNU Privacy Guard (GPG)   123
S/MIME   123
SSL and TLS   124
HTTPS   125
IPsec   126
SSH (Secure Shell)   127
CHECKPOINT   128
REVIEW QUESTIONS   128
REVIEW ANSWERS   131

5   Public Key Infrastructure 133

Objective 5.01   **Explain the Core Concepts of Public Key**
      Infrastructure **135**
      Digital Certificates 135
      Certificate Authorities 136
      Trust Models 137
            Web of Trust 137
            Third-Party (Single Authority) Trust 137
            Hierarchical Model 138
      Key Management and Storage 139
            Centralized vs. Decentralized Storage 139
            Key Storage and Protection 141
            Key Escrow 142
            Key Recovery 143
            Multiple Key Pairs 144
            Key History 145
Objective 5.02   **Implement PKI, Certificate Management,**
      and Associated Components **146**
      Certificate Life Cycle 146
            Certificate Requested, Issued, Published,
                  and Received 147
            Certificate Suspension and Revocation 147
            Certificate Expiration 149
            Key Destruction 149
      Certificate Renewal 150
      CHECKPOINT 151
      REVIEW QUESTIONS 151
      REVIEW ANSWERS 153

III   **Access Control and Identity Management** 155

6   Access Control 157

Objective 6.01   **Explain the Fundamental Concepts and Best**
      Practices Related to Authentication, Authorization,
      and Access Control **158**

Users and Resources 159
  Levels of Security 160
  Access Security Grouping 160
Access Control Best Practices 163
  Separation of Duties 163
  Rotation of Job Duties 164
  Mandatory Vacations 164
  Implicit Deny 164
  Least Privilege 165
Access Control Models 165
  Mandatory Access Control 166
  Discretionary Access Control 166
  Role-Based Access Control 166
  Rule-Based Access Control 167

Objective 6.02 **Implement Appropriate Security Controls When Performing Account Management** **167**
User Account Policies 167
  Using Appropriate Naming Conventions 168
  Limiting Logon Attempts 168
  Setting Account Expiry Dates 168
  Disabling Unused Accounts 168
  Setting Time Restrictions 169
  Setting Machine Restrictions 169
  Using Tokens 169
Password Management 170
  Password Policies 170
  Domain Accounts and Single Sign-on 171
Security Roles and Privileges 171
  User 171
  Group 172
  Role 172
File and Print Security Controls 172
  File and Print ACLs 173

Objective 6.03 **Analyze and Differentiate among Types of Mitigation and Deterrent Techniques** **175**
Physical Barriers 175
Lighting 176
Video Surveillance 176
Locks 177
  Hardware Locks 177

Man-Trap   178
Access Logs   179
Personal Identification Verification Card   179
Smart Card   179
Common Access Card   180
CHECKPOINT   181
REVIEW QUESTIONS   182
REVIEW ANSWERS   184

7 Authentication and Identity Management 187

Objective 7.01 **Explain the Fundamental Concepts and Best
Practices Related to Authentication, Authorization,
and Access Control** **188**
Authentication Models   188
      Single-Factor Authentication   189
      Two-Factor Authentication   189
      Three-Factor Authentication   189
      Single Sign-on   190
Authentication Methods   190
      Remote Access Authentication   191
      Remote Access Applications   195
      Remote Access Protocols   197
      VPN Protocols   198
Objective 7.02 **Explain the Function and Purpose
of Authentication Services**. **200**
PAP   200
CHAP   200
LANMAN   201
NTLM and NTLMv2   201
Extensible Authentication Protocol (EAP)   201
RADIUS   202
LDAP   202
TACACS   203
Kerberos   203
802.1X   204
Certificates (Mutual Authentication)   205
Biometrics   205
CHECKPOINT   206
REVIEW QUESTIONS   207
REVIEW ANSWERS   209

IV Network Security 211

8 Securing Networks 213

Objective 8.01 **Explain the Security Function and Purpose of Network Devices and Technologies....................** **214**

Firewalls 214
Routers 217
Switches 218
Load Balancers 218
Proxy Servers 219
Antimalware and Content
    Security Appliances 219
        Antispam Filter 220
        Content Filtering 221
Web Security Gateway 222
        URL Filtering 222
Intrusion Detection and Prevention 223
        Active Detection 225
        Passive Detection 226
        Monitoring Methodologies 226
Protocol Analyzers 229

Objective 8.02 **Distinguish and Differentiate Network Design Elements and Compounds...........................** **229**

Security Zones 230
        DMZ 231
        Intranet 233
        Extranet 233
Networking Security Techniques 234
        NAC (Network Access Control) 234
        NAT (Network Address Translation) 235
        Internal Network Addressing 235
        Subnetting 237
VLAN 237
Remote Access 238
        Modems 239
        VPN 240
Telephony 241
VoIP (Voice over IP) 241

Virtualization 242
Cloud Computing 243
CHECKPOINT 244
REVIEW QUESTIONS 245
REVIEW ANSWERS 247

9   Secure Network Administration **249**
Objective 9.01 **Implement and Use Common Protocols** **250**
TCP/IP 250
ICMP 252
HTTP and HTTPS 252
Telnet 253
SSH (Secure Shell) 253
FTP 254
    TFTP 254
    FTPS and SFTP 255
    SCP 255
DNS 255
SNMP 256
IPsec 257
NetBIOS 257
Objective 9.02 **Identify Commonly Used Default**
Network Ports **258**
TCP/IP Network Ports 259
Objective 9.03 **Analyze and Differentiate among Types**
of Network Attacks **261**
Denial of Service 261
    Distributed Denial of Service 261
    Ping Attack 262
    SYN Flood 262
    Flood Protection 263
Back Door 263
NULL Sessions 264
Spoofing 264
Smurf Attack 265
TCP/IP Hijacking 266
Man-in-the-Middle 267
Replay 267
Xmas Attack 268
DNS Poisoning 268

ARP Poisoning 269
Domain Kiting 269

Objective 9.04 **Apply and Implement Secure Network
Administration Principles** **270**
Networking Device Configuration 271
ACL Rules 272
Network Device Threats and Risks 274
Weak Passwords 274
Default Accounts 274
Transitive Access and Privilege Escalation 274
Network Loops 275
Network Device Hardening 275
Secure Remote Access 276
Disable Unused Services 276
Firmware/OS Updates 277
Log Files 277
CHECKPOINT 277
REVIEW QUESTIONS 278
REVIEW ANSWERS 280

10 Securing Wireless Networks 283
Objective 10.01 **Apply and Implement Secure Network
Administration Principles** **284**
Wireless LAN Technologies 285
Narrowband Technology 285
Spread-Spectrum Technology 285
Infrared Technology 286
Wireless Access 286
Site Surveys 287
WLAN Topologies 289
Wireless Protocols 289
Wireless Access Protocol 290
Bluetooth 291
802.11 292
Securing Wireless Networks 294
Access Point Security 294
Service Set Identifier (SSID) 295
MAC Address Filtering 295
WEP Security 296

WPA and WPA2 Security 296
Wireless Authentication Protocols 297
    EAP 297
    LEAP 298
    PEAP 298
VPN Wireless Access 298
Personal Firewall 300
Objective 10.02 **Analyze and Differentiate among Types**
of Wireless Attacks.................................. 300
Data Emanation 300
Bluetooth Vulnerabilities 301
War Driving 302
Rogue Access Points (Evil Twin) 302
War Chalking 303
Packet Sniffing and Eavesdropping 303
WEP IV Attack 304
CHECKPOINT 304
REVIEW QUESTIONS 305
REVIEW ANSWERS 307

V   **Application, Data, and Host Security 309**

11   **Securing Host Systems 311**
Objective 11.01 **Analyze and Differentiate among Types**
of Malware....................................... 312
Viruses 313
    Types of Viruses 313
    File Types That Commonly Carry Viruses 315
Trojan Horses 316
Logic Bombs 317
Worms 317
Adware and Spyware 318
Rootkits 319
Botnets 320
Objective 11.02 **Carry Out Appropriate Procedures**
to Establish Host Security.......................... 321
Host Software Security Baseline 321
Operating System Hardening 322

Operating System Updates 322
Server and Workstation Patch Management 323
BIOS Security 323
Services and OS Configuration 324
File System Security 324
System User Accounts and Password Threats 325
Management Interface Security 326
Host Internet Access 326
Software Access and Privileges 327
Host Security Applications 327
Antivirus and Antispyware Software 328
Antispam Software 329
Host-Based Firewalls 330
Web Browser Security 332
Host-Based Intrusion Detection System 334
Mobile Device Security 335
Protection from Theft 336
Password/Screen Lock 336
GPS Tracking 336
Remote Wipe 336
Device Encryption 336
Voice Encryption 337
Mobile Camera Security 337
CHECKPOINT 337
REVIEW QUESTIONS 338
REVIEW ANSWERS 340

12 Securing Applications and Data 343

Objective 12.01 **Analyze and Differentiate among Types
of Application Attacks**............................... **344**
Web Application Vulnerabilities 345
JavaScript 345
ActiveX 346
Buffer Overflows 346
Privilege Escalation 347
Cookies and Session Hijacking 348
HTML Attachments 348
Malicious Add-ons 349
CGI Scripts 349

Cross-Site Scripting 350
Cross-Site Request Forgery (XSRF) 350
Header Manipulation 351
XML Injection 351
Command Injection 351
Directory Traversal 352
Zero-Day Attacks 352
Internet Server Vulnerabilities 352
FTP Servers 353
DNS Servers 354
DHCP Servers 355
Database Servers 356
LDAP and Directory Services 356
E-Mail Servers 357
Objective 12.02 **Explain the Importance of Application
Security**. **359**
Secure Coding Concepts 359
Input Validation 359
Escaping 359
Fuzzing 360
Error and Exception Handling 360
Transitive Access 360
Application Hardening 361
Application Configuration Baseline 361
Application Patch Management 362
Objective 12.03 **Explain the Importance of Data Security** **362**
Data Loss Prevention (DLP) 362
Data Encryption 363
Trusted Platform Module 364
Hardware Security Module (HSM) 364
Whole Disk Encryption 365
Database Encryption 365
Individual File Encryption 365
Removable Media and Mobile Devices 366
CHECKPOINT 366
REVIEW QUESTIONS 367
REVIEW ANSWERS 369

VI   Threats and Vulnerabilities 371

13   Monitoring for Security Threats 373

`Objective 13.01`   **Analyze and Differentiate among Types**
   of Mitigation and Deterrent Techniques 374
   Security Posture 374
   Detecting Security-Related Anomalies 375
       System and Performance Monitoring 375
       Protocol Analyzers 377
       Network Monitor 379
       Intrusion Detection and Intrusion Prevention Systems ... 379
       Bypass of Security Equipment 380
   Monitoring Logs 382
       System Logs 382
       Performance Logs 383
       Access Logs 384
       DNS Logs 384
       Firewall Logs 385
       Antivirus Logs 386
       Security Logging Applications 387
       Reports and Trend Monitoring 387
       Alarms and Notifications 389
   System Auditing 389
       System Baselines 389
       Auditing Event Logs 390
       User Access Rights Review 391
       Reviewing Audit Information 392
       Auditing the Administrator 392
       Storage and Retention Policies 393
   CHECKPOINT 393
   REVIEW QUESTIONS 394
   REVIEW ANSWERS 396

14   Vulnerability Assessments 399

`Objective 14.01`   **Implement Assessment Tools and Techniques**
   to Discover Security Threats and Vulnerabilities 400
   Vulnerability Assessment Tools 402

Network Mappers 403
Port Scanners 404
Vulnerability Scanners 406
Protocol Analyzers 407
OVAL 407
Password Crackers 408
Honeypots and Honeynets 410
Application Code Assessments 412

Objective 14.02 **Within the Realm of Vulnerability Assessments,**
Explain the Proper Use of Penetration Testing Versus
Vulnerability Scanning **414**
White, Black, and Gray Box Testing 417
White Box Testing 417
Black Box Testing 417
Gray Box Testing 418
CHECKPOINT 418
REVIEW QUESTIONS 419
REVIEW ANSWERS 421

A   About the CD-ROM 423
System Requirements 424
Installing and Running MasterExam 424
MasterExam 424
Electronic Book 425
Help 425
Removing Installation(s) 425
Technical Support 425
LearnKey Technical Support 425

B   Career Flight Path 427
Recommended Prerequisites 429
Security+ and Beyond 429
Getting the Latest Information on Security+ 430

Index.. 431

Check-In

May I See Your Passport?

What do you mean, you don't have a passport? Why, it's sitting right in your hands, even as you read! This book is your passport to a very special place. You're about to begin a journey, my friend, a journey toward that magical place called *certification*! You don't need a ticket, you don't need a suitcase—just snuggle up and read this passport, because it's all you need to get there. Are you ready? Let's go!

Your Travel Agent: Mike Meyers

Hello! I'm Mike Meyers, president of Total Seminars and author of a number of popular certification books. On any given day, you'll find me replacing a hard drive, setting up a web site, or writing code. I love every aspect of this book you hold in your hands. It's part of a powerful book series called Mike Meyers' Certification Passports. Every book in this series combines easy readability with a condensed format—in other words, it's the kind of book I always wanted when I went for my certifications. Putting a huge amount of information in an accessible format is an enormous challenge, but I think we have achieved our goal and I am confident you'll agree.

I designed this series to do one thing and only one thing—to get you the information you need to achieve your certification. You won't find any fluff in here. T.J. and I packed every page with nothing but the real nitty gritty of the CompTIA Security+ certification exam. Every page has 100 percent pure concentrate of certification knowledge!

Your Destination: CompTIA Security+ Certification

This book is your passport to CompTIA's Security+ Certification, the vendor-neutral industry-standard certification developed for foundation-level security professionals. Based on a worldwide job task analysis, the structure of the exam focuses on core competencies in network security, compliance and operational security, threats and vulnerabilities, application, data, and host security, access control and identity management, and cryptography.

Whether the Security+ certification is your first step toward a career focus in security or an additional skill credential, this book is your passport to success on the Security+ Certification exam.

Your Guides: Mike Meyers and T.J. Samuelle

You get a pair of tour guides for this book, both me and T.J. Samuelle. I've written numerous computer certification books—including the best-selling *CompTIA A+ Certification All-in-One Exam Guide*—and written significant parts of others, such as the *CompTIA Network+ Certification All-in-One Exam Guide.* More to the point, I've been working on PCs and teaching others how to make and fix them for a *very* long time, and I love it! When I'm not lecturing or writing about PCs, I'm working on PCs, naturally!

T.J. Samuelle is from Southwestern Ontario, Canada and is an Information Technology consultant.

About the Tech Editor

Chris Crayton is an author, editor, technical consultant, and trainer. Chris has authored several print and online books on PC Repair, CompTIA A+, and CompTIA Security+. He has served as technical editor on numerous professional technical titles for leading publishing companies, including the *CompTIA A+ Certification All-in-One Exam Guide,* the *CompTIA Network+ Certification All-in-One Exam Guide,* and the *Mike Meyers' CompTIA Network+ Certification Passport.*

About LearnKey

LearnKey provides self-paced learning content and e-learning solutions to enhance personal skills and business productivity. LearnKey claims the largest library of rich streaming-media training content that engages learners in dynamic, media-rich instruction complete with video clips, audio, full-motion graphics, and animated illustrations. LearnKey can be found on the Web at www.LearnKey.com.

Why the Travel Theme?

The steps to gaining a certification parallel closely the steps to planning and taking a trip. All of the elements are the same: preparation, an itinerary, a route, even mishaps along the way. Let me show you how it all works.

This book is divided into 14 chapters. Each chapter begins with an *Itinerary* that lists the objectives covered in that chapter, and an *ETA* to give you an idea of the time involved in learning the skills in that chapter. Each chapter is broken down by the objectives, which are either those officially stated by the certifying body or our expert take on the best way to approach the topics.

Each chapter contains a number of helpful items to call out points of interest:

Exam Tip
Points out critical topics you're likely to see on the actual exam.

Local Lingo
Describes special terms, in detail and in a way you can easily understand.

Travel Advisory
Warns you of common pitfalls, misconceptions, and downright physical peril!

Travel Assistance
Directs you to additional sources, such as books and web sites, to give you more information.

The end of the chapter gives you two handy tools. The *Checkpoint* reviews each objective covered in the chapter with a handy synopsis—a great way to review quickly. The end-of-chapter *Review Questions* test your newly acquired skills.

CHECKPOINT

But the fun doesn't stop there! After you've read the book, pull out the CD-ROM and take advantage of the free practice exam! Use the full practice exam to hone your skills, and keep the book handy to check answers. Appendix A explains how to use the CD-ROM.

When you reach the point that you're acing the practice questions, you're ready to take the exam. Go get certified!

The End of the Trail

The IT industry changes and grows constantly, *and so should you*. Finishing one certification is just a step in an ongoing process of gaining more and more certifications to match your constantly changing and growing skills. Read Appendix B, "Career Flight Path," to determine where this certification fits into your personal certification goals. Remember, in the IT business, if you're not moving forward, you're way behind!

Good luck on your certification! Stay in touch.

Mike Meyers
Series Editor
Mike Meyers' Certification Passport

Organizational Security

Chapter 1   Organizational Security and Compliance

Chapter 2   Security Training and Incident Response

Chapter 3   Business Continuity and Disaster Recovery

Organizational Security and Compliance

ITINERARY

○ **Objective 1.01** Explain risk-related concepts
○ **Objective 1.02** Carry out appropriate risk mitigation strategies

	NEWBIE	SOME EXPERIENCE	EXPERT
ETA	3 hours	2 hours	1 hour

As part of an overall company strategy, security should be officially recognized as a critical business objective just like any other important business objective. In the past, the IT department had to define security and access controls for the company network and data. In today's Internet world, corporate management adapts the legalities of the business world to computer networks by ensuring that electronic transfer of information is secure to protect both the company and their customers.

To protect their assets, employees, and customers from security risks, organizations must analyze their security practices to identify the threats to their operations and protect themselves in the most cost-efficient way. Risks to your organization must be assessed based on their probability and impact (both quantitative and qualitative), and then security measures are implemented based on this risk analysis.

To ensure security across the organization, and to assure customers that the company can be trusted, overall security policies must be implemented to include several component policies and procedures that govern how the organization uses computer networks, protects and distributes data, and offers services to customers. Each component of the security policy defines specific security best practices for a particular topic, such as a password policy. These policies and procedures include rules on company Internet use, customer data privacy, company structure, and human resources hiring and termination practices. Many companies, such as those in the financial and health care sector, must now comply with several government regulations for the protection and privacy of customer data in their industry. Organizations must be diligent in crafting their policies to adhere to these regulations, and they must employ risk mitigation techniques to avoid violating these strict standards.

For a company's security policies to be effective, they must be communicated properly to the employees to ensure companywide knowledge and compliance. Rules won't be followed if nobody knows they exist. Many companies make use of consultants to create and draft security policies and procedures, but these policies often aren't communicated to the user community and aren't used. Employees need to be aware of security issues and procedures to protect not only themselves but also the company's services and data.

This chapter describes general risk assessment and mitigation strategies, and organizational policies that should be in place to protect an organization, its networks and data, its employees, and its customers.

Objective 1.01
CompTIA Security+
Objective 2.1

Explain Risk-Related Concepts

R isk management is the act of identifying, assessing, and reducing the risk of security issues that can impact your organization's operations and assets. The following sections describe these risk-related concepts:

- **Risk Control Types**   Risk control types can be separated into three logical divisions: *management, operational,* and *technical.* Each risk control type is a separate but cooperative layer in your overall risk management strategy.
- **Risk Assessment**   Use risk assessments to understand your current risks, their probability and impact, and the solutions to prevent them.
- **Risk Management Options**   Depending on the type of risk, you have several options based on the nature and probability of the risk, and the cost of the solution: *avoidance, transference, acceptance, mitigation,* and *deterrence.*
- **Using Organizational Policies to Reduce Risk**   Your organizational security is critical for ensuring that your company's risk management plan is properly detailed, communicated, and adhered to by your employees in all its activities through the use of policies.

Risk Control Types

Risk control types can be separated into three basic functions: *management, technical,* and *operational.*

Management

Risk management is an ongoing high-level function within your organization. Risk management begins with the risk assessment and analysis to identify the risk of security breaches against company assets, assessing the probability of a risk and estimating its impact, and defining the steps to reduce the level of that risk. The solutions to these risks must be properly analyzed and budgeted to ensure that the probability and impact of the risk are properly factored into a cost-effective solution.

Technical

Technical risk control describes the actual technical measures used to prevent security risks in your organization. From physical access controls (perimeter fencing, security passes, surveillance) to environmental controls (fire suppression, temperature controls), and deep-level network and system security (firewalls, antivirus scanning, content filters, and other network security devices), these controls perform the risk mitigation and deterrence that have been defined in your organization risk analysis.

Operational

Finally, there is an overall operational risk control that must be created and implemented throughout your company. This risk control strategy is concerned with how you conduct your daily organizational business to minimize the security risk to your organization and its business activities. These include company-wide policies that must be created, distributed, and used to educate your employees on how to conduct their day-to-day activities while being vigilant about organization security. Operational risk management also includes user education and vigilant monitoring and testing to make sure your plans are being adhered to by your organization and its activities are constantly analyzed to protect against new threats.

> **Exam Tip**
>
> Management risk controls the high-level risk management, assessment, and mitigations plans that define your overall organization security. Technical risk controls are the technical measures deployed to prevent security risks. Operation risk controls deal with security for your day-to-day organizational business activities.

Risk Assessment

Risk assessment and mitigation deals with identifying, assessing, and reducing the risk of security breaches against company assets. By assessing the probability of a risk and estimating the amount of damage that could be caused as a result, you can take steps to reduce the level of that risk.

Suppose, for example, that your company file server contains confidential company data. The file server asset is considered extremely valuable to the company, its clients, and its competitors. A considerable amount of financial damage would be incurred by the company in the event of loss, damage, or theft of the server. The risks and threats posed to the server could be physical—such as damage caused by a natural disaster or a hardware malfunction—or nonphysical—such as viruses, network hacker attacks, and data theft if the server is easily accessible through a network. The costs associated with reducing these risks are mitigated by the potential costs of losing data on the file server.

To help reduce these risks, you can take several actions:

- Use multiple hard drives and power supplies for fault tolerance.
- Implement a good backup scheme.
- Protect the server through physical security such as door access controls.
- Install antivirus software.
- Disable unused network services and ports to prevent network attacks.

To identify the risks that pose a security threat to your company, you can perform a risk analysis on all parts of the company's resources and activities. By identifying risks and the amount of damage that could be caused by exploiting a system vulnerability, you can choose the most efficient methods for securing the system from those risks. Risk analysis and assessment can identify where too little or even too much security exists, and where the cost of security is more than the cost of the loss because of compromise. Ultimately, risk analysis and assessment is a cost/benefit analysis of your security infrastructure.

Risk analysis and assessment involves three main phases:

- **Asset identification**   Identify and quantify the company's assets.
- **Risk analysis**   Identify and assess the possible security vulnerabilities and threats.
- **Risk likelihood and impact**   Rate your various risks according to how likely they are to occur and their impact.
- **Cost of solutions**   Identify a cost-effective solution to protect assets.

Asset Identification

Company assets can include physical items such as computer and networking equipment, and nonphysical items such as valuable data. *Asset identification* involves identifying both types of assets and evaluating their worth. Asset values must be established beyond the mere capital costs—acquisition costs, maintenance, the value of the asset to the company, the value of the asset to a competitor, what clients would pay for the asset or service, the cost of replacement, and the cost if the asset were compromised should also be considered. For example, a list of a company's clients can be easily re-created from backup if the original is lost or destroyed, but if the list finds its way into the hands of a competitor, the resulting financial damage could be devastating. Ultimately, the value of the assets you're trying to protect drives the costs involved in securing that asset.

Risk Analysis

Risk analysis deals with identifying, assessing, and reducing the risk of security breaches against company assets. By assessing the probability of a risk and estimating the amount of damage that could be caused as a result, you can take steps to reduce the level of that risk. To identify the risks that pose a security threat to your company, you can perform a risk analysis on all parts of the company's resources and activities.

Quantitative risk analysis is a strict dollar-amount calculation of the exact cost of the loss or a specific company asset because of a disaster. This is a straightforward method that can be applied for simple situations. For example, if a hard drive in a RAID (redundant array of inexpensive disks) system fails, it is simply replaced with a new hard drive. There is no loss of data because the information is rebuilt from the rest of the array.

Qualitative risk analysis must take into account tangible and several other, intangible factors in determining costs. Consider a denial-of-service network attack on your company's web store server that causes four hours of downtime and corrupted data on a back-end transactional database. You are not only faced with the monetary loss from your web site being down and customers not being able to order products for many hours, but the time it takes to perform countermeasures against the attack, get your web server back into operation, recover any lost data from your database, and also take into account data that cannot be recovered. The costs in this scenario include the manpower hours in recovering from the attack, the loss of orders from the web store during the downtime, monetary loss from corrupted data that cannot be restored, and even potential loss of future business from disgruntled customers.

Exam Tip

Quantitative risk analysis is a dollar-amount calculation of the exact cost of the loss due to a disaster. Qualitative risk analysis includes intangible factors, such as loss of potential business, in determining costs.

There are additional risks often ignored in a risk analysis in regard to virtualization technology and cloud computing. Using virtualization technology, a computer can host multiple instances of an operating system environment all running from the same computer on the same hardware. The consolidation of many different types of services on the same hardware creates a security risk that if that system is hacked or fails, it will take down every virtualized server that runs on the system.

The risk of a single point of failure for cloud computing is very similar. Cloud computing aggregates services in a virtual environment where all aspects of the cloud, from the platform, to the software, to the entire infrastructure, are based on a distributed web service. If the cloud service fails, you may lose all access to your services and data until the cloud service is restored.

Travel Assistance
See Chapter 8 for more detailed information on virtualization and cloud computing.

Overall, your risk assessment must be wide in scope to use both quantitative and qualitative analysis to determine your risk factors from all aspects of your company's operations.

Risk Likelihood and Impact

As part of your risk assessment and mitigation strategy, you will need to rate your various risks according to how likely they are to occur and their impact. The risks more likely to occur and their calculated impact are ranked toward the top of the list to indicate where solution efforts should be most concentrated. For example, within a company that already practices strict physical security and access control methods, the priority of risk scenarios could be geared toward nonphysical threats, such as viruses and network hackers, because this would have a greater impact on their ability to operate.

The likelihood and impact of a risk has a strong measure on your cost analysis for budgeting funds for risk countermeasures and mitigation. A calculation used to determine this factor is *annual loss expectancy (ALE)*. You must calculate the chance of a risk occurring, sometimes called the *annual rate of occurrence (ARO)*, and the potential loss of revenue based on a specific period of downtime, which is called the *single loss expectancy (SLE)*. By multiplying these factors together, you arrive at the ALE. This is how much money you expect to lose on an annual basis because of the impact from an occurrence of a specific risk. Using the ALE, you can properly budget the security measures to help protect against that particular risk from occurring.

For example, if a file server is at 25 percent risk of being infected by a virus, its ARO is 0.25. During the time the file server is down and data is being recovered, none of your employees can work. For a downtime of two hours, you calculate $8000 of lost time and productivity. By multiplying these two factors (0.25 and $8000), you get an ALE value of $2000. You can use this amount to budget for additional antivirus software protection to help lower this risk and save money in your next annual budget.

Exam Tip
The Annual Loss Expectancy (ALE) is calculated by multiplying the annual rate of occurrence (ARO) and the single loss expectancy (SLE).

Solutions and Countermeasures

After you've assessed and defined risk and management procedures, you'll have collected the following information:

- **Asset identification**   A list of your assets, including physical assets such as server hardware and hard disks, and nonphysical assets such as the valuable customer data stored on the hard drives.
- **Threat profiles**   A list of every possible threat against your assets.
- **Risks**   An evaluation of the potential risk of each threat—such as the risk of a malicious hacker being able to compromise a database server. If the server itself is compromised, but the valuable and confidential data on the database server is leaked by the hacker, the risk is far greater for this asset.
- **Impact**   The potential loss in the event your assets are attacked or compromised by threats, including the asset's capital value (such as hardware cost), plus how much it will cost to replace that asset, especially lost customer data. A failed hard drive can be a relatively low cost to recoup, but if you have no backup of customer data that was stored on that hard drive, you might have lost tens of thousands of dollars' worth of data.
- **Probability**   The risks more likely to occur are ranked toward the top of the list to indicate where solution efforts should be most concentrated. For example, within a company that already practices strict physical security and access control methods, the priority of risk scenarios could be geared toward nonphysical threats, such as viruses and network hackers.

Once this process is complete, a list of solutions and countermeasures to protect against each threat should be reviewed and documented. Examine your solutions with respect to what current security measures are in place and what needs to be done to make them more effective. Ensure that the functionality and effectiveness of the solution is sufficient to reduce the risk of compromise. Purchasing a fire extinguisher for the server room could seem like a fire-prevention solution, for example, but only an automatic fire detection and suppression system can fully protect a room full of servers from a large, out-of-control fire that occurs in the middle of the night. Similarly, buying a firewall to protect your servers from outside Internet traffic is a great idea for network security, but if the network administrator hasn't been trained to configure it properly, the firewall might not be effective at all.

Any solutions must be cost-effective to ensure that the benefits of the solution are in line with the actual value of the assets. For example, there's no point in spending $100,000 on a security solution to protect data that's worth only $40,000 to the company if it's lost or damaged. Ongoing maintenance also needs to be factored into the final calculations. Although a large initial cost is incurred for a tape backup solution, costs of purchasing new tapes as they're needed will be ongoing, and you'll pay for offsite storage of used tapes.

Exam Tip
The cost of the risk management solution shouldn't exceed the value of the asset if it's lost. For example, if a file server and its data are valued at $35,000 and the proposed security solution to protect it costs $150,000, then it doesn't make sense to implement the proposed solution.

Risk Management Options

When you have completed your risk analysis, and depending on your operations and budgets, you have several options for dealing with each risk:

- **Avoidance**   Depending on the type of risk, you can opt to avoid the risk altogether. This option is typically used when the cost to mitigate a threat, especially if it is unlikely or has little impact, means it is not worth implementing. This can also mean you take certain steps to avoid a risk altogether, such as disabling a rarely used feature in a web application because the benefits aren't worth the great security risk it causes.

- **Transference**   The organization can also transfer or "pass on" the risk to a third party, for example, an insurance company who will pay out your damages in the event a certain risk occurs, or trusting a third-party provider to store your offsite backup media.

- **Acceptance**   In most cases in information security, there is a level of risk that must be accepted with any type of information system network. For example, your organization may want to sell its products directly from their web site, and the potential revenues greatly outweigh the potential network security risks involved. On the other hand, if the risk is deemed too great in comparison to the benefit, the service may not be offered, or additional mitigation techniques required.

- **Mitigation**   Based on your risk analysis, there are specific risks that must be mitigated using countermeasures—for example, implementing a network firewall for network security, installing desktop and server antivirus protection, and implementing fault-tolerant systems to mitigate the impact of failed hardware.

- **Deterrence**   Risk deterrence is an extension of mitigation in which more active levels of control are used to deter security threats. On the network level, this can include intrusion detection systems and threat prevention devices that proactively monitor and deter network and system attacks. This can also include honeypot devices that attract network attacks to specific "false" devices and services to ward away attacks from vital networking and service infrastructure.

False Positives and Negatives

A *false positive* is a legitimate action that is perceived as a risk or threat. A false positive is a term often used in e-mail security scanning to indicate a legitimate message that was classified as a security issue such as spam, content violation, or poor reputation check. False positives can be applied to almost any type of security scenario where security controls block what is essentially a legitimate action. For example, an intrusion detection system may send out constant alarms even though the traffic it's detecting is legitimate traffic. The administrator becomes lax in responding to alarms because he knows they are more likely than not false positives. This can allow other more serious intrusions to be ignored.

Occasional false positives are a fact of life when it comes to strict security controls, but too many can become difficult to manage and put a lot of burden on both the administrators and the end users to manage. Excessive false positives in your environment means that your security controls are too aggressive and need to be reconfigured.

Most security systems can be fine-tuned to allow future attempts from the legitimate action, as long as you can verify it is being performed by an authorized user or process in a secure way. In the example of legitimate e-mail messages being blocked, end users can create lists of trusted known senders so that future messages from the same sender can bypass certain types of scanning such as content filtering. Intrusion detection systems can have their thresholds redefined to a lower value to prevent an increase in false positives.

Security controls that are not aggressive enough can result in false negatives. A *false negative* is a security issue that has passed your security controls as legitimate. For example, an e-mail message that is spam or contains illegal content may pass through your e-mail security controls and content filters as if it were legitimate mail. An intrusion detection system may let through a denial-of-service attack because it detects the event as normal operation.

Security controls require continuous baselining and adjustments to properly set their thresholds to detect the difference between normal behavior and serious security issues. The baseline provides you with a report of what is considered normal activity, and then you set your thresholds on your security controls to detect anomalies to that normal activity. This period of recording baselines and making configuration adjustments can take several weeks to result in ideal security thresholds, but this ensures that you will have fewer issues with false positives and negatives in the future.

Exam Tip

A false positive is a legitimate action that is perceived as a risk or threat. A false negative is a security issue that has passed your security controls as a legitimate action.

Use Organizational Policies to Reduce Risk

To provide effective security, security policy and procedure creation must begin at the top of an organization with senior management. These policies and procedures must then flow throughout the company to ensure that security is useful and functional at every level of the organization. Understanding company security must begin with an understanding of the basic laws, regulations, and legal liability issues to which the company must adhere to protect the company and its assets, as well as the employees and customers.

Security policies and procedures are official company communications that are created to ensure that a standard level of security guidelines exists across the entire organization. These policies define how the employees interact with company computer systems to perform their job functions, how to protect the computer systems and their data, and how to service the company's clients properly. The upcoming sections outline policies and procedures in the following areas:

- Security policies
- Network access policies
- Human resources policies

Security Policies

The following policies concern general organizational security, including physical access, access control to data, and security through proper organizational structures and data security principles.

Physical Access Security Policy   As part of your organization's overall access control policy, you must have a strong physical access policy and ensure that all employees are educated on its use.

Depending on the security level of the company, physical security may include guarded or nonguarded entrances. Even on guarded premises, the use of security access cards makes sure that only identified and authenticated employees can enter a facility. Security access cards are coded with the authorization level of the user, who will be able to access only areas of the facility that are required by his job function. For example, only network and systems administrators would be able to access a server and networks communications room with their access card.

Employees must be trained to always close automatically locking doors behind them, and not allow other, unidentified people to follow them through. Most security access cards have photographs on them to further identify users in the event they are challenged for their identity. Employees must be encouraged to report suspicious individuals within the premises who are unfamiliar and do not have proper identification.

A published organizational security policy for physical access allows your employees to have proper knowledge of security procedures and be equally active in the responsibility for physical security.

Access Control Policies   The following access control policies help provide a consistent organizational structure and procedures to prevent internal fraud and corruption in your organization.

- **Least privilege**   The *least privilege* principle grants users only access rights they need to perform their job functions. This requires giving users the least amount of access possible to prevent them from abusing more powerful access rights.

- **Separation of duties**   A *separation of duties* ensures that one single individual isn't tasked with high-security and high-risk responsibilities. Certain critical responsibilities are separated between several users to prevent corruption.

- **Job rotation**   *Job rotation* provides improved security because no employee retains the same amount of access control for a particular responsibility for a period of time. This prevents internal corruption from employees that take advantage of their long-term position and security access.

- **Mandatory vacations**   *Mandatory vacation* policies require employees to use their vacations at specific times of year or use all of their vacation days allotted for a single year. This policy helps detect security issues with employees, such as fraud or other internal hacking activities, because the anomalies might surface while the user is away.

Travel Assistance
These access control concepts and best practices are discussed in more detail in Chapter 6.

Network Security Policies

Several policies provide standard guidelines for network security within a company and encompass areas such as the Internet and internal network use, data privacy, security incident response, human resources issues, and document security.

Acceptable Use Policy   An *acceptable use policy* is a set of established guidelines for the appropriate use of computer networks within an organization. The policy is a written agreement, read and signed by employees, that outlines the terms, conditions, and rules of the Internet and internal network use for the company.

An acceptable use policy helps educate employees about the kinds of tools they will use on the network and what they can expect from those tools. The policy also helps to define boundaries of behavior and, more critically, specify the consequences of violating those boundaries. The policy also specifies the actions that management and the system administrators may take to maintain and monitor the network for unacceptable use, and they include the general worst-case consequences or responses to specific policy violation situations.

Exam Tip
An acceptable use policy is a set of established guidelines for the appropriate use of computer networks within an organization.

Developing an acceptable use policy for your company's computer network is extremely important for organizational security and to limit legal liability in the event of a security issue. Acceptable use policies should cover the following issues:

- **Legality**   The company's legal department needs to approve the policy before it's distributed for signing. The policy will be used as a legal document to ensure that the company isn't legally liable for any type of Internet-related incident and any other transgressions, such as cracking, vandalism, and sabotage.

- **Uniqueness to your environment** The policy should be written to cover the organization's specific network and the data it contains. Each organization has different security concerns—for example, a medical facility needs to protect data that differs significantly from that of a product sales company.
- **Completeness** Beyond rules of behavior, your policy should also include a statement concerning the company's position on Internet use.
- **Adaptability** Because the Internet is constantly evolving, your policy will need to be updated as new issues arise. You can't anticipate every situation, so the acceptable use policy should address the possibility of something happening that isn't outlined.
- **Protection for employees** If your employees follow the rules of the acceptable use policy, their exposure to questionable materials should be minimized. In addition, it can protect them from dangerous Internet behavior, such as giving out their names and e-mail addresses to crackers using social engineering techniques.

The focus of an acceptable use policy should be on the responsible use of computer networks. Such networks include the Internet—including web, e-mail, and instant messaging access—and the company intranet. Most acceptable use policies contain the following components:

- A description of the strategies and goals to be supported by Internet access in the company
- A statement explaining the availability of computer networks to employees
- A statement explaining the responsibilities of employees when they use the Internet
- A code of conduct governing behavior on the Internet
- A description of the consequences of violating the policy
- A description of what constitutes acceptable and unacceptable use of the Internet
- A description of the rights of individuals using the networks in your company, such as user privacy
- A disclaimer absolving the company from responsibility under specific circumstances
- A form for employees to sign indicating their agreement to abide by the policy

---

Travel Advisory

Many company web sites contain an acceptable use policy or Terms of Use statement that protects the company from any liability from users of the site.

Due Care, Due Diligence, and Due Process   *Due care, due diligence,* and *due process* are terms that apply to the implementation and enforcement of companywide security policies. A company practices *due care* by taking responsibility for all activities that take place in corporate facilities. A company practices *due diligence* by implementing and maintaining these security procedures at all times to protect the company's facilities, assets, and employees. Although many companies outline plans for security policies and standards, they often never officially implement them, or the information isn't properly shared with the employees. Without training, guides, and manuals, and without employee input and feedback, no guidance comes from management regarding the policies and their use.

By practicing due care, the company shows it has taken the necessary steps to protect itself and its employees. By practicing due diligence, the company ensures that these security policies are properly maintained, communicated, and implemented. If the company doesn't follow proper due care and due diligence initiatives, it might be considered legally negligent if company security and customer data are compromised.

Due process ensures that in the event of a security issue by an employee, the employee receives an impartial and fair inquiry into the incident to ensure the employee's rights are not being violated. If, in the course of an investigation and inquiry, the employee's rights are violated, the company may face legal ramifications via lawsuits or governmental employment tribunals.

Exam Tip

Due care is taking the necessary responsibility and steps to protect the company and the employees. Due diligence ensures these security policies are properly implemented. Due process ensures an impartial and fair inquiry into violations of company policies.

Privacy Policy   *Privacy policies* are agreements for protecting individually identifiable information in an online or electronic commerce environment. A company engaged in online activities or e-commerce has a responsibility to adopt and implement a policy for protecting the privacy of personally identifiable information. Organizations should also take steps to ensure online privacy when interacting with other companies, such as business partners.

The following recommendations pertain to implementing privacy policies:

- A company's privacy policy must be easy to find, read, and understand, and it must be available prior to or at the time that individually identifiable information is collected or requested.

- The policy needs to state clearly what information is being collected; the use of that information; possible third-party distribution of that information; the choices available to an individual regarding collection, use, and distribution of the collected information; a statement of the organization's commitment to data security; and what steps the organization takes to ensure data quality and access.

- The policy should disclose the consequences, if any, of an individual's refusal to provide information.

- The policy should include a clear statement of what accountability mechanism the organization uses, such as procedures for dealing with privacy breaches, including how to contact the organization and register complaints.

- Individuals must be given the opportunity to exercise choice regarding how personally identifiable information collected from them online could be used when such use is unrelated to the purpose for which the information was collected. At a minimum, individuals should be given the opportunity to opt out of such use.

- Where third-party distribution of information is collected online from the individual, unrelated to the purpose for which it was collected, the individual should be given the opportunity to opt out.

- Organizations creating, maintaining, using, or disseminating personally identifiable information should take appropriate measures to assure its reliability and should take reasonable precautions to protect the information from loss, misuse, or alteration.

Each company must evaluate its use of the Internet to determine the type of privacy policy it needs to protect all involved parties. The privacy policy will protect the company from legal issues, raising customers' comfort levels regarding the protection of their information. A privacy policy should include the following elements:

- **Information collection**   Collect, use, and exchange only data pertinent to the exact purpose, in an open and ethical manner. The information collected for one purpose shouldn't be used for another. Notify consumers of information you have on them, as well as its proposed use, handling, and enforcement policies.

- **Direct marketing**   The company can use only non–personally identifiable information for marketing purposes and must certify that the customers' personal information won't be resold to third-party marketing firms.

- **Information accuracy**   Ensure the data is accurate, timely, and complete, and that it has been collected in a legal and fair manner. Allow customers the right to access, verify, and change their information in a timely, noncumbersome fashion. Inform customers of the data sources and allow them the option of removing their names from the marketing lists.

- **Information security**   Apply security measures to safeguard the data on databases. Establish employee training programs and policies on the proper handling of customer data. Limit the access to a need-to-know basis on personal information and divide the information, so no one employee or unit has the whole picture. Follow all government regulations concerning data handling and privacy.

Exam Tip

Privacy policies must be easy to find and provide information on how to opt out of any use of personal information.

Service Level Agreement Policy   A *service level agreement (SLA)* is an understanding among a supplier of services and the users of those services that the service in question will be available for a certain percentage of time. For example, a web-hosting company could have an SLA with its customers that states the web servers that host the customer's web pages will be available 99.8 percent of the time. If the service level drops below this percentage, the customer might be reimbursed for business lost during the downtime.

The SLA policy describes the policies and procedures that a company performs to support the SLA agreement, including the services performed to preserve the SLA uptime and the contingency plans and communications that must be performed if the availability of the organization's services exceeds the thresholds agreed to in the SLA.

Human Resources Policies

A company's human resources (HR) department is an important link regarding company and employee security. The HR department is responsible for hiring employees, ensuring employees conform to company codes and policies during their term of employment, and maintaining company security in case of an employee termination. The following sections outline the responsibility of human resources during the three phases of the employment cycle.

Hiring Policy   When hiring employees for a position within the company, the HR department is responsible for the initial employee screening. This usually takes place during the first interview: an HR representative meets with the employee to discuss the company and to get a first impression of the employee's personality, gauging whether this person would fit into the company's environment. This interview generally is nontechnical and personality-based. Further interviews are usually more skill-oriented and are conducted by the department advertising the position. The employee could possess excellent technical skills for the position, but his personality and communications skills might not be conducive to integration with the work environment.

During the interview process, HR also conducts background checks of the applicant and examines and confirms her educational and employment history. Reference checks are also performed, where HR can obtain information on the applicant from a third party to help confirm facts about the person's past. Depending on the type of company or institution, such as the government or the military, the applicant might have to go through security clearance checks or even health and drug testing.

To protect the confidentiality of company information, the applicant is usually required to sign a nondisclosure agreement, which legally prevents the applicant from disclosing sensitive company data to other companies in case of her termination. These agreements are particularly important with high-turnover positions, such as contract or temporary employment.

When an employee is hired, the company also inherits that person's personality quirks or traits. A solid hiring process can prevent future problems with new employees.

Codes of Conduct and Ethics Policy   The HR department is also responsible for outlining a company's policy regarding codes of conduct and ethics. The codes are a general list of what the company expects from its employees in terms of everyday conduct—dealing with fellow employees, managers, and subordinates, including people from outside the company, such as customers and clients.

This code of conduct could include restrictions and policies concerning drug and alcohol abuse, theft and vandalism, and violence in the workplace. If an employee transgresses any of these codes of conduct and ethics, that employee could be disciplined, suspended, or even terminated, depending on the severity of the infraction.

Termination Policy   The dismissal of employees can be a stressful and chaotic time, especially because terminations can happen quickly and without notice. An employee can be terminated for a variety of reasons, such as performance issues; personal and attitude problems; or legal issues such as sabotage, espionage, or theft. Or the employee could be leaving to work for another company. The HR department needs to have a specific set of procedures ready to follow in case an employee resigns or is terminated. Without a step-by-step method of termination, some areas might have been ignored during the process that compromise company security.

A termination policy should exist for each type of situation. For example, you might follow slightly different procedures for terminating an employee who's going to work for an industry-unrelated position with another company than with an employee who's going to work for a direct competitor. In the latter case, the employee might be considered a security risk if he remains on the premises for his two-week notice period, where he could transmit company secrets to the competition.

A termination policy should include the following procedures for the immediate termination of an employee:

- **Securing work area**   When the termination time has been set, the employee in question should be escorted from his workstation area to the HR department. This prevents him from using his computer or other company resources once notice of termination is given. His computer should be turned off and disconnected from the network. When the employee returns to his desk to collect personal items, someone should be with him to ensure that no private company information is taken. Finally, the employee should be escorted out of the building.

- **Return of identification**   As part of the termination procedure, the employee's company identification should be returned. This includes identity badges, pass cards, keys for doors, and any other security device used for access to company facilities. This prevents the person from accessing the building after being escorted from the premises.

- **Return of company equipment** All company-owned equipment must be returned immediately, such as desktops, laptops, cell phones, PDAs, organizers, or any other type of electronic equipment that could contain confidential company information.

- **Suspension of accounts** An important part of the termination procedure is the notification to the network administrators of the situation. They should be notified shortly before the termination takes place to give them time to disable any network accounts and phone access for that employee. The network password of the account should be changed, and any other network access the employee might have, such as remote access, should be disabled. The employee's file server data and e-mail should be preserved and archived to protect any work or important communications the company might need for operational or legal reasons.

Exam Tip

All user access, including physical and network access controls, needs to be disabled for an employee once they have been terminated. This prevents the employee from accessing the facility or network.

Objective 1.02
CompTIA Security+
Objective 2.2

Carry Out Appropriate Risk Mitigation Strategies

As a result of your risk analysis, many of the risks identified require security controls if you have decided to budget resources to mitigate the risk. The policies and procedures described previously help you implement security controls at the managerial, operational, and technical levels of your organization.

Security policies and procedures provide the template and framework for employees to follow and implement risk mitigation controls across your organization. To ensure these policies are being followed, however, requires continued monitoring and auditing to make sure they are in use and being adhered to.

The following sections describe additional aspects of risk mitigation that require security policies and continued monitoring to ensure the policies are being followed and do not result in additional risks for the organization. These risk mitigation strategies and policies include change management, incident response, auditing, user permission reviews, and data loss prevention.

Change Management Policy

Change management policies are official company procedures used to identify and communicate current or forthcoming changes to some aspect of the company's networks and communications services. For example, the IT department might issue a change control document to all employees to notify them of a network outage because of an upgrade to networking equipment, or that an application will be down for several hours for a software upgrade. More detailed change control communications describe longer-term outages for specific technical changes to the company's systems or network infrastructure, such as taking down part of the network for a weekend for router and switch upgrades.

Tracking, controlling, and communicating outages and changes to your network infrastructure, systems, and applications are important to keep all departments in your organization up-to-date with IT maintenance activities to prevent accidental loss of data and services. For security reasons, this activity also ensures any unplanned changes or outages are quickly detected and investigated. System and network changes without prior knowledge or approval of management and the IT department could indicate a hacker or an intruder has compromised the network.

Incident Management and Response Policy

Incident management and response should be part of a company's overall security policy. In the event of some form of security incident, be it physical intrusion, network attack, or equipment theft and vandalism, some form of procedure should be in place to deal with these events as they happen. Without any clear directives, the aftermath of a security breach can cause even more damage if employees don't know how to handle an incident properly. A clearly defined incident response policy can help contain a problem and provide quick recovery to normal operations.

The policy should cover each type of compromised security scenario and list the procedures to follow when they happen. For example, in case a server is hacked, procedures might be in place to deal with removing the server from the network, shutting down related network servers and services, and preserving evidence, such as audit trails and logs. The incident response policy should cover the following areas:

- Contact information for emergency services and other outside resources
- Methods of securing and preserving evidence of a security breach

- Scenario-based procedures of what to do with computer and network equipment depending on the security problem
- How to document the problem and the evidence properly

Travel Assistance

Incident response is described in greater detail in Chapter 2.

Perform Routine Audits

Routine audits of your security procedures and policies are an integral part of continuous security awareness. Until serious incidents occur, you will not know if your policies are being followed and adhered to, which leaves your organization and its activities at risk. Recording and collecting logs of security activity isn't helpful unless you are able to review and analyze the data, and compare it to your current policies and the level of incidents that occur.

Security and access logs should be carefully preserved and analyzed in case of a security compromise or policy violation. For example, there may be evidence of attempts at network intrusion that go completely unnoticed because of notifications and alerts in the security logs that went unnoticed or unheeded. In this case you must review your IT incident response policies and procedures to understand why these activities went unnoticed and the risk continued. By auditing and re-evaluating your policies, you can identify additional monitoring and mitigation measures that need to be put into place.

Audits of policies and procedures need to be performed at all levels of your organization, including deep level network and account management policies, physical access policies, and human resource procedures. You may find that your current policies are correctly defined but are not implemented properly or communicated efficiently to all users. Employees can become lax, and often republication and retraining for specific types of policies may be required.

User Rights and Permissions Reviews

While auditing and reviewing overall organizational policies and procedures are critical for security maintenance, you must also regularly review and audit the rights and permissions granted to your users. While at a specific moment in time, the rights and privileges you have assigned for users may be accurate and secure, over longer periods of time, employees leave the company, move to different positions and responsibilities, and may possess higher or lower security clearances than what they had previously.

Regularly auditing user security rights and permissions is extremely important in ensuring that existing security lapses in user rights policies can be resolved before a user accesses or damages data to which that user should not be allowed access. Group, geographical, and department-based policies are very important to audit because users change their locations and departments frequently. For example, a user who recently switched from the sales department to the marketing department needs her permissions reviewed to remove her from any access to shared sales department data.

User rights and permission reviews need close cooperation with human resources and department heads to be proactively notified when employees' positions and responsibilities change.

Data Loss Prevention and Regulatory Compliance

Data loss prevention (DLP) is a major growing trend for organizational security. While most security is concerned with inbound risks and threats, such as malware, network attacks, and hacker intrusions, internal data security and outbound data loss have also now become a primary security targets.

DLP is a security concept focused on preventing the loss of data and protecting its confidentiality and privacy. This includes a company's own data, and also any customer data that it stores and communicates. Data must be protected from theft, loss, and interception in storage and in transit. DLP mitigation techniques require the use of both inbound security through the use of standard network security techniques such as firewalls and antimalware appliances to prevent inbound threats, and also security for outbound traffic through the use of content filtering and encryption technology.

| Travel Assistance |
Data loss prevention techniques are discussed in more detail in Chapter 12.

There are now several government-directed regulations and policies regarding the protection of data for companies in specific industries. For example, companies in the medical industry must prevent confidential patient information from being compromised. Financial organizations such as banks and insurance companies must provide several layers of security for protecting financial transactions and the confidential financial information of customers such as credit card and bank account data.

The most common data protection regulations include:

- **Health Insurance Portability and Accountability Act (HIPAA)** HIPAA is a set of compliance regulations for the protection of confidential patient data in the medical, health care, and health insurance industry.
- **Sarbanes-Oxley Act (SOX)** In the financial services industry, the Sarbanes-Oxley Act defines standards for publicly held companies and accounting firms for storage, access, communications, and auditing of financial data.
- **Payment Card Industry (PCI)** This set of standards is defined for companies that process credit card financial transactions to help prevent fraud and identity theft. PCI defines several concepts that should be complied with when storing and communicating financial data.
- **EU Data Protection Directive (EUDPD)** This European Union regulation requires organizations, including multinational companies, to provide privacy protection for stored and transmitted user data.

Generally, most compliance regulations and standards include these key factors for data security:

- Proper protection of data through network security principles and technology, such as firewalls and antimalware devices
- Strong user account and password management for access control
- Use of encryption when storing and transmitting confidential data
- Extensive logging and auditing to be able to monitor and analyze reports and have audit trails for forensic evidence

CHECKPOINT

✔ **Objective 1.01: Explain risk-related concepts.** An acceptable use policy is a set of established guidelines for the appropriate use of computer networks. The company practices due care by taking responsibility for all activities that take place in corporate facilities. The company practices due diligence by implementing and maintaining these security procedures at all times to protect the company's facilities, assets, and employees. A service level agreement (SLA) is an understanding among a supplier of services and the users of those services that the service in question will be available for a certain percentage of time. A specific separation of duties ensures that one individual isn't tasked with high-security and high-risk responsibilities. Users should have only the access rights they need to perform their job functions. The employee termination process includes securing the work area, returning identification and company equipment, and suspending computer accounts.

✔**Objective 1.02: Carry out appropriate risk mitigation strategies.** Security policies provide the template and procedures for risk mitigation, but these policies need to be implemented and adhered to. Use change management policies for communication of network changes and outages. Unplanned changes in your network could indicate security breaches. Use an incident response policy so that procedures are in place to deal with security incidents. Perform routine audits of your policies and procedures to make sure they are being adhered to. Constantly review user rights and permissions to deal with security issues deriving from changing roles and responsibilities for end users. Use DLP techniques to protect the integrity and privacy of data, and adhere to government-regulated compliance policies for data protection.

REVIEW QUESTIONS

1. After a few incidents where customer data was transmitted to a third party, your organization is required to create and adhere to a policy that describes the distribution, protection, and confidentiality of customer data. Which of the following policies do you create?

   A. Privacy

   B. Due care

   C. Acceptable use

   D. Service level agreement

2. You are performing a risk analysis for a complex web-based application. Based on your conclusions regarding the probability, impact, and mitigation cost of an attack based on DNS manipulation or poisoning against your web domain, you decide to place the responsibility of the risk on your ISP, which handles your DNS services. Which risk management option is this an example of?

   A. Acceptance

   B. Deterrence

   C. Avoidance

   D. Transference

3. As the centralized management location from which you provide Internet-based application services to several external clients, which of the following policies do you provide to your clients as an agreement for service uptime?

   A. Code of ethics

   B. Privacy

   C. SLA

   D. Due care

4. There is a suspicion that a specific employee is performing illegal activities on your company's networks. In an effort to gather evidence about his activities, which of the following principles and techniques could you employ?

   A. Password rotation

   B. Mandatory vacation

   C. Need-to-know

   D. Separation of duties

5. As part of a risk analysis of a very large and extensive back-end database, you need to calculate the probability and impact of data corruption to the data. Which of the following impact factors allows you to calculate your annualized losses due to data corruption?

   A. SLE

   B. SLA

   C. ARO

   D. ALE

6. You need to create an overall policy for your organization that describes how your users can properly make use of company communications services, such as web browsing, e-mail, and FTP services. Which of the following policies do you implement?

   A. Acceptable use policy

   B. Due care

   C. Privacy policy

   D. Service level agreement

7. After the initial configuration of an antispam e-mail filtering appliance on your network, users are complaining that too many legitimate messages are being flagged as spam in their mailboxes. Which of the following concepts is this an example of?

A. Baseline threshold

B. False negative

C. False positive

D. Legitimate positive

8. Your organization deals with sensitive health insurance information for patients that is covered by the HIPAA compliance policies. Which of the following DLP security techniques would you implement to help protect the confidentiality and privacy of your patient's health insurance data when communicating the information between health care facilities?

   A. Encryption of outbound data containing health insurance information

   B. A firewall to protect from inbound network attacks

   C. Antivirus scanning of patient data

   D. Strong physical access control of your facility

9. It has been discovered that a former member of the IT department who switched to the development team still has administrative access to many major network infrastructure devices and servers. Which of the following mitigation techniques should be implemented to help reduce the risk of this event recurring?

   A. DLP

   B. Incident management and response policy

   C. Change management notifications

   D. Regular user permission and rights reviews

10. A high-level executive has been terminated due to sharing company confidential data with competitors. Which of the following actions should be immediately performed?

   A. Encrypt all outbound data sent from the user.

   B. Change the password and disable all user accounts for the user.

   C. Scan the user's computer for compliance violations.

   D. Encrypt all data in storage that the user has access to.

REVIEW ANSWERS

1. **A**   A privacy policy concerns the protection and distribution of private customer data. Any company, especially one engaged in online activities or e-commerce, has a responsibility to adopt and implement a policy for protecting the privacy of individually identifiable information.

2. **D** The risk of DNS attacks occurring against your web domain is something that can only be assumed by your ISP, which takes care of your DNS services. In this part of your risk analysis, you are transferring the responsibility of the risk to your ISP to protect your web services from DNS-based attacks.

3. **C** A service level agreement (SLA) is an understanding among a supplier of services and the clients of those services that the service in question will be available for a specific percentage of time. In this case, you may guarantee your clients a 99.5 percent uptime of communications services.

4. **B** When a user is forced to take a vacation, his activities can be audited and any suspicious behavior will be more likely to be noticed and detected, because the user is not there to prevent its discovery. You may also discover that the illegal activities completely cease while the user is away, and then resume when he returns.

5. **D** ALE (annual loss expectancy) describes how much money you expect to lose on an annual basis because of the impact from an occurrence of a specific risk. ALE is calculated by multiplying the annual rate of occurrence (ARO) by the single loss expectancy (SLE).

6. **A** An acceptable use policy establishes rules for the appropriate use of computer networks within your organization. The policy describes the terms, conditions, and rules of using the Internet and its various services within the company's networks.

7. **C** A false positive is a legitimate action that is perceived as a risk or threat. A false positive is a term often used in e-mail security scanning to indicate legitimate mail that was classified as spam.

8. **A** To comply with the HIPAA regulations, you must protect the confidentiality of your patient's health insurance information. When communicating this data, you must encrypt it to ensure that it cannot be read if intercepted or stolen.

9. **D** User rights and permissions must be constantly reviewed to make sure that users have only the rights they require for their current responsibilities. When users change roles and responsibilities in the organization, you must review their permissions and modify their access accordingly.

10. **B** When a user is terminated, the first action that should be performed is to have that user's passwords changed and his user accounts disabled. This immediately prevents the user from gaining access to his accounts, data, and e-mail.

Security Training and Incident Response

ITINERARY

○ **Objective 2.01** Explain the importance of security-related awareness and training

○ **Objective 2.02** Analyze and differentiate among types of social engineering attacks

○ **Objective 2.03** Execute appropriate incident response procedures

	NEWBIE	SOME EXPERIENCE	EXPERT
ETA	3 hours	2 hours	1 hour

Security is not only about technological security controls. While network devices such as firewalls, antivirus and antispam appliances, and intrusion detection systems, can help protect against most types of security issues, they cannot completely protect your users from social engineering attacks.

Social engineering uses behavioral manipulation to trick users into bypassing security controls and providing elevated access or confidential data to the attacker. Hackers using social engineering techniques can result in victims unknowingly providing their login credentials or confidential information such as personal credit card numbers or bank account information. Social engineering techniques cover a variety of mediums, including networking, web sites, e-mail, instant messaging, telephone calls, and even person contact.

User education is key in preventing security issues arising from social engineering attacks. Awareness training helps users to understand the dangers of various social engineering hacking techniques, and to be wary of intrusions when working through their day-to-day activities. Users communicate with other, external users every day when using e-mail, phones, social media, instant messaging, and file sharing applications, and each application has its share of security issues, including the risk of malware and phishing. While technological security controls help, user education and awareness are the most effective security measures against the risks of social engineering attacks.

In preparing for security incidents, organizations must also create policies and procedures in regard to incident response. By taking into account the legalities of prosecuting computer crimes, most companies have trained their employees in collecting and preserving forensic evidence of such crimes. Because the evidence is usually electronic in nature, it can easily be tampered with, causing it to be legally invalid in a court of law. Therefore, the art of computer forensics is a critical part of preventing and prosecuting computer crimes.

This chapter describes user security training and policies, provides an overview of the most common social engineering attacks, and covers best practices for incident response and data forensics.

Objective 2.01
CompTIA Security+
Objective 2.4

Explain the Importance of Security-Related Awareness and Training

Security awareness and training are critical business objectives that must be directed from senior management and filtered throughout the company to every single employee. Different departments and divisions within a company need different forms of security education, depending on their job tasks and area of influence. The security procedures used by the financial department could be different from those used by sales or engineering, for example. Finance might need special procedures to protect confidential company and employee financial data from being exposed to other employees or companies. Engineering's security efforts will revolve around the protection and integrity of the source code or research data. Front reception could be specially trained on security practices with incoming calls or the physical security of the main entrance. Each department must interpret the company's high-level goals into the functional procedures specific to a job function.

To propagate security policies and procedures effectively to the user community, the company must make a diligent effort to communicate these policies. If no one knows about the security policies, there's no point creating them. The best methods for overall user-security awareness are though proper documentation and training.

Accessing Policy Documentation

The first step in user security awareness is creating and maintaining proper documentation of all your security policies and procedures. Policies that apply to the company as a whole should be distributed to each employee. These policies might include such areas as acceptable Internet use, employee codes of ethics and conduct, and safety and emergency contact information. More department-specific policies could be distributed only to employees in that department. The HR department wouldn't publish policies for the protection of employee salary information to other departments of the company, so it wouldn't reveal or undermine any security procedures. The IT department would have different security policies because one of its main job functions is to be responsible for the security and protection of the company's network infrastructure and data.

As security policies tend to change over time, manual distribution isn't always the most efficient and timely way to communicate security information. Employees should have a way to access the most current versions of these documents in a conspicuous place, such as in a binder located outside the HR area. Another more efficient method is to publish these documents on a company intranet, so that employees can easily access the most current versions. Printed versions should still be available, but because this documentation frequently changes, only a few central copies should be created to prevent excessive paper waste. The advantages of online versions of documents are that they're instantly available through employees' computers and they're always the most recent versions.

Exam Tip
The best place to store company documentation for easy access by employees is through the corporate intranet.

Awareness Training

Providing access to documentation is only one part of user awareness. Although printed documentation might be handed out to all employees or electronic versions could be made available online, no guarantee exists that they'll be read, understood, or implemented. To supplement the documentation and to ensure employee awareness, provide education and training sessions.

Training sessions should be mandatory for all employees and are especially critical for new employees. The training courses ensure that employees know the security policies and procedures the company has created and, most important, that they understand these policies and know how to enact them within their specific positions. Any policies or procedures of which employees are not sure can be discussed. Classes can be based on overall security procedures, such as virus awareness and dealing with outside clients and inquiries. These should be attended by all employees to ensure they know how to handle security problems properly with communications media used companywide, such as e-mail or the telephone.

General security items, such as facility access control, can include training on identifying and authenticating users in the facility, so that they can spot employees or strangers who are somewhere they shouldn't be. Network authentication standards, such as proper login and password management, are also applicable to all employees.

Specialized training can be presented to laptop and mobile device users who'll be traveling to ensure they protect company equipment and data when they're not on the premises. Other education initiatives can be more specific to an individual user or department, depending on their job function. The HR department can be given training on the security practices involved with hiring and terminating employees. The IT department should be given special training on specific networking security issues.

Threat Awareness

Virus and phishing threat awareness training can educate users on proper use of company communications, such as e-mail, IM, and personal usage of social media, to prevent viruses and malware from infecting the company network.

While a company's security controls, such as firewalls, antivirus programs, and antimalware devices, can block most threats at the network border before they reach the end users, there is still the possibility that new types of viruses, malware, or other zero-day types of threats can evade security controls. *Zero-day* threats are those that are so new that there is no published, active defense for them, such as a new virus with no current antivirus signature to compare it to.

In these cases, the user is the last line of defense for protecting against new types of threats, and through training, users can recognize the signs of suspicious messages, viruses, malware, and phishing links that should be brought to the attention of the administrator before they spread through the company's network.

> ### Exam Tip
> A zero-day attack takes advantage of existing software security vulnerabilities before a security fix has been developed or applied.

Data and Documentation Policies

Your company produces a wide variety of documentation, from publications for internal use, to confidential papers for senior management, to publicly available documents. Without proper controls, that documentation could be used to compromise company security. The company's document control standards and guidelines must ensure all documents produced by the company are classified, organized, and stored securely to prevent their loss, damage, or theft.

To ensure control over the protection and distribution of data, it needs to be classified with a certain designation. This data *classification* indicates what type of document it is, if the information it contains is confidential or can be made public, and to whom it can be distributed. The classification also defines what levels of data retention and storage are needed for that particular document. Finally, policies must exist on the legal status of documents concerning which can be destroyed and which need to be retained.

Standards and Guidelines

To ensure the continuity of documentation across the company as a whole, a set of documentation standards and guidelines should be introduced. These standards and guidelines can serve as templates for all documentation to ensure they have the same look and feel, and to ensure they'll all be distributed and stored securely, according to their scope or sensitivity.

The standards and guidelines should address the following topics:

- Data classification
- Document retention and storage
- Disposal

Data Classification   A company's documentation can be voluminous, comprising a variety of documents of varying value and importance. Depending on the type of document, the amount of security and types of procedures used in storing and distributing that document can greatly vary. Some documents might be considered public, so they can be posted in a public form or distributed freely to anyone. Other documents can be extremely confidential and contain information that only certain individuals should be allowed to see.

To aid in this effort, documents need to be assigned security classifications to indicate the levels of confidentiality of the document. Each classification requires different standards and procedures of access, distribution, and storage. The classification also sets a minimum standard of privileges required by a user to access that data. If you don't have the necessary access privileges for that classification of data, you won't be able to access it.

Several levels of classification can be assigned, depending on the type of company or organization and its activities. A typical company could have only two classifications: private and public. *Private classified documents* are only for the internal user of the company and can't be distributed to anyone outside the company. *Public documents,* however, would be available to anyone. Government and military institutions might have several levels of confidentiality, such as "Unclassified," "Confidential," "Secret," "Top Secret," and so on. Each level of classification represents the level of severity if that information is leaked. For example, the lowest level, "Unclassified," means that the document is not considered confidential or damaging to security and can be freely distributed. At the highest, "Top Secret" level, documents are highly restricted and would be severely damaging to national security if they fell into the wrong hands. Each document needs to be assigned a classification depending on the sensitivity of its data, its value to the company, its value to other companies such as business competition, the importance of its integrity, and the legal aspects of storing and distributing that data.

Exam Tip

The type of security protections, access controls, data retention, and storage and disposal policies to be used depends on a document's security classification.

Document Retention and Storage   Depending on the classification of a document, the procedures and policies for storing that document can be quite different. For example, a particular document might incur certain legal liabilities if it isn't properly stored, distributed, or destroyed. To ensure proper document management, depending on its classification, companies have implemented data-retention policies to help reduce the possibility of legal issues.

Certain documents are required to be archived, stored, and protected, while others should be disposed of after a certain period of time. These policies must be created by senior management and the legal department, which can define what retention policies apply to different classifications of documents. The data retention policy needs to be specific about your company's data. It also needs to take into account items that could be legally damaging and information that can be damaging to the business if it's lost or falls into the wrong hands.

To protect documentation properly, it should be stored offsite at a special document storage facility. In case of a disaster, such as a fire at the company facility, this will ensure all important documentation is secure and can be recovered.

Document Disposal   Document disposal can often be a tricky issue. In some cases, to prevent future legal or confidentiality ramifications from the existence of a certain document, it needs to be destroyed. In other cases, it's illegal to destroy certain documents that are required by law as evidence for court proceedings. Only your company's legal department can decide on retention and disposal for particular documents. Once decided on, these policies need to be communicated to the employees to ensure that sensitive documents are either destroyed or retained as per their classification.

When data is to be disposed of, the job must be done completely. When destroying paper documentation, most companies use a shredder to cut the document into pieces small enough that they can't easily be put back together. Simply putting documents in the trash or recycle bin isn't acceptable because anyone can sift through the garbage or recycle containers for these documents, a practice called *dumpster diving*. As part of corporate espionage, some companies hire private investigators to examine garbage dumpsters of a target company, and these investigators try to discover any proprietary and confidential information.

Travel Advisory

To combat the problems of dumpster diving for confidential company documents, the physical security of your facility should include your garbage disposal and recycling operations.

Data Retention Policy

Many companies have been affected legally by archived e-mail or data that offers evidence against them during court proceedings. To prevent legal liabilities, companies have implemented *data retention* policies to help reduce the possibility of legal problems arising from past messaging communications and data.

Data retention policies should apply to electronic information, such as files, e-mails, instant messages, and traditional paper documentation. Some clashes might occur between data retention policies and backup policies, where certain files are required to be archived, while others should be disposed of after a certain period of time. Only management and the legal department can define which data is covered under either policy. The data retention policy needs to be specific about your information and take into account items that could be damaging legally, as well as information that can be damaging to business if the data is lost. In the case of e-mail, the concept of data retention becomes complicated because e-mail can contain file attachments. Part of your policy might require that e-mail be retained for a certain amount of time before deletion, while the policy for actual electronic files could be different.

Hardware Disposal and Data Destruction Policy

Any policies must also include the disposal of old hardware. As the turnaround time for the life of computers is very low (three to five years), older equipment is constantly swapped out for newer, faster machines with more capabilities and resources. However, a critical security issue is apparent in regard to the proper disposal of these systems. Servers and personal computers are typically returned with their original hard drives, which could contain sensitive and classified data. System administrators must follow a specific policy for the removal and disposal of hardware to ensure that any media containing data is completely erased or overwritten.

When data is to be disposed of, the job must be done completely. When destroying paper documentation, most companies use a shredder to cut the document into pieces small enough that they can't easily be put back together. For electronic files, this process is more complicated. Merely deleting a file or e-mail from a hard drive doesn't necessarily delete the data. Many operating systems (OSs) use a special recovery method that enables you to recover deleted files easily. When a file is deleted, it usually still exists in its original location; only the locator for the file in the hard drive directory has been removed. To ensure complete destruction of data on magnetic media such as hard drives, the media should be overwritten or the drive physically destroyed. Many "shredder" utilities are available that can overwrite the contents of a hard drive with random data to ensure any information on the drive is unrecoverable. Also, a number of high-security organizations, such as the military, opt to destroy the drives physically instead of using a shredding application.

IT Documentation

Beyond standard company documents, such as policies, procedures, guidelines, and training manuals, some specialized document sets require added attention regarding security and storage. Network architecture diagrams, change logs, and system logs and inventories are all documents created and managed specifically by the company's IT department. Because these documents can contain specific information on system and network devices such as logs, audit trails, network addresses, and configuration data, they are usually accessible only by authorized persons within the IT department and aren't accessible by other employees in the company.

Systems Architecture The IT department should always have current diagrams of your overall company network architecture on hand. When troubleshooting network problems or security issues, engineers who have network diagrams are ready to identify devices and overall data flow within the company's network.

A variety of diagrams are needed to show different aspects of the architecture. Overall diagrams should be general and show the company network as a whole. These diagrams should possibly indicate offices only by name—with wide area network (WAN) links in between them—for companies that have geographically distant offices. More detailed diagrams can be made of the internal network structure, showing all the routers, switches, firewalls, hubs, printers, and servers.

Each device should be clearly labeled with identifying information, such as the system name and the network address. Including end-user workstations on systems architecture diagrams is rare, because too many could exist to include on a single diagram. The general network used by the end users should be indicated, however.

As a security precaution, network diagrams shouldn't be generally published, because the information can be used maliciously by a hacker to give him a road map of the company's network, including IP addresses of the most critical network devices and servers. Network architecture diagrams should be accessed only by authorized individuals from the IT department. Printouts of diagrams should never be posted in public places, such as on a notice board or even the office of the network administrator. The diagram can be easily stolen by someone walking by the area, or a person can use a digital camera to quickly take a picture of it for later use.

> **Exam Tip**
>
> System architecture diagrams should never be displayed or stored in a public area, especially if they contain system IP addresses and other information hackers can use to compromise a network.

Logs and Inventories   General application logs, audit logs, maintenance logs, and equipment inventory documentation are also important documents within an IT department. Most of this documentation is related to the maintenance and operation of the company's computer equipment, but certain logs, such as system activity logs, should be carefully archived and preserved as evidence in case of a security compromise.

System and audit logs provide snapshots of what's happening on a system at a specific point in time. These logs need to be retained for auditing in case of some security compromise. For example, the hacking of a certain server could have gone unnoticed for a long period of time. But if the logs of that system are retained and archived, they can be audited to reveal when the compromise began and how it happened. To ensure the company's backup procedures and policies are being followed, the IT department might have to retain and store copies of backup application logs, which indicate when certain data was backed up and where it's now stored. Inventories of computer equipment enable the company to keep track of its assets and know where they're located. Maintenance logs also provide important evidence for service and warranty claims.

Best Practices for User Habits

Beyond security awareness training, you must enact several policies and best practices that users should adhere to during their day-to-day activities within the office. Security is an ongoing practice, and concepts learned in awareness training must be enacted within the office to make them effective. The following sections describe several areas of interoffice security techniques and practices that should be followed by your users.

Password Policy

A strong password policy should be created that must be followed by all employees in an organization. Password policies ensure that all network administrators and users are aware of the rules and procedures in place for managing the user accounts and passwords that allow access to company resources. Password policies should be part of the company's overall security policy.

Typically, users create passwords that are easy to remember—such as the names of family or pets, phone numbers, and birth dates, all of which can be easily discovered by someone who knows the user or even by a complete stranger who, through simple social engineering, has to ask the user only a few questions about his or her personal life. Other types of passwords that aren't secure are those based on any word found in the dictionary. Many password-cracking programs based on dictionary attacks are available that can find out any password in a short time if it's based on a common dictionary word.

The minimum length for a password should be enforced for all employees. This prevents users from using small, easy-to-guess passwords of only a few characters in length. The recommended minimum password length is six to eight characters. Password complexity must be part of your password policies to ensure that beyond a minimum length, the password is not easy to guess, such as a dictionary word, and does not contain information specific to the user, such as a birth date. Passwords should contain a mix of uppercase and lowercase characters, numbers, and symbols, and they should not be based on any word that can be found in a dictionary.

Most login and password authentication systems can remember a user's last five to ten passwords and can prevent the user from using the same one over and over again. If this option is available, it should be enabled, so a user's password will always be different. Also, the longer a password has been in existence, the easier it is to discover eventually, simply by narrowing the options over time. Forcing users to change their passwords regularly (password aging) prevents the discovery of a password through brute-force attacks

Clean Desk Policy

Users should be aware of the risk of leaving confidential papers, sticky notes, cell phones, portable devices, and removable media on their desks when unattended. These items can be quickly stolen or copied while a user is away from his desk. A clean desk policy maintains that any such items should be always kept in locked drawers. Users should also never write down login credentials and leave them on their desk or stuck on the front of the monitor, where they can be easily found by other, unauthorized users. Whiteboards or drawings should be wiped clean or removed after they are used in the event confidential information is left on the board for any passerby to view.

Personally Owned Devices

Users may bring a variety of personally owned devices, such as laptops, USB keys and drives, cameras, and other peripherals, into the workplace. Your company must have a defined security policy in place to educate users on the use of personally owned devices to protect organizational security and cover the con ditions under which they may be used. For example, you may have a policy in place (and enforced through technological controls) that prevents personal laptops from connecting to a corporate wired or wireless network unless a full vi rus scan is performed. Smartphones that are able to access corporate messaging servers should be protected with a password so that if a user ever loses her per sonal phone, an unauthorized user could not access her company e-mail account. These security controls ensure that all devices have a minimum standard of secu rity before they can connect to company resources and access data.

In very high-security environments, personal devices, especially cameras and smartphones with cameras, are banned and must be turned in to security before entrance into the facility.

Workstation Locking and Access Tailgating

Users must ensure that they lock and password-protect their workstation ses sions while away from their desk. If the user leaves his current computer session open, he is still logged in to the network and any passerby can "tailgate" on to his privileges and access confidential data, e-mail messages, and shared network re sources. Network-wide policies implemented by the network administrator should automatically make sure workstations lock after a period of inactivity such as ten minutes, but even that is enough time for a malicious user to find what she needs on an unprotected workstation.

Instant Messaging

One of the most popular Internet services is *instant messaging (IM),* which al lows users to send real-time messages to each other via their PCs. Web links, files, and other types of multimedia can also be exchanged between IM users.

While e-mail messages can be protected by authentication and encryption tools, IM applications reside on a user's hard drive and are usually not protected by a firewall by default. This is even more critical in corporate environments, where IM programs used by employees make the corporate network vulnerable to attack because these programs are often not part of a company's traditional network security plan. To prevent users from using IM in the workplace, the ad ministrator can configure the firewall to block specific IM ports. In certain cases, it may be necessary to allow IM within the company network, but not al low it to connect to clients outside of the network.

IM can be used to send files to another user, and the same risks associated with attachments exist, such as receiving virus-infected files. When receiving a message with an option to download the file, the user must always establish the identity of the sender before replying or downloading the file. The best practice is simply to ignore the message unless the user has no doubt about its origin. Some IM programs enable the user to create a list of users whose messages will be automatically rejected. This is helpful if the unknown user continues to send a user messages even after being ignored the first time. Of course, an antivirus scanner should always be running on the system to protect against any type of virus, spyware, or malware in downloaded files.

P2P Applications

Peer-to-peer (P2P) networking allows two computers to connect to each other directly and share files, rather than through an intermediary server or service.

The most popular application using P2P Internet file sharing is the trading (usually illegally) of music, movies, and videos. Unfortunately, many of these P2P programs can contain a number of security vulnerabilities that can give unauthorized users access to your system. The P2P application enables you to configure a specific directory on your hard drive that can be accessed by other users. The P2P servers can scan the contents of this directory to create a centralized master database that can be searched by users of the service. Once the user finds the file he is looking for, he connects directly to your computer to download the file. Insecure P2P software may put your system at risk by opening it up to network attacks and the possibility that other remote users can gain access to your nonshared files.

The biggest issue with P2P sharing is that the files you download may be disguised viruses or Trojan horse programs. The open nature of this type of networking and file sharing means little trust and control exists over what files are offered for download. When using these types of file-sharing programs, you must ensure your computer is fully protected with a current antivirus program and a personal firewall to protect against network attacks.

Exam Tip
P2P applications have no place on a corporate network, and any P2P protocols and ports should be closed off at the firewall to prevent these applications from operating on the network.

Social Media

With the massive increase in social media use, such as Facebook, Twitter, and LinkedIn, security administrators are beset with a number of new avenues of risk with their organization. The same security risks that affect other communications mediums such as e-mail, web, IM, and P2P are also inherent in social media applications; however, phishing and the spread of malware can be more prevalent in social media because most malicious links are spread by trusted users on the social network. When one person's social media application is affected with malware, it can quickly spread to other users as automatic messages are spread from the victim's computer to all his social media contacts. These types of social engineering attacks are very effective on social media users.

To provide a strong layer of security, many organizations have included social media with other restricted applications such as instant messaging and P2P apps and block their use on the network. If users do have access to social media sites, they require social engineering awareness training to educate them on the types of behavior to look out for when using social media.

Analyze and Differentiate among Types of Social Engineering Attacks

Objective 2.02
CompTIA Security+
Objective 3.3

The easiest way to discover someone's password often is simply to ask for it. *Social engineering* is defined as using and manipulating human behavior to obtain a required result. A user might be easily led to reveal her password or to provide personal information that might reveal her password. For example, someone might call a user on the phone, pretending to be from another department, asking for the user's password to retrieve a file. The user, thinking she knows who she is talking to, might give the unauthorized user the password without officially authenticating who the caller is or why he needs the information. The caller might make small talk with the user and trick her into revealing names of family members or her birth date, so the attacker can try out this information as a password to the user's account.

Another typical example of this type of security breach occurs when an unauthorized user calls a help desk operator and impersonates a high-level user, and asks to reset his password. The user insists he is a high-level manager who needs access into his account immediately. The help desk operator, if not trained properly, could instantly give this user a new password without properly identifying the user. Now the hacker can log in using the account of a high-level person who could have access to sensitive information.

Protecting against social engineering security abuses requires user education and emphasis on the need to follow security procedures at all times, even when dealing with someone an employee knows within the company. Social engineering involves nontechnical methods of attempting to gain unauthorized access to a system or network. This typically means the hacker tricks a person into by-passing normal security measures to reveal information that can help the at-tacker access the network. The hacker, in effect, acts much like a con man, who tries to uncover sensitive information through manipulating someone's basic human nature.

Exam Tip
Be able to differentiate between the different types of social engineering attacks.

Phishing

A *phishing* scam is a type of e-mail or web security threat that tries to use social engineering to trick an unsuspecting user into visiting a web site or replying to an e-mail with confidential personal information such as a user name and ad-dress, login and password, and banking or credit card details.

Phishing e-mails often contain logos, messages, and links to well-known trusted sites, such as a real bank or credit card company. In reality, any links in the message will actually redirect to the web site of the phishing scam operator. These web sites are often made to look just like a real bank or credit card site. The user then unknowingly enters his login and password information and per-sonal details into the web site, when in reality it is being entered into the data-base of the phishing web site operator.

This activity is most commonly related with identify theft, where the unau-thorized user is able to collect enough personal information about his target victim that he can perform forged credit card and banking transactions using the victim's financial and personal details.

A variant attack called *spear phishing* is a targeted type of phishing attack that includes information familiar to the user and could appear to be from a trusted source such as a company that the user has previously purchased a product from, or a financial service that the victim has used previously, or even a specific trusted user. A spear phishing attack is much more sophisticated than regular phishing; in this kind of attack, the information targeted at the victim offers a greater inducement to click the links in the message and serves to gain the user's trust to enter confidential information. The user's personal information, such as full name and postal address, could have been stolen from a mailing list, or the name of the user's bank manager could appear as the sender of the e-mail.

To help protect end users, many web browsers, e-mail clients, and antivirus software applications can detect behavior that may indicate the presence of a phishing e-mail or web site. This is typically accomplished by parsing the URL links in a message and comparing them to lists of known phishing web sites.

User education and awareness is the most important tool to protect against phishing attacks. Users must be aware that financial institutions will never ask personal details, especially bank account numbers and credit card details, in an e-mail to a user. When a suspicious e-mail is received, it is also helpful to check the destination of any clickable links within the message to determine the location to which it is actually redirecting. If the destination site is not recognized, it is likely a phishing attempt. Many browsers can automatically check links for suspicious or obfuscated URL redirect links and warn the user before connecting to the site.

Travel Assistance

For detailed information and resources on phishing and best practices for reducing the risk of phishing attacks, see the Anti-Phishing Working Group web site at www.antiphishing.org.

Whaling

Whaling is a type of phishing attack that is targeted at a specific high-level user. Most phishing attempts are general in nature and are sent to thousands of users hoping that some of those users will fall prey to the attack. In a whaling attack, the victim is usually a high-profile member of the organization, such as an executive who has much more critical information to lose than the average user.

Many executives have their profile information posted on the organization's public web site. Hackers can use this information to craft a unique phishing message so specific to that user that it may seem legitimate enough for the victim to act and click a link containing malware that is installed on her computer, or else it may redirect to a web site under the hacker's control where the executive may enter sensitive credentials or banking information.

Whaling requires the same sort of protections as other social engineering attacks such as proper malware and antivirus protection on the computer, as well as user education on social engineering techniques.

Shoulder Surfing

End users must always be aware of their environment and the people in their surroundings when entering login names and passwords or accessing sensitive data. It is very easy for an unauthorized person to casually glance over the shoulder of an employee who is concentrating on the work at hand and watch the user as she enters user names and passwords into the computer. The person who is *shoulder-surfing* can easily see which keys the employee is typing on the keyboard and will use the user name and password when attempting to access that account at a later time.

The issue of viewing sensitive and confidential data, such as human resources records, while other employees are present is also important. An unauthorized person can watch from behind an unsuspecting employee and view the data the authorized person is accessing on the monitor, especially today's monitors with large and wide screens.

Users must examine their surroundings before entering or viewing confidential data. If a user has her own office, she should ensure that her monitor is not easily read from a distance from the hallway and is situated in such a way that a casual passerby cannot see the monitor screen. In many environments, the desk can be oriented to face away from the doorway to ensure that a monitor screen is always facing the back of the office. Blinds can be installed on windows to prevent outsiders from looking in to the office. Special "privacy" monitor screen guards also prevent prying eyes. In open-concept office spaces, this is more difficult, and it is up the user to ensure that no one is standing behind her or viewing over her shoulder while she is entering and working with sensitive data.

Tailgating

Tailgating is one of the simpler forms of social engineering that describes gaining physical access to a facility by following another authorized user through the security check point. For example, a user can swipe her access card to open a door to enter the facility, but an unauthorized user can follow the authorized person through while the door is still open. The unauthorized user may try to use conversation to gain trust and then entry by saying he has lost or forgotten his access card.

Organizations must have strict access control rules that prevent tailgating incidents and allowing unauthorized users into a facility without proper authentication or identification. All employees should be encouraged to report unknown individuals within the facility, and never let an unknown user within the premises without proper authentication, including photo ID if possible. Many security access cards also include photos as additional identification in case the card is lost or stolen. Visitors must always be accompanied by an employee and be properly signed in and given a temporary access card. The visitor must be signed out and the access card returned when he has left the facility.

As mentioned earlier in the chapter, tailgating can also refer to using another user's access rights on a computer. For example, a user might leave on her lunch break and forget to lock her office or log out of her session on her computer. An unauthorized user could get access to her computer and be able to read her e-mail messages, access her files, and gain access to other company network resources. Users must always log out of sessions or lock their workstations before they leave the work area.

Pharming

Pharming is a type of social engineering attack where a user is misdirected to an attacker's web site without his knowledge. While similar to phishing, where a user may click a link in a seemingly legitimate e-mail message that takes him to an attacker's site, pharming occurs when code is installed on the computer that actually modifies the destination URL to that of the attacker, even if the URL is entered correctly or chosen from a web browser bookmark. In some cases the malicious code can change the hosts file on the victim's computer to point legitimate web domains to alternate IP addresses of the hacker. Through these methods, the user is tricked into browsing to the attacker's web site even though he thinks he has gone to a legitimate destination. Just as in phishing, pharming can result in loss of confidential data such as login credentials and credit card and banking details; it can lead to identity theft as well.

Spim

Spim is instant messaging spam, and just like the more common e-mail spam, it occurs when a user receives an unsolicited instant message from another user, including users that are known and in the client's contact list. Instant messaging services provide a lot of information about users, including demographic sex and age information, that can be used for targeted spam advertising. These messages can contain ads, or links to viruses, malware, and phishing sites.

Users can protect themselves from spim and other IM-security-related issues by making sure that only people on their contact list can send the user messages. In many cases, organizations have completely blocked access to external IM chat services.

Vishing

Vishing is a type of social engineering phishing attack that takes place over phone systems, but most commonly over VoIP (Voice over IP) lines. Using tools specific to VoIP systems, hackers can program their autodialers to send recorded messages from spoofed VoIP addresses. The recorded message can claim to be from a bank call center asking the customer to call back and verify her financial information. Because the VoIP source is difficult to trace, unsuspecting users may trust the call as legitimate and provide their private financial details to the hacker inputted on the phone keypad.

Like other social engineering attacks, vishing requires user education to recognize the warning signs of scams, including any attempt to get financial information such as credit cards and bank account numbers over the phone.

E-Mail Spam

Spam is a deliberate attempt to mass e-mail a large number of users with unsolicited advertisements. Any time you enter your e-mail address on a public web site or a newsgroup, you open yourself to the possibility of having your e-mail address added to spam mailing lists. These mailing lists are shared among Internet spam advertisers, and sometimes, you can receive multiple junk e-mails every day. This annoys not only users but also networking administrators because of the amount of space and bandwidth these mass mailings can consume. Many Internet service providers (ISPs) and corporate networks use antispam mail filters that block incoming spam e-mail from reaching users' inboxes.

Travel Assistance
For details on antispam and e-mail content filtering devices, see Chapter 8.

E-mail spam continues to be one of the prime nuisances and security issues affecting organizations. Spam has evolved from the early years of simple text adverts to full HTML messages with clickable links, images, and even spam messages hidden in attached images and document files. The links in spam messages are often redirected to malicious sites containing spyware, malware, and phishing activities.

E-Mail Hoaxes

One of the most annoying problems, hoaxes are typically some kind of urban legend users pass on to others via e-mail because they feel it is of interest. The most common types of these e-mails tell the user to forward the e-mail to ten friends to bring the user good luck. Others claim to be collecting e-mails for a sick person. Of course, this activity merely consumes network and computer resources, as the number of e-mails grows exponentially as users send them to all their friends, and so on.

Travel Assistance

See www.hoax-slayer.com for an exhaustive list of known e-mail hoaxes.

Hoaxes are generally harmless and are caused more by social engineering than maliciousness; however, some hoax e-mail messages can be phishing attempts that try to get the user to visit a link in the e-mail message that redirects to a malicious web site. The only cure for the spreading of hoax e-mails is user education to make sure that users know the typical characteristics of a hoax message and know to ignore the message and not forward it to another user.

Exam Tip

Know how to spot an e-mail hoax and how to handle it properly. The best solution is to delete it immediately and do nothing more at all.

Objective 2.03
CompTIA Security+
Objective 2.3

Execute Appropriate Incident Response Procedures

When a security incident or disaster scenario occurs, the initial incident response can make all the difference—either it quickly mitigates a threat, preventing it from spreading and causing further issues, or the incident spins out of control, causing irreparable damage to your organization's ability to function. Incident response must be planned in advance to ensure that your front-line employees are prepared in the event of a disaster to quickly contain the incident, preserve any evidence in the event of a security breach, and escalate issues as appropriate to company management or third-party authorities.

After the discovery of the incident, company personnel must report the incident to the appropriate person, and this person should be identified ahead of time. The incident could have been discovered by a security guard, an employee working late, or in many cases the network or security administrator themselves. The company's incident response policy needs to define the first responders from the incident response team that can be deployed to respond to the incident.

First Responders

A *first responder* is the first person or persons who are notified and respond to a security incident. For example, the network administrator may receive notifications from an intrusion detection system that a security breach has taken place, and therefore the network administrator is typically the first person to respond to the incident. A first responder must follow several responsibilities and procedures when he or she is the first person on the scene of a security incident.

The company's incident response policy should describe the exact tasks and responsibilities of the first responder. If a computer crime occurs, an effort must be made by the first responders to the incident to contain any damage and prevent further asset or data loss. The first responders must also try to leave the original environment and evidence intact and unaltered as best they can until the authorities have been contacted. If people begin to pick apart the crime scene after a physical crime, or if the network administrator begins poking around the file system or reboots the system, the evidence could be disturbed and considered inadmissible in court. Finally, first responders need to follow an escalation policy to notify other company officials or the authorities.

Damage and Loss Control

A major initial aspect of incident response is being able to contain an incident and the damage it is causing to prevent it from spreading or causing further damage. A company must create an incident response policy that indicates what can and cannot be touched if a security compromise occurs. For example, a worker at a company undergoing a denial-of-service (DoS) attack might panic and pull the plug on its Internet connection. This, of course, stops the attacks, but it brings down the entire network and no communication exists with the outside world, effectively stopping all e-mail and Internet business communications. If the business runs its operations through a web page, this can be fatal.

In other cases, such as a virus-infected server, immediately disconnecting it from the network so that it does not infect other systems might be the best response. The incident handling and response procedures provide information on what to do in certain scenarios. In the example of the DoS attack, to prevent the entire network from going down and to preserve any evidence of the attacks, the company might let the attack continue, so that the network administrator can save logs and audit trails to help trace the source of the attack. Decisions must be made on how critical specific services are, such as e-mail, file and print services, and web services. If a file server is specifically attacked, it may be less critical to take that system offline than to disconnect an e-mail service that must be running to provide communications to the organization, even though it might be under a DoS or spam attack.

Forensics

In adjusting to the legalities of prosecuting computer crimes, most companies have trained their employees from the incident and response team in collecting and preserving forensic evidence of computer crimes. Because the evidence is usually electronic in nature, it can easily be tampered with by an uneducated investigator, which would cause the evidence to be legally invalid in a court of law. Therefore, the art of computer forensics is a critical part of evidence collection necessary for prosecuting computer crimes.

Forensics is the act of collecting and preserving evidence to use in a court of law for legal proceedings. Typical forensics of crimes, such as theft or murder, includes gathering evidence to help prosecute a suspect, such as fingerprints, weapons, and even DNA samples. In the computer world, evidence of a cybercrime can be difficult to obtain, preserve, and allow into a court of law. Because of its nature, most computer crime evidence is electronic, which can easily be erased, modified, and tampered with. After a computer crime—such as a server attack—is committed, initial investigation by the network administrator can quickly ruin evidence the attacker left behind.

Travel Advisory
If a system is rebooted after a security compromise, certain evidence could be destroyed in the process, such as memory contents and system logs.

The following sections outline some of special procedures required when preserving and collecting evidence of a computer crime, which includes preserving the incident environment, collecting evidence, data volatility, and retaining a chain of custody of the evidence.

Collection and Preservation of Evidence

Collecting evidence is a crucial aspect of incident response. Depending on the type of incident, there could be physical evidence, logs, system images, screen captures, and camera video, each of which needs to be carefully collected and preserved, and protected from tampering.

Order of Volatility   When collecting forensic data evidence, it is important to realize that any type of digital data has a specific volatility, meaning that over time the veracity or ability to recall the data declines. Some data is more persistent and less volatile; for example, a printout of a log file or a copy of the file on backup tape is less volatile than a live data log file on hard disk that is constantly being modified and overwritten. The RAM (random access memory) of a computer system is extremely volatile, as the data is not persistent and can change at any time within a matter of seconds.

When capturing data for forensics, especially in the initial stages directly after an incident, you must take into account the levels of volatility and focus your efforts on preserving the most volatile types of data before moving on to less volatile data. Your early focus should be on system memory or crash dump files, error messages on the screen, and log files, before moving on to less volatile data.

Capture a System Image   In many cases, the entire contents of your hard drive, or an entire server with an array of hard drives, needs to be saved as evidence of your security incident. It is a best practice to create a system image, which is a snapshot of your entire data system at a specific time. The system image allows you to preserve the state of your data after the incident so that you can resume operations with your server, while the image of your hard drive is stored elsewhere.

If you do not make a system image, you could lose important log files, network traces, and crash dump files that get overwritten over time. You must also adhere to legal requirements to ensure that the digital evidence is not tampered with after the incident.

System images are typically saved to an external hard drive with MD5 hashing (discussed later in this chapter) to preserve its integrity, and then stored in a secure place. Your disk imaging software and image drive need to provide bit-for-bit accuracy to create an exact image of your original drive and prevent alteration after the image is created for legal reliability.

Network and System Logs   Collecting and preserving evidence from a computer crime primarily concerns keeping and storing any logs or audit trails that detail step-by-step what the attacker was doing. Log files will contain specific date and time stamps with each aspect of an intruder's activity, including login credentials, commands used, and files accessed.

When an incident occurs, avoid panicking. If you suddenly reboot a network device or server to ward off the attacker, you not only disrupt access to that server for legitimate users, but you could also destroy valuable evidence in the form of audit trails and time stamps on files that might have been changed by the intruder.

Make sure you preserve copies of your log files before letting too much time elapse from the incident. Log files, especially network logs from firewalls and routers, can roll over very quickly; older log files may be deleted to make resources available for new ones. By immediately making copies of the log files, you ensure they are not accidentally deleted or lost.

Time Offsets When collecting data evidence from your systems, be aware that not all network devices or servers may have their clocks synchronized, and the time stamp that one device puts on an action that appears in the logs may be different than that of another device. There is also the issue of time zones, and how different types of devices stamp times. One device may use UTC (Coordinated Universal Time) without time zone offsets, while other systems may insert their own time zone offsets, depending on their configuration. When collecting and organizing your evidence, be aware of the issue of time offsets between different devices and time zone issues. Legally, you need to account for any time discrepancies in your evidence.

Use Hashing to Protect Evidence Integrity For legal reliability, you need to be able to prove the logs haven't been altered in any way from the time of the original data capture. To help preserve data integrity, you can create an MD5 hash of the file immediately after the incident. A *message digest* hash is used in encryption systems to create a "fingerprint" for a message. Hashing preserves message integrity by ensuring that the original data has not been tampered with. MD5 is a complex message digest algorithm that is widely used for data integrity checking.

The resulting checksum can be matched to the MD5 hash at a later time. If the MD5 hash does not match, the file has been altered since the original capture.

Travel Assistance

For more details on hashing and MD5, see Chapter 4.

Take Screenshots In certain cases, evidence of an attack may only occur as an error or diagnostic image that appears on the screen. You may even have a full transcript of the command-line instructions entered by an intruder during their attack. In this case, you will have to use a screen capture image program to take a snapshot of your current screen. This must be performed before any other action. If you clear the message, you may lose your evidence if it does not also appear in the log files. Screen capture files should be accurately labeled and time-stamped, and you should also use hashing to preserve the integrity of the file to prove that it was not altered or tampered with.

Capture Video   If the crime was physical in nature, such as the theft of equipment, the evidence required would be surveillance videos. If the theft took place in a secured area, it might be possible to analyze the access logs of employees who logged in to the secured area at the time. If the company uses magnetic access cards for doors, a log can be created showing who went in and out at a certain time. In this case, only the video surveillance could show who was in possession of the access card, as the card might have been lost or stolen from the original user.

Make multiple copies of the video evidence to make sure you have additional copies if the original is damaged or lost. Surveillance video on tape should be transferred to a computer as a digital video file for backup purposes and more efficient retrieval.

Chain of Custody   When collecting evidence of a computer crime, maintaining a proper chain of custody is extremely critical. A *chain of custody* requires that all evidence be properly labeled with information on who secured and validated it. This process must also occur for each individual who comes in contact with the evidence. Unfortunately, electronic evidence can be volatile, and in a court of law it can be easily dismissed because of possible tampering. Computer media can be easily destroyed, erased, or modified, so handling this evidence requires strict procedures.

If additional copies of data need to be made, reliability and integrity must be assured so the copies can be considered tamperproof. Perform an MD5 hash of the data so that a checksum can be created for comparison at a later time to prove the data was not tampered with. Any devices or media containing data need to be carefully catalogued and labeled, and then sealed away to prevent tampering. Magnetic media should be write-protected to prevent the data from being overwritten.

If all evidence has been properly secured, identified, labeled, and stored, then it can be considered solid and admissible in court. A clear chain of custody log ensures this process was completed without the possibility of data modification.

Exam Tip

A chain of custody ensures that evidence has been handled with the utmost care and lists the persons who have had access to the evidence.

Interview Witnesses   It is possible that, depending on the nature of the incident, you may have witnesses who need to have their statements recorded as evidence. For example, in the case of a physical theft, an employee might have caught sight of an unidentified person in the building. You must take a statement of where they saw the individual and at what time, and provide a detailed description. It is also possible that a witness might have noticed screen activity on a server that resulted in the initial incident alarm.

What is most important is interviewing and recording the witness statements as soon as possible after the incident. Over time the witnesses may forget specific details, and it is important to have as much information recorded as possible while the incident is fresh in their memory.

Escalation Policy

An escalation policy must be enacted and followed to provide a specific list of management or other authorities that must be contacted in the event of a security incident. Depending on the department or area of the incident, one or more direct managers should be notified, along with any central security for the organization, and the incident should be escalated to various executives such as directors, vice presidents, and so on, as required for the type of incident and the downtime it has caused. For example, if a web server has been attacked overnight and the attack was discovered by the network administrator in the morning, she should notify her direct manager and the security administrator.

In the event the attacking suspect is an internal employee, the human resources department should be contacted immediately as part of the incident response policy. From there, it can be decided whether to keep the organization's investigation internal or to contact the authorities and any other outside agencies to aid in the investigation.

In the event that the security threat was external, external authorities may need to be contacted if the organization holds that the security breach or damage that it causes is serious enough to warrant notification of the police.

Reporting and Disclosure

When investigating a security incident, every single detail should be meticulously documented to ensure that every aspect of the incident, from the specific details of the security breach to every step taken during the incident response process, is recorded.

Keep careful track of the number of man-hours and expense required to respond to, investigate, and provide mitigation for the security incident. These statistics are very useful for future risk analysis and security budgeting, and they help assign a real dollar value as a cost for the incident beyond the costs incurred for loss of data and system downtime.

During the post-incident response phase, your organization must determine whether to keep the investigation and response internal or to issue a public announcement to notify customers or users of the security issues. By keeping the information of a security breach from the public, the organization can ensure that details of its internal security (or lack thereof) are not published. For example, if an organization sent out a press release that one of its web servers had been hacked using a known exploit, other hackers who heard this information might try the same exploit on the organization's other web servers if they knew the servers were vulnerable.

The decision to internalize or release publicly information on a security incident becomes very sensitive when dealing with security breaches that occur in financial institutions, such as a bank or stock trading firm, and especially for medical institutions that have strict guidelines for protecting clients' data. In these cases, the decision is often regulated by the government, and any security breaches that affect the privacy of clients must be published. For example, if a hospital computer is hacked and confidential patient records are stolen or damaged, or an Internet banking system is hacked and leaks tens of thousands of their customers' bank account and credit card numbers, it is necessary or even mandatory that the company release details of the incident to ensure customers know that data has been leaked. In the case of the bank, customers should be told to contact the bank to help secure their current accounts and lock them down before they can be abused.

Reporting and disclosure are also critical issues for companies that manufacture software or hardware systems that are found to contain security vulnerabilities. Many companies are embarrassed by such security breaches in their products, and they quietly release patches to the product to fix the security breach in an effort to ensure the vulnerability does not become well known. In other cases, companies try to protect the customers by not disclosing or discussing any known security issues until they have researched the issue and released a patch to deal with it. Many companies take a very proactive approach and welcome information from third parties that test their software for vulnerabilities, which actually helps the company solve the issue and prevent it from being exploited before news of the vulnerability reaches the public.

CHECKPOINT

✔**Objective 2.01: Explain the importance of security-related awareness and training.**   An organization's policies must be communicated to employees through training and documentation to be effective. Training documentation must be easily available via company intranet sites. Use data classification to indicate levels of data confidentiality. Destroy documents to prevent dumpster diving. Create user policies for password management, clean desk initiatives, and personally owned devices. Be wary of social engineering attacks for IM, P2P, and social media applications.

✔**Objective 2.02: Analyze and differentiate among types of social engineering attacks.**   Perform employee awareness training to educate users on the security issues of social engineering. Make sure no one is looking over your shoulder when you're entering sensitive data or login credentials. Be wary of tailgating users passing through an access door behind you. Educate your employees to recognize the characteristics of phishing e-mails and web sites. Ignore hoax e-mails and do not forward them.

✔**Objective 2.03: Execute appropriate incident response procedures.**   Perform damage and loss control to isolate an incident and the damage it is causing to prevent it from spreading or causing further damage. To preserve evidence, leave the original system environment intact. Gather information based on order of volatility. Save audit and activity logs, take screen shots, and make a system image for evidence. Use hashing to preserve data evidence integrity. Keep a chain of custody of evidence to prevent tampering.

REVIEW QUESTIONS

1. You have enacted a new policy to combat the issue of confidential data and documents being stolen or leaked internally within the office after a user had confidential HR papers taken from their office. Which of the following policies helps prevent these security issues?

    A. Antiphishing policy

    B. Clean desk policy

C. Acceptable use policy

D. Tailgating policy

2. You are the first responder to a security incident in which a database server has been compromised and has crashed. Which of the following should be performed to help preserve evidence of the incident?

A. Save access logs and a current memory dump.

B. Restart the system to restore operations.

C. Perform a backup of the database.

D. Perform a restore of the database.

3. You are collecting forensic evidence from a recent network intrusion, including firewall logs, access logs, and screen captures of the intruder's activity. Which of the following concepts describes the procedures for preserving the legal ownership history of evidence from the security incident?

A. Damage control

B. Audit trail

C. Escalation

D. Chain of custody

4. A network administrator has discovered the company's FTP server has been hacked. Which of the following items would be the most important to collect and preserve as evidence?

A. Server memory dump

B. List of user accounts

C. List of files on the FTP server

D. Access activity log

5. You have been contacted by your company's CEO after she received a personalized but suspicious e-mail message from the company's bank asking for detailed personal and financial information. After reviewing the message you determine that it did not originate from the legitimate bank. Which of the following security issues does this scenario describe?

A. Dumpster diving

B. Phishing

C. Whaling

D. Vishing

6. During your user awareness training, which of the following actions would be the best security practice for your users to help prevent malware installation from phishing messages?

   A. Forwarding suspicious messages to other users

   B. Not clicking links in suspicious messages

   C. Checking e-mail headers

   D. Replying to a message to check its legitimacy

7. After recent security issues with certain types of development documents being leaked out of the organization, what security policy can you implement to help improve user awareness of what types of documents can be transmitted outside of the organization?

   A. Document security classifications

   B. Clean desk policy

   C. Tailgating policy

   D. Antiphishing policy

8. A web server recently crashed because of a denial-of-service attack against it. Based on the order of volatility, which of the following pieces of evidence would you preserve first?

   A. Web site data

   B. Screen capture of crash error message

   C. Printout of web access logs

   D. Web server configuration files

9. After collecting several log files as evidence for a hacking incident against your web server, what should you do to help preserve the legal integrity of the logs to prove they have not been tampered with?

   A. Print a hard copy of the log files.

   B. Encrypt the logs.

   C. Perform a hash on each file.

   D. Save the logs to backup tape.

10. To help prevent security issues within the office, you have implemented blinds for all windows and also screen guards for all your computer monitors. Which of the following security issues will be mitigated through these security controls?

    A. Shoulder surfing

    B. Tailgating

    C. Phishing

    D. Whaling

REVIEW ANSWERS

1. **B**   A clean desk policy means that users should not leave out any documents or devices with confidential data on them on their desk when they are away from their work area. These items should be locked within a drawer or file cabinet and only brought out when required.

2. **A**   Any current logs and memory dumps should be saved to make sure you have evidence of all activity during the time of the incident. If you reboot the server to get it functioning again, you can lose valuable log data or data residing in memory.

3. **D**   Keeping a chain of custody requires all evidence to be properly labeled with information on who secured and validated the evidence. This can ensure the evidence wasn't tampered with in any way since the time it was collected.

4. **D**   The activity log will show what times the attacker was performing hacking activities and what those activities were. This evidence might be able to be used in court to help prosecute the attacker if he is caught.

5. **C**   Whaling is a type of phishing attack that is targeted at a specific high-level user. The victim is usually a high-profile member of the organization who has much more critical information to lose than the average user. These messages are usually crafted and personalized toward the specific victim user.

6. **B**   To help prevent malware from being installed, it is a best practice to make your users aware that they should never click links in a suspicious message. The link can take the user to a malicious web site that could automatically install malware on their computer through their web browser.

7. **A**   By classifying all your documents, you will inform users as to which types of documents are marked "confidential" and must never be transmitted outside of the organization through e-mail, fax, or other communications. Other document types that do not contain confidential information can be marked as "public" and freely distributed.

8. **B**   When collecting forensic data evidence, be aware that certain types of data are more volatile over time. In this case, the error message on the web server should be captured as a screen shot before restarting the server. The message will disappear, and unless it appears in the logs, you may have no other record of it.

9. **C** You must be able to prove that the log files have not been tampered with since they were captured. You can create an MD5 hash of the file immediately after the incident to create a "fingerprint" for a message that you can compare to the original file at a later time.

10. **A** Shoulder surfing occurs when an unauthorized user can view a user's actions while she is working on her computer. You can mitigate shoulder surfing by using screen guards on computer monitors that allow only viewing from directly in front of the monitor, and installing window blinds to prevent users from seeing into your office and viewing important documents or files on the computer screen.

Business Continuity and Disaster Recovery

CHAPTER 3

ITINERARY

- **Objective 3.01** Compare and contrast aspects of business continuity
- **Objective 3.02** Execute disaster recovery plans and procedures
- **Objective 3.03** Exemplify the concepts of confidentiality, integrity, and availability (CIA)
- **Objective 3.04** Explain the impact and proper use of environmental controls

ETA	NEWBIE	SOME EXPERIENCE	EXPERT
	3 hours	2 hours	1 hour

Business continuity and disaster recovery constitute a subject often avoided by management personnel because of the additional costs and time required to put together a disaster recovery plan that adds little value to the company's bottom line. Unfortunately, if a company is unprepared for natural disasters such as fires, floods, earthquakes, and tornadoes, as well as unnatural disasters such as vandalism, theft, hacking, and virus attacks, and a disaster strikes, the final costs of implementing no disaster protection could prove fatal.

The most difficult task is analyzing your company's weaknesses to such risks and identifying the impact each risk will have on your business operations. When it becomes obvious that even a small-scale disaster can send your operations into a tailspin, you must begin planning an overall disaster recovery plan to prevent a disaster from fully impacting your ability to function as a business. A disaster recovery plan must be created so that representatives from each department know exactly what to do if an emergency occurs. Representatives must be trained thoroughly and the procedures documented carefully, and the plan should be tested at least once a year or when company changes require alterations to the original procedures.

Travel Advisory

A disaster recovery plan is a step-by-step plan for recovering your networks and systems after a disaster. It is essential to protect employees, the company's ability to operate, its facilities and equipment, and its vital data.

Protecting your data from corruption, lack of access, or data loss is vital in maintaining your ability to provide vital services to your organization and your customers. As part of a company's overall information security, disaster preparedness, and business continuity plans, redundancy planning is concerned with preventing your systems from downtime caused by failed equipment, interrupted communications, and environmental issues.

The key components of redundancy planning are *high availability* and *fault tolerance.* Maintaining high availability is the premier goal of most businesses that guarantee access to data and provide host services and content that must be always available to the customer. Fault tolerance defines how able your system is to recover from software or hardware errors and failure. For example, a server with only one hard drive and one power supply isn't fault-tolerant: If the power supply fails, the entire server will be rendered useless because there's no power to the system. Similarly, if your file server's hard drive crashes and is unrecoverable, all data on that hard drive will be lost. Fault-tolerant systems are important for maintaining business continuity.

This chapter describes the components of business continuity and disaster planning, including creating a disaster recovery plan, fault tolerance and redundancy, backup policies, and the importance of environment controls in an organization's security strategy.

Compare and Contrast Aspects of Business Continuity

Objective 3.01
CompTIA Security+
Objective 2.5

Any disaster, however rare, can be fatal to a business that doesn't prepare for the emergency. Even interruptions on a small scale, such as system or network outages, can quickly incur huge financial costs and a damaged reputation. Many studies have shown that a majority of businesses that suffer a service interruption lasting more than one week are never able to recover and, consequently, go out of business. Critical to a company's preparedness is having a proper business continuity and disaster recovery plan.

Recovery Plans

Although the chances of a large disaster, whatever the cause, interrupting or halting business operations are fairly slim, all companies should be prepared for disastrous events.

The overall business continuity plan is a detailed document that provides an initial analysis of the risks involved to the business because of a disaster, the potential business impact, and a disaster recovery plan for restoring full operations after a disaster strikes. The specific purpose of a disaster recovery plan is to prepare your company with a step-by-step plan to recover your networks and systems. The plan is a technologically oriented part of the overall business continuity plan, detailing specific steps to take to return and recover systems to an operational state.

The process of creating a business continuity plan includes the following phases:

- Creating a disaster recovery team
- Performing a risk analysis
- Performing a business impact analysis
- Creating a disaster recovery plan
- Preparing documentation
- Testing the plan

Disaster Recovery Team

A disaster recovery team is responsible for creating and executing business continuity activities and a disaster recovery plan that outlines the goals for restoring company operations and functionality as quickly as possible following a disaster. The team is also available to provide for the safety and support of the rest of the company's personnel and the protection of company property.

The team should include members from all departments, including management. Including all areas of the company's operations is important because each department has its own objectives and goals, depending on its function. Disaster recovery duties should be included in the job description of each department, even though these duties go over and above regular duties. Designated backup team members should also be assigned in case the original member isn't available to perform the appropriate function.

In a disaster, each team member is responsible for certain priorities and tasks, which could include coordination of other department personnel, and contact with outside emergency agencies and equipment and service vendors. The bulk of the work will be the responsibility of the IT staff that needs to coordinate the creation of a communications and networking infrastructure, as well as restore all system functionality, including the restoration of lost data.

Risk Analysis

A *risk analysis* identifies the areas of your facility and computer network that are vulnerable to certain types of disasters. The entire business operation of the company must be broken down and analyzed, so the impact of a disaster on a critical business function can be ascertained.

As part of your risk analysis, you examine and identify any areas of your operations that stand out as a single point of failure. For example, you may realize that although you have several redundant web servers that process customer orders, the back-end database is located on a single server. If that single server were to fail or is damaged in a disaster, your web servers would not be able to connect to the database causing all customer transactions to halt. Through this process, you identify areas where you can remove single points of failure with redundant and fault-tolerant systems.

A risk analysis evaluates the potential outcome any type of disaster could have on your company's infrastructure. You need to analyze all possible scenarios in full. For example, in case a flood strikes the area where your main company building is located, the facility must be carefully examined for areas that would be affected by this particular disaster. Similar analysis must be made for other potential natural disasters, such as earthquakes and fire, and nonnatural disasters, such as software and hardware failure, network attacks, or virus attacks.

Create or obtain diagrams of the facility layout, such as building blueprints, seating plans, network cabling maps, and hardware and software inventory. The effect of each disaster scenario should be more easily ascertained with the aid of these diagrams. When you finish, you'll have a detailed document outlining the possible risks for each type of disaster that might occur. Using this information, you can formulate a business impact analysis that will show how those risks can affect your business functionality.

Business Impact Analysis

A *business impact analysis* will outline your most critical functions and how they'll be affected during a disaster. The analysis will examine the loss of revenue, legal obligations, and customer service interruption that can arise as the result of a disaster. Your most important business functions should be prioritized so that during the disaster recovery process they'll receive the attention they need to become operational before any noncritical aspects of the business.

Exam Tip

Business functions should be prioritized so that in case of a disaster they'll be made operational before other, less-critical functions.

The business impact analysis should also include timelines on how long it will take to get the company operational again if a disaster occurs. The resources, equipment, and personnel required should be carefully detailed, especially the ability to recover and restore vital company information from backups.

Most important will be examining the total financial loss incurred through certain types of disasters. If the company isn't prepared, it might not survive a disaster that completely halts its operations. This information can be provided to other managers, who might help fund and organize a disaster recovery plan, based on the statistics of the impact of a disaster. Many companies don't like spending the time or money on disaster recovery, but when the cost of the impact is analyzed and calculated, the ability to be prepared for a disaster will quickly pay for itself, if and when a disaster strikes.

Types of Disasters

Many types of disasters can befall a company. Many are small and inconvenient, affecting only a certain part of the company or only one network server. They might affect only communications or software applications. Larger disasters can be devastating, causing the destruction of most or all of the company's physical facility. The following sections describe the different types of disaster scenarios that can affect an organization's operations.

Natural   The types of natural disasters that can occur depend on the location of the company facilities; natural disasters can be the most devastating emergency to affect a business. You must be aware of the types of natural disasters that can happen in your specific geographic area. A fire, flood, earthquake, tornado, or hurricane can destroy your building and its infrastructure within minutes. The only way the company can be truly protected is if its data is regularly backed up and sent to an offsite location. Your company furniture and computer equipment can be relatively quickly replaced, but sensitive company data collected over many years can't.

Human Error and Sabotage   Something as simple as a mistakenly deleted file can cause a company much grief if the data in that file is critical to the business operation. A spilled cup of coffee can render a server unusable within seconds. Human errors and mistakes can be expected and are much more common than natural disasters. Vandalism and sabotage, however, can be quite unexpected but cause great damage. Theft or malicious destruction of company equipment by a disgruntled employee can cause as much damage as any natural disaster. The need for access controls and physical security is emphasized with these types of disasters.

Network and Hacking Attacks   Cyber theft and vandalism are an increasingly annoying and dangerous problem for companies, especially those whose business is Internet-related. When a company is permanently connected to the Internet, the door is open for unauthorized users to attempt to gain access to company resources. Some malicious hackers simply try to gain access to a system for fun. More malicious unauthorized users might cause widespread damage within the company's network if they gain access. Some attacks could come from within the network. A security professional will need to analyze threats coming from both outside and inside the network.

Viruses   Computer viruses are special programs able to replicate themselves, and they often perform malicious activities on networks, servers, and personal computers. Viruses can be extremely destructive, causing massive network outages, computer crashes, and corruption or loss of data. Once one computer is infected with the virus, the virus can quickly spread to other computers and servers on the network. E-mail-based viruses can spread quickly in a short amount of time. Protection against viruses includes the use of special antivirus software at both the personal computer and server levels, and user education about computer virus prevention.

> **Travel Advisory**
>
> Hacking and viruses are probably the most common disasters that befall a business. An e-mail virus can spread so fast it can overload your e-mail servers within a matter of minutes after initial infection.

Disaster Recovery and Contingency Plans

You must devise disaster recovery and contingency plans to establish the procedures that can quickly recover critical systems after a service disruption. Specific tasks are defined and prioritized to aid in the recovery process to define clear objectives that must be met during the recovery phase.

Responsibilities must be clearly defined for those important individuals participating in the recovery as part of the disaster recovery team. Tasks should be divided and assigned to the appropriate people and departments. Each individual must be trained on the specific procedures and have these procedures properly documented. Team leaders must be established, and central authorities can guide the recovery process through each of its critical steps.

You also need to decide which aspect of the business is the most critical and must be up and running first if a disaster occurs. Different departments in the company have unique objectives and priorities, but certain functions can be delayed if they don't immediately impact the ability of the company to function.

The most important part of the company to get operational is basic communications, such as desk phones, mobile phones, networking connectivity, and e-mail. Until these communication lines are functional, the company's ability to coordinate the disaster recovery effort will be greatly reduced, causing much confusion and chaos. Business-critical items should come next, such as file servers, database servers, and Internet servers that run the company's main applications or anything specifically needed by customers. Most of these responsibilities come under the IT department's contingency plan.

The ability for the company to restore full operations as quickly as possible depends on the efficiency with which objectives and goals, outlined in the disaster recovery plans, are met.

Your disaster recovery plans must also contain information on *succession planning* for key employees. Depending on the type of disaster, specific employees may not be available or are directly affected by the disaster. You must identify key positions that can be filled in by another employee that can take over and execute the same responsibilities. These positions can be very technical in nature, such as a network administrator, or at the executive level to provide direction during a disaster.

Documentation

Each phase of your recovery plans should be carefully documented and the resulting document should be readily available to all members of the disaster recovery team. The document should also be safely stored in both hard copy and software copies to reduce the potential for damage or loss. In case of a real disaster, a lack of documentation will cause nothing but chaos because no one will know how to get all aspects of the company running again, especially during a stressful and frantic time.

The disaster recovery plan must be precise and detailed, so anyone can follow the instructions without requiring further clarification. Each person on the disaster recovery team will have clear responsibilities and duties that must be performed in the most efficient manner possible.

The plan should include the following items:

- **Notification lists**   A list of people and businesses to notify in case of a disaster
- **Contact information**   Phone numbers and contact information for employees, vendors, data recovery agencies, and offsite facilities
- **Networking and facilities diagrams**   Blueprints and diagrams of all networking and facilities infrastructure, so it can be re-created on the new site
- **System configurations**   Configuration information for all servers, applications, and networking equipment
- **Backup restoration procedures**   Step-by-step information on how to restore data from the backup media
- **Backup and licensing media**   To reinstall the servers, you will need the operating system software, the appropriate license keys, and the backup media. These should be stored in a safe location so that they are ready and available during the installation process.

Finally, copies of the disaster recovery plan should be stored and secured both onsite and in an offsite facility, especially any designated alternative company site. If a physical disaster strikes your main facility, the plan will be useless if it's destroyed along with the building.

> **Exam Tip**
>
> Be aware of the types of information that should be documented in your disaster recovery plans.

Testing

To complete your disaster recovery plan, you must fully test it to ensure all parts of the plan work as they should. Re-creating a disaster without affecting the current operations of your company might be difficult, but some form of test should be performed at least once a year.

Most disaster recovery tests involve the choice of a scenario, such as a fire in a certain part of the building. Your disaster recovery team must consult the recovery plan documentation and execute it accordingly. Depending on the size of the company, it might be feasible to involve only certain departments, but the IT department should always be included because its main responsibilities are the network infrastructure and data recovery. During the testing, every phase should be fully documented through the use of a checklist. Any exceptions or problems encountered during the procedure should be thoroughly documented.

When the test has been completed, the original disaster recovery plan should be reviewed for any procedures that didn't work correctly or that need to be modified as a result of the test. The plan should be updated with any new information as a result of the testing. Any changes to the existing facilities or infrastructure should initiate a review of the current disaster recovery procedures. Any changes should be made immediately to reflect the new environment.

Objective 3.02
CompTIA Security+
Objective 2.7

Execute Disaster Recovery Plans and Procedures

Disaster recovery planning is extremely important in preventing downtime for your organization in the event of equipment or communications failure. Your system's ability to recover from a disaster is greatly dependent on the facilities and equipment available if your main facility is heavily damaged or destroyed. Backup equipment and facilities are vital elements in planning for recovery, and each should be examined for both onsite and offsite strategies.

High availability, redundancy planning, and *fault tolerance* are extremely important factors in ensuring business continuity, and they are implemented at the system and network levels to protect the confidentiality and integrity of data, and to maintain data availability.

High Availability and Redundancy Planning

The ability to provide uninterrupted service consistently is the goal of maintaining a high-availability system. This initially requires that you identify systems that need to provide services at all times. Answer the following questions to help you in planning for high-availability systems:

- What is the monetary cost of an extended service downtime?
- What is the cost to a customer relationship that can occur as a result of an extended service downtime directly affecting that customer?
- Which services must be available at all times? Rank them in order of priority.

If your company hosts a number of services required by customers, these services should be given higher priority than your own systems because the service level promised to customers must be maintained at all times.

Service Levels

Many companies measure their ability to provide services as a *service level*. For example, a web server–hosting company might promise 99 percent service availability when the systems and services it hosts are available. The other 1 percent of the time, the systems might be unavailable because of maintenance, equipment failure, or network downtime.

> ### Local Lingo
>
> **service level** Specifies in measurable terms the level of service to be received, such as the percentage of time when services are available. Many Internet service providers (ISPs) provide a service-level agreement to guarantee customers a minimum level of service. Some IT departments now provide a measured service level to the rest of the company.

The most common examples of servers and services that require high availability and high service levels include the following:

- **Internet servers** These include Internet services, such as web and FTP servers. These types of servers usually require that the information and data stored on them be available at all times.
- **E-mail** E-mail is the most commonly used Internet service because all users need and use e-mail. Therefore, mail servers and gateways must maintain high levels of service availability.

- **Networking** As the backbone of all computer communications, the networking equipment that provides the infrastructure for private and public networks must be available at all times.
- **File servers** File servers house all data and information needed by the users. Without access to this data, users can't perform their job functions.
- **Database servers** Database servers are typically required as back-end servers to web servers and other applications that use database transactions. Data stored on database servers, just like file servers, must be available at all times.
- **Telecom** Even in an Internet-centric organization, phone and other voice telecommunications systems are still a service that requires availability at all times. In the event of a disaster, your voice communications will be of the highest critical priority to be available to coordinate disaster recovery efforts.

Reliability Factors

There are several industry-standard terms used in the IT world to refer to the reliability of services and hardware products. These terms are often used in maintenance contracts that identify how long it takes a manufacturer or a service company to repair a failed service or server. They can also refer to service levels provided by a company to customers depending on their services, such as a web hosting company that hosts and services thousands of web sites for a large number of customers.

- **Mean Time to Restore (MTTR)** Mean Time to Restore is the average time from the moment of a service failure until when the service is restored. For spare parts for a failed server hard drive, your service contract may state that they can provide a new hard drive within 4 hours, but in other cases, this could be 24 to 48 hours. A web hosting company may promise that for any failed web site or service, the mean time to restore could be 60 minutes.
- **Mean Time Between Failures (MTBF)** This is the average time for when a specific device is expected to work until it fails. A mathematical formula is used to determine how long a specific product should last based on previous measurements of failure rates. For example, a mechanical or electrical device such as a hard drive or power supply may have an MTBF rating of 500,000 hours when it is more likely to fail.
- **Recovery Time Objective (RTO)** This is the maximum amount of time that is considered tolerable for a service or certain business function to be unavailable. Organizations use this as a key factor in

their ability to provide specific guaranteed service levels. Different functions and services may have different recovery time objectives. For example, it may be determined that a company web site where customers purchase their products from is of the highest importance, and the Recovery Time Objective is set as 60 minutes. These objectives are typically defined in the business impact analysis of the business continuity and disaster recovery plan.

- **Recovery Point Objective (RPO)**   This is the maximum accepted amount of lost data as a result of an outage or disaster. This is defined in terms of time, such as one hour. For example, if a database server fails, up to one hour of data can be considered an acceptable loss. These policies are defined in the business impact analysis of your business continuity and disaster recovery plan. This objective can help define other security policies such as the backup frequency to make sure that a data backup occurs at least every hour to preserve the RPO.

Spare Equipment Redundancy

Most disasters and disruptions are localized in nature and typically involve only one room or one particular piece of equipment. Failed hardware is the most common type of service interruption, such as blown power supplies, damaged network cabling, failed hard drives, and broken tape backup drives. Having spare hardware onsite to fix these small problems is vital to handling these smaller disruptions quickly. Many companies have vendor maintenance contracts that require the vendor to replace failed hardware, but in case of an emergency, the spare parts might not be delivered for many hours or even days. It's critical for hardware components that are commonly prone to failure to be switched quickly with an onsite spare.

The following spare components should be kept onsite at all times:

- Hard drives
- Redundant Array of Independent Disks (RAID) controllers
- SCSI controllers
- Hard-drive cabling
- Memory
- CPU
- Network cards
- Keyboard/mouse
- Video cards

- Monitor
- Power supplies
- Network switches, hubs, and routers
- Phone sets

It is also highly recommended that you have a contact list on hand for the manufacturers of your components in the event a replacement part needs to be ordered.

Redundant Servers   In high-availability environments such as e-commerce or financial web sites, where servers must be up and running 24 hours a day and 7 days a week, a downed server can cause a company severe financial damage. Customers will be unable to make purchases online while the server is down, and critical stock trades or financial transactions cannot take place. In these environments, redundant servers are installed that will take over in the event the primary server is unavailable. For example, an organization with a critical web server can install a secondary identical web server that can be swapped with the primary if the primary is down. In the event redundant servers are not running concurrently, having spare servers and workstations on hand means that if the primary server goes down, the failed file server hardware can be quickly replaced and the data restored from backup. This is often the preferred method for smaller organizations that do not have the resources or budget to run live redundant systems.

Exam Tip

High availability ensures that a service, such as a web or database server, is always available. Redundancy via live or spare replacement servers is a recommended method of ensuring availability.

Clustering   For more advanced high-availability purposes, the use of *clustering* technology enables you to use several servers to perform the services of one. Clustering greatly enhances load balancing, as the resources of all the servers can be used to perform the same task as one server. For fault tolerance purposes, if one system goes down, one of the other servers in the cluster can take over seamlessly without any interruption to the clients.

Two primary types of clusters are used: active/active, and active/passive. *Active/active* means that both servers in the cluster are up and running and actively responding to requests. In the event one server is unavailable, no drop in availability occurs, as the other server is still actively responding to requests. In an *active/passive* arrangement, one server is actively responding to requests, while the other server acts as a live standby. In the event the active server is unavailable, the other passive server can be triggered into becoming the active server and begin responding to requests.

For major disaster recovery scenarios, failover systems and redundant servers can be located in buildings of other company locations. For example, a company operating in Los Angeles might have another facility operating in New York. This allows the servers in New York to take over the services offered by the Los Angeles servers if LA suffers an interruption or disaster.

System Configuration Backups   The use of backups in a business continuity sense involves not only the backup of important information and data, but also backing up the system files and configuration settings of your server and network equipment.

When equipment failure causes the loss of your server, you not only lose the data and services housed on that server, but you lose all your system settings and configuration. Depending on the type of server, these configuration settings can be complex and can take many hours, or even days, to restore. For example, an e-mail server is usually configured with many options and settings that are unique to your location. If the server has failed or is destroyed and needs to be rebuilt, you'll need to reinstall the OS, install your e-mail server applications, and configure the system properly before you can restore your mail files that were backed up. If you didn't back up your system files, you'll need to recall and enter your system settings manually, which can take up too much time when a high-availability server is down.

Most modern backup applications have disaster recovery options that save important elements of the OS and application configuration files that can be instantly restored in case of a disaster. If you're recovering a server, you need only install the OS and the required media device drivers for your backup media device to retrieve the rest of your server files and system configuration from the backup media.

Redundant Internet Lines   It might be surprising to learn that many organizations rely on only one Internet service provider (ISP) to host their connections to the Internet. If any communications issues occur with the Internet line, or the ISP itself, the organization's communications are instantly crippled. No users will be able to access the Internet or e-mail, and for companies that have deployed Voice over IP (VoIP) telephony applications that rely on the Internet, the telephones will not be operational. It is difficult to think that so much time and money can be spent on redundant servers and equipment, while no thought is put into communications redundancy.

It is a best practice to have two or even three completely different ISP services and connections to provide a backup line of communication or to run concurrently with your current ISP line. In the event one of the ISPs or lines goes down, you will still be able to communicate to the Internet via the redundant connection. The ISP lines must be from different companies, or else your supposedly redundant Internet lines will be going to the same point of failure at the same ISP, and if the central router fails at the ISP, both your connections to the Internet will be down.

Many organizations also use redundant ISPs to provide some bandwidth control. For example, critical applications and services can be routed to one ISP, while general company connectivity (such as e-mail or web browsing) can be directed to the second ISP to ensure critical applications receive the maximum bandwidth they require from their own dedicated Internet connection.

Alternative Site Redundancy

In the event of a physical disaster such as a fire or a flood at your main company site, you need alternative facilities to house backup equipment to get your company operational again. In some cases, your original server and networking equipment could be damaged or destroyed, and then a new infrastructure must be created at a new site. For a company with no alternative site in its disaster recovery plan, this could mean many weeks before a facility is secured and new equipment is set up in the new building. The purpose of an alternative site is to have a facility already secured and, in some cases, already populated with a network and server infrastructure to minimize downtime. The choice of alternative sites will come down to how time-sensitive your company's product or services are and how fast you need to be operational again.

Hot Site   A *hot site* is a facility that's ready to be operational immediately when the primary site is unavailable. All equipment and networking infrastructure the company requires are already in place and can be activated quickly. The equipment duplicates the setup installed in the original building. The hot site facility is usually provided by another company, which hosts your company's equipment. Hot sites should be tested frequently to ensure the switchover runs smoothly and quickly. This is an expensive solution, but for companies that offer critical services, the costs of losing money and customers during an extended downtime warrant the expense of a hot site.

Warm Site   A *warm site* is similar to a hot site, but without most of the duplicate servers and computers that would be needed to facilitate an immediate switchover. The warm site is there to provide an immediate facility with some minimal networking in place. In the event of a disaster, a company will transport its own equipment to the new facility, or if the original equipment is destroyed with the facility, new equipment can be purchased and moved there. A warm site could take several days to restore and transfer data and bring the business back to full operation, so this option makes sense for companies that don't offer time-critical services. This is the most widely used alternative site option because of its relatively lower price compared to hot sites and its flexibility. The disadvantage of a warm site is that it's not immediately available after a disaster and it isn't easily tested.

Cold Site   A *cold site* merely offers an empty facility with some basic features, such as wiring and some environmental protection, but no equipment. This is the least expensive option, but this also means in case a disaster strikes, it might take several weeks before the facility and equipment are ready for operation, as almost all the networking and server infrastructure will need to be built and configured.

Exam Tip
Be aware of the advantages and disadvantages of the different types of alternative sites, depending on your environment.

Fault Tolerance

To protect your systems and network equipment and to provide redundancy for maintaining high-availability service, you must implement *fault-tolerant* systems. To make a system fault tolerant, it should contain a number of redundant components that will allow it to continue functioning if an equipment failure occurs. For example, a file server can be configured with two network cards. In case one network card fails, network communications can continue uninterrupted through the second network card. To ensure data integrity, it isn't enough to implement redundant hardware components, such as power supplies and network cards. The use of fault-tolerant RAID systems is required to allow multiple copies of the same data to be saved across multiple disk media, so data won't be lost if one of the hard drives fails.

Local Lingo
RAID (redundant array of independent disks)   Defines the concept of using a number of separate hard drives to create one logical drive. If one of the drives fails, the system can rebuild the information using the remaining disks.

Some fault tolerance concepts must be understood before implementation:

- **Hot swap**   Refers to the ability to insert and remove hardware while the entire system is still running. Most types of hardware require that the system be shut down before removing or inserting components. Hard drives in RAID systems are the most common type of hot-swap device.

- **Warm swap**   Refers to the ability to insert and remove hardware while a system is in a suspended state. Although less flexible than a hot-swap device, warm swap means you needn't shut the entire server down to replace hardware components. When the swap is complete, the server resumes its normal operations. Although services are shut down during the suspend period, time is saved by not having to reboot the entire system.

- **Hot spare**   Refers to a device already installed in the system that can take over at any time when the primary device fails. There's no need to physically insert or remove a hot spare device.

The following sections outline the types of system components that can be made fault tolerant.

Hard Drives

Hard drives are partly mechanical in nature. This makes them one of the most common components prone to failure on a server. The hard drives contain all the data and information, and if the hard drive fails, that data can be irretrievably lost.

Travel Advisory

If a hard drive fails or its data is corrupted, the information it contains can sometimes be retrieved by special hard-drive recovery specialists. This recovery process can be both time-consuming and expensive.

The most common method of hard-drive redundancy is to use a RAID system. RAID allows data to be spread across two or more hard drives, so if one hard drive fails, the data can be retrieved from the existing hard drives.

RAID can be implemented via hardware or software. Hardware RAID is based on a disk controller that controls the redundancy process across several physical hard drives. Software RAID relies on operating system kernel processes to control the RAID redundancy process, and while less expensive, it requires much more CPU processing power to manage the RAID process, and a software problem could put your data at risk compared to a dedicated hardware solution.

Mirroring the contents of one hard drive on another is called *RAID 1*. Several RAID levels can be implemented, depending on the number of disks you have and the importance of the information being stored. Other RAID techniques include *striping,* which spreads the contents of a logical hard drive across several physical drives and includes parity information to help rebuild the data. If one of the hard drives fails, parity information is used to reconstruct the data. Most RAID systems use hot-swap drives, which can be inserted and removed while the system is still running. To increase the fault tolerance of a RAID system, redundant RAID controllers can be installed to remove the disk controller as a single point of failure. Table 3-1 describes the most common RAID levels and their characteristics.

Power Supplies

Because of their electrical nature, power supplies are another important common computer component prone to failure. As the central source of power for any computer or network device, a power supply that fails can instantly render a critical computer system useless. Most modern servers come with multiple power supplies, which are running as hot spares. In case one of the power supplies fails, another will immediately take over without an interruption in service. Some high-end servers have as many as three extra power supplies. Many network devices, such as switches and routers, now come with dual power supplies. Replacing a single power supply on such a small, enclosed device would be difficult.

TABLE 3.1	RAID Levels	
RAID Level	**Minimum Number of Hard Drives**	**Characteristics**
0	2	Striping only, no fault tolerance
1	2	Disk mirroring
3	3	Disk striping with a parity disk
5	3	Disk striping, distributed parity
6	4	Disk striping, double distributed parity
0+1	4	Disk striping with mirroring

Network Interface Cards

One of the most overlooked fault-tolerant-capable devices in a server system is the *network card*. Typically, little thought is given to the scenario of a failed network card. In the real world, losing connectivity to a server is the same as having the server itself crash because the server's resources can't be accessed. Many modern servers now come preinstalled with redundant network cards. Extra network cards can also be used for load balancing, as well as being available to take over if another network card fails.

CPU

Although CPU failure is unlikely, failure is still a scenario that requires fault-tolerance capabilities, especially for high-availability systems. Many large-scale server systems have multiple CPUs for load-balancing purposes to spread the processing across all CPUs. Extra CPUs, however, can also be used for fault tolerance. If a CPU happens to fail, another one in the system can take over.

Uninterruptible Power Supply

Although redundant power supplies can provide fault tolerance in a server if one of the power supplies fails, they can't protect against the total loss of power from the building's main-power circuits. When this happens, your entire server will immediately shut down, losing any data that wasn't saved or possibly corrupting existing data. In this case, a battery backup is needed. An *uninterruptible power supply (UPS)* contains a battery that can run a server for a period of time after a power failure, enabling you to shut down the system safely and save any data.

Travel Advisory

Most UPSs come with software that can configure your server to automatically shut down when it detects the UPS has taken over because of a power failure.

Backups

Critical to a company's preparedness is having a proper backup and disaster recovery plan. Without any sort of data backup, a company risks having its entire data store wiped out forever. In most cases, this would cause the company to go under immediately or face a long rebuilding stage until it can become operational again. A well-defined disaster recovery plan is coupled with a backup strategy. Although the expense and planning for such a large disaster can be costly and time-consuming because of the dedication of resources and equipment costs, it must be compared to the costs involved with losing the ability to do business for many days, weeks, or months.

Planning

A good backup strategy must be clearly planned, defined, executed, documented, and tested. The first step in establishing your backup strategy is to draft a plan that covers the following points: the *type of data* to be backed up, the *frequency* in which backups will occur, the *amount of data,* and the *retention period* for the backups.

Type of Data   Your company's data must be separated into mission-critical data and more constant data that doesn't change much over time. Obviously, the most important data is the information the company requires during its daily business activities, especially if this information is something frequently accessed by customers. For example, a database company will ensure that it fully protects its customers' data. If the company loses that data without any procedure for disaster recovery, its business is essentially lost.

Frequency   Depending on the type of data your company stores, a wide range of backup frequency schedules can be implemented. For example, a transactional database used every day by customers would be considered critical data that must be backed up every day. Other files such as operating system (OS) and application program files that don't change often can be backed up on a lighter schedule—say, once a week. Backup frequency should depend on the critical nature of the data as well as the costs involved with losing and re-creating data from the same point in time. Some high-end transactional databases, for example, need to be backed up many times a day because of the high rate of transactions.

Amount of Data   The amount of data to be backed up will have a large bearing on the type of backup strategy you choose. Depending on how much information you need to save on a daily basis, you might be unable to perform a completely full backup of all your data every night because of the time it takes to perform the operation. To create a backup plan that can meet your objectives, you must achieve a balance between the type of data and the frequency with which it needs to be backed up. Instead of using full backups, you can try other alternatives, such as performing incremental or differential backups on information that has only recently changed.

Retention   You must decide how long you need to keep backed-up data. Depending on the type of business and the type of data, you might need to archive your backup data for long periods of time, so it will be available if you need to perform a restore. Other data might be needed only in the short term and can be deleted after a certain period of time.

Travel Advisory

The legal policy of some companies is to retain information for a certain period of time before the information must be destroyed. Check with your legal department to create a policy for backup media retention.

Backup Hardware

Several types of backup hardware and devices are available to suit the needs of the backup strategies of most companies. In the past, the most common type of backup system used was magnetic tape. These can be simple devices that contain only one tape drive, to large jukebox tape libraries with robotic autoloaders. Magnetic tape drives and media are flexible and offer relatively inexpensive storage, combined with speed and ease of use.

The vast amount of data storage used by today's hard drives that are into the terabyte (TB) territory, and the speed required to back up such a vast amount of data is slowly making tape backups a thing of the past. Today's backup systems use hard drives, including removable hard drives, or network-attached storage (NAS) that provide an array of disks to back up your data quickly over the network to secure storage and backup servers. Backup to tape, however, is still popular as a long-term archiving method.

Backup hardware should be routinely inspected for faults. Because of its mechanical nature, tape backup hardware is more prone to failure than typical electrical devices. Magnetic tape drives should be cleaned periodically with a special tape to clean the magnetic heads, which become dirty over time. Network-attached storage devices need to be monitored for failing hard drives that should be immediately replaced.

Backup Types

An important part of your backup strategy is deciding what type of backup you'll perform. Depending on the size of all the data you need to back up on a daily basis, a full backup of everything every night might be impossible to do. The amount of backup media required and the time needed to perform the backup can render this option unfeasible. The goal is to achieve the most efficient backup and restoration plan possible, depending on your environment and the type of data to be backed up.

Each file on a computer system contains a special bit of information, called the *archive bit.* When a file is modified or a new file is created, the archive bit is set to indicate the file needs to be backed up. When a backup is performed, the archive bit is either cleared or left as is, depending on the type of backup method chosen.

Full Backup   A *full backup* includes all files selected on a system. A full backup will clear the archive bit of each file after every backup session to indicate the file has been backed up. The advantages of a full backup include the fact that all data you selected is saved during every session, so all your system's data is backed up in full. If you need to restore all the information back on to the server, the recovery time is much shorter because it's saved in a specific backup session and can be restored with a single restore operation. For example, if you perform a full backup on Wednesday night and the server crashes Thursday morning, your data loss will be minimal. The disadvantages of using a full backup are that, depending on the amount of data you have, the backup could take up a large amount of media, and the time it takes to perform the backup could intrude on normal working hours, causing network delays and system latency.

Incremental Backup   With an *incremental backup,* only those files that have been modified since the previous full or incremental backup are stored. The archive bit is cleared on those files that are backed up. Incremental backups are much quicker to perform than full backups, and they use up much less space on backup media because you're saving only files that have been changed. The disadvantage of incremental backups is that to restore an entire system, you need to restore the last full backup and every incremental backup since then.

Differential Backup   A *differential backup* saves only files that have been changed since the last full backup. In this method, the archive bit isn't cleared, so with each differential backup, the list of files to save grows larger each day until the next full backup. The advantage of differential backups is that to restore an entire system, you need only the last full backup and the most recent differential backup. The disadvantage is the backups will take more time and use more media with each differential backup that takes place.

Exam Tip

Be aware of the advantages and disadvantages of each type of backup method, depending on the environment.

Media Rotation and Retention

Another important factor in your backup plan is determining the length of time that backup media and their data should be retained. Theoretically, you could save every backup you create forever, but this increases costs because of the large amount of backup media you'll need to purchase on a routine basis. Magnetic tape media usually deteriorate over time, and if you use the same tapes over and over, they'll quickly wear out. The integrity of your backups might be compromised if you continue to use the same tapes. Media rotation and retention policies must be defined to form the most efficient and safe use of your backup media. Several methods can be used for rotation and retention, from simple to the most complex.

Son Backup Method   The *son backup method* is the simplest method to use because it involves performing a full backup every day, using the same backup media each time. This method is used only for small backup requirements. The media can quickly wear out and must consistently be replaced. The son method doesn't allow for archiving, and if you need to perform a restore, you can use only the last backup as a source—so if the file you're looking for was deleted months ago, the data can't be recovered.

Father-Son Backup Method   The *father-son backup method* uses a combination of full and differential or incremental backups on a weekly basis. For example, daily media are used for a differential or incremental backup from Monday to Thursday, while Friday or weekend media are used to perform a full backup that can be archived away as a weekly backup. This method enables you to retrieve files archived from the previous week, using the weekly full backup. Additional backup media can be added to the strategy if further archiving is needed.

Grandfather-Father-Son Backup Method   The most common backup strategy is the *grandfather-father-son method.* This method is easy to administer and offers flexible archiving. Similar to the father-son method, daily backup media are assigned for incremental or differential backups. At the end of the week, a full backup is made, which is kept for one month. At the end of the month, a special monthly backup can be made, which is then kept for one year. This method enables you to archive data for at least a year.

Backup Documentation

Your backup plan should be carefully documented, so if the primary backup operator is unavailable, another person can perform the backup operator's functions, such as changing backup media, sending backup media offsite, performing restores, and examining backup log files. The document should outline what systems are backed up, how often they're backed up and by what method, and the location and directories of the data. The documentation should also describe any special media labeling used and contact information for any offsite storage facilities. The documentation should be constantly reviewed and updated when new hardware and software are installed. New systems with new data must be added to your backup routine immediately.

> **Travel Advisory**
>
> When adding a new system or a directory/file to a network server, ensure that it's added to your backup schedule.

Restoration

The ultimate goal of any backup system is the ability to restore lost or corrupted data from the backup media. It's amazing to think that most companies don't test the backups they've made. The only true way of testing a backup system is to perform routine test restores. Although your backup application logs might show that no problems exist and that backups have completed successfully, a hardware problem could exist with a tape drive or hard drive storage that causes the written data to be corrupted.

> **Travel Advisory**
>
> One of the most important aspects of a backup strategy is regularly testing backups by performing test restores. Remember that your backups are no good unless you know the information can be restored.

When performing regular file restoration, the best practice is not to overwrite any original files of the data you're trying to restore. Create a separate directory and restore the file there. This way, the user can decide which version is required. If the original file and directory have been completely deleted, there's no need for this extra step.

All your backup media should be properly labeled, so that in case of an emergency—where time is of the essence—the correct media containing the data can be quickly located and restored.

Offsite Storage

In the event of a disaster at your primary site, such as fire or a flood, any backup media stored there could also be destroyed. All the data that's saved to backup will be lost, and you won't have other backups available. This is why you should store copies of the backup media offsite. Offsite storage is an important part of your overall disaster recovery plan. Using an offsite storage facility means after you successfully complete your backups, they're sent to a different location, which could be another office building or a special storage company facility.

> ### Travel Advisory
> In case you want to keep your most recent backup media onsite, you can make two copies of your full backup, and then send one of them to the offsite storage company and keep the other. However, creating the extra backup requires extra time and backup media.

When choosing an offsite storage facility, you must ensure it follows the same basic rules of facility security measures that you follow at your own site. You should visit the location where your backup media will be stored to examine the environment. For example, the storage area should be regulated for temperature, humidity, fire prevention, and static electricity prevention. Access control should be strictly enforced, so only authorized employees of your company can retrieve backup media from the facility. Depending on the type of data you're sending offsite, you should identify how quickly you'll need access to the media, if and when this is necessary. The storage facility should allow access at all hours in case you need a backup in an emergency.

Online Backup

With the vast increase in Internet bandwidth speed and capacity, online backup services that back up your data over the Internet are a popular alternative for offsite storage of physical backup media. Client software is installed on your system, and an initial upload takes place of your data. Depending on the size of data, this can take many days before the full body of data is synchronized. After the initial synchronization, your file system is constantly scanned, and changed files are automatically synchronized over the Internet to a secure server.

Some online servers only offer synchronization services that only keep a copy of your data in its current state. There is no way to retrieve a file that was changed two weeks ago but modified several times since that initial change, or files that have been deleted. Other services offer version control, where you can restore a deleted file, or a version of a file several weeks old.

For security, you must make sure the online backup server stores your data in encrypted form, and that all network communications with the service are over encrypted channels such as an SSL connection.

Online backup services are geared toward individual systems or small business servers, and they cannot scale to back up the vast amount of data for a large company or datacenter. For these larger networks, the same online backup principles can be applied and the data kept securely within the company's networks by synchronizing or backing up data between geographically different sites.

Objective 3.03
CompTIA Security+
Objective 2.8

Exemplify the Concepts of Confidentiality, Integrity, and Availability (CIA)

Ensuring data protection and business continuity in the event of a disaster utilizes these major concepts of information security.

- **Confidentiality** Confidentiality prevents sensitive and private data from being intercepted or read by unauthorized users. Data must be protected in its primary storage location, when data is backed up, and when it is transmitted to another user over a network.

- **Integrity** Integrity ensures that your data is consistent and never modified by unauthorized persons or manipulated in any intentional or accidental manner. Data integrity includes the use of proper authentication and authorization security techniques for protecting against data manipulation, but it also includes redundancy planning and fault-tolerant systems that protect data from corruption.

- **Availability** Availability ensures that your systems and networks are always operational and providing service to users. Your organization's networks and data must be available to authorized users as required at all times without interruption. Your disaster recovery and business continuity plans make sure through the use of redundancy and fault tolerance that interruptions do not happen, and if there is downtime, it can be resolved very quickly.

Objective 3.04
CompTIA Security+
Objective 2.6

Explain the Impact and Proper Use of Environmental Controls

Security is often considered as protection against theft, vandalism, or unauthorized access to a company's computer systems. Typically, not enough thought and planning are put into the security of your actual facility, which is the first line of defense for your employees and your company's assets. Threats from unauthorized network access are a great concern, but protecting your facilities from environmental concerns, such as fires and floods, is equally important.

At the minimum, the facility itself must adhere to any local and national safety standards as they pertain to building construction, fire ratings, and electrical code. Many of these issues need to be resolved before and during the time the facility is being constructed.

To protect your employees and sensitive equipment that resides inside the building, a regulated environment should be provided that controls and monitors the temperature, humidity, electrical systems, ventilation, and fire-suppression systems.

Facility Construction Issues

Before the foundation of a new company facility is laid, an incredible amount of planning goes into the construction process. Part of that process should involve the physical security and safety of the new facility. Several issues must be considered, often even before the new location is chosen. These main issues include location planning, building construction, and computer room construction.

Location Planning

When planning the location for a proposed company facility, several factors must be considered. Unless secrecy of the facility is desired, the building should be in a visible area and situated comfortably within the surrounding terrain. The building should be easily accessible from major roads, highways, or even railway or coastal ports, depending on the type of business. The building facility should have proper lighting for its entrances, both for the security of the employees and for adequate light for security camera recording. Most important, the site should be analyzed in respect to its susceptibility to natural disasters. If the building is located in a valley, could flooding occur? Is the building situated in an area prone to tornadoes, hurricanes, or earthquakes? All these factors should be incorporated into an overall site plan.

Facility Construction

After the site has been chosen, the actual construction of the facility must be carefully planned and executed. The construction materials need to be studied for their compliance with local and national safety standards, including fire and structural-strength ratings. Building security must also be a high priority during construction. The following outlines some of the key components of building construction, including some recommendations to enhance security:

- **Walls** Walls must be examined for fire and strength ratings. For high-security areas, walls might need to be reinforced with stronger materials.
- **Doors** Doors should be resistant to forced entry and fitted with security mechanisms, such as basic or electronic locks. Emergency doors must be carefully placed for access during an emergency.
- **Ceilings** Ceilings should be examined for their fire rating, and materials should be made of noncombustible materials. The decision to use a drop ceiling is a balance between security and convenience. Although a drop ceiling is good for cable management, it also inadvertently provides access to other areas and rooms.
- **Windows** Windows should be resistant to shattering and placed accordingly to prevent access to sensitive areas of the building. For added security, the windows can be made opaque or reflective, so no one can see into them from the outside. Computer screens should face away from the windows so that they cannot be viewed from the outside.
- **Flooring** Flooring should be carefully chosen for its fire rating and susceptibility to combustion. The flooring surfaces should be conducive to a nonconductive, nonstatic environment.

Computer Room Construction

To preserve the integrity and security of sensitive computer and networking equipment, these components should be housed in a separate environmentally and security controlled room. This room should not be accessible by other doors, rooms, corridors, or stairs. Only one secured doorway should exist, which employees can enter and exit.

Inside, servers and networking equipment are usually stacked in a rack or cabinet that can be secured by a lock. Cabling is typically run up to the ceiling, down through the floor, or high up on the walls using special cable management trays. This prevents people from tripping over equipment or wiring that might be strewn haphazardly over the floor.

The room should also be designed for maximum air ventilation and installed with environmental controls to regulate both temperature and humidity.

Exam Tip

Ensure that you know the special considerations for computer network room security compared to other parts of the building.

Environmental Issues

Computers and electronic equipment are sensitive to environmental factors such as temperature, humidity, and air and power quality. Imbalances in any of these utilities can result in severe damage to computer equipment, and they can potentially cause even greater perils to both the people and the facilities. Environmental controls must be installed and continuously monitored for proper operation.

Temperature

Sensitive computer and electronic equipment must operate in a climate-controlled environment. To provide a proper operating environment, the temperature and humidity of a computer facility must be carefully controlled and maintained. In addition, computer facilities should be equipped with an industrial air conditioner to keep the entire room at a steady, cool temperature. Overheating of computer equipment can cause disruption or even total equipment failure. When devices overheat, their components expand and retract, which can eventually damage them permanently. In a computer system itself, several fans circulate the air and cool the components inside.

Hot and Cold Aisles   *Hot and cold aisles* are an air circulation technique often used in large data centers with rows and rows of equipment racks, as shown in Figure 3.1. A cold aisle has the front of the two adjoining rows of equipment facing each other over a vented floor with cool air passing upward. This allows the cool, air-conditioned air to flow into the front of the equipment racks to cool them down. The backs of each row of equipment face into a hot aisle, where the fans from the equipment racks on each side of the row push out hot air.

Through the use of cool air vents and hot air intakes from the HVAC (heating, ventilation, and air conditioning) units, this creates a constant flow of air circulation to prevent buildup of heat emanating from the back of the equipment racks and allows cool air to flow into the front of the equipment racks.

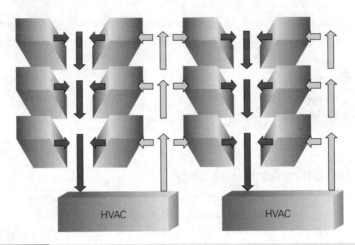

FIGURE 3.1   Hot and cold aisles

Humidity

Humidity levels are important to the overall operating health of computer equipment because high humidity can cause corrosion of the internal parts of a system. Low humidity levels create a dry environment where the buildup of static electricity can cause great harm to electronic equipment, so humidity levels should be set between 40 and 50 percent. Static electricity can also be minimized in the environment through the use of special antistatic mats and wrist bands, which can be used by technicians who regularly touch the equipment.

Ventilation

The quality of the air circulating through the computer facility must be maintained through the proper use of ventilation techniques. Without proper ventilation, a risk of airborne contaminants occurs. These contaminants could be dust or other microscopic particles that can get inside and clog such critical equipment as the fans, which need to be running to keep the system cool.

Monitoring

The temperature and humidity of your equipment rooms must be constantly monitored to make sure they are maintaining a safe environment for your computer equipment. A failed air conditioning unit can cause your computer equipment room temperature to soar immediately, causing equipment shutdown and failure within several minutes.

The monitoring equipment must be able to actively generate alarms so that you will be alerted to a significant change in temperature. This gives you time to quickly shut down systems before they overheat. Individual devices may also have diagnostic tools that can alert you to changes in the temperature of a device.

Electrical Power

Another important environmental concern is the electrical power system that runs your equipment. Electrical power must be provided with consistent voltage levels and a minimum of interference. Even small fluctuations in power can cause irreparable damage to sensitive electronic equipment. Power protection has two aspects: ensuring the consistency and quality of your primary power source, and maintaining the availability of alternate power in a power outage.

Several types of fluctuations can occur:

- **Blackout**   A prolonged period without any power
- **Brownout**   A prolonged period of lower than normal power
- **Spike**   A momentary jump to a high voltage
- **Sag**   A moment of low voltage
- **Surge**   A prolonged period of high voltage

To protect your equipment against these different types of perils, you can use several devices. Simple power-surge protectors generally aren't rated for expensive types of computer equipment. Usually, these types of power bars contain some type of fuse or circuit breaker that cuts off the power in a spike or a surge. By the time the breaker cuts in, the moment of high voltage has already been reached and has possibly damaged the equipment that's plugged into the power bar. The recommendation is for most computer systems, servers, and network infrastructures to use a UPS that works on a variety of levels as both a high-end surge protector and during a power failure.

Travel Advisory

Don't plug power bars or high-load peripherals, such as laser printers, into UPS power outlets, because they can quickly overload the UPS.

To provide clean and consistent power to computer equipment, a device called a line or power conditioner can be used. It plugs directly into the power supply outlet and ensures that the power that reaches the computer equipment is free of voltage fluctuations and interference.

For large organizations with critical high-availability requirements, a more expensive option for backup power is the use of a backup power generator that runs on a battery or fuel. When using batteries, a power generator has a finite

time that it can run until the battery power runs out. With fuel-based generators, the generator can be kept operational as long as it continues to be filled
with fuel, and it provides electricity even for very long blackout periods as long
as fuel is available.

Cable Shielding

Network cabling can be extremely sensitive to environmental electrical interference. This type of disruption can cause loss of information, network latency,
and the complete disabling of the network. These types of problems are most
pronounced in manufacturing environments where computers and networking
cabling run side-by-side with large machines. The following are the most common type of problems that affect network cabling:

- **EMI**   *Electromagnetic interference* is caused by the electrical "noise"
  created by motors, lighting, and any type of electronic or mechanical
  equipment. This interference can potentially disrupt communications
  on network cabling because of the noise in the line that distorts the
  network signals.
- **Crosstalk**   *Crosstalk* is caused by the electrical signals of one wire
  disrupting the signals of another wire. Without proper shielding,
  network cabling is susceptible to crosstalk, especially twisted-pair wiring.
- **Attenuation**   As an electronic signal travels, it slowly degrades over a
  certain distance. The longer a network cable, the more susceptible it is
  to this type of signal degradation. The rate of *attenuation* increases
  when the type of network signaling is using higher frequencies for
  faster data transfer. Attenuation can also be caused by damaged or
  faulty network cabling.

To prevent these problems from affecting your network communications,
the cabling you use should be properly shielded. Different types of cabling use
different kinds of shielding methods.

Exam Tip

Be aware of the different types of interference that can affect
network cabling.

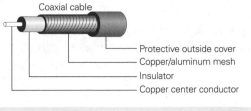

FIGURE 3.2 Coaxial cabling

Coaxial

Coaxial cabling consists of a special copper core wire that's surrounded by several layers of protection. The copper wire is insulated by PVC or Teflon-based material, as shown in Figure 3.2. This, in turn, is wrapped with a braided shielding material, and then the cable is covered with a protective outer sheath. This cabling is resistant to EMI and, most often, is installed in manufacturing environments because of the large amounts of interference that can result from nearby electrical and mechanical equipment.

Twisted Pair

Twisted-pair cabling consists of several insulated copper wires, surrounded by a protective sheath. The copper wires are twisted together to protect them from EMI and to balance the crosstalk between the individual wires. Two types of twisted-pair cabling exist: shielded and unshielded. Shielded twisted-pair (STP) cabling contains an extra layer of foil shielding for added protection, as shown in Figure 3.3.

Unshielded twisted-pair (UTP) cabling, which doesn't have this protection, is shown in Figure 3.4. UTP is the most common form of cabling because the extra shielding of STP makes it much more expensive.

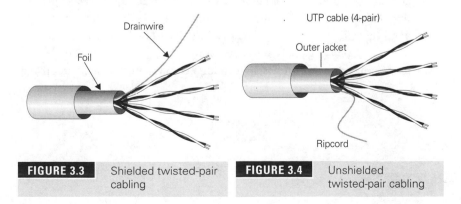

FIGURE 3.3 Shielded twisted-pair cabling

FIGURE 3.4 Unshielded twisted-pair cabling

Fiber-Optic

Because fiber-optic technology uses light as the medium for communication, it isn't susceptible to electromagnetic interference, crosstalk, or attenuation. Fiber-optic cabling is expensive and is typically used in large local area networks (LANs) as the backbone among smaller networks using coaxial or twisted-pair cabling. Figure 3.5 shows a cross section of a fiber-optic cable.

Wireless Networks and Cells

Although no physical wires are involved with wireless communications, wireless networks can still be disrupted in many ways. Because wireless networks use a common frequency band—typically in the 2.4 or 5.8 GHz range—they can suffer from interference from other devices that use those frequencies, such as cordless phones and microwave ovens.

Another problem is that the overlapping of *wireless cells* can cause disruptions in communications, especially when a user is tied to a specific access point. An *access point* is a wireless base station that connects the wireless clients to a wired network. A *cell* is a specific area of influence of that access point or other cellular system base station. Users suffer signal degradation as they travel farther from the access point. The ranges for wireless access points are typically 500 feet indoors and 1000 feet outdoors.

Local Lingo
wireless cell   A division of wireless networks containing a certain range of frequencies that can be used.

Fire Suppression

Although fire suppression is typically already part of the facility plans, fire suppression for a computer environment can differ from techniques used to protect building structures and their contents. The most obvious difference is that suppressing a fire with water in a computer facility that's filled with a large number of electronic servers, personal computers, laptops, printers, and network devices can be as damaging as the fire itself. Although computer equipment–approved

FIGURE 3.5   Fiber-optic cabling

fire extinguishers are available, other effects of a fire, such as smoke and high temperatures, can also be damaging to computer equipment.

The key elements of fire protection are early detection and suppression. Early detection is a must in preventing fires from escalating from a small, minor fire to a raging inferno. Timing is of the essence, and you can detect a fire in several ways.

- **Smoke detectors**   Smoke detectors are the most common form of warning device. Through the use of optical or photoelectric technology, a beam of light is emitted, and the smoke detector sets off an alarm if it detects a change in the light's intensity. As smoke filters into the unit, it senses the changes in the light pattern.
- **Flame detectors**   A flame detection unit can sense the movements of a flame or detect the energy that's a result of combustion. Flame detection units tend to be more expensive than other options, and they're typically used in high-security environments that require advanced fire-detection techniques.
- **Heat detectors**   A heat detector can detect fires by sensing when a predetermined temperature threshold has been reached. When the temperature from the fire grows to a certain level, an alarm is triggered. Heat detector units can also detect rapid changes of temperature that indicate the presence of a fire.
- **Video monitoring**   A video monitoring system allows you to look for any visible environmental concerns in a computer equipment room, such as smoke or flames that indicate a fire. Full time video monitoring requires a dedicated security team, and this is typically reserved for protection of larger data centers.

When a fire is detected, a mechanism must be initiated to suppress the fire. A fire can be suppressed in several ways, each with its own positive and negative aspects, depending on the type of fire and the environment of the location.

Water

Water is the most common type of fire suppressant, but for computer facilities that contain a large amount of electrical equipment, water can be damaging. The use of water during an electrical fire can make the fire worse, causing even more damage. Water sprinkler systems usually consist of sprinkler heads that are distributed evenly throughout the area to provide maximum coverage. In some cases, the detection system can be configured to shut down the electrical supply before the water sprinklers turn on.

Chemical-Based Fire Suppression

Older fire suppression units for computer facilities used *Halon,* a special fire-suppressing gas that can neutralize the chemical combustion of a fire. Halon acts quickly and causes no damage to computers and electrical equipment. Unfortunately, because of its environmental drawbacks, including depletion of ozone and the possibility of danger to humans when used in large amounts, Halon is no longer manufactured. Halon still currently exists in some building installations, if they were installed before restrictions on Halon were put in place.

Several more environmentally safe chemical-based replacements exist for Halon, such as FM-200 and Argon, which work the same way to neutralize a fire.

CHECKPOINT

✔**Objective 3.01: Compare and contrast aspects of business continuity.** Create a disaster recovery plan that documents your risks, the business impact of a disaster, a contingency plan, succession planning, and network and facility documentation. Test your business continuity and disaster recovery plans on a regular basis.

✔**Objective 3.02: Execute disaster recovery plans and procedures.**   Perform backups to save and archive critical company data. Full backups are recommended if time and space permit, but if not, use incremental or differential schemes. Test your backups by performing a restore on a scheduled basis. Consider using alternative sites for disaster recovery purposes. Maintain high availability of your services by implementing redundancy, data integrity protection, and fault tolerance. Use RAID for disk storage systems. Determine the level of RAID redundancy appropriate to the importance of the data you're protecting. Keep spare parts of common hardware on hand, so it can be replaced immediately.

✔**Objective 3.03: Exemplify the concepts of confidentiality, integrity, and availability (CIA).**   Confidentiality prevents sensitive and private data from being intercepted or read by unauthorized users. Integrity ensures that your data is consistent and never modified by unauthorized persons or manipulated in any intentional or accidental manner. Availability ensures that your systems and networks are always operational and providing service to users.

✔**Objective 3.04: Explain the impact and proper use of environmental controls.** Environmental protection for your computer equipment rooms involves temperature and humidity management, proper ventilation (hot and cold aisles), electrical protection with UPS and power conditioners, and fire detection and suppression. Be aware of electromagnetic interference attenuation with network cabling.

REVIEW QUESTIONS

1. You need to set up an alternate backup site that contains networking and server equipment that is ready immediately for operation in the event of a disaster. Which of the following sites is required?

   A. Warm site

   B. Hot site

   C. Cold site

   D. Offsite

2. Which of the following disaster recovery concepts describes the ability to provide uninterrupted services?

   A. Fault tolerance

   B. High availability

   C. Contingency planning

   D. Business impact analysis

3. You are installing a database server that requires several hard drives in a RAID array. In the event one of the drives fails, you need to be able to swap out a failed hard drive with no downtime. Which of the following types of hard drives do you require?

   A. Cold swap

   B. Suspend swap

   C. Warm swap

   D. Hot swap

4. Your company is in the middle of budgeting for disaster recovery. You have been asked to justify the cost for offsite backup media storage. What is the primary security purpose of storing backup media at an offsite storage facility?

   A. So that the facility can copy the data to a RAID system

   B. So that, if the primary site is down, the offsite storage can reload your systems from backup at their facility

   C. For proper archive labeling and storage

   D. To prevent a disaster onsite from destroying the only copies of your backup media

5. You have implemented a backup plan for your critical file servers, including proper media rotation, backup frequency, and offsite storage. Which of the following must be performed on a regular basis to ensure the validity and integrity of your backup system?

   A. Periodic testing of restores

   B. Multiple monthly backup media

   C. Purchasing of new media

   D. Updating the backup application software

6. As part of your organization's contingency plan in the event of a disaster, which of the following would be the primary component of the organization to make functional after an initial disaster incident?

   A. Check all file servers and make sure they are running.

   B. Retrieve all backup tapes from the offsite storage facility.

   C. Ensure basic communications such as phone and Internet connectivity are functional.

   D. Ensure that web servers are able to accept requests from customers.

7. You must ensure that power is always available (24/7) for a critical web and database server that accepts customer orders and processes transactions. Which of the following devices should be installed?

   A. Power conditioner

   B. UPS

   C. Power generator

   D. Redundant power supply

8. You are installing network cabling for the main backbone of a manufacturing facility network. The manufacturing machinery generates a significant amount of EMI. Which of the following network cabling types should you use?

   A. STP

   B. Fiber-optic

   C. UTP

   D. Coaxial cable

9. You are performing a risk analysis of the environmental factors for your primary server equipment room. Which of the following environmental issues is most likely to affect an enclosed server room?

    A. Average humidity levels

    B. Cool temperatures

    C. Flooding

    D. High temperatures

10. During disaster recovery planning, you must ensure you have plans in place for succession planning. Which of the following concepts describes succession planning?

    A. Replacing key employees who are unavailable during a disaster

    B. Organizing an emergency contact list

    C. Having an alternate hot site facility in place

    D. Availability of onsite spare parts and servers

REVIEW ANSWERS

1. **B** A hot site contains enough networking and server equipment to continue your business operations in case a disaster strikes your primary facility. Warm sites and cold sites contain little to no existing equipment or infrastructure.

2. **B** The ability to provide uninterrupted service is referred to as high availability. This is important for businesses that require the services or products they offer to be available at all times.

3. **D** A hot swap device, such as a hard drive, can be inserted or removed without the need to shut down the server. This enables you to retain the availability of the services on that server.

4. **D** All backup plans should require backup media to be sent to an offsite storage facility. If a disaster destroys your physical location, the backup media will be safe.

5. **A** Regularly testing your backups by performing a test restore is the only way to ensure that your backup data is valid and the data intact. If the information cannot be restored, your backup plan is not providing any benefit for a disaster recovery scenario.

6. **C** The most important part of the company to get operational is basic communications, such as phones, networking connectivity, and e-mail. Until these communication lines are functional, the ability to coordinate the disaster recovery effort will be greatly reduced.

7. **C** A power generator is required to ensure that there is always power for your server. A UPS battery typically contains only enough power to run a system for about 10 to 20 minutes, while a power conditioner or redundant power supply will not help if there is no power to run them.

8. **B** Because fiber-optic cabling uses light to transfer information over the cables, they aren't susceptible to electromagnetic interference.

9. **D** Server rooms can quickly rise in temperature with so many systems running in an enclosed area. At high temperatures, CPUs and hard drives can shut down due to the excessive heat. Most server rooms contain air-conditioning systems that keep the temperature regulated and cooler than normal. If this air-conditioning system fails, the heat can dramatically rise within minutes.

10. **A** Succession planning makes sure that you have replacements for key employees in the event they are unavailable during the disaster recovery phase. This requires that employees will have the same security clearance and be able to immediately take over the responsibilities of another employee's position.

Cryptography

Chapter 4   Cryptography and Encryption Basics

Chapter 5   Public Key Infrastructure

Cryptography and Encryption Basics

ITINERARY

- **Objective 4.01** Summarize general cryptography concepts
- **Objective 4.02** Use and apply appropriate cryptographic tools and products

	NEWBIE	SOME EXPERIENCE	EXPERT
ETA	3 hours	2 hours	1 hour

Cryptography is the conversion of communicated information into secret code that keeps the information confidential and private. The protection of sensitive communications has been the basis of cryptography throughout history. Modern cryptography performs essentially the same function, but with added functionality to accommodate personal and business communications and transactions in the digital world, such as *authentication, data integrity,* and *nonrepudiation.*

The central function of cryptography is *encryption,* the transformation of data into an unreadable form. Encryption ensures privacy by keeping the information hidden from those for whom the information is not intended. *Decryption,* the opposite of encryption, transforms encrypted data back into an intelligible form. Even though someone might be able to read the encrypted data, it won't make any sense until it's been properly decrypted.

The encryption and decryption process involves taking data in *plain text,* which is readable and understandable text, and manipulating its form to create *ciphertext.* When data has been transformed into *ciphertext,* the plain text becomes inaccessible until it's decrypted. The entire process is illustrated in Figure 4.1.

This process enables the transmission of confidential information over an insecure communications path, greatly decreasing the possibility of the data being compromised. In a file storage system, data is protected by *authentication* and *access controls* that prevent unauthorized users from accessing some files. When this data is transmitted over a network, these controls no longer exist, and the data becomes vulnerable to interception. If the information or the communications channel itself is encrypted, the chance of someone intercepting and deciphering the data is extremely slim.

This chapter details the subjects of cryptography and encryption, including mathematical algorithms, public key infrastructure systems, and encryption standards and protocols.

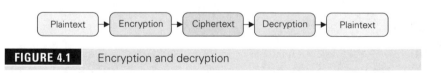

FIGURE 4.1   Encryption and decryption

Summarize General Cryptography Concepts

Today's cryptography involves more than hiding secrets with encryption systems. With the world using more technological means to perform business and legal functions, such as purchasing items from a web-based store, conducting online banking, and digitally signing documents, the need for strong and secure encryption systems to protect these transactions is vital.

Information Assurance

Information assurance is a method of protecting information and information systems by providing confidentiality, integrity, authentication, and nonrepudiation.

Confidentiality

Confidentiality is the concept of ensuring that data is not made available or disclosed to unauthorized people. Processes such as encryption must be used on the data, network infrastructure, and communication channels to protect against data interception and disclosure.

Integrity

Data *integrity* is the protection of information from damage or deliberate manipulation. Integrity is extremely critical for any kind of business or electronic commerce. Data integrity guarantees that when information has been stored or communicated, it hasn't been changed or manipulated in transit. The cryptological function of hashing is often used to create signatures for files that indicate if the file has been tampered with if the hashed value does not match the original.

Authentication

Authentication is the concept of uniquely identifying individuals to provide assurance of an individual user's identity. It is the act of ensuring that a person is who he claims to be. Typical physical and logical authentication methods include the use of identification cards, door locks and keys, and network logins and passwords. For modern e-commerce and legal applications, this type of authentication needs to be tightly controlled. Encrypted digital certificates are used to identify users electronically on a network. Encrypted forms of authentication can also be used in smart cards, which are a more secure medium than a typical ID badge.

Nonrepudiation

Nonrepudiation is the term used to describe the inability of a person to deny or repudiate the origin of a signature or document, or the receipt of a message or document. For example, a user could legally prove that an electronic document or transaction did not originate with her. The user could have digitally signed a contract that was transmitted through e-mail, but if the data or transmission wasn't considered secure because of the lack of encryption, the user might legally claim it was tampered with and call its integrity into question. By implementing nonrepudiation processes, a cryptographic system can be considered secure for business and legal transactions.

Exam Tip

A specific type of encryption scheme, algorithm, or protocol may cover only certain parts of the information assurance objectives. For example, certain encryption protocols concern themselves only with authentication, while others cover all the objectives of confidentiality, integrity, authentication, and nonrepudiation.

Algorithms

A system that provides encryption and decryption services is called a *cryptosystem*. The cryptosystem uses a mathematical encryption *algorithm*, or *cipher*, to turn data into ciphertext. An algorithm is a complex mathematical formula that dictates how the encryption and decryption process takes place. Because these mathematical algorithms are usually publicly known, the cryptosystem is strengthened with the addition of a secret key, as shown in Figure 4.2.

A *key* is like a password that's combined with an algorithm to create the ciphertext. The encryption can't be deciphered unless the key is used to decrypt it. No one can simply unravel the algorithm to decode the message, because the key is also needed. Depending on the encryption mechanism used, the key might be used for both encryption and decryption, while different keys might be used for encryption and decryption for other systems.

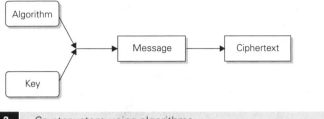

FIGURE 4.2 Cryptosystem using algorithms

The strength of the key depends on the algorithm's *keyspace,* which is a specific range of values—usually measured in bits—that's created by the algorithm to contain keys. A key is made up of random values within the keyspace range. A larger keyspace containing more bits means more available values exist to use for different keys, effectively increasing the difficulty for someone to compromise the system. The smaller the keyspace, the greater the chance someone can decipher the key value.

The strength of the cryptosystem lies in the strength and effectiveness of its algorithm and the size of the keyspace. Most attackers use some method of brute-force attack to figure out the cryptosystem by processing large numbers of values to subvert the algorithm. No matter how strong the algorithm, it will be rendered useless if someone obtains the key, so the key must be protected, and one of the methods is by encryption protocols for secure key delivery.

Travel Advisory

Most attacks on encryption center on the interception of keys rather than on attempts to subvert the algorithm, which requires large processing resources.

Two main types of cipher encryption can be used:

- **Substitution** In its most simplified form, a *substitution* cipher takes plain text and substitutes the original characters in the data with other characters. For example, the letters *ABC* can be substituted by reversing the alphabet, so the cipher form will read *ZYX*. Modern substitution encryption ciphers are much more complex, performing many types of substitutions with more than one alphabet.

- **Transposition** In a *transposition* cipher, the characters are rearranged through mathematical permutations. When used with difficult mathematical formulas, these ciphers can be extremely complex.

Most modern ciphers use a combination of long sequences of substitution and transposition schemes. The data is filtered through an algorithm that performs these complex substitution and transposition operations to arrive at the ciphertext.

Two main types of encryption use key values and complex algorithms: *symmetric* and *asymmetric.*

Symmetric Keys

In a *symmetric* encryption scheme, both parties use the same key for encryption and decryption purposes. Each user must possess the same key to send encrypted messages to each other, as shown in Figure 4.3. The sender uses the key to encrypt the message and then transmits it to the receiver. The receiver, who is in possession of the same key, uses it to decrypt the message.

The security of this encryption model relies on the end users to protect the secret key properly. If an unauthorized user were able to intercept the key, she would be able to read any encrypted messages sent by other users by decrypting the message with the key intercepted. It's extremely important that a user protect the key itself as well as any communications in which he transmits the key to another user.

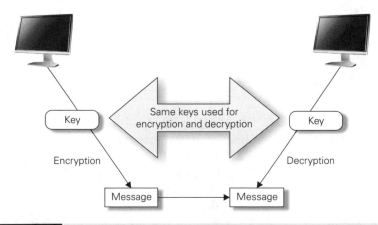

FIGURE 4.3 Symmetric key encryption

One of the main disadvantages of symmetric encryption schemes is that they don't scale well with large numbers of users. A user needs different keys depending on the person with whom he is communicating—with a large number of users, the number of keys that need to be distributed and tracked can become enormous. Another disadvantage is that the system needs a secure mechanism to deliver keys to the end users. Symmetric systems can offer confidentiality only through encryption; they offer little in the way of authentication and nonrepudiation.

Symmetric systems, however, can be difficult to crack if a large key size is used. A symmetric system is also much faster than asymmetric encryption because the underlying algorithms are more simple and efficient.

Two main types of symmetric encryption can be used:

- **Stream cipher** A *stream cipher* encrypts data one bit at a time, as opposed to a block cipher, which works on blocks of text. Stream ciphers, by design, are fast compared to block ciphers. The encryption of any plain-text data with a block cipher results in the same ciphertext when the same key is used. With stream ciphers, each bit of the plain-text stream is transformed into a different ciphertext bit. A stream cipher generates a key stream that's combined with the plain-text data to provide encryption.

- **Block cipher** A *block cipher* encrypts entire blocks of data, rather than smaller bits of data as with stream cipher methods. A block cipher transforms a particular block of plain-text data into a block of ciphertext data of the same length. For many block ciphers, the block size is 64 bits.

Popular symmetric algorithms include Advanced Encryption Standard (AES), Data Encryption Standard (DES), Blowfish, Twofish, International Data Encryption Algorithm (IDEA), and RC5 (Rivest Cipher).

Asymmetric Keys

In an *asymmetric* encryption scheme, everyone uses different, but mathematically related, keys for encryption and decryption purposes, as shown in Figure 4.4.

Even though the keys are mathematically similar, they can't be derived from each other. An asymmetric scheme is the basis for the *public key* system. Two keys are created for encryption and decryption purposes: One key is the public key, which is known to all users, while the private key remains secret and is given to the user to keep private. To use this system, a user will encrypt a message or file with the intended receiver's public key. To decrypt this message, the receiver

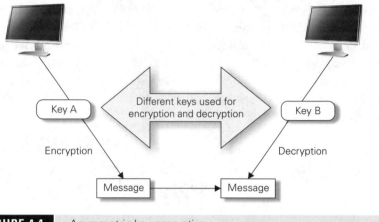

FIGURE 4.4   Asymmetric key encryption

will use a private key that only he possesses. No one else can decrypt the message without this private key. Public keys can be passed directly among users or found in directories of public keys.

Another encryption concept related to asymmetric cryptography is that of key escrow. Key escrow involves a third party, such as a government agency or an authorized organization, that holds a special third key on top of your private and public key pair. The third key is used to encrypt the private key, which is then stored in a secure location. This third key can be used to unlock the encrypted copy of the private key in case of loss or the theft of the original key.

Travel Assistance

Key escrow is described in more detail in Chapter 5.

The advantage of this system over symmetric schemes is that it offers a level of authentication. By decrypting a message with a sender's public key, the receiver knows this message came from the sender. The sender is authenticated because, to be decrypted with a public key, the private key had to be used to perform the initial encryption.

Exam Tip

Recognize how the different combinations of key-pair encryption methods can provide different levels of information assurance such as authentication, confidentiality, and integrity.

The main disadvantage of asymmetric encryption is that it can be much slower than symmetric schemes. Unlike symmetric systems, however, asymmetric schemes offer confidentiality, authentication, and also nonrepudiation, which prevents a user from repudiating a signed communication. Asymmetric schemes also provide more manageable and efficient ways for dealing with key distribution.

Popular asymmetric algorithms and applications include RSA (named for creators Rivest, Shamir, and Adleman), Elliptical Curve, Digital Signature Standard (DSS), and Diffie-Hellman.

> **Exam Tip**
>
> In a symmetric encryption scheme, both parties use the same key for encryption and decryption purposes. In an asymmetric encryption scheme, everyone uses a different (but mathematically related) key for encryption and decryption.

Steganography

Steganography does not involve algorithms to encrypt data; it is a method of hiding data in another type of media that effectively conceals the existence of the data. This is typically performed by hiding messages in graphics images such as bitmap (BMP) files or other types of media files such as digital music files. Many companies hide a watermark (a hidden image) within a company image to be able to prove it is owned by the company in the event it is being used by another company or person. Unused sectors of a hard disk can also be used in steganography. These types of files contain insignificant data bits that can be replaced by the data to be hidden without affecting the original file enough to be detected.

Digital Signatures

A *digital signature* is an encrypted hash value used to ensure the identity and integrity of a message. The signature can be attached to a message to uniquely identify the sender. Like a written signature, the digital signature guarantees the individual sending the message is who he claims to be. The sender runs a hash function on his message, takes the resulting hash value, encrypts it with his private key, and sends it along with the message. When the receiver gets the signed message, he first decrypts the encrypted hash with the corresponding public key (verifies the sender) and then performs his own hashing function on the message. The calculated hash is then compared against the unencrypted hash, and if they are the same, the receiver knows the message hasn't been altered in transmission.

Basic Hashing Concepts

A *hashing* value is used in encryption systems to create a "fingerprint" for a message. This prevents the message from being improperly accessed on its way to its destination. In the overall information assurance model, hashing is used to protect the integrity of a message and is most often used with digital signatures.

The most commonly used hashing function is the *one-way hash,* a mathematical function that takes a variable-sized message and transforms it into a fixed-length value referred to as either a *hash value* or a *message digest.* This function is *one-way* because it's difficult to invert the procedure, and the procedure is never decrypted. The hash value represents the longer message from which it was created. This hash value is appended to the message that's sent to another user, as shown in Figure 4.5. The receiver then performs the same hashing function on the message and compares the resulting hash value with the one sent with the message. If they're identical, the message was altered.

Attacks against one-way hash functions can be prevented by longer hash values that are less susceptible to brute-force attacks. A good minimum starting point for the size of a hash value is 128 bits. The most common problem with weak hashing algorithms is the possibility of *hash value collisions* that occur when two hashed messages result in the same hashing value. When these collisions are discovered, they can be used to reveal the underlying algorithm. *Birthday attacks,* a class of brute-force attacks, are often used to find collisions of hash functions. The birthday attack gets its name from this surprising result: The probability that two or more people in a group of 23 share the same birthday is greater than one half. Such a result is called a *birthday paradox.* In encryption terms, if an attacker finds two hashed values that are the same, she has a greater chance of cracking the algorithm with this information.

The following sections describe some of the common hashing algorithms in use today.

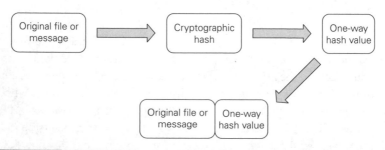

| | FIGURE 4.5 | One-way hash appended to a message to protect its integrity |

Message Digest Hashing

Message digest hashing algorithms are used for digital signature applications when a large message must be hashed in a secure manner. A digital signature is created when the digest of the message is encrypted using the sender's private key. These algorithms take a message of variable length and produce a 128-bit message digest.

Exam Tip	
Remember that a digital signature is created when the digest of the message is encrypted using the sender's private key.	

Message Digest 4 (MD4)

Message Digest 4 (MD4) is a one-way hash function that produces a 128-bit hash message digest value. Developed in 1990, MD4 is fast and optimized for 32-bit machines. The message is padded to ensure its length in bits plus 448 is divisible by 512. Next, a 64-bit binary representation of the original length of the message is added to the message. The message is then processed in 512-bit blocks, and then each block is processed in three rounds. Over time, though, MD4 has been shown to be easily broken.

Message Digest 5 (MD5)

Message Digest 5 (MD5), developed in 1991, is a slower but more complex version of MD4. MD5 is popular and widely used for security applications and integrity checking. For example, downloaded software usually includes an MD5 checksum that the user can compare to the checksum of the downloaded file. MD5 produces a 128-bit hash value using a hexadecimal 32-character string. Its complex algorithms make it much more difficult to crack than MD4. The algorithm consists of four distinct rounds that have a slightly different design from that of MD4. Vulnerabilities have been found in MD5 in which techniques are used to reverse-engineer the MD5 hash, and Secure Hash Algorithm (SHA) hash functions are often considered better alternatives to MD5 hashing.

Secure Hash Algorithm (SHA)

SHA was developed by the U.S. National Security Agency (NSA) for use with digital signature standards and is considered a more secure successor and alternative to MD5.

Travel Advisory

The NSA web site (www.nsa.gov) provides an excellent overview of the history of cryptography for American national security.

SHA produces a 160-bit hash value that is run through the Digital Signature Algorithm (DSA), which adds the signature for the message. The sender encrypts the hash value with a private key, which is attached to the message before it's sent. The receiver decrypts the message with the sender's public key and runs the hashing function to compare the two values. If the values are identical, the message hasn't been altered. Other variants of basic SHA (sometimes called SHA-1) exist, such as SHA-224, SHA-256, SHA-384, and SHA-512, which indicate their larger bit values. SHA is used in several popular security applications such as Transport Layer Security (TLS), Secure Sockets Layer (SSL) and Internet Protocol Security (IPsec). SHA is considered fairly secure, although published theoretical attacks have been able to break the hash.

RIPEMD

RIPEMD (RACE Integrity Primitives Evaluation Message Digest) is a hash function message digest. Originally based on MD4, RIPEMD comes in several different bit versions, including 128-, 160-, 256-, and 320-bit, although the 256- and 320-bit versions don't necessarily increase security; they only reduce the chance of hash value collisions. The original weak 128-bit version has been primarily replaced by RIPEMD-160, but it is slower than and not as popular in use as SHA-1 or MD5.

HMAC

HMAC (Hash-based Message Authentication Code) is used as an algorithm for message authentication purposes where the authentication is applied using hash functions and a secret key to create an authentication code value. HMAC is used to authentic a message and provide data integrity. The Message Authentication Code (MAC) is sent along with the message itself so that the receiver can authenticate the sender of the message and verify the integrity of the message contents. The strength of HMAC depends on the size and type of hash it uses, such as MD5 or SHA-1, and the key size.

Exam Tip

Be aware of the different types of hashing algorithms available and their strengths, weaknesses, and applications.

Use and Apply Appropriate Cryptographic Tools and Products

Objective 4.02
CompTIA Security+
Objective 6.2

In a symmetric encryption scheme, both parties use the same key for encryption and decryption purposes. Each user must possess the same key to encrypt and decrypt messages sent to each other.

In an asymmetric scheme, two keys are created for encryption and decryption purposes: one key is the public key, which is known to all users, while the private key remains secret and is kept private by the user to which it is assigned. Asymmetric encryption schemes are widely used in public key cryptography systems.

Symmetric Encryption Algorithms

The following sections describe examples of symmetric-based algorithms.

DES and 3DES

The Data Encryption Standard (DES) is a block cipher defined by the U.S. government in 1977 as an official standard. The actual encryption system used was originally created by IBM. DES has become the most well-known and widely used cryptosystem in the world. This symmetric cryptosystem uses a 64-bit block size and a 56-bit key. It requires both the sender and receiver to possess the same secret key, which is used both to encrypt and decrypt the message. DES can also be used by a single user for encrypting data for storage on a hard disk or other medium.

After DES was used for many years, the government ceased to authorize it as a standard and moved on to more secure methods of encryption, such as Triple DES (3DES) and the AES standard. Using the same standard with a weak 56-bit key for so long increased the chances for the encryption scheme to be broken.

Travel Advisory

Despite being criticized for published weaknesses, DES-based encryption such as 3DES is still in wide use today.

Over time and after tests with multi-CPU systems proved the standard could be broken through brute force, DES encryption was considered insecure. A Double-DES encryption scheme was created that contained a key length of 112 bits, but its susceptibility to being cracked wasn't considered much different from the original DES.

Triple DES is a 168-bit encryption standard that's resistant to cryptanalysis because it uses 48 rounds of cryptographic computations. 3DES is considered 2^{56} times stronger than DES. The main disadvantage of 3DES is that encryption and decryption are almost three times slower than for DES. Nevertheless, 3DES is considered powerful enough to be implemented in many banking and financial applications.

AES

The *Advanced Encryption Standard (AES)* (also often called Rijndael) is the government-defined encryption standard created to replace DES, which was considered vulnerable. The new standard uses a symmetric-block cipher supporting variable block and key lengths, such as 128, 192, and 256 bits. In 2003, the U.S. government stated that the AES encryption standard could be used for nonclassified documents, while AES using 192–256 bits was required for top secret purposes.

AES itself has not been compromised, but a number of speculative theoretical attacks have been published. Some attacks, called "side channel attacks," have compromised AES encrypted data, but only because the implementation of the encryption scheme itself was weak, not the encryption algorithm. These cases are rare, and they typically involved attacking an application server using AES that had weaknesses in its timing and caching mechanisms that accidentally leaked data, which led to discovery of the AES key.

Blowfish

Blowfish is a symmetric block cipher that uses 64-bit blocks of data. Its key length is 448 bits, and it uses 16 rounds of cryptographic computations. Blowfish was designed specifically for 32-bit machines and is significantly faster than DES.

Twofish

Twofish is also a symmetric key block cipher that is very similar to Blowfish but uses a block size of 128 bits and key sizes up to 256 bits. Twofish is a free public domain encryption cipher and is often used in open-source projects such as OpenPGP.

IDEA

International Data Encryption Algorithm (IDEA) is a symmetric block cipher that uses 64-bit blocks of data, with a key length of 128 bits. The data blocks are divided into 16 smaller sections, which are subjected to eight rounds of cryptographic computation. The speed of IDEA in software is similar to that of DES. IDEA is the cipher used in the popular encryption program Pretty Good Privacy (PGP).

RC4

RC4 (Rivest Cipher) is a symmetric stream cipher created by RSA Data Security in 1987. With its speed and simplicity, it has been used in popular encryption protocols such as Secure Sockets Layer (SSL), Transport Layer Security (TLS), and also 40-bit and 128-bit WEP (Wireless Encryption Protocol). It utilizes the secure exchange of a shared key. There are weaknesses in some implementations of RC4, such as 40- and 128-bit WEP, and early implementations of WPA. This means you should always use proven technologies for wireless encryption, such as WPA2, which uses Counter mode with Cipher Block Chaining Message Authentication Code Protocol (CCMP) with AES-128.

Asymmetric Encryption Algorithms

The following sections describe examples of asymmetric-based algorithms.

RSA

RSA, one of the most popular asymmetric public key algorithms, is the main standard for encryption and digital signatures and is widely used for electronic devices, operating systems, and software applications. The acronym RSA stands for Rivest, Shamir, and Adleman, the inventors of this technique. RSA is also used in many web servers that use SSL, and its algorithm is based on the factoring of prime numbers to obtain private and public key pairs. RSA is used primarily for encryption and digital signatures.

Elliptic Curve Cryptosystems

Elliptic Curve Cryptosystems (ECC) provides functionality similar to RSA, such as encryption and digital signatures. The ECC cryptosystem uses complex mathematical structures to create secure asymmetric algorithms and keys. ECC was created for devices with smaller processing capabilities, such as cell phones, PDAs, and other wireless devices. ECC uses smaller keys than the similar RSA; larger keys need more processing power to compute.

Diffie-Hellman

Diffie-Hellman isn't an actual encryption algorithm: it's a key agreement protocol that enables users to exchange encryption keys over an insecure medium.

The Diffie-Hellman protocol depends on the discrete logarithmic formulas for its security. The main vulnerability with the basic protocol is that the key exchange doesn't authenticate the participants. Further enhancements to the Diffie-Hellman protocol allow the two parties to authenticate each other through the addition of digital signatures and public-key certificates. This system is used in the Public Key Infrastructure (PKI).

| **Travel Assistance** |

Public Key Infrastructure is described in more detail in Chapter 5.

DSA (Digital Signature Algorithm)

The *Digital Signature Algorithm (DSA)* was published by the National Institute of Standards and Technology (NIST) in the Digital Signature Standard (DSS), which is a part of a U.S. government project. The DSS was selected by NIST, in cooperation with the NSA, as the digital authentication standard of the U.S. government. DSA is based on discrete logarithms and is used only for authentication. The algorithm is considered secure when the key size is large enough. DSA was originally proposed with a 512-bit key size and was eventually revised to support key sizes up to 1024 bits. Because of DSA's lack of key exchange capabilities, relative slowness, and public distrust of the process and the government involvement that created it, many people prefer RSA for digital signatures and encryption, but both standards are used widely.

One-Time Pad

A *one-time pad* is a type of encryption scheme that, when implemented correctly, is considered secure and theoretically impossible to compromise. The pad is generated from random values and uses a mathematic function called an *exclusive-OR (XOR)* to encrypt the plain-text message into ciphertext. One-time pads are secure because they are only ever used once, a pad is as long as the message it is encrypting, the pad values are completely random, and the communication of the pad is secure.

One-time pads are difficult to implement within computerized environments, as not all of the requirements can be successfully met, and they are often used as a manual backup encryption method for extremely high security areas such as military and government environments.

Quantum Cryptography

Quantum cryptography is an extremely advanced technique to protect key distribution through light-based quantum computing. The technique uses the quantum effect of light waves over fiber-optic cable to transmit code within theoretically unbreakable light pulses to distribute a shared key between two users.

Unfortunately, the expensive hardware required to support quantum cryptography means it is limited to only the most advanced and secure of environments such as scientific research or military applications.

Implementing Encryption Protocols

Securing communication between systems is an important part of security that prevents malicious users from capturing data in transit. The following sections outline some of the various encryption protocols and their implementations in communications security.

Wireless Encryption

The following encryption protocols and techniques are specifically designed for the security of wireless communications.

Wireless Encryption Protocol

For wireless networks, the *Wireless Encryption Protocol (WEP)* security protocol provides encrypted communication between wireless clients and access points. WEP uses a key encryption algorithm to encrypt communications between devices. Each client and access point on the wireless LAN must use the same encryption key. The key is manually configured on each access point and each client before either can access the network. Basic WEP specifies the use of up to 64-bit keys (a 40-bit key plus a 24-bit initialization vector); however, 64-bit WEP encryption has been proven to be vulnerable to attack because of a weak algorithm. Most devices now support up to 128-bit encryption (a 104-bit key plus a 24-bit initialization vector); however, this has also been proven to be vulnerable. If your wireless access point supports only WEP, you should use 128-bit WEP encryption in conjunction with other security controls such as MAC address filtering and network identifiers.

Travel Assistance

For more details on wireless security, see Chapter 10.

WPA and WPA2 Security

Wi-Fi Protected Access (WPA) is the most recent and secure form of encryption for wireless networks. It was created to fix several weaknesses in the WEP standard.

WPA can use a pre-shared key, or it can use an authentication server that distributes the keys. In the pre-shared key method (also called Personal WPA), all devices on the wireless LAN must use the same passphrase key to access the network. The authentication server method (also called Enterprise WPA) is more suited for environments with hundreds of clients, where using a single passphrase key for each device is not scalable, and the authentication server takes care of key management between the wireless devices on the network.

Using WPA, data is encrypted using a 128-bit key that is actually routinely changed during sessions using the Temporal Key Integrity Protocol (TKIP). With WPA, a single session key cannot be hacked by the time the protocol changes keys. WPA also provides for improved integrity checking of the data traversing the wireless network to make sure that data cannot be intercepted and changed on the way to its destination. This provides much more protection than the original WEP.

The strength of a WPA network, however, is only as strong as the passphrase used. A WPA passphrase can be from 8 to 63 characters and should be as strong as possible and not based on known dictionary words: it should include numbers, uppercase and lowercase characters, and special characters such as the @ symbol. All devices on the WPA network must share the same passphrase, including all access points.

WPA2 is the most recent version of WPA and adds Robust Security Network (RSN) support that includes added protection for ad hoc networks, key caching, pre-roaming authentication, and the Counter Mode with Cipher Block Chaining Message Authentication Code Protocol (CCMP) that uses the AES cipher to replace TKIP. All currently manufactured devices support WPA2 in addition to WPA. If your network devices support WPA2, they should use this type of encryption. However, many older devices do not support WPA2, and you will have to use WPA or some other common encryption method, such as WEP, that can be supported by all your clients.

Exam Tip

You should use the highest level of encryption available for wireless networks, such as WPA2. Older levels of encryption, such as WEP and WPA, have proved to be vulnerable. Use proven technologies such as WPA2 to maximize your security.

Pretty Good Privacy (PGP)

By default, a mail server doesn't encrypt e-mail messages. This means anyone who might have access to your account, who has hacked the system, or who is capturing the unprotected network traffic can read your private e-mail messages. E-mail messages, once sent, can relay among a large number of e-mail servers until they arrive at their destination. If any one of these servers is insecure, e-mail could be captured and viewed. Users can protect themselves with encryption products or through the use of digital certificates. Once the e-mail is encrypted, there's no way for an unauthorized user to view the contents of the e-mail. The destination user must also have the matching encryption key, so he or she can unlock the message when it arrives.

PGP is one of the most common encryption tools used to protect messages on the Internet, because it's both easy to use and effective. PGP uses its own decentralized type of digital certificates using an RSA-based public-key encryption method with two keys: One is a public key you give to anyone with which you share messages, and the other is a private key you use to decrypt messages you receive. A passphrase is used to encrypt the user's private key, which is stored on the local computer. Each PGP user distributes his own public key, creating a "web of trust" with other users. Each user keeps a collection of other user's public keys on a *key ring*. PGP is different from a centralized certificate authority, where one authority is used to authenticate users; using PGP, users rely on each other to establish trust between other users and their keys.

GNU Privacy Guard (GPG)

GNU Privacy Guard (GPG) is a free, open-source implementation of the OpenPGP standard. Intended as a free replacement for PGP, GPG does not contain any patented encryption algorithms, and it supports many technologies, including DSA, RSA, AES, 3DES, Blowfish, Twofish, MD5, SHA-1, and RIPE-MD-160.

GPG utilizes asymmetric keys that are generated by GPG end users. Public keys can be exchanged with other users using Internet key servers. You can also use digital signatures to verify the sender and integrity of the message.

Travel Assistance
For detailed information on PGP, see www.pgp.com. For detailed information on GPG, see www.gnupg.org.

S/MIME

Multipurpose Internet Mail Extensions (MIME) is a specification for transferring multimedia and attachments through e-mail. This specification offers a standard way for all mail clients and mail transfer systems to handle certain types of attachments. For example, if a user sends an audio clip to another user through e-mail, the MIME header will include information on the attachment. When the audio clip reaches the destination user, the user's computer will understand what type of file it is and what application can be used to open it.

Secure MIME (S/MIME) is an extension of the MIME standard that is used for digitally signing and encrypting e-mail using certificates. S/MIME is used for sending confidential e-mail that needs to be secured so that other users can't capture the message and read its contents. By encrypting the e-mail, an unauthorized user will be unable to decipher the contents of the message and its attachments. S/MIME requires the use of public key certificates for authentication and provides message confidentiality and integrity via the user's encryption and hashing algorithms.

SSL and TLS

Although the data on a server might be secured from unauthorized access, the communications pathways between the server and client systems might not be. The SSL (Secure Sockets Layer) protocol enables communication between systems to be encrypted.

Many web sites have both secured and unsecured areas. The secured areas might provide access to a financial bank account or a database of personal information, for example. This secured area of the site usually requires user authentication to proceed. To increase security when switching from the unsecured public part of a web site to a secured area, SSL encryption is invoked. SSL must be supported by both the web server and the client browser to function. SSL is also often used in e-mail systems to secure the message communications between mail servers and mail clients.

In an SSL communication, a process known as a *digital handshake* occurs. The handshaking phase begins when the server sends a message to the client indicating a secure session must be set up. The client then sends its security information and encryption key to the server, which compares the credentials with its own to find the right match. Next, the server sends authentication information, so the client knows the web server with which it is communicating is the correct one. This is an important step, because it's possible, through redirection or other methods, that a user can be switched from one web site to another without the user's knowledge. So, for example, as you enter your username and password, you might be entering the information into a bogus web site that collects this information to perform unauthorized activity with your accounts. This handshake confirms not only that you are who you say you are, but that the site with which you're connected is the actual site you expect it to be. The SSL protocol uses public key cryptography in the handshake phase to securely exchange symmetric session keys that are then used to encrypt communications for the duration of the session, as shown in Figure 4.6. When the client moves to another web site, the encrypted session is closed.

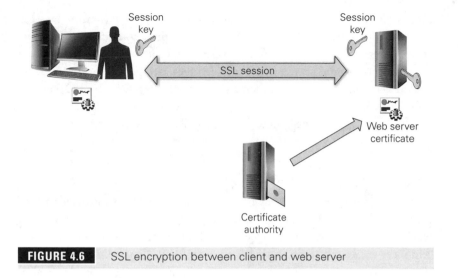

FIGURE 4.6 SSL encryption between client and web server

TLS (Transport Layer Security) is the next generation of the SSL protocol. Although the two protocols are similar, TLS builds on the strong security of SSL with more enhanced encryption and authentication techniques to secure communications between a client and a server. However, TLS is not interoperable with SSL.

TLS is a widely implemented protocol used to secure connections to web sites, secure e-mail connections between e-mail servers and clients, secure instant messaging and VoIP applications, and also secure connections to LDAP servers.

HTTPS

Hypertext Transfer Protocol over Secure Socket Layer (HTTPS) is a secure means of communicating HTTP data between a web browser and a web server. All HTTP communications are sent in clear text, so no messages are secure, and they can be easily viewed using a protocol analyzer. This makes HTTP unusable for communications requiring security and privacy, such as web-based banking and other online financial transactions. HTTPS protects the communication channel by using SSL and certificates to provide encrypted and protected communications. When connecting to a web site that uses a secured channel, the URL begins with *https* instead of *http*, such as *https://secure.website.com*. HTTPS is typically used in banking and online shopping transactions, where the transfer of credit card and personal information must be encrypted to prevent an unauthorized user from stealing the information while it's in transmit between the client and the server. When a client connects to the secure site, the web server sends a certificate to the web browser to establish its identity. If the browser accepts the certificate and finds no validation issues with the certificate, SSL is activated between the server and client. This ensures that the web site is genuine (who it says it is), and that the client is not connecting to a *rogue* site. In many web browsers, a secure site is indicated by a small padlock icon in the application taskbar. HTTPS uses TCP port 443 for communications.

IPsec

IPsec (IP Security) is a standards-based suite of protocols that provide privacy, integrity, and authenticity to information transferred across IP networks. IPsec works on the IP network layer to encrypt communications between the sender and receiver. IPsec is most often used to secure VPN communications over an open network such as the Internet; however, because IPsec operates at lower levels than most application security protocols (such as SSL), it offers greater flexibility in its implementation, as applications do not need to be aware of IPsec to make use of its benefits. IPsec ensures that communications cannot be read by a third party, that traffic has not been modified in transit, and that messages received are from a trusted source.

IPsec uses two types of encryption modes: transport and tunnel. In *transport* mode, IPsec encrypts the data portion of each packet, but not the header. This can be used only in host-to-host communications. *Tunnel* mode encrypts both the header and the data of the network packet. This is used to host VPN gateway communications, the most common form of VPN. The receiver of the packet uses IPsec to decrypt the message. For IPsec to work, each communicating device needs to be running IPsec and share some form of public key. Key management is provided by the Internet Key Exchange (IKE), formerly ISAKMP/Oakley. IKE enables the receiver to obtain a public key and authenticate the sender using digital certificates.

IPsec consists of component protocols, including *authentication header (AH)* and *encapsulating security payload (ESP)* headers. The AH is an IP header that is added to a network packet and provides its cryptographic checksum. This checksum is used to achieve authentication and integrity to ensure that the packet has been sent by a specified source and has not been captured and changed in transit. ESP is a header applied to an IP packet after it has been encrypted. It provides data confidentiality so that the packet cannot be viewed in transit. In newer IPsec implementations, the AH functionality is always performed within the ESP header, resulting in a single combined ESP/AH header.

Security associations (SAs) are the basic building blocks of IPsec communications. Before any two devices can communicate using IPsec, they must first establish a set of SAs that specify the cryptographic parameters that must be agreed upon by both devices before data can be transferred securely between them, including the encryption and authentication algorithms and keys.

The primary way of establishing SAs and managing VPN keys is via the Internet Security Association and Key Management Protocol (ISAKMP) and Internet Key Exchange (IKE). ISAKMP/IKE is the protocol for performing automated key management for IPsec. The ISAKMP/IKE process automatically negotiates with the remote VPN device to establish the parameters for individual SAs. An SA is established so that all key exchanges can be encrypted and no keys need to be passed over the Internet in clear text. Once the SA is established, a session SA is negotiated for securing normal VPN traffic, referred to as IKE Phase-1 and Phase-2 negotiations. The session SAs are short-lived and are renegotiated at regular intervals, ensuring that the keys are discarded regularly. The same keys are used only for a small amount of time and for limited amounts of data.

SSH (Secure Shell)

SSH is a secure remote access utility that lets a user log in to a remote machine and execute commands as if they were working at the console of that system. Other remote access utilities like Telnet are insecure because the data isn't encrypted when communicated. SSH provides a secure, encrypted tunnel to access another system remotely. SSH is sometimes used as a low-cost alternative to normal VPN communications because of its simple installation and delivery of well-encrypted, secure communications.

SSH uses public key cryptography for authentication, and when a client connects to a system using SSH, an initial handshaking process begins and a special session key is exchanged. This starts the session, and a secure channel is created to allow the access.

Vulnerabilities have been discovered in some versions of SSH, so make sure that you are using the latest version. Early versions of SSH were susceptible to man-in-the-middle attacks because a hacker could capture the headers of the handshaking phase to intercept the session key.

CHECKPOINT

✔ **Objective 4.01: Summarize general cryptography concepts.**   Information assurance protects information and information systems by securing their confidentiality, integrity, authentication, and nonrepudiation. An algorithm is a complex mathematical formula that dictates how the encryption and de-cryption process takes place. Because these mathematical algorithms are usually publicly known, the cryptosystem is strengthened with the addition of a secret key. A key is like a password that's combined with the algorithm to create ciphertext, and encrypted data can't be deciphered unless the same key is used to decrypt it. In a symmetric encryption scheme, both parties use the same key for encryption and decryption purposes. In an asymmetric en-cryption scheme, everyone uses different, but mathematically related, keys for encryption and decryption purposes.

✔ **Objective 4.02: Use and apply appropriate cryptographic tools and products.** A hashing value is used in encryption systems to create a "fingerprint" for a message. This prevents the message from being accessed and changed on the way to its destination. In the overall information assurance model, hashing is used to protect the integrity of a message and is most often used with digi-tal signatures. A one-way hash is a mathematical function that transforms a variable-sized message into a fixed-length value, referred to as either a hash value or a message digest. Popular hashing algorithms include MD5 and SHA. Use AES-256 and RSA algorithms as secure encryption algorithms. A one-time pad must be used only once, must be truly random, must be com-municated securely, and must be as long as the message it is encrypting. Use WPA2 for encrypting wireless networks, as the WEP and WPA technologies have become vulnerable. Encryption protocols include SSL/TLS and HTTPS for secure web communications, and IPsec for VPN communica-tions. Use SSH as an encrypted alternative to Telnet or other mechanisms that use clear text in their communications.

REVIEW QUESTIONS

1. You have encrypted an e-mail message that is only meant to be seen by the recipient. A hacker has intercepted the message. When he views the message, what does he see?

   A. The plain text of the e-mail

   B. One-way hash of the message

    C. The recipient's certificate information

    D. Ciphertext

2. You have been tasked to implement information assurance principles within your organization's security and encryption functions. Which of the following isn't a function of information assurance within encryption systems?

    A. Efficiency

    B. Confidentiality

    C. Integrity

    D. Nonrepudiation

3. You have sent your friend a secret, encrypted message. The key you used to encrypt the message is the same key with which your friend will decrypt the message. What type of encryption scheme is used?

    A. Asymmetric

    B. Symmetric

    C. RSA

    D. Diffie-Hellman

4. Which of the following encryption schemes would you use if your company wants to create an invisible watermark hidden within the images on their web site to identify the images if they are used by another company?

    A. One-time pad

    B. Elliptical curve

    C. One-way hash

    D. Steganography

5. Your organization wants you to implement an encryption system that ensures the sender and receiver of the encrypted message use different keys for encryption and decryption. Which type of encryption scheme would you use?

    A. Elliptical curve

    B. Non-symmetric

    C. Asymmetric

    D. Symmetric

6. Which of the following protocols would you use for message authentication and integrity in your encryption systems?

   A. Steganography

   B. Elliptical curve

   C. HMAC

   D. One-time pad

7. You have been asked to implement hashing protocols that have a low possibility of a hashing collision. Which of the following describes a hashing collision?

   A. The greater probability that two or more people in a group of 23 share the same birthday

   B. That the hash values of two different messages result in the same value

   C. An invalid digital signature

   D. When a 128-bit message digest is mixed with a 256-bit message digest

8. When you connect to a secure web site, you are asked to accept the server certificate. What is the function of the digital certificate?

   A. Securely validates the identity of the server and its public key

   B. Identifies you to a certificate authority

   C. Provides your ID required by the government to request a public key

   D. Allows you to encrypt your web sessions

9. You want to start a secure web session to your banking web site to prevent your credentials and financial information from passing as clear text. Which of the following protocols do you use?

   A. SSL

   B. SSH

   C. HTTPS

   D. HTTP

10. When you connect to a secure HTTPS web page, which of the following actions is performed first?

   A. The username and password are sent for authentication.

   B. A digital certificate establishes the web site identity to the browser.

   C. The web page is displayed, and then authentication is performed.

   D. The client establishes its identity to the web server.

REVIEW ANSWERS

1. **D** Clear text is transformed into ciphertext after being put through some type of cipher or encryption algorithm system. The ciphertext is unreadable unless it is decrypted back into clear-text form.

2. **A** Efficiency is not a function of information assurance within encryption systems. The four basic functions pertaining to information assurance are confidentiality, integrity, authentication, and nonrepudiation.

3. **B** In a symmetric encryption scheme, both parties use the same key for encryption and decryption purposes. Both users must possess the same key to send encrypted messages to each other.

4. **D** Steganography hides data in another type of media that effectively conceals the existence of the data.

5. **C** An asymmetric encryption scheme relies on the sender and receiver of a message to use different keys for encryption and decryption. The keys are mathematically related but can't be derived from each other.

6. **C** HMAC (Hash-based Message Authentication Code) is used to authentic a message and provide data integrity. The Message Authentication Code (MAC) is sent along with the message itself so that the receiver can authenticate the sender of the message and verify the integrity of the message contents.

7. **B** A collision occurs within a hashing algorithm when the hashed values of two different messages result in the same value. Collisions can be used to aid in cracking a hacking algorithm.

8. **A** A digital certificate is a credential required by PKI systems that can securely identify an organization's server, as well as create an association between the server's authenticated identity and its public keys.

9. **C** HTTP communications send all data in clear-text form. For secure web communications, HTTPS is a secure means of communicating HTTP data between a web browser and a web server. HTTPS protects the communication channel by using SSL to provide encrypted and protected communications.

10. **B** When a client connects to the secure HTTPS site, the web server sends a certificate to the web browser to establish its identity. If the browser accepts the certificate and finds no validation issues with the certificate, SSL is activated between the server and client. No other communication can occur between the server and client until the certificate is validated and accepted.

Public Key Infrastructure

ITINERARY

- ○ **Objective 5.01** Explain the core concepts of Public Key Infrastructure
- ○ **Objective 5.02** Implement PKI, certificate management, and associated components

	NEWBIE	SOME EXPERIENCE	EXPERT
ETA	2 hours	1.5 hours	1 hour

Traditional cryptography methods based on symmetric key cryptography use the same secret key by both the sender (to encrypt the message) and the receiver (to decrypt the message). Unfortunately, it can be difficult to transmit the secret key securely from one user to another. If an unauthorized user intercepts the key, he can decrypt, read, forge, and modify all messages encrypted using that key. Key management is a challenge for these systems, especially for systems that serve large numbers of users.

Public key cryptography was introduced in 1976 by Diffie and Hellman, whose public key protocol was created to solve the key management problem. In public key cryptography, each user receives two keys: the public key and the private key. The private key is kept secret, while the public key can be published for any user to see or use. The problem faced using symmetric keys is solved because no need exists to share a secret key. All transmissions involve only the public keys; no private key is ever transmitted or shared. With public key cryptography, *asymmetric cryptography* is used to exchange symmetric keys. The sender encrypts the message with the receiver's public key. The receiver then decrypts the message with his own private key, as shown in Figure 5.1. The security mechanism is safe as long as the private keys aren't compromised.

Public key cryptography is efficient, is secure, and scales well with a large amount of users, making it ideal for all types of critical personal and business communications and transactions. This chapter describes the core concepts and implementation of public key cryptography, including certificate authorities and the certificate life cycle.

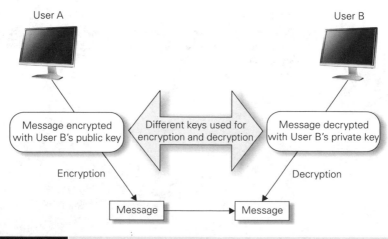

FIGURE 5.1   Public key cryptography

Objective 5.01
CompTIA Security+
Objective 6.3

Explain the Core Concepts of Public Key Infrastructure

The *Public Key Infrastructure (PKI)* is a standard infrastructure consisting of a framework of procedures, standards, and protocols, based on public key cryptography. A hybrid of asymmetric and symmetric key algorithms, PKI provides the full range of information assurance objectives for confidentiality, integrity, authentication, and nonrepudiation. The asymmetric keys are used for authentication, and then one or more symmetric keys are generated and exchanged using asymmetric encryption.

Travel Assistance

See Chapter 4 for detailed information on the differences between asymmetric and symmetric cryptography.

A message is encrypted with a symmetric algorithm, and that key is then encrypted asymmetrically using the recipient's public key. The entire message (symmetrically encrypted body and asymmetrically encrypted key) is sent together to the recipient. The message can also be digitally signed through the use of digital certificates.

Exam Tip

Public key cryptography uses a hybrid of symmetric and asymmetric encryption systems. A message is encrypted using a symmetric algorithm, and that key is then encrypted asymmetrically using the recipient's public key. The entire message (symmetrically encrypted body and asymmetrically encrypted key) is sent together to the recipient.

Digital Certificates

A *digital certificate* is a credential required by PKI systems that can securely identify an individual as well as create an association between the individual's authenticated identity and public keys. A trusted party, called a *certificate authority (CA)*, is used to sign and issue certificates. The CA is responsible for verifying the identity of a key owner and binding the owner to a public key. This enables users who have never met to exchange encrypted communications because the authentication is performed by the CA. Each certificate contains a unique serial number, an identity, and public key information for the user, as well as the validity dates for the life of the certificate.

Certificate Authorities

A CA is an organization or entity that issues and manages digital certificates and is responsible for authenticating and identifying users who participate in the PKI. This service doesn't necessarily involve a third party; it can be internal to an organization. A CA server can be set up to act as the manager of certificates and the user's public keys.

Third-party CAs are special organizations dedicated to certificate management. Some of the larger companies that offer this service, such as VeriSign and Entrust, have their functionality built in to popular web browsers to perform certificate services automatically.

Exam Tip

A certificate authority is an organization or entity that issues and manages digital certificates. The CA is responsible for authenticating and identifying users who participate in the Public Key Infrastructure (PKI).

Some of the actual authentication and identification services for certificates are managed by other organizations called *registration authorities (RAs)*. These organizations offload some of the work from CAs by confirming the identities of users, issuing key pairs, and initiating the certificate process with a CA on behalf of the user. The RA acts as a middleman between the user and the CA and doesn't issue certificates on its own.

To verify a user's identity, the CA and RA usually require some form of identification, such as a driver's license, Social Security number, address, or phone number. Once the user's identification is established, the CA generates public and private keys for the user. A certificate is then generated with the identification and public key information embedded within it. Once the user is registered and receives his certificate, he can begin using his certificate to send encrypted messages. When the receiver receives the message, her software can verify the certificate to ensure the message is from the stated sender. Certificates can also be revoked if the certificate's original subscriber information has changed, has been compromised, or is no longer valid.

Exam Tip
A certificate contains the authenticated identification of a user and his public key information.

Trust Models

Trust models define how users trust other users, companies, CAs, and RAs within the PKI. These models provide a chain of trust from a user's public key to the root key of a CA. The validated chain then implies authenticity of all the certificates. The following are the most common trust models used in PKI.

Web of Trust

The *web of trust* is a simplistic trust model that relies on each user creating and signing her own certificate, as shown in Figure 5.2. This is the basis for encryption applications, such as Pretty Good Privacy (PGP) or Gnu Privacy Guard (GPG), where no central authority exists. With this model, each user is responsible for authentication and trust, and anyone can sign someone else's public key. When User A signs User B's key, User A is introducing User B's key to anyone who trusts User A. Each user is then considered a trusted introducer in the model.

Third-Party (Single Authority) Trust

A *third-party central certifying agency* signs a given key and authenticates the owner of the key. Trusting that authority means, by association, that you trust all keys issued by that authority, as shown in Figure 5.3. Each user authenticates the

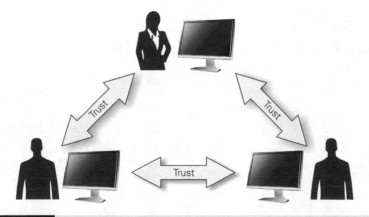

FIGURE 5.2 Web of trust model

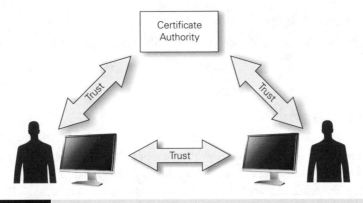

FIGURE 5.3   Third-party single authority trust model

other through the exchange of certificates. The users know the CA has performed all the necessary identification of the owner of the certificate and can therefore trust the owner of the message.

Hierarchical Model

The *hierarchical model* is an extension of the third-party model, in which root CAs issue certificates to other, lower-level CAs and RAs, as shown in Figure 5.4. Each user's most trusted key is the root CA's public key. The trust inheritance can be followed from the certificate back to the root CA. This model allows enforcement of policies and standards throughout the infrastructure, producing a higher level of overall assurance than other trust models. A root certificate is trusted by software applications on behalf of the user.

Local Lingo

root certificate   A root certificate is the highest certificate in the hierarchical tree, which is used to sign other, lower-level certificates. These certificates inherit the trust of the root certificate.

For example, web browsers will create trusted connections to secure servers using the Secure Sockets Layer (SSL), using root certificates that identify to the user that this web site and its certificate are trusted.

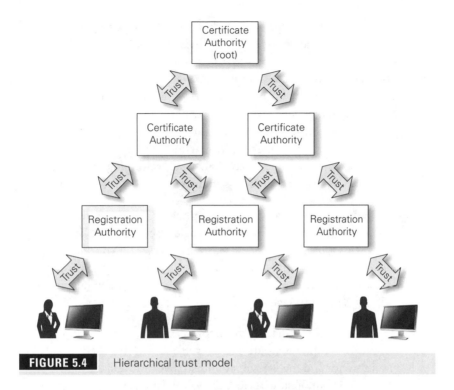

FIGURE 5.4   Hierarchical trust model

Key Management and Storage

Encryption key management deals with the generation, distribution, storage, and backup of keys. Securing encryption keys is an extremely important aspect of encryption and cryptography. Once a key is generated, it must be secured to avoid an unauthorized user discovering the key. Attacks on public-key systems are typically focused on the key management system, rather than on attempts to break the encryption algorithm itself. No matter how secure or difficult a cryptographic algorithm, the entire process can be compromised by poor key management.

Centralized vs. Decentralized Storage

Keys need to be generated and securely sent to the correct user. The user must then store that key in a secure place so that it can't be accessed by another user. The key can be encrypted and stored on a hard drive, a DVD, a flash device, a USB key, or a trusted platform module (TPM). The keys should also be recoverable if they're lost or damaged, or if passwords to use them are forgotten. Key storage is an important aspect of secure key management, which can be centralized either to a particular server or a third-party service. Key storage can involve both hardware and software storage methods.

In the early days of encryption key management, cryptographic keys were stored in secure boxes and delivered to users by hand. The keys were given to the systems administrator, who distributed them from a main server or by visiting each workstation. This type of administrative overhead for key management could almost be a job in itself, and it obviously didn't scale well in large enterprise networks. In today's networks, key distribution and storage are typically performed automatically through a special key management system, such as a key management server, or through a third-party service such as VeriSign or Entrust. Key management can be an extremely time-consuming process for network administrators in a large enterprise network.

Centralized Storage   Most modern encryption infrastructures use a *centralized storage system* for key management, a single place where all key management occurs. This typically involves a centralized server on your network that takes care of key management for you. The server can issue key pairs, store and back them up, and take care of certificates. A centralized key management system offers several advantages:

- **Administration**   Managing the accounts and keys of users at one centralized location is secure and convenient, relieving the administrator and the users of administrative overhead. Signature verification is automatic because the validity information is co-located with the actual key and other account information.
- **Scalability**   Key management servers are built to scale to any size enterprise network.
- **Integrity**   Keys stored at a server can be easily backed up, eliminating the potential for the loss of a vital verification or an encryption key.
- **Security**   Unlike a decentralized storage system in which keys can be insecure because of lack of user education or operating system (OS) vulnerabilities, a key storage server is a secure environment where audited controls are required for access to the physical hardware and the keys are protected with specialized cryptographic devices.

Exam Tip

Centralized key storage solutions provide greater security and integrity of keys than decentralized solutions. They're also far more manageable and scalable.

Decentralized Storage   A *decentralized storage system* is typically used by individual users or a small network. Once the user has created her keys, her private key is stored locally on her system or some other secure device. She then sends her public key with a certificate request to a CA that, after authenticating the user, sends her a certificate, which is again stored locally.

The advantage for end users is that they're always in control of their private keys and certificates. The users trust themselves with the security, rather than trusting a server or a third-party service that might not properly protect their information or that could divulge their private keys to third parties, such as government authorities.

A decentralized storage method has many disadvantages as well. For example, if the user encrypts data on her hard drive and misplaces her private key, she won't be able to recover any information encrypted with her private key. Another concern involves users in a corporate network: After a disgruntled employee leaves an organization, he might not reveal the key needed to decrypt information that was protected on the corporate network, denying access to the information from other people who need it.

Keys can also be damaged or lost, and if the user didn't properly back them up, those keys will be permanently lost. This means the data the user encrypted will also be lost permanently, because no key exists to decrypt the information.

Travel Advisory

Decentralized methods are typically used by individual users. Centralized types of key storage are used for larger networks of users, for which individual key management would be insecure and time-consuming to manage.

Key Storage and Protection

Once a key pair has been generated, the private key must be safely stored to protect it from being compromised, lost, or damaged. The type of security used to encrypt and protect the private key should be as strong as the security used to encrypt and protect the actual message or files. A number of methods for protecting the private key can be used, including both hardware and software methods.

The most important aspect of hardware key protection is the ability to protect the hardware itself. Many users store their private keys on their computers' hard disks. Their computers might be part of a network, potentially allowing access to anyone on that network. To prevent this sort of access, private keys are usually stored on removable media that can be more easily protected and can be physically carried with the user. This hardware can be typical media, such as a DVD or a USB device. However, these small media devices can be easily lost or stolen, which is why the stored key should always be encrypted. You can also use a trusted platform module (TPM), which is a special hardware chip that is installed within a computer system or device, such as on the system motherboard of a computer desktop or laptop. This protected, encrypted module can store encryption keys that are specific to that system hardware.

Travel Assistance

Trusted platform modules are discussed in more detail in Chapter 12.

A private key should never be stored in its plain-text form. If an unauthorized user manages to find the file or steals the device in which the file is located, that user could uncover the private key. The simplest method of protection is to secure the encrypted private key with a password and store it locally on disk or a USB key. The password should be as carefully crafted as your network password so that it can't be guessed easily or discovered through brute-force attack methods.

Exam Tip

A private key should never be stored in plain-text form. It needs to be encrypted and protected with a password.

For enterprise-level networks, the installation of a key management system takes the burden of key storage and protection away from the user and lets the OS or application manage key storage on a centralized server.

An additional method of protection includes the generation of another key pair to be used to encrypt the private key. This key is usually kept with a third party using a key escrow–type service.

Key Escrow

The concept of *key escrow* has been heavily overshadowed over the years by debates between privacy groups and the government, because it concerns the issues of data privacy versus national security. Key escrow involves a third party, such as a government agency or an authorized organization, that holds a special third key on top of your private and public key pair. The third key is used to encrypt the private key, which is then stored in a secure location. This third key can be used to unlock the encrypted copy of the private key in case of loss or the theft of the original key. Although the main concern of privacy activists is the possible abuse by the government regarding individual data privacy, the main security issue for most companies is the idea of a third-party entity controlling a crucial part of the company's security infrastructure.

Exam Tip

Key escrow involves a trusted third party that holds a special key in addition to your private and public key pair. This third key is used to encrypt the private key, which is then securely stored. In the event the private key is lost or stolen, the third key can be used to unlock the encrypted copy of the private key.

Another common key escrow entity is the CA, which is responsible for authorizing and distributing certificates and encryption key pairs. As part of your overall security plan, the ability for the CA to protect your information is crucial. CAs are a popular target of malicious hacker attacks because of the valuable information they store. Attacks are usually targeted at the CA's own private keys.

The CA's key pairs are common targets of cryptanalytic attacks that attempt to break weak keys through brute force. CAs need to be both secure and practical because their public key might be written into software used by a large number of users. If the key needs to be changed, every user's software will need to be updated to accept the new key.

Travel Advisory

When examining a key escrow service, pay careful attention to its methods of security, including the secure storage and transfer of keys and certificates.

Key Recovery

As the main key to unlocking the encryption on a file or other critical data, the private key must be carefully protected. If the private key is lost or destroyed, nothing that's been encrypted with that key will be accessible. With the storage and backup of private keys, a balance must be maintained between the security of the key and the ability to archive it in the event of the need for recovery.

Unfortunately, the concept of key recovery has been clouded by the issue of governmental control and the possibility that the government, in the interest of national security, would require a mandatory key recovery system. Such a mandatory key recovery system might enable the government to decrypt private data through the use of key escrow and key management companies. Whatever the outcome of that debate, secure methods of key recovery are available that keep the responsibility and capability of key recovery within the end user's hands.

Recovery Agent One method gaining in popularity is for a company to maintain protection of the backup of its private keys, but to use a third-party company, called a *recovery agent,* to store a unique key that can be used to unlock the backup of the private keys. This system prevents any of your private keys from leaving your premises and offers little room for compromising the security of those keys. The private keys are stored on your site, while the key to unlock those private keys is stored offsite.

M of N Control Another method uses what is known as *M of N control,* which refers to a method of storing a private key, protected and encrypted with a separate unique key. The key used for recovery is split into different parts and distributed to various individuals, called *key recovery operators,* and is usually stored in a smart card or other memory device. To use the recovery key, a certain number of the operators must be present with their part of the key.

Travel Advisory

M of N control can be somewhat difficult to maintain, especially with employee turnover where new replacements must be entered into the scheme.

The term *M of N control* refers to the number of operator keys that must be present to create the recovery key, such as *2 of 3* or *4 of 7.* For example, in a 4 of 7 scheme, a recovery key is split into seven parts and only four of those parts are needed to create the recovery key that will decrypt the backup of the private key.

Exam Tip

M of N control refers to the number of keys that must be present to create the recovery key, such as 3 of 5.

Multiple Key Pairs

The issue of using multiple key pairs in a PKI implementation greatly increases both the security and the complexity of data encryption. Using multiple keys directly involves the problems associated with backing up certain types of key pairs for recovery.

In a typical PKI setup, a private key and a public key are generated to be used for encryption and digital signatures. These keys can be used for three basic purposes:

- **Encryption**   To encrypt data to protect its contents.
- **Authentication**   To identify users through their public keys and certificates.
- **Nonrepudiation**   To make it impossible for someone to deny having signed a transaction or file.

The problem with using a single key pair for these functions is that the single key pair can often conflict with the backup and recovery requirements of the organization. A key pair used for encryption should be backed up in case the private key is lost or destroyed, so it can be recovered to decrypt the locked data. The backup of the same key pair used for nonrepudiation purposes, however, could be harmful. A digital signature intended to be legally binding can be repudiated if the signer proves it could be invalid because of the existence of another copy of the private key.

To solve this conflict, a dual key pair system can be used that can satisfy all security and backup requirements. One key pair can be used for encryption and decryption, while the second key pair can be used exclusively for digital signatures and nonrepudiation needs. The key pair used for encryption can be safely backed up for recovery purposes, while the second key needn't be backed up, in conformance with nonrepudiation procedures.

Exam Tip

Know the concept of nonrepudiation and how a dual key system can resolve the conflict with key backup.

Key History

Another important concept is the problem of *key history*. When using multiple keys and discarding old keys in favor of new ones, you might have archived data protected with encryption keys that you no longer use. As part of your key backup strategy, you need to retain copies of keys for encryption still in use on your network.

Travel Advisory

Without some form of key history, you won't be able to recover data files that have been encrypted with older keys you no longer possess.

Implement PKI, Certificate Management, and Associated Components

In the overall encryption trust model, all aspects, including users, administrators, the key management server, and any third-party key management company, must be able to trust one another so that the keys and identities of those using the keys are secured. As part of identifying users of keys, certificates are created, so users' identities and their public keys can be fully authenticated. If the public keys corresponding to a certain certificate have been compromised, any messages or files that were encrypted might be vulnerable. The only way to ensure the validity of the key is to check the status of the certificate.

Certificates go through a life cycle that identifies how long they're valid, how the certificate is renewed, when they can be suspended and revoked if compromised, and when they can be destroyed when no longer needed.

Certificate Life Cycle

The life cycle protects and secures the certificate mechanism itself, because the entire key infrastructure could be undermined if it is compromised. The life cycle of a certificate goes through the following stages, as detailed in Figure 5.5:

1. Certificate is requested.
2. Certificate is issued.
3. Certificate is published.
4. Certificate is received.
5. Certificate is suspended/revoked.
6. Certificate is expired.
7. Key is destroyed.

If the certificate is renewed prior to being revoked or suspended, the life cyle is extended.

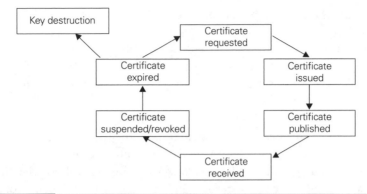

FIGURE 5.5   Certificate life cycle

Exam Tip

Know the various aspects of the certificate life cycle and what scenarios can cause certificates to be suspended or revoked.

Certificate Requested, Issued, Published, and Received

In the first steps of the certificate life cycle, the user makes a request to a CA for a certificate. In this request, the user must submit certain identity details. A CA cannot issue a certificate without verifying the identity of the requester. As part of the request, the user can generate his own public key pair when he submits his request, or the CA can perform the key generation when the user's identity is established.

If the process is followed correctly, the requester's identity is established and pubic key pairs are generated; then the CA can issue the certificate, and then publish and distribute it. The user will then receive his certificate, which authorizes him to use the certificate for its intended purpose.

Certificate Suspension and Revocation

A particular certificate can be suspended and revoked before its expiration date for a number of reasons. The most common reason for revocation is that the user who is using that certificate isn't authorized to use it anymore, as in the case of a company employee who quits his job or is fired. Alternatively, the certificate subscriber's data, such as the name of the company, might have changed, or it could have been incorrect on the certificate application. Other reasons for revocation include the problem of a key pair or certificate being compromised. If the private key is lost or compromised, the details in the corresponding certificate will no longer be valid. By immediately revoking the certificate, it can't be used for any authentication, encryption, or digital signature purposes. *Suspension* is a temporary revocation of the certificate until the problem concerning the certificate or the certificate owner's identity can be corrected. A suspension of a certificate can be undone, but a revocation is permanent.

The owner of the certificate must initiate communication with the CA to begin the revocation process. This needs to be performed in a secure way, through a signed message, in person, or via another authenticated channel. The private key corresponding to the certificate being revoked can be used to authenticate a revocation request, but if the revocation is a result of the key being compromised, the key can't be used to support authentication for a new certificate.

When a certificate is revoked, it's placed on a CA's Certificate Revocation List (CRL), which includes certificates that have been revoked before their expiration date by the CA. A CRL is used by other users and organizations to identify certificates that are no longer valid.

CRLs can be distributed in two main ways:

- **Pull model** The CRL is downloaded from the CA by those who want to see it to verify a certificate. In this model, the user or organization is responsible for regularly downloading the latest CRL for the most recent list.
- **Push model** In this model, the CA automatically sends the CRL out to verifiers at regular intervals.

These models can also be hierarchical in nature, in which a specific CRL of a CA is pushed to other sites, where other users and organizations can download it. CRLs are maintained in a distributed manner, but various central repositories contain the latest CRLs from a number of CAs.

Web sites and companies that deal with large numbers of secure transactions might need their own local version of a CRL that can quickly be compared to the large number of certificates accepted.

To check the status of a certificate, the CRL can be obtained from the specific CA or from a centralized database of CRLs released by a collection of authorities. To help automate this process, certificate status checks have been built into software applications, such as e-mail programs and web browsers that automatically check the status of a received certificate. Status checks can also be made manually by checking the web site of a CA and entering the serial number of a certificate.

> **Exam Tip**
>
> Know the purpose of a CRL and how it can be used to verify certificates.

Certificate Expiration

Within each certificate is a specific date for the beginning and ending of that certificate's life cycle. Most certificates are valid for approximately one to three years. The length of time the certificate is valid depends on the type of certificate issued and its purpose. A high-security defense contractor might switch its key pairs on a regular basis, meaning the certificates it uses could be valid for a short time.

The purpose of certificate expiry is to protect certificates from brute-force attacks. The longer certificates are in use, the greater the risk that they will be cracked. This is similar to a password expiry and retention scheme for a network in which users must regularly change their passwords to prevent them from being compromised.

If you want to use a certificate after its time of validity is complete, you'll need to renew the certificate. See the section "Certificate Renewal" a little later for more information.

> **Exam Tip**
>
> Once a certificate has expired, it can't be renewed. A new certificate and key pair need to be generated.

Key Destruction

If a certificate and key pair have been compromised or are no longer in use, the key pair (the private and public keys) should be destroyed to prevent further use. Because the public key has been distributed many times during its lifetime, it can obviously be difficult to destroy completely. Therefore, the destruction of the private key is essential to ensure certificates or digital signatures can no longer be created with those keys.

Some private keys, however, need to be retained—for example, if they're used for key management or data privacy, such as an encrypted file on a corporate network file server. The private key might need to be maintained as part of a key history, so items being stored with an older encryption key can be unlocked if necessary. A balance must be struck between the security need for key destruction and the need to access archived information.

Another aspect of key destruction involves the certificate that validates those keys. If the certificate is still valid, according to its creation and expiry date, then it needs to be revoked by contacting the CA, which will include the certificate's serial number in its CRL.

Destroying the private key can be a fairly simple process, but it must be thorough to ensure that the private key can't be recovered in any way. If the key is simply stored on a local hard disk, it can be deleted. The drawback to this method, however, is that many OSs don't delete the file; they delete only the file-name from the disk directory, while the actual file is still stored on disk, so it can be retrieved through a data recovery program such as the Recycle Bin. In some cases, such as if the computer were stolen, an unauthorized user could analyze the hard drive or send it to a special recovery lab that can restore the data still residing on the disk.

To prevent such discovery, many utilities can delete files permanently from magnetic media. Other options include the actual physical destruction of the media itself, whether it is a hard drive, DVD, USB key, or flash memory device.

Certificate Renewal

To continue to use a certificate, it must be renewed before its expiry date. Typically, the CA will contact the owner of the certificate when the certificate's expiration date is impending. The certificate owner has the responsibility of renewing the certificate before the expiration date. If this renewal isn't performed before the expiry date, the certificate will become invalid, and anyone trusting the source of that certificate will be unable to transact or communicate with the certificate owner. For companies that rely on certificates for digital transactions, this could be fatal. In addition, a request for a new certificate will need to be issued, which might take time to process before you receive the new certificate and keys.

The policies and procedures of the CA must be examined carefully to ensure that certificates are renewed on time, especially because CAs usually require extra time before the expiry date to register the renewal properly. As a rule, you should renew certificates at least 30 days before they expire.

One important aspect of renewal is deciding whether or not to generate a new key pair to go along with the new certificate. Many CAs, in the process of renewal, merely repackage the certificate with the same public key. Because cryptographic keys can be compromised over time through sustained computational brute-force methods, the longer you keep the same key pair, the more insecure it will become. Therefore, it's extremely important for cryptographic security to generate a new key when renewing a certificate. This might not be so important for an individual who uses encryption only sparingly for personal purposes, but for companies with high-security needs, this is vital.

CHECKPOINT

✔**Objective 5.01: Explain the core concepts of Public Key Infrastructure.**
Decentralized storage is used by individual users, and centralized storage is used for enterprise networks. Private keys need to be stored securely and, preferably, encrypted with a password. Key escrow companies can store the encryption key that can unlock the encryption on your private key, which is stored at your location. Backups need to be made of keys to prevent loss of data because of lost, stolen, or damaged keys. Keys for digital signing shouldn't be backed up because of nonrepudiation requirements. A dual-pair key system can generate separate keys for encryption and digital signing. M of N control stores different parts of a key distributed among several people, or a third-party recovery agent can be used to store your keys. Only a certain number of key parts are needed to provide the key.

✔**Objective 5.02: Implement PKI, certificate management, and associated components.** Certificates need to be renewed before expiry, or else a new certificate must be generated. A certificate should be suspended or revoked if the keys related to that certificate are compromised. Check the CRL for certificates that have been revoked.

REVIEW QUESTIONS

1. To protect its customers from logging in to unauthorized web sites, your company wants you to implement the use of digital certificates to satisfy which of these information assurance requirements?

   A. Confidentiality

   B. Nonrepudiation

   C. Authentication

   D. Integrity

2. For your organization's encryption systems, which of the following should you implement to act as a centralized server to store and distribute your public and private keys?

   A. Key management server

   B. Digital certificate

   C. CRL

   D. Certificate authority

3. To improve the integrity and authentication of your encryption systems, you have contacted a certificate authority to generate which of the following items for you?

   A. Digital certificate and public/private key pair

   B. Public key and a private hash

   C. Private key and a certificate

   D. Secret key for local encryption server

4. You need to store your company's private key in a safe, secure place. Which of the following would you use?

   A. Save it on a hard drive in plain text.

   B. Seal it in an envelope and store it at your home office.

   C. Encrypt it on a flash memory device.

   D. Store it on a portable USB device in plain text.

5. You have started using a third-party key escrow company to protect your encryption keys. Which of the following do you send to them?

   A. Encryption key to decrypt a private key file

   B. Encryption key to decrypt a public key file

   C. Copy of a public key

   D. Copy of a certificate

6. Your recovery encryption key is split between seven of your co-workers, of which four are only required to be present to decrypt the private key. Which of the following methods are you using for key recovery?

   A. Steganography

   B. Certificate authority

   C. Key escrow

   D. M of N control

7. During a legal battle with another company, they have denied that they sent and signed a file with their encryption key, but you have proven that they did through their digital signature information. What information assurance function has been satisfied?

   A. Nonrepudiation

   B. Authentication

   C. Encryption signing

   D. Digital signature

8. You have been tasked to contact your certificate authority and revoke your company's current web server certificate. Which of the following is the most likely reason to revoke the certificate?

   A. You renewed your certificate after it expired.

   B. The previous network administrator who created the certificate was fired.

   C. You installed a new web server.

   D. Your current certificate expires in less than 30 days.

9. You need to look up the details of a certificate that was revoked. Where can you find this information?

   A. Certificate Expiry List

   B. Registration Suspension List

   C. Certificate Revocation List

   D. Registration Expiry List

10. You need to renew your company's certificate for its public web server. When should you renew the certificate?

   A. On its expiry date

   B. After it expires

   C. After it's revoked

   D. Thirty days before expiry

REVIEW ANSWERS

1. **C**   A digital certificate is a credential required by PKI systems that can securely identify an organization's server as well as create an association between the server's authenticated identity and public keys. When a user connects to your company web site, the certificate confirms the identity of the server.

2. **A**   A key management server is a centralized storage system that takes care of the process of distributing, storing, and backing up keys for users of an enterprise network.

3. **A**   When a user's identification is established, the CA generates public and private keys for the user. A certificate is then generated with the identification and public key information embedded within it. Once the user is registered and receives his certificate, he can begin using his certificate to send encrypted messages.

4. **C**   Private keys should never be stored in plain text. If they're stolen, an unauthorized user will be able to use them to decrypt messages and files.

5. **A**   In a key escrow storage scheme, an encryption key used to encrypt and decrypt the private key file is stored offsite with a third party. If access is needed to the backup copy of the private key, the encryption key needs to be obtained from the third-party company after you've been properly authenticated.

6. **D**   In this key recovery scheme, a prescribed number of the key owners must be present with their parts of the key. M of N control refers to the number of operator keys that must be present to create the recovery key, such as 2 of 3 or 4 of 7. For example, if a recovery key is split into seven parts, only four of those are needed to create the recovery key that will decrypt the backup of the private key.

7. **A**   Nonrepudiation refers to an information assurance concept that defines the inability of a user to deny having signed a transaction or file with his or her encryption key. For example, they could try to prove that another copy of the private key exists. Digital signatures and certificates provide the function of nonrepudiation.

8. **B**   The certificate should be revoked because the user assigned to that certificate is no longer with the company. This prevents the user from continuing to use that certificate for encryption and authentication.

9. **C**   A Certificate Revocation List (CRL) is published by a CA to show certificates that have been revoked. A verifier can examine the list to check the validity of another user's certificate.

10. **D**   Most certificate authorities require that a certificate be renewed a certain amount of time before the actual expiry date. This provides the CA with enough time to renew the certificate and deliver it back to the client for distribution.

Access Control and Identity Management

| Chapter 6 | Access Control |
| Chapter 7 | Authentication and Identity Management |

Access Control

ITINERARY

○ **Objective 6.01** Explain the fundamental concepts and best practices related to authentication, authorization, and access control

○ **Objective 6.02** Implement appropriate security controls when performing account management

○ **Objective 6.03** Analyze and differentiate among types of mitigation and deterrent techniques

	NEWBIE	SOME EXPERIENCE	EXPERT
ETA	3 hours	2 hours	1 hour

157

Two simple and often overlooked aspects of security are access control and authentication. In many business environments, access involves a single login to a computer or a network of computer systems that provides the user access to all resources on the network. This access includes rights to personal and shared folders on a network server, company intranets, printers, and other network resources and devices. These same resources can be quickly exploited by unauthorized users if the access control and associated authentication procedures aren't set up properly.

Access control refers to permissions applied to resources that determine which users can access those resources. *Authentication* goes hand-in-hand with access control by identifying users to be sure they are exactly who they claim to be. After a user has been authenticated, the resources for which the user has appropriate permissions become accessible.

As an administrator, you must carefully consider system and network security when creating access and authentication policies. Basic security practices such as login IDs and passwords must be augmented with advanced logical access control techniques, such as the use of long, nondictionary, alphanumeric passwords; regular password rotation and expiration; and password aging. Finally, the protection of personal and shared data resources on network file servers must be maintained through the use of directory and file access control permissions on a per-user or per-group basis.

Access control also pertains to physical access to your organization's buildings or computers. Physical access control is a first-level barrier that prevents unauthorized users from entering your facility or accessing vital company equipment.

This chapter describes the basic concepts and models of access control, user account and privilege management, and physical access control security.

Objective 6.01
CompTIA Security+
Objective 5.2

Explain the Fundamental Concepts and Best Practices Related to Authentication, Authorization, and Access Control

Access control methods determine how users interact with resources and computer systems. Resources must be protected from unauthorized modification or tampering. Access controls must be enforced on a network to ensure that unauthorized users cannot access its resources or the network and computer system infrastructure.

Users and Resources

Your first task is to define who are the *users* and to what *resources* they need access. A *user* in this sense doesn't always mean a specific person. A computer might act as a user when it tries to connect to the resource of another computer system. A *resource* can be anything from a simple text file on a file server, to a network laser printer, to an Internet proxy server. A user of a resource might also be a computer account used by a system to back up other computer systems' resources and data to a tape drive. This *backup* user account must also have its access control defined properly so that it can securely perform its job function.

Just as your users must be carefully defined, the resources offered by your computer network need to be categorized and access controls defined for the resources' security. Your resources must be categorized with the following attributes in mind:

- **Sensitivity**   How confidential is the data from this resource? Should it be seen only by certain users, or should access be open to anyone? An example of sensitive data would be payroll or human resources data. The ability to access this resource should be available only to users from those departments. Sensitivity issues can be secured via access controls.

- **Integrity**   Should users only be able to read from this directory, or can they modify the files within? If the integrity of the data is vital, this resource should have its access permissions set to read-only. For example, a datasheet of released company financials to shareholders should never be modified after distribution. Integrity issues can be addressed via access controls, primarily file and directory security.

- **Availability**   How available should the data be as a resource? Does this data need to be available at all times or only during certain time periods? Is this information so critical that it must be available whenever a user requests it? Typically, availability decreases with increased security, so the needs of protecting the data must be balanced with the necessary level of availability. Availability issues can be addressed via backups, clustering, and redundancy solutions.

Travel Advisory

In real-world situations, friction can exist between management and the information technology (IT) department over the need for availability against the need for security. IT departments must emphasize the need for security over ease of availability and balance the requirements accordingly.

Levels of Security

Before a user is allowed access to a facility or resource, three main levels of security must be passed:

- **Identification**   The user must initially identify herself as a valid user for that network, usually with a login user name or account name. *Identification,* also referred to as *identify proofing,* ensures that a user (which could also be an application program or process) is who she claims to be. For example, before performing any type of online banking, a customer must identify who she is and have sufficient physical identification (such as bank cards, passwords, PINs, and so on) to be able to prove her identity before the process goes any further.

- **Authentication**   The user must then pass the *authentication* phase using her logon user name or account number and a password. If these two criteria are matched with the global database of login user names and passwords stored on the network, the user is authenticated and is granted access to the network. To be authenticated properly, the user must provide proof that she should be using the login name by supplying a password, PIN, or token. If the identity and password or PIN match the central database, the user is authenticated.

- **Authorization**   Finally, when a user tries to access a resource, the system must check to see if that user ID is authorized for that resource and what permissions or privileges the user has when using it. Just because a user has been identified and authenticated to a network doesn't mean she should be able to access all resources. If the system determines that the user may access the resource, the user is authorized and allowed access with the privileges she has been granted.

Exam Tip

Be aware of the differences between identifying a user, authenticating, and authorizing. In a secure, access-controlled environment, these terms specifically correspond to different steps in the process.

Access Security Grouping

Administrators need to visualize the relationships among users and groups and the resources they need to perform their jobs. A network administrator assigning access permissions individually to resources on a per-user basis would likely be inefficient and extremely time-consuming. For small networks, this might be a viable option, but for mid-sized to large corporate networks, it would be an unwieldy strategy. Grouping users, depending on similarities in their attributes, is far more efficient. Typically, you can identify groups of users in three main ways: by job function, department, and physical location.

Job Function   Users who perform the same job will most likely need access to the same resources. For example, a number of financial analysts might need access to the same data directory on a specific file server. By grouping these users into one entity, you can assign the resulting group access to the data without needing to perform this configuration for each user. This model can also be defined hierarchically, as shown in Figure 6.1, where management might have more access to resources than nonmanagement personnel.

Department   Users who belong to the same department in an organization will probably need access to the same data and resources. All employees within a department aren't always working in the same physical location. Because of the virtual nature of many large corporate networks, a sales employee in the United States might need access to the same sales database used by a sales employee in Japan. All users from the sales department can be assigned to the same group: Sales. The network administrator has to configure access only to the sales database once for the Sales group, without having to assign access for each individual salesperson. This model is shown in Figure 6.2.

Physical Location   A company could be located in a single building, in several buildings, or in different cities and countries. Many companies divide their resources among physical locations, so, for example, an office in New York might

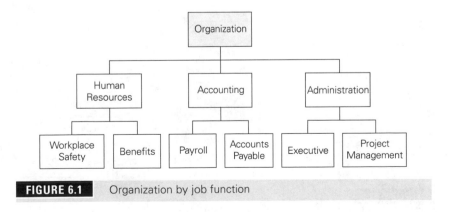

FIGURE 6.1   Organization by job function

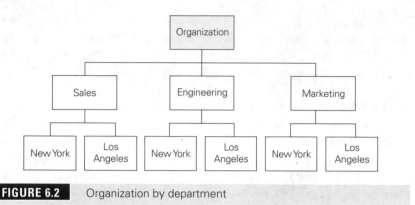

FIGURE 6.2   Organization by department

not need access to resources to a file server in Los Angeles. In this way, the security model can be set up by physical location, where users are grouped depending on the office to which they belong, as shown in Figure 6.3.

In the most efficient security model, data resources are organized based on need-to-know criteria. Resources should be available only to users who need access to that information. In most cases, the users in a sales department wouldn't need access to the data resources of accounting or human resources, for example. Each resource must have its access controls specifically set to allow access only to users authorized for that resource. This also flows down into more granular levels of security, in which a user might have access to read a file, but not modify or execute it. For example, an employee assigned to print a directory of documents should need only read and print access to the file; he does not need access to modify or delete. The best practice is to grant only the lowest level of access permissions a user needs to perform their job.

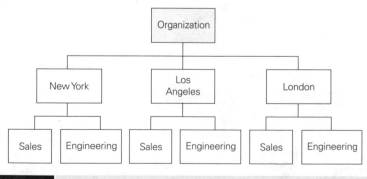

FIGURE 6.3   Organization by physical location

Travel Advisory

When setting up a new network, you should create a user hierarchy based on one of the previous security models. Trying to change the model down the road can be difficult after it is already in place.

Access Control Best Practices

There are several best practices for access control to data that increase security through proper organizational structures and data security principles.

Separation of Duties

To make sure that all employees and management personnel know their roles in the company, the organization's structure should be clear, with positions properly defined with formal job titles and descriptions, definitions of responsibilities, and reporting structures that define the lines of authority.

To increase security and reduce risk from security compromises, part of the effort should be directed toward both a clear organizational structure and a specific separation of duties. A *separation of duties* can ensure that one individual isn't overtasked with high-security and high-risk responsibilities and that users aren't accessing restricted resources because of jobs that haven't been properly defined.

To separate duties that involve high-security situations, a certain amount of collusion must take place. *Collusion* means that to proceed with a certain task, more than one person is required to allow the procedure to take place. In a banking situation, for example, opening the main safe could require the authorization of at least two people, because each authorized person possesses a key, and both keys are needed to open the safe. This prevents a single individual from opening the safe without supervision. Like a safe, a computer system must have protected access. The more people involved, the less chance of a single person making a poor security decision that could compromise the entire network.

Exam Tip

Separation of duties ensures that one individual isn't tasked with high-security and high-risk responsibilities, and that users aren't accessing restricted resources because of jobs that haven't been defined properly. Collusion requires that more than one person allow a specific procedure to take place to ensure that important security decisions are not relegated to a single person.

Rotation of Job Duties

Job rotation provides employees with workforce skills improvement and increased job satisfaction, but it also enhances the security of an organization. Job rotation exposes employees to new skills and opportunities by allowing them to perform different jobs within an organization. Job rotation also ensures better security, as no single employee retains the same amount of access control for a particular area for an extended period of time. This can prevent internal corruption that can occur, for example, when a long-term employee, because of her deep knowledge of a particular area of duty, might take advantage of the position and security access. Job rotation also boosts accountability when another person takes over a specific job duty and examines potential inefficiencies or evidence of security lapses.

Suppose, for example, that a server administrator and network administrator switch roles. Each administrator has an opportunity to increase her knowledge by applying her security skills and knowledge of security procedures to a different part of the organization. The switch also allows each administrator to scrutinize the security aspects of the other role with a fresh perspective.

Mandatory Vacations

Mandatory vacations are a security measure that requires employees to use their vacations at specific times of year or requires that they use all of their vacation days instead of not using them and carrying over unused vacation days to a following year. This policy is most often used to detect security issues with employees, such as fraud or other internal hacking activities, as typically the employee must be present every day to continue to perpetuate or erase the evidence of malicious activities. When a user is forced to go on vacation, his on-the-job activities may be more likely to be noticed and detected because the user is not present to prevent their discovery. When the user is away, the person filling in for him will be able to audit the user's activities and reveal any suspicious behavior. For example, an unscrupulous employee in a financial institution may be performing illegal activities related to customer bank account details, and manually cleaning up log files to erase traces of her activity. When she is forced on vacation, this activity may be noticed in the logs, as she is not able to cover her tracks while she is away.

Implicit Deny

Implicit deny refers to the security principle of starting a user out with no access rights and granting permissions to resources as required. This principle states that a security policy must implicitly deny all access to provide a fully secure baseline. Only then can the administrator grant a user access to resources.

The implicit deny principle is more secure than starting out with a policy that grants a user default access to all resources and then denies access permissions to certain resources. It is too easy for administrators to overlook several aspects of resources that require access to be controlled and denied as appropriate.

The implicit deny policy should be applied to all aspects of an organization's security, from physical security and access control, to file and resources permissions on a file server, and to network firewall and router rules. By starting out with the strongest security policy and then creating access permissions, administrators know that all access is denied by default, and each access control permission granted is an exception to that policy.

> **Exam Tip**
>
> Implicit deny means that all access is denied by default, and access permissions are granted only to specific resources as required.

Least Privilege

The *Least Privilege* principle grants users only access rights they need to perform their job functions. This requires giving users the least amount of access possible to prevent them from abusing more powerful access rights. For example, a user might need access to certain files to print them for a manager. The network administrator should give the user only enough access rights to read the file and print it, without including privileges to delete, modify, or add information to the file.

The function of management is to decide exactly what a person needs to know or for what areas the person requires access for a particular position. The network administrator must enact the decision. When in doubt, the network administrator should be cautious and allow only minimal access until someone can authorize more privileges on behalf of the user. Increased privileges should never be handed out at the request of the user who needs them.

> **Exam Tip**
>
> Data access should be based on the least privilege principle, which ensures that users have the minimal access rights available to perform their job function and nothing more.

Access Control Models

Access control models are policies that define how users access data. These policies form a framework based on the security and business goals of the organization.

The rules of the framework are enforced through access control technologies. The following sections cover the main access control types.

Mandatory Access Control

In a mandatory access control (MAC) model, the operating system (OS) is in control of access to data. Most data owners can assign permissions to their own files and share them however they see fit, but OS access controls override any data owner settings. Users have little freedom to adjust access controls, except for specific data under their control. When defined on the system, users are given certain access rights representing a certain level of trust. The data resources themselves also have security classifications that define the level of trust a user must have to access the data. If a user doesn't have the appropriate access rights to use the data, he is denied access. This type of model is centralized and is often used in high-security environments, such as the military or government offices, where access control is tightly guarded through strict OS security policies. Military classifications such as Classified, Secret, and Top Secret are examples of MAC in which specific security access is restricted depending on the classification of the data.

Discretionary Access Control

Discretionary access control (DAC) enables data owners to specify which users can access certain data. Access to resources is allowed only for authorized users through permissions on the resource. This is the most common model used in Windows and Unix environments in which administrators create a hierarchy of files, directories, and other resources that are accessed based on user privileges and access rights. Resource owners are typically allowed to control who accesses their resources. For example, an individual user can share specific files or directories with users they authorize. This model is a less-centralized version of the mandatory access control.

Role-Based Access Control

Role-based access control (RBAC) is also referred to as nondiscretionary access control. This centrally controlled model allows access to be based on the role the user holds within an organization. Instead of giving access to individual users, access control is granted to groups of users who perform a common function. For example, many organizations have special "contractor" roles comprising employees who work on a contract basis and are not full-salaried employees; these workers are given less access to certain resources or parts of the network. In an IT department, for example, a user given the role of "backup administrator" might have access to controlling backup and restore operations, but he would not have privileges to add users or assign access permissions, which are reserved for a system administrator. No matter who is assigned the backup administrator role, access permissions will be the same. Database servers such as SQL servers often use role-based permissions to restrict access to certain portions of the database.

Rule-Based Access Control

Rule-based access control provides enhanced granularity when specifying access control policies and indicates specifically what can and cannot happen between a user and the resource. This type of access control policy is typically defined by an access control list (ACL), which specifies a set of rules that must be followed before access is granted. Unlike the DAC method, rule-based access control does not necessarily have to be tied to an authorized identity and could involve access permissions based on network location, content of messages (such as e-mail text or attachments), and other types of content filtering. These rules are typically implemented in network access devices such as routers, firewalls, and content-filtering systems, and they apply to all users regardless of their identity.

Objective 6.02
CompTIA Security+
Objective 5.3

Implement Appropriate Security Controls When Performing Account Management

L̲ogical access controls are software-based components that control user access to resources. These access controls are typically an integral part of an operating system or software application to provide user account, password, and access privileges management. By using a strong user account policy, you can greatly diminish the ability of a hacker to break into a user's account.

User Account Policies

Several policies can be created for account use to strengthen the security of the login process. Some of the most effective restrictions include the following:

- Using appropriate naming conventions
- Limiting logon attempts
- Setting account expiry dates
- Disabling unused accounts

- Setting time restrictions
- Setting machine restrictions
- Using tokens

Using Appropriate Naming Conventions

When you configure and set up a company network, a best practice is to enact some form of account naming conventions. A common naming convention is employing a user's first initial and last name, or variations of it, as his account ID. Never use account names that represent job functions: A user account named *admin* is much more likely to attract the attention of an unauthorized user who is trying to hack into a system, because he knows the user ID could be the main administrative account for the network. If he's able to compromise that account, he will have full control over the network. Other names such as *human_resources* or *accounting* will also be more likely targets for an unauthorized user.

Limiting Logon Attempts

This parameter sets the maximum amount of incorrect logon attempts before disabling an account. This is an important feature because many hackers simply repeat attempts at accessing an account using different passwords each time. If no logon attempt restrictions exist, hackers can continue this brute-force attack until the account is eventually compromised. A best practice is to set a limit of three to five failed attempts, after which the account is locked out and the user must contact the administrator to enable the account again.

Setting Account Expiry Dates

Setting an expiry date on a user account will disable it when the target date is reached. This is useful for contract workers who are employed for a limited period of time. When the contract date is reached, the user's login is immediately disabled. By setting an expiry on the account when a contractor is first hired, disabling the account won't be forgotten, and the account will be automatically disabled when the expiration date is reached. If the contract is renewed, the account can simply be re-enabled and the expiration date changed.

Disabling Unused Accounts

When an employee leaves the company, his account should be immediately disabled. This is especially important for any employee who is suddenly terminated for any reason. By immediately disabling the account, you deny access to further attempts by that user to access his account. Another best practice is to disable accounts you don't recognize as valid. Unauthorized users could have broken into the system and created their own "dummy" accounts to perform malicious activities unnoticed. If the account is valid, the user will contact you, because he can't log in. You can then verify whether the user should have access to the system.

Setting Time Restrictions

If your company operates only during certain hours each day, you can set time restrictions for access to the network. After hours, only a select few users might need access. You can set time restrictions on other users' accounts so that they are able to log in only during operating hours. This will reduce the risk of unauthorized users trying to use an employee's account off-hours to break into the system.

Setting Machine Restrictions

You can allow logins only from certain machines on the network. Any computer on your current internal network can be set up to prevent anyone trying to access the system using an outside computer or laptop. Machine restrictions are usually set using a computer's network card MAC address, computer name, or the network IP address.

Using Tokens

To provide additional access control and authentication protection, many organizations use a two-tier form of authentication: in addition to an account name and password, the user also requires a physical or logical *token,* such as a special Universal Serial Bus (USB) key, that needs to be connected to their computer before she is allowed access. Certain types of physical tokens, such as RSA SecurID and CRYPTOCard, provide a logical token number that is generated in conjunction with the access control server that must be entered, along with a user name and password, to grant access.

Tokens provide an extra layer of security, because even if an unauthorized user has access to the physical token (if it was stolen from the user, for example), he still requires a user name and password to access the system. Similarly, if the unauthorized user knows a user name and password he can use, he still needs the physical or logical token to complete the authentication and access control process.

Exam Tip

Be aware of the different types of account restrictions and access control methods that can be used to increase the security of user accounts.

Password Management

Password management, although typically created and enforced by the network administrator, is becoming a special area of network security that should be covered in specific company policies. All users must be aware of the company's rules and procedures for managing user accounts and passwords that allow access to company resources.

Password Policies

Following are some basic, but important, password policies that can be set by the administrator to enforce strong passwords:

- **Minimum Length and Complexity**   The minimum length for a password can be enforced by the network administrator. This prevents users from using small, easy-to-guess passwords of only a few characters in length. The password should be at least six to eight characters and contain a mix of uppercase and lowercase characters, numbers, and special characters.

- **Password History**   Most login and password authentication systems are able to recall a user's last several passwords and can prevent the user from using the same one over and over again. This is often referred to as *password aging*. If this option is available, it should be enabled, so a user's password will always be different.

- **Password Rotation and Expiration**   The longer a password has existed, the easier it is for a hacker to eventually discover the password simply by narrowing the options over time. Forcing users to change their passwords regularly can prevent a hacker from discovering a password through brute-force attacks and ensures that if the account password has been compromised, the hacker will lose access the next time the password is changed. Most organizations expire passwords and force their users to change their passwords every one to three months.

- **Password Recovery**   If a user forgets the password, the administrator must reset the password to a secure temporary value, and force the user to change that password the first time she logs in. More secure password recovery schemes include sending a temporary password to a user's e-mail address. This provides some verification of the user's identity, as only that user would be able to check her e-mail account.

Domain Accounts and Single Sign-on

In environments that use the *single sign-on* type of account and password, such as a Microsoft Active Directory domain account, account and password security mechanisms must be strictly enforced, as each user will use one account and password to access all file and print resources for her domain. This strengthens security, as both administrators and users only need to define, enforce, and utilize a single account and password policy for the entire domain. In the past, users had different accounts and passwords for each resource they needed to access, which usually meant that one or more of these resources was inadequately protected with a weak password. Having an overall domain account and password policy allows administrators to manage the security of these accounts using a single policy and allows end users to have to remember only one user name and password to access any resource.

Security Roles and Privileges

Privilege management involves the creation and use of policies defining the users and groups that access company resources, such as data files or printers. To control how users access data, employees need to be logically structured to define access privileges depending on the type of user, the groups to which the user belongs, or the user's specific role in the company.

When designing a company's security infrastructure, you must visualize the relationships among users and groups and the resources they need to perform their jobs. Although assigning access permissions individually to resources on a per-user basis might be viable for small networks, it would be an inefficient and extremely time-consuming strategy for mid-sized to large corporate networks. Grouping users according to similarities in job functions is much more efficient. Beyond this, user security can be designed according to user roles within the company.

User

A single user's access rights and privileges revolve around the data that person creates, modifies, and deletes. In addition to the user's own user access control privileges, he can also be part of a group, be assigned a specific role, and be assigned that role's privileges as well. For example, a user can have individual access rights to files in his home directory, but he can also have access to the Sales and Marketing group directory, as he also belongs to that group. In addition, the user might have an additional role such as auditor, so he has access to additional resources beyond his user and group access rights.

Group

In this model, several users who need access to the same data are organized in a group. Privileges can be distributed to the entire group of users, rather than to each individual user. This is much more efficient when applying permissions and provides greater overall control of access to resources. For example, users who are part of the same Sales and Marketing group would typically have access to and share the same data on a file server and, depending on their location, would share rights to the same printers. Group privileges typically provide additional access rights to users beyond their own individual access permissions to access shared data.

Role

A user might have different security privileges according to his role in the company. For example, a user who is also a database administrator might have extra privileges accorded to that role, on top of or replacing those privileges acquired as a user or part of a group. Predetermined permissions for a role can be created and then applied to users or groups that fit that role.

File and Print Security Controls

Use of file and print servers can be involved in much of a user's daily work routine. *File servers* are used to store the user's data, including personal work files and departmental or company-wide information. *Print servers* are used to administer print services and print queues, in which a user's print jobs are organized and sent to the appropriate printer.

Security concerns with file and print servers center around authentication and access permissions. File servers should be configured so that no user can access the server through the network without first being authenticated via a user name and a password. Beyond that, various directories and files, depending on their ownership and confidentiality, need to be secured with access permissions.

Most file servers have directories arranged in hierarchies, typically according to user and departmental or group directories. For example, each user would have her own personal data directory, in which only she has access to create, delete, and modify the files and directories within. This prevents other users from accessing her files. Or the CEO of the company can store her personal and important company files in a personal directory that only she can access.

Typically, some directories are set up as departmental or group directories that provide a separate area for each department to store files to which everyone in that department needs access. For example, a directory could be set up for the finance department that allows each person in the finance group to access the confidential accounting files in that directory. The access permissions would be set so that no user or department could access that directory except those in the finance group. Other directories could allow only read-only permissions, such as a directory of company policy and benefit files that all employees need to access for reference but shouldn't be allowed to modify or delete.

This same methodology should be used for printing services. Most printers are configured to allow any user to send print jobs to them. For more confidential printers, such as a printer used in the human resources department, where employment or termination notices might be created, the printer's access permissions would allow only HR department employees to print. The printer itself should also be physically located in a secure area with controlled access. More granular security-access permissions can be set, so users can't modify or delete jobs after they've been sent to the printer. Most of these controls are handled by the administrator, who controls the flow and access of print queues.

File and Print ACLs

Several different permissions can be assigned to files and directories on a computer system. This is typically defined in the ACL, which contains a list of permissions granted to users for each resource. Following are the most common permissions that can be assigned:

- **Read** View the contents of a file or directory.
- **View** View the contents of a directory; users can see that a file exists, but they won't necessarily have permission to read the contents of the file.
- **Write** Create and save a new file or write to an existing file.
- **Print** Print a file.
- **Copy** Copy a file from one location to another. The Write permission would also be required in the destination directory.
- **Delete** Delete a file or directory.
- **Execute** Execute a program file or script.
- **Modify** Modify the attributes of a file or directory.
- **Move** Move a file from one location to another. The Write permission would be required in the destination directory. The Delete permission would be required to remove the file after the move is completed.

Exam Tip

Be aware of the differences between the various access permissions, especially those pertaining to files, directories, and file attributes.

The most basic types of security that can be set at the resource level are *full access* or *no access* at all. Using these settings is a bad practice, however, and must be avoided through the use of more granular security. An ACL should be created for every resource and applied for all users. When you first create an ACL for a resource, start with *no access* as a default. This lets you begin with a clean slate, where no access is the default permission. Then add access permissions based on the needs of the particular user or group, granting only the access permissions necessary to perform their job functions. Never grant Write or Modify permissions unless users need to make changes to a file.

Consider the following example. A sales database is used to keep track of clients and their pertinent information. Employees in the sales group must be able to read and modify this information and delete and add new users to the database. The administrative staff will initiate or take calls from clients, and they need access to the database to look up client information and print the results. The administrative staff doesn't need access to modify the contents of the client records in the database, however. To perform system maintenance and administration on the database, the database administration group needs access to perform all functions, including changing the file attributes of the database file. The sales group, however, doesn't want the database administration group to have Delete access. In this scenario, the following access rights should be defined for each group:

User	Access Rights Assigned
Sales	Read, Write, Delete, Copy, Move
Admin	Read, Print
Database Admin	Read, Write, Copy, Move, Modify

Travel Advisory

If a user asks to be given access rights to a file or directory, never grant it without first verifying the user's need for the access with his or her manager.

Objective 6.03
CompTIA Security+
Objective 3.6

Analyze and Differentiate among Types of Mitigation and Deterrent Techniques

Physical access control security differs from computer security: When securing a computer system or network, you're attempting to prevent unauthorized users from accessing the resources of your system. Physical security, however, is implemented to prevent unauthorized users from accessing an environment—anything from the entire facility to a small network closet that contains networking equipment and wiring.

Much time and expense is spent on securing a computer network from unauthorized external access, but typically not enough resources are used on physical security to prevent unauthorized internal access. The possible result of lax physical security and access control includes equipment theft, physical damage and vandalism, service interruptions, and the unauthorized release of confidential data. Physical security is required to protect employees, company data, equipment, and the facility itself.

To secure access to the facility, access systems should be installed to identify employees and control what areas of the facility they can enter. Access control security also includes surveillance and monitoring of company property and the installation of physical barriers to prevent unauthorized intruders from trespassing on a company's property.

Your first line of defense is the security of the perimeter of the facility or the boundaries of its property. It's critical that unauthorized people be prevented from accessing the property or its buildings. This could involve unique security mechanisms for use during daily working hours and for use when the facility is closed. Building security includes the use of physical barriers, surveillance, and access control.

Physical Barriers

To deter unauthorized people from accessing a facility, physical barriers can be the most effective form of security. *Fencing* can close off the perimeter from people who are simply passing by and could be inclined to trespass on company property. Depending on the level of protection required, fencing can be as simple as a four-foot fence that protects against casual trespassers or animals. Higher fences of at least eight feet should be constructed to make it difficult for the average person to climb over them. For the most protection, barbed wire can be installed at the top of the fence.

Lighting

In the interest of security and safety, all areas of the property—including all the company's buildings and the parking lot—should have proper lighting installed to discourage intruders and provide a safe environment for employees. Floodlights are an effective way to illuminate a large area. The entire lighting system should also be set on a timer, or photoelectric technology can be used to detect outside light levels.

Video Surveillance

To maintain the physical security of the property, surveillance and monitoring devices should be employed. The simplest form of surveillance is the use of common security procedures, such as using security guards. Cameras can be set up throughout the facility, which can be constantly monitored by security guards. Although effective, these options can be costly because of the high price of surveillance equipment and the ongoing wages that must be paid to security guards. Camera surveillance can be coupled with recording equipment that can monitor and record all activity 24 hours a day. If a burglary or vandalism occurs, the culprits could be captured on video, which can then be analyzed to identify the unauthorized intruders.

Camera placement is of primary importance, both in terms of efficiency of surveillance and equipment costs, and at a minimum all entrances, doors, and access ways should be included in the coverage. All people who enter and exit the facility will be recorded on the cameras. In high-security environments, additional cameras are typically placed inside server rooms and other networking equipment areas that form the hub of the communications network.

The use of intruder detection equipment can ensure that a surveillance and monitoring system is proactive by alerting you to suspicious behavior without the need and expense of constant monitoring by security guards. Several intrusion detection technologies options are available:

- **Proximity detector** Senses changes in an electromagnetic field that surrounds a small area or object; when a change is detected, an alarm will sound.

- **Motion detector** Detects motion in a certain area; most often used in conjunction with floodlights that turn on when motion is detected. The light serves as a warning that an intruder has been detected.

- **Photoelectric detector** Senses changes in light patterns that indicate someone is in the area. The photoelectric device emits a beam of light, which, when disrupted, sounds an alarm.

- **Infrared detector** Senses changes in the heat patterns of an area that indicate the presence of an intruder.

- **Sound detector** Senses sounds and vibrations, and can detect changes in the noise levels in an area.

Travel Advisory

The main drawback of most intrusion-detection systems is the large number of false alarms that can occur because of abnormal weather conditions, animals, and improper calibration.

Locks

The most basic and least expensive type of physical-access control is the use of a lock and key. Unfortunately, in large environments this can quickly become an administrative nightmare, because the number of keys that must be distributed for each lock can grow quickly. In addition, employees lose keys, duplicate them, and let other users borrow them. When an employee is terminated, he might not always return his keys, and then every lock has to be changed.

Depending on the environment, different types of locks can be used. For perimeter security, a simple padlock on a chained fence might suffice. For more high-security areas, electronic or mechanical locks with programmable keys can be installed. These require a combination or key code to open, instead of a physical key.

Travel Advisory

Electronic locks should be linked with the alarm system. In case of a fire or other emergency, the locks should automatically disengage to allow people to leave the building.

Hardware Locks

It's easy for an unauthorized user to walk by an unattended desk or system rack and quickly remove expensive equipment. Not only does the stolen equipment need to be replaced, but the sensitive data saved on that equipment must be recovered. If the item was stolen for the purpose of corporate espionage, the results of the theft can be devastating.

Any expensive or sensitive equipment—especially portable items such as laptops, mobile devices, and networking equipment, should be kept out of sight or locked up when unattended. Device locks are available for both desktop computers and portable laptops. A desktop computer can be housed in a lockable cage that would require a great deal of effort to open. Also, alarm cards, which will sound a loud alarm whenever the computer is moved, can be installed in computers. Peripheral devices attached to a computer can be protected with cable traps that prevent their removal. Laptop computers should be fitted with special cables and locks that can securely attach them to a current work area. If the user will be away from a laptop for an extended period of time, it should be locked inside a desk or cabinet.

Physical access to special network and computer equipment rooms should be secured as carefully as access to company facilities. These rooms are the brains of company operations, concentrating a variety of critical functions, such as network communications, database servers, and backup systems. If an unauthorized user gains access to the central network room, the damage she can cause could be considerable.

The main door to the network or server room should be secured with some type of lock, preferably with some sort of smart access system, as described earlier. Only those employees who need to be in the room to perform their job functions should be allowed access. Inside, servers and other sensitive equipment should be housed inside a lockable cage or rack and not left running in an open area where they could be accessed or accidentally damaged. Many types of networking equipment servers come with their own locks that require keys to open them for access.

Man-Trap

A *man-trap* describes a two-tier physical access control method with two physical barriers, such as doors, between the person and the resource he is trying to access. A person must be authenticated to be able to get in the first door, and then when that door is closed, the person is physically caught between doors and must pass an additional form of authentication to gain entry through the second door. In high-security environments, the person is effectively trapped if he cannot be properly authenticated by the second door. The first door will be locked down and he will not be able to leave until security arrives to examine his credentials.

A more basic example of this is a bank whose cash machines are located in a lobby between the outside doors and the internal bank doors. To access the first door, the person must swipe his card for that bank. Once inside, the person must use his bank card in conjunction with a PIN to access the ATM.

Access Logs

As part of an overall security plan, access logs should contain the names of all visitors to the facility and the in and out times of their visits. Most organizations have some type of policy that requires all nonemployees to sign in at the front lobby of a building and indicate who they are visiting, including the times they entered and exited. This allows the organization to keep a record of all nonemployees, contractors, and visitors to the building. If any security issues arise, a list is available of everyone who was in the building at that time.

Access logs are also important for highly sensitive areas of an organization such as the main server and telecommunications room that houses the primary system and networking equipment. Each administrator should record times of entry and departure of the server room to perform duties or maintenance. Any security issues that arise in regard to activities in the server room can be tracked to whoever was in the room at the time.

Most electronic card systems automatically record this information as employees typically use their ID cards to enter and exit various parts of the building. These electronic logs can be easily obtained and scanned to determine who was at a certain location in times of a security lapse.

Personal Identification Verification Card

More advanced personnel-access control techniques include the use of *personal identification verification cards.* The ID card provides photo identification that can immediately identify the wearer as an authorized user. ID cards should be worn at all times where they can be seen by other employees. The card should identify the person and his job function. By listing job function, that person's access clearance into a certain part of the facility can be quickly determined. Simple ID cards, however, require the use of security guards and security-conscious employees.

Smart Card

The most common method of personnel access control used today is the *smart card.* Typically, each employee receives a card with a magnetic strip or computer chip that contains their access information. These cards are swiped in magnetic card readers that are stationed outside important access points, such as doors and elevators, or if the card uses a chip, it is inserted into a card reader. The information on the card is then compared with the security access of the area the person is about to enter. If she doesn't have access to that particular area, the door won't open.

Travel Advisory
Smart cards should include no company identification. If a card is lost or stolen, the unauthorized user would have no idea from which company or facility the card came.

Another type of access card system is the proximity reader, which doesn't require the physical insertion of a card. The reader can sense the card if it's within a certain minimum distance. The information is read through an electromagnetic field.

The card can also be used as a requirement to log in to sensitive networks and computers. Using a card reader, the computer will not allow you to log in until you have inserted your smart card to verify your identity and access level.

Exam Tip
Smart cards can be complemented with access codes or PINs. In the event the card is lost or stolen, it can't be used for access if the proper corresponding PIN is not keyed in.

Common Access Card

A *Common Access Card* is a special type of smart card issued by the United States Department of Defense. It is primarily used for military and government personnel as an identification and authentication card for physical access to military and government buildings, and also for computer and network access. For example, you would not be able to log in to a military network computer without inserting your card into the card reader for identification and authorization to the resources available for your level of access. The card also contains a digital certificate for a user that allows that user to encrypt messages and perform digital signing.

CHECKPOINT

✔**Objective 6.01: Explain the fundamental concepts and best practices related to authentication, authorization, and access control.** Use separation of duties, job rotation, implicit deny, and least privilege principles when organizing your security infrastructure and grouping users and resources into appropriate security groups and zones. In a mandatory access control model (MAC), the OS of the network is in control of access to data. Discretionary access control (DAC) allows the data owners to specify what users can access certain data. Role-based access control (RBAC) allows access to be based on the role the user holds within an organization. Privileges can be assigned by user, group, or role in the company. Rule-based access control is based on ACLs and is not necessarily tied to the identity of a user; it provides access rules that are applied to all users in the organization.

✔**Objective 6.02: Implement appropriate security controls when performing account management.** Some of the most effective account restrictions include limiting logon attempts, using expiry dates, disabling unused accounts, setting time restrictions, restricting machine access, and using tokens. Use password policies such as regular password rotation, enforce strong passwords, and employ password aging to prevent password weaknesses. Each user should have his own personal data directory, where only he has access to create, delete, and modify the files and directories within. When you first create an ACL for a resource, use no access as a default. This enables you to start with a clean slate, and you can add access permissions based on the needs of the particular user or group, giving them only enough access permissions to perform their job function.

✔**Objective 6.03: Analyze and differentiate among types of mitigation and deterrent techniques.** Physical access control security includes video surveillance and monitoring, ID cards, locks, man-traps, and access logs. ID cards should be complemented with access codes or PINs. In case the card is lost or stolen, it can't be used for access unless the user keys in the corresponding PIN.

REVIEW QUESTIONS

1. You are defining your overall access control model for a new network. To provide a strong default access policy, you want to make sure that users are given the absolute minimum access rights they need to perform their job function. Which access control principle does this follow?

   A. Implicit deny

   B. Separation of duties

   C. Least privilege

   D. Role-based access control

2. You are creating an access control model that will allow you to base specific access policies depending on which network a user is on, and not necessarily the actual identity of the specific user. Which privilege management access control model would you use?

   A. Rule-based access control

   B. Discretionary access control

   C. Role-based access control

   D. Mandatory access control

3. You must create an access control mechanism for your server and network room, which houses all your organization's servers and primary networking equipment. Which of the following methods would be the most secure?

   A. Access list

   B. Smart card access

   C. ID badge

   D. Video surveillance

4. You are designing file security for a new file server for your sales department. Each user will have his own private and secure directory, and a shared group directory. Which of the following should be the initial default access level for each user before you assign permissions?

   A. Full access

   B. Read and Write access

   C. No access

   D. Only Read access

5. You have recently had several laptops stolen after hours when employees leave unattended laptops on their desks after they leave work. Which of the following policies should you implement to increase security and prevent theft?

   A. Enforce the use of cable locks.

   B. Make sure users are logged out of laptops before they leave.

   C. Set a hardware password.

   D. Lock all unattended laptops in a cabinet after hours.

6. Which of the following best practices discourages corruption by ensuring that users do not have the same amount of access and privileges for too long a time?

   A. Least privilege

   B. Separation of duties

   C. Job rotation

   D. Implicit deny

7. Your company has defined working hours for a call center department. There have been several instances of employees using company resources for downloading Internet content after work hours. Which of the following can you implement to improve security?

   A. Use MAC address filtering to prevent access on suspect computers.

   B. Set access time restrictions.

   C. Shut down all computers after work hours.

   D. Implement job rotation.

8. You have had a rash of hacking incidents where weak employee passwords are being hacked through brute-force methods and unauthorized users are gaining access to the network. Which of the following security policies is most efficient for preventing brute-force hacking attempts on employee passwords?

   A. Password rotation

   B. Password length and complexity restrictions

   C. Password expiration

   D. Limiting logon attempts

9. You have already implemented a password expiration and rotation policy that forces your users to change their password every 60 days. However, you find that many users are simply using their same password again. Which of the following can you implement to improve security?

    A. Password history

    B. Password complexity

    C. Limiting logon attempts

    D. Password expiry

10. A military building uses strict access control where a user must use smart card access to enter the main door of the facility. Then he must meet a security guard at a second door to present an ID badge and enter his PIN number. What security feature is used in this access control mechanism?

    A. Mandatory access control

    B. Implicit deny

    C. Three-tier access control

    D. Man-trap

REVIEW ANSWERS

1. **C**   The least privilege concept ensures that a user has only the access rights they need to perform their job functions. By granting users the least amount of privileges possible, this prevents the user from abusing more powerful access rights.

2. **A**   Rule-based access control is defined with an access control list (ACL), which specifies a set of rules that must be followed before access is granted. Rule-based access control does not necessarily have to be tied to an authorized identity and could involve access permissions based on network location, content of messages (such as e-mail text or attachments), and other types of content filtering.

3. **B**   Smart card access would provide the most security. The server room door will not unlock unless a user inserts her smart card and has the proper authorization to enter the room.

4. **C**   You should use the principle of implicit deny, which means that by default, a user should have no access permission at all unless explicitly permitted. You can then assign read/write access for each user to his

own home directory, and read/write access to the shared directory. This ensures you start with the most secure default configuration.

5. **D**   If employees are not taking their laptops home with them, they should be removed from their desks and put in a locked cabinet until the users return the next day. Cable locks are useful for security during office hours, but can be cut by a determined thief. Logging out of the laptop or setting hardware passwords can prevent unauthorized access but will not deter theft.

6. **C**   Job rotation ensures greater security, as no single employee retains the same amount of access control for a particular area for an extended period of time. This can prevent internal corruption, whereby long-term employees, because of their deep knowledge of their area of duty, might be more inclined to take advantage of their position and enhanced access.

7. **B**   By setting time restrictions on network access, you prevent employees from being able to log in and access the network after working hours are complete.

8. **D**   You can limit logon attempts to lock out the user's account if an incorrect password has been entered too many times. While password length, complexity, rotation, and expiration are helpful security measures, brute-force attacks can most efficiently be stopped by limiting the number of attempted logons.

9. **A**   When password history is enabled, the system can remember a user's former passwords. When the current password expires, the system forces the user to use a new password that is not the same as one of her previous passwords.

10. **D**   When you use a man-trap, a user must be authenticated to be able to enter the first door of a facility. When he has entered the first door, it is closed, and the user is physically trapped between the first and second doors. The user must pass an additional round of authentication to gain access through the second door.

Authentication and Identity Management

ITINERARY

- **Objective 7.01**   Explain the fundamental concepts and best practices related to authentication, authorization, and access control
- **Objective 7.02**   Explain the function and purpose of authentication services

	NEWBIE	SOME EXPERIENCE	EXPERT
ETA	2 hours	1 hour	0.5 hour

To use the resources of a computer system or network or enter a secure facility, a user must first be *authenticated*. Identification and authentication verifies that the user is who he says he is and has the credentials to access these resources. The most common form of authentication requires a user name and password, but more secure schemes can use multiple factors to strengthen the authentication process and confidence in the identity and credentials of a user.

Methods such as security cards, tokens, personal identification numbers (PINs), and more advanced techniques, such as biometric voice or fingerprint recognition, offer additional forms of authentication. When a user logs in to a system, he supplies a set of credentials or login identifiers that must be matched against credentials stored in an authentication database. If any of the information doesn't match, the user is refused entry or access to the system. Authentication and access control methods are only as efficient as the amount of time and planning spent setting up and configuring the system. The more complex the login process, the more difficult it will be for an unauthorized user to gain access to a system.

This chapter describes the types of authentication models, services, and protocols available that help to provide secure, authenticated access to your networks.

Objective 7.01
CompTIA Security+
Objective 5.2

Explain the Fundamental Concepts and Best Practices Related to Authentication, Authorization, and Access Control

Before a user can access a resource, the user must initially *identify* himself as a valid user for that resource. The user must then be *authenticated* using additional criteria that verify that the identify presented by the user is valid. If these criteria are matched, the user is granted access. The following sections describe the basic authentication models and methods that can be used to verify an identity.

Authentication Models

A user authentication system must be able to confirm a user's identity and level of authorization. Three basic authentication components can be combined to provide the highest level of assurance in authenticating a user's identity:

- Something the user has in his possession (ID badge, smart card)

- Something the user knows (user name, password, PIN)
- Something that is a unique physical aspect of the user (biometrics, fingerprint)

The following sections describe how these factors or multiple sets of factors can be used to identify a user.

Single-Factor Authentication

Single-factor authentication refers to requiring only one factor (such as a password) to authenticate a user. The system compares the password for the account with the database of known user names and passwords and then authenticates the user if they match. This is the simplest but weakest form of authentication, because users' passwords tend to be weak.

Single-factor authentication can also involve a magnetic swipe card or token used to open a locked door. This is also a weak form of authentication, as the card or token can be easily lost or stolen and an unauthorized user can simply use the card or token to access the door without needing to provide any other credentials.

Two-Factor Authentication

Two-factor authentication typically combines two single-factor authentication types, such as something the user knows and something the user possesses. For example, most ATM banking transactions require two-factor authentication: the user inserts a physical banking card into the machine and then types a PIN, which is matched with the electronic information contained on the card's magnetic strip. One authentication factor should be physical, such as a smart card or access token (something the user possesses) or a biometric factor (something physically unique about the user), and the second factor should be a password or PIN (something the user knows). Without these two items, no access can be granted.

Three-Factor Authentication

Three-factor authentication is the strongest form of user authentication and involves a combination of physical items such as a smart card, token, or biometric factor, and nonphysical items such as passwords, passphrases, and PINs. Typically, the biometric factor is the third and deciding factor used in combination with an access card and password. For example, before he can enter a high-security facility, a user might have to insert a smart card into a door, enter a PIN on a keypad, and then insert his finger into a scanner.

Single Sign-on

In early computer systems, when networking wasn't as available as it is today, each computer contained a set of resources the user could access. To access the resources of a computer system, she used a specific login and password. Each specific computer needed a separate login and password. This was tedious for computer users and administrators alike, because of the frequency with which login accounts and passwords needed to be reset for each computer if a user forgot them.

Nowadays, modern networks provide resources that are spread throughout the computer network and that can be accessed by any user from any location. The user can be onsite on her own computer, or she can be logged in from home or on the road by using dial-up methods or via the Internet. With the vast amount of resources that can be contained on a large computer network, the concept of different logins and passwords for each resource has been eliminated in favor of a *single sign-on* to the network; the user has to be authenticated only once on the network to access the resources for that network. This type of centralized administration is a much more efficient way for a network administrator to control access to the network. User account policy templates can be created and used network wide to remove the need to configure each user's account settings individually, except for a unique login and password.

An example of single sign-on is a Microsoft Active Directory user name and password required for accessing directories, files, and printers on a network, along with MS Exchange mail servers and SQL database servers. LDAP is also a popular authentication database used for single sign-on purposes. LDAP is discussed in more detail later in this chapter.

Authentication Methods

The methods used for authentication depend on the resources that these security mechanisms are trying to protect. Most computer networks rely on a login and password–type system. The use of remote access or virtual private network (VPN) accounts might require the use of encrypted communications beyond the typical user login and password process. Each authentication system must be geared specifically to the circumstances that define a user and resources and how those resources need to be protected. The following sections describe several authentication methods and their components, including remote access authentication.

Remote Access Authentication

Remote access is an important network feature for companies and organizations that require users to access network resources from anywhere offsite. With the evolution of telecommunications, a variety of methods can allow a user to access a network remotely. Early methods included attaching a serial cable between two computers via their serial interfaces. The use of modems enabled users to dial into a system or network over a common phone line. Modern access methods include complex VPNs that let users access their corporate network from a public network, such as the Internet. Fast home networking technologies have enabled home users to break free of the bandwidth limitations of modems and phone lines to create fast and secure communications channels to remote networks.

The most important factor in securing remote communications is the ability both to authenticate a client to a remote network and to encrypt the communications so that they can't be captured. With the explosive growth of high-bandwidth home networks that communicate over the Internet with remote systems, the need for secure communications is critical.

Each type of communication system depends on the medium used by the client user to connect to the remote machine. A user in a hotel in another country could be trying to access his corporate LAN via a public wireless connection. Another user might be connected to the Internet from home through a digital subscriber line (DSL) connection, using a virtual private network to communicate with a remote network. A network administrator might use Telnet or Secure Shell (SSH) to log in to a server remotely from home.

Each remote access method must be carefully examined for security vulnerabilities to make sure that users are properly authenticated to access the network's resources and that communications are encrypted to prevent someone from tapping into the transmitted information.

Dial-up   For many years, the most common way of accessing remote services to a corporate local area network (LAN) or the Internet was through the use of a dial-up connection using a modem over a common phone line. A modem, short for modulator-demodulator, is used to convert the digital signals of a computer to analog for transmission over an analog phone line. A modem at the receiving end converts the signal back into digital for the remote computer. Many companies don't properly protect their remote access services because they think their regular company firewall will protect them. Unfortunately, the firewall protects the network only from traffic that comes from the Internet—not traffic that dials into the network.

Travel Advisory

One of the oldest modem-hacking methods is the use of war dialing, in which a malicious hacker uses a program to call phone numbers in quick succession to look for those attached to a modem. Once a number is found, the hacker can dial in to the modem and try to break the authentication to gain access.

For remote access to a network, a client machine initiates a connection to a remote access server. The remote access server is connected to a modem, or several banks of modems, to provide enough connections for multiple remote users, as shown in Figure 7.1.

When the client and remote modems are connected, the server typically requires some form of authentication, often user name and password, before granting the client access to the network's resources. The authentication system could be built into the remote access server itself, or it could be a separate service running an authentication protocol, such as Terminal Access Controller Access-Control System (TACACS) or Remote Authentication Dial-In User Service (RADIUS). Additional forms of authentication that can secure communications even more include the use of security tokens, a type of card or token that displays a key code that cycles every few minutes. When synchronized with the server, the token creates another form of authentication that's tied to a user account. Because the sequenced number is cycled with a defined algorithm, the same number can't be used twice within a certain period of time.

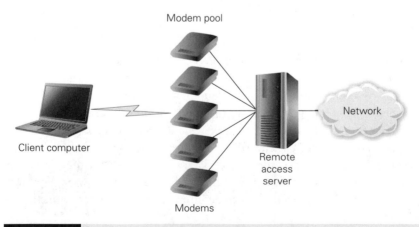

FIGURE 7.1   Remote access via modem

> ### Travel Advisory
>
> Security tokens are combined with traditional user names, passwords, and PINs; if the token card is stolen, the unauthorized user still needs the other credentials to gain access.

Another type of dial-in security check is the use of a *call-back feature*: When the client first connects, the remote access server will hang up and try to dial back the client with a preconfigured phone number. Once the client answers, a user name and password can authenticate the client for access. This call-back feature ensures the caller is who he says he is and allows the company to absorb any long-distance charges incurred because of the call.

ISDN   *Integrated Services Digital Network (ISDN)* technology was created to replace the use of common phone lines for network communications. A special ISDN line must be run to your location, and both your client computer and the remote computer must use a special ISDN adapter. Unlike a modem, an ISDN adapter doesn't convert signals from digital to analog and back again; instead, ISDN connects digitally between the two adapters over the ISDN line.

Each ISDN connection is divided into channels:

- **B-Channels**   These channels transmit data, such as voice or computer data communications. The channels can be used individually or combined to create higher bandwidth.
- **D-Channels**   These channels transmit control and signal information for managing the transmission of data.

Three main types of ISDN implementations exist, depending on the level of bandwidth a customer requires:

- **Basic Rate Interface (BRI)**   This interface is targeted for lower bandwidth home installations and can run over conventional phone lines. It uses one 16 Kbps D-Channel, and two 64 Kbps B-Channels. The data channels can be combined to provide 128 Kbps communications.
- **Primary Rate Interface (PRI)**   This interface is for business customers who have higher bandwidth needs. It contains one 64 Kbps D-Channel and twenty-three 64 Kbps B-Channels for data, providing bandwidth up to 1.544 Mbps.

- **Broadband ISDN** This interface can handle many different services at the same time and is usually used within a telecommunications carrier backbone. Broadband ISDN is most often used in fiber-optic and radio-type networks, such as Fiber Distributed Data Interface (FDDI), Asynchronous Transfer Mode (ATM), and Synchronous Optical Networking (SONET).

ISDN has generally been passed over in favor of cable modem and DSL communications. These methods are much less expensive and easier to set up and configure because they use the existing cabling infrastructure in the home.

Cable Modem *Cable modems* are one of the most popular ways of connecting home computers to the Internet. Cable modems are misnamed, though, because they don't operate like a typical modem, which translate signals between analog and digital. A cable modem enables you to connect to your home's coaxial cable lines, which are then connected by common Ethernet cable to your computer's network interface card (NIC).

The speed of cable modem communications decreases when more homes are connected to the same cable line. For example, in most neighborhoods, several homes are connected to the same segment of a coaxial cable run. If many people are using the Internet at the same time, the bandwidth is shared among them, so the individual connections are slower.

The security risk involved with cable modems is that, unlike dial-up connections, the connection to the Internet is permanent and always on, until the system is turned off or unplugged from the cable network. As long as a system is connected to the Internet, it's open to attacks from hackers, who continually scan networks for security vulnerabilities in online systems. To secure these connections, the use of a firewall is recommended to protect your computer against these intrusions.

Travel Advisory

Malicious hackers make use of port scanner programs to analyze a bank of IP addresses on a network, looking for open service ports and applications that can be compromised. To prevent a port scanner from viewing your system while you're connected to a cable modem or DSL network, a firewall can be installed, which prevents your system from replying to such scans.

DSL DSL (Digital Subscriber Line) is another popular method of connecting a home computer or small business to the Internet. DSL runs over common copper telephone lines but requires the connection to be in close proximity to a phone company's access point. The closer your system is to the access point, the faster your connection.

DSL can be used for communicating voice and data transmissions over the same phone line. Home users can talk on the phone while still connected to the Internet. This type of communication was impossible over normal dial-up modem methods. DSL also differs from a typical modem in that it doesn't require modulating the signal from digital to analog and vice versa. DSL uses the entire bandwidth of the phone line for digital transmission.

Like cable modems, a DSL network connection is always on until the system is switched off or unplugged from the DSL network. To protect your system, use a firewall.

Remote Access Applications

Remote access applications are used to provide access to a machine from an external client system. The communication that connects the two systems can be anything from a dial-up modem connection, to a direct cable connection, to a TCP/IP network. Typically, these applications consist of server and client components. The server software is installed on the system made available for remote access. Sometimes the client and server computers are connected with a simple network or serial cable. The server software is then configured to accept communications as a host server. When the client connects to the server, it must be authenticated before it is granted access.

When connected, the remote user can remotely control the machine as if they were sitting in front of it on the console. This type of application can create severe security vulnerabilities if it isn't properly secured. This security should include strong authentication and encryption methods.

Telnet *Telnet* allows you to connect remotely to a system and execute commands is if you were on the console of the system.

Telnet only provides basic authentication security consisting of a user name and password on the remote system. Telnet communications are not encrypted but are sent in clear text and can be discovered by a hacker monitoring network traffic.

Telnet use should be limited to communications within an already secure network, but other more secure methods of remote access that use encryption and stronger authentication methods are recommended.

SSH   *SSH* is a secure form of remote access to a remote computer. Like Telnet, SSH allows you to connect to a remote system and perform commands as if the remote user were on the console of the system. SSH uses a secure, encrypted tunnel to the remote system.

During the initial SSH connection, a special session key is exchanged during the connection negotiations and authentication. This creates an encrypted secure channel for the communications between the client and the server.

Encrypted remote access solutions such as SSH should always be used in place of Telnet and other insecure remote access utilities.

Travel Advisory

Other utilities that send their information in clear text include remote login (rlogin), File Transfer Protocol (FTP), and remote shell (rsh). Whenever possible, a secure method, such as SSH, should be used for remote console access and file transfer.

VPN   A *VPN* is a secure and private connection over a public network. The connection between the client and the remote network is provided by an encrypted tunnel between the two points, as shown in Figure 7.2.

In addition to remote access, VPNs are also used for connecting two remote routers to form a secure wide area network (WAN). For a VPN to work properly, the sender and receiver must be running the same type of VPN, with the same protocols and encryption settings.

The VPN enables the remote user to be connected locally to a public network such as the Internet, while also being directly connected to the corporate network through the use of the encrypted VPN tunnel. This connection can be a dial-up through a modem or a direct Internet connection, such as a cable modem or DSL.

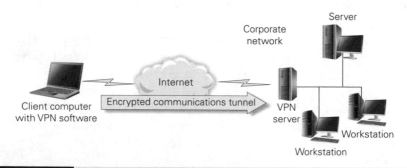

FIGURE 7.2   VPN connection

The user must first establish her connection to the Internet and then start the VPN software, which creates a virtual connection to the VPN access server on the corporate network. After the connection is negotiated, the client must authenticate itself using a user name and password before the VPN will grant access to the corporate network. A VPN is only as secure as the tunneling and encryption protocols used on the connection. Early types of VPNs used older encryption methods, which can be cracked by today's savvy attackers.

Remote Access Protocols

For remote access communications to work, the data must be transmitted using one or several network protocols. These protocols must be able to travel through different networks and different physical infrastructures. A home user who wants to connect their computer to the Internet must use an analog modem, cable modem, or DSL line to connect with an ISP. Different protocols are needed both to facilitate the transmission of digital data over cable and analog phone lines and encapsulate TCP/IP (the protocol used for Internet communications) over these mediums.

Exam Tip

Know the advantages and disadvantages of the protocols discussed here, as well as with what types of communications they can be used.

SLIP   The *Serial Line Internet Protocol (SLIP)* is one of the earliest Internet protocols used for encapsulating IP packets for transmission over serial communications, such as a phone line or serial cable. SLIP is able to work with most types of protocols, such as IP, Internetwork Packet Exchange/Sequenced Packet Exchange (IPX/SPX), and NetBIOS Extended User Interface (NetBEUI), and does not require a static network address; however, SLIP is considered difficult to configure, inefficient, and unreliable. SLIP isn't used much these days and has been replaced by PPP.

PPP   The *Point-to-Point Protocol (PPP)* is used to enable a connection between two computers using a serial interface, usually over a phone line. PPP is the most popular protocol used by an ISP to enable users to dial into the Internet network from home using a modem attached to a home computer. The main function of PPP is to encapsulate IP packets and send them over the Internet. PPP is considered much more reliable and easier to use than SLIP, because it contains error checking and the ability to run different types of protocols over a variety of media methods. Common authentication protocols used with PPP are Password Authentication Protocol (PAP), Challenge Handshake Authentication Protocol (CHAP), Microsoft Challenge Handshake Authentication Protocol (MSCHAP), and Extensible Authentication Protocol (EAP), which are discussed later in this chapter.

VPN Protocols

The following types of protocols are used by VPNs to tunnel network data over a public network and to provide encryption to protect transmitted data.

PPTP The *Point-to-Point Tunneling Protocol (PPTP)* is a Microsoft implementation of secure communications over a VPN. Because PPTP is an extension of PPP, it has become one of the most widely used tunneling protocols and allows network packets to be encapsulated within PPP communications for transfer over another network, such as the Internet.

Previous remote access technologies allowed remote access only through a dial-up modem to the corporate network. Depending on where this user is located, the long-distance charges could be enormous, and sometimes, a company would need to create its own expensive toll-free phone service for long-distance dial-in access. Tunneling protocols allow users connected to a public network, such as the Internet (through fast cable modem or DSL service), to create their own private connections to their corporate LANs.

PPTP decrypts and encapsulates PPP packets to create the VPN connection. The security mechanisms within PPTP include authentication and data encryption. One major security problem with PPTP is that when a connection is negotiated, the communication is transmitted in clear text. This data can be captured by an unauthorized user who can use the information to try to hack the connection. PPTP connections for VPNs are typically authenticated using Microsoft Point-to-Point Encryption (MPPE), which uses the RSA RC4 encryption algorithm with support for 40-bit, 56-bit, and 128-bit session keys. These keys are changed on a regular basis, which greatly improves security and lessens the chance of the keys being broken.

L2TP The *Layer 2 Tunneling Protocol (L2TP)* combines the best features of PPTP with the Layer 2 Forward (L2F) protocol created by Cisco Systems. L2TP is most often used with other media technologies, such as Frame Relay.

L2TP consists of two main components:

- **L2TP Access Concentrator (LAC)** The LAC is responsible for terminating the local network connection and tunneling PPP packets to the LNS.

- **L2TP Network Server (LNS)** The LNS is situated on the remote end of the connection and terminates the PPP connection originating from the LAC.

Through the use of the LAC and LNS, the connection can be localized, because the L2TP components terminate the endpoints of the PPP connection, as shown in Figure 7.3.

The main difference between L2TP and PPTP is that L2TP can run on top of and tunnel through other network protocols, such as IPX and Systems Network Architecture (SNA), while PPTP can run only on top of IP networks. L2TP, however, doesn't provide any type of native encryption, so it must be combined with another encrypted protocol, such as Internet Protocol Security (IPsec). Unlike PPTP, L2TP supports authentication services such as RADIUS and TACACS+ (discussed later in this chapter).

IPsec *IPsec* is a suite of protocols used primarily to encrypt VPN communications over the Internet. IPsec provides several security benefits for authentication, data integrity, and confidentiality for remote VPN access.

IPsec utilizes a shared public key encryption method to create an encrypted communications tunnel between two VPN endpoints, including client-to-server and server-to-server connections. The client can remotely connect to a network from anywhere it has Internet access, and all its network traffic is sent through the encrypted tunnel while the IPsec VPN is activated. The connecting client can be authenticated to an authentication service, such as a RADIUS or LDAP server, before the connection is established.

Travel Assistance

For detailed information on IPsec, see Chapter 4.

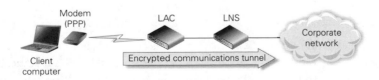

FIGURE 7.3   L2TP deployment

Explain the Function and Purpose of Authentication Services

Your authentication services not only protect your networks for internal users on your wired LAN but also remote access users who access your network resources over an Internet VPN or wireless network. Protection of the authentication phase of your communications is vital to prevent your users' logins and passwords from being captured. A good remote access method needs to secure the password database and the communications over which the client sends their credentials. The following sections describe some popular authentication services.

> **Exam Tip**
>
> Be aware of the authentication protocols discussed here, including their uses and strengths and weaknesses.

PAP

The *Password Authentication Protocol (PAP)* is the most basic type of authentication that consists of comparing a set of credentials, such as a user name and a password, to a central table of authentication data. If the credentials match, the user is granted access. PAP is most often used with dial-up remote access methods using PPP, such as connecting to an ISP or Remote Access Services (RAS) that supports PPP.

Although the password tables used by PAP are encrypted, the actual communications between the client and authentication server are not, allowing the user name and password to be sent over the network in clear text. This can easily be captured by an unauthorized user monitoring the network. Typically used for dial-up authentication, PAP is also the default authentication protocol within HTTP. Because of PAP's weaknesses, CHAP is usually used in place of PAP.

CHAP

The *Challenge-Handshake Authentication Protocol (CHAP)* is much more secure than PAP. Once the communications link is completed, the authenticating server sends a random value to the client. The client sends back the value combined with the user name and password credentials, plus a predefined secret, calculated using a one-way hash function. The server compares the response against its own calculation of the expected hash value. If the values match, the client is granted access.

CHAP provides protection against *replay attacks,* which are used by hackers to capture data and then resend it again. To prevent this type of attack, CHAP uses an incrementally changing identifier and a variable challenge value, and the authentication can be repeated any time while the connection is open using the new identifiers.

Microsoft has its own version of CHAP called MSCHAP, which extends the functionality of CHAP for Microsoft networks. The latest version, MSCHAPv2, provides stronger security for remote access connections and resolves issues present in earlier versions of MSCHAP.

LANMAN

Windows LANMAN (LAN Manager) is used by older versions of Windows Server (such as Windows NT) for encrypting user passwords for authentication purposes. The hashing system used (LM hash algorithm) is easily subverted via a brute-force attack in which a password can be cracked in only a few minutes or hours.

LANMAN has been replaced by NTLM (NT LAN Manager) in Windows NT 3.1 Server and later operating systems, although LANMAN is still available for backward compatibility. As of Windows Vista, LANMAN is completely disabled, but it can be enabled manually. In general, LANMAN should be disabled if all of your systems are running Windows 2000 or later.

NTLM and NTLMv2

NTLM (NT LAN Manager) was created as an improvement to the original Microsoft LANMAN implementation and combines challenge/response authentication with message digest–hashed passwords that are transmitted between the clients and authenticating servers. NTLM version 1 uses MD4 hashing, while version 2 (introduced in Windows NT Service Pack 4) uses keyed–Hash Message Authentication Code (HMAC)–MD5 hashing and is more secure than version 1.

Since Windows 2000 and the growth of Active Directory–based implementations, Microsoft has implemented Kerberos authentication, but NTLM is still used for authentication purposes in cases where Windows networks are run without Active Directory domains or any other type of third-party authentication service.

Extensible Authentication Protocol (EAP)

The *Extensible Authentication Protocol (EAP)* is primarily used in wireless networks, but it can also be used in traditional LANs and remote access methods to extend PPP authentication. The EAP framework provides an extension of the types of authentication protocols that are typically used in PAP and CHAP methods. For example, instead of a simple user name and password, additional methods can be used such as tokens, Kerberos, biometrics, and Transport Layer Security (TLS).

RADIUS

The *Remote Authentication Dial-In User Service (RADIUS)* is the most common Internet standard used for authenticating clients in a client/server environment. When the remote user accesses a network through a remote access device, the user is authenticated by a RADIUS server that compares the user's authentication credentials against those of the server's database. If the credentials match, the user is granted access to the rest of the network. The client's credentials that are sent to the RADIUS server are encrypted to prevent someone from capturing the transmission. RADIUS servers also include accounting and reporting functions that can monitor and log data on each connection, such as packet and protocol types, as well as length of time connected. Figure 7.4 shows an example of how a RADIUS server authenticates a remote access client.

LDAP

The *Lightweight Directory Access Protocol (LDAP)* is used to look up information in a database for other users and network resources. A *directory* is a database that's often compared to the telephone white pages or the yellow pages because the information can be searched and quickly found within the indexed database. The directory database itself can consist of a wide variety of information, including not only basic user contact information, such as e-mail addresses or phone numbers, but also objects, such as printers and computers. Some directory services are used to configure and control access to every single network resource object on the entire network or to contain a centralized database of logins and passwords. With such a critical collection of network data, security is of prime importance when using directory access protocols such as LDAP.

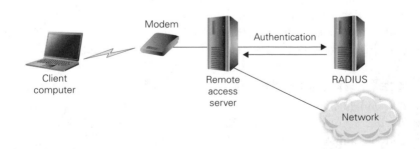

| FIGURE 7.4 | RADIUS server authentication |

All LDAP servers have some security controls in place for allowing read and update access to the directory database. Typically, all users can read most of the information held in the database, but only a few users have update privileges. Large directories usually have multiple information administrators who have access to update only information pertaining to their departments or regions.

For a client to access an LDAP server, it must first be authenticated, unless the server allows anonymous connections. This type of access control allows the LDAP server to decide exactly what that client can access and what information it can update.

Most LDAP servers support the use of encrypted secure channels to communicate with clients, especially when transferring information such as user names, passwords, and other sensitive data. LDAP servers use the Secure Sockets Layer (SSL) protocol (also called LDAPS) for this purpose.

> **Exam Tip**
>
> Remember that LDAP (unencrypted) uses TCP port 389, LDAP over SSL uses TCP port 689, and LDAP over TLS uses TCP port 636.

TACACS

The *Terminal Access Controller Access Control System (TACACS)* is an older type of authentication protocol that's similar to RADIUS. A remote access user connects to a network and is authenticated by the TACACS server before being allowed access to the network's resources. Three versions of TACACS have been used:

- **TACACS** The original protocol, which performs both authentication and authorization.
- **XTACACS** Extended TACACS, which builds on TACACS by separating the functions of authentication, authorization, and accounting.
- **TACACS+** This added the use of both a user name and password for authentication or other authentication methods, such as Kerberos or dynamic passwords through security tokens. All communications are encrypted.

Unfortunately, the TACACS protocols have several security vulnerabilities, including a weak encryption algorithm. This has decreased its use in favor of the standards-based RADIUS authentication protocol.

Kerberos

Kerberos is an authentication system that uses a special key ticket assigned to the client that is embedded in all its network data to identify the client to other clients on a nonsecure network. Kerberos uses symmetric key cryptography, where the same key used to encrypt a message is used to decrypt the message. The Kerberos client needs to authenticate only once to the Kerberos server, which provides the client with a ticket that proves to other clients on the network that it has been authenticated. This type of authentication requires a Kerberos server to authenticate clients and manage the tickets assigned to them. This is also its weakness, as all the keys are stored on the Kerberos server; if it is compromised or crashes, the security of the entire Kerberos authentication system is compromised or unavailable to authenticate clients.

802.1X

The *IEEE 802.1X* standard is a port-based authentication mechanism for devices connecting to wired or wireless networks. Its goal is to provide a centralized authentication framework for LANs and wireless LANs (WLANs) that includes wired clients, wireless clients, and the wireless access points that connect them to the network.

For wired LANs, 802.1X is implemented on network devices such as switches to provide access control by authenticating connecting clients based on the user or system identity. You can then allow or block network connectivity, and apply network access policies based on this authentication.

In WLANs, a client automatically connects to the closest access point and then authenticates to the network by directly communicating with the network's native authentication. Unfortunately, unless the LAN is protected with a strong encryption method, the client can perform certain network functions without authentication, such as a ping request.

Using 802.1X, when a client connects to an access point, the wireless port is set to an unauthorized state, so it can't perform any network functions, which include receiving an IP address from a DHCP server. The access point then asks the client for authentication credentials. Once received, this data is forwarded to an authentication server running a service such as RADIUS. If the client is accepted as an authorized user, then the client port on the access point is switched to an authorized state, and normal communications can commence.

802.1X can be helpful in allowing WLANs to scale upward in size easily, while maintaining a centralized authentication system. This authentication, however, should be coupled with a strong communications encryption mechanism to provide full security.

Travel Assistance

See Chapter 10 for more detailed information on wireless security.

Certificates (Mutual Authentication)

Certificates are a form of *mutual authentication* that use a third party to establish the identity of a user for access control purposes. A certificate is like a digital piece of paper that contains a user's credentials. Digital certificates are used primarily with secure web communications and encryption. Each user needs another user's certificate to authenticate the other user before exchanging secure confidential information.

A user obtains a certificate by registering with a third-party service called a certificate authority (CA). To receive the certificate, the user must supply credentials such as a driver's license, Social Security number, address, and phone number. The certificate authority then issues a certificate to the user, along with the encryption keys she'll be using. This certificate proves the user's legitimacy.

Biometrics

Although typically available only to extremely high-security installations because of the high costs, biometric access control offers the most complete and technologically advanced method for securing access. *Biometrics* uses a unique physical attribute, such as a fingerprint, voice scan, or retinal scan, to identify a user.

Initially, the user requesting access must have the respective attribute scanned, so a perfect copy is on file for comparison when the user tries to gain access in the future. These types of biometric systems are complex and sensitive, and they can often result in false permissions and denials for access. They must be constantly calibrated, and repeated measurements of users' biometric data are required.

The following are the most common types of biometric access systems:

- **Palm/fingerprint scan** No two fingerprints are alike. A user must place his hand on a biometric scanner that compares it to the palm scan and fingerprints on file for that user. This is the most effective of all biometric methods.
- **Hand geometry scan** The size and shape of a person's hand vary significantly among different people. Similar to a fingerprint scan, the user places his hand on a biometric scanner, which measures the length and width of the hand, including the sizes of the fingers.
- **Retinal/iris scan** A person's retina is a unique attribute, similar to a fingerprint. The user must place his eye up to a device that projects a light beam into the eye to capture the retinal pattern.
- **Voice scan** The voice is also a unique characteristic for each user. By recording the user speaking a set of access words, the captured voice print can be compared to the same spoken words the next time the user tries to gain access.

- **Face scan** A facial scan records the unique characteristics of each user's face, such as bone structure and the shape of the eyes and nose. These characteristics can be captured in the scan and compared to the facial scan on file.

- **Signature scan** Considered one of the weakest types of biometric security, a signature scan records the written signature of a user and then compares it to subsequent signatures when the user attempts to gain access. Two types of signature scans exist: static and dynamic. A static scan merely compares the two signatures for accuracy and can't be considered accurate. A dynamic scan can record the motions of the signature using electrical signals. These unique characters make a dynamic signature scan much more reliable.

Exam Tip

Be aware of the characteristics of a biometric access control system that differentiate it from other traditional access control methods.

CHECKPOINT

✔ **Objective 7.01: Explain the fundamental concepts and best practices related to authentication, authorization, and access control.** Identification ensures that a user (which could also be an application program or process) is who he claims to be. The user must then pass the authentication phase using his logon user name or account number and a password. If these two criteria are matched with the global database of login user names and passwords stored on the network, the user is granted access to the network. Finally, when a user tries to access a resource, the system must check to see if that user ID is authorized for that resource and what permissions or privileges the user has when accessing it. Two- and three-factor authentication schemes build upon single-factor by combining multiple single-factor authentication types, such as something the user knows (a password or PIN) and something the user possesses (a magnetic swipe card or token).

✔ **Objective 7.02: Explain the function and purpose of authentication services.** Remote access via VPN is typically the most secure method, as it encrypts communications while ensuring that users are authenticated before being granted access. Other methods include RADIUS, Kerberos, TACACS, LDAP, and certificates. LDAPS offers secure encrypted authentication to an LDAP server. Biometric systems offer the most complete and advanced methods to identify people through a unique physical attribute, such as a fingerprint, voice scan, or retinal scan.

REVIEW QUESTIONS

1. You must set up a secure authentication and encryption method for your remote users. Most users are remote salespeople who connect to the company's networks from home networks or hotel Internet connections. Which of the following methods would you use?

   A. 802.1X

   B. VPN

   C. Kerberos

   D. TACACS

2. You are tasked to create a high-security authentication system for physical access control to a military installation? Which of the following authentication systems would be most appropriate?

   A. Biometric eye scan

   B. Security badge

   C. Smart card and PIN

   D. Encrypted login and password

3. You are setting up an LDAP server that will provide secure, encrypted authentication services. Which of the following protocols and ports do you use?

   A. LDAP on TCP port 689

   B. LDAPS on TCP port 389

   C. LDAPS on TCP port 689

   D. LDAP on TCP port 389

4. You are at home and have received a call from your office that one of your mail servers is down. You have set up a secure, encrypted remote access method to an administrative computer at your office. Which of the following remote access methods do you use?

   A. HTTP web login

   B. Dial-up

   C. Telnet

   D. VPN

5. You have several home users with Internet access who require remote access to your organization's network. Which of the following remote access and authentication technologies would be the most secure?

   A. Dial-up access to a Kerberos server

   B. VPN authenticated to a RADIUS server

   C. Telnet access to a local password database

   D. Wireless access to an LDAPS server

6. You have a specific user who needs to remotely access a legacy application server from home using dial-up access to a modem attached to the server. Which of the following security measures can you use to verify the user's identity when she is calling from her home office?

   A. User name and password authentication to a local database

   B. Only providing the modem phone number to that user

   C. Voice recognition

   D. Call-back verification

7. You are creating an authentication mechanism for physical access to a high-security government building. The high-security nature of the facility requires at least a three-factor authentication model. Which of the authentication types do you use?

   A. Biometric eye scan

   B. Smart card and PIN

   C. Smart card, PIN, and fingerprint scan

   D. ID badge and password

8. After a user is identified and authenticated to the system, what else must be performed to enable the user to use a resource?

   A. Authorization

   B. Authentication by token

   C. Encryption of network access

   D. Biometric scan

9. You want to set up a simple remote access method for your desktop computer to be able to access the console of a server located on the other side of your building in a secure server room. Which of the following remote access protocols would be the most secure?

   A. FTP

   B. SSH

   C. Dial-up

   D. Telnet

10. You are setting up a single sign-on authentication system for a large, enterprise network of 5000 users. Which of the following authentication methods would you use?

   A. Local login and password database

   B. Login and password with a security token

   C. LDAP server

   D. Smart card with PIN number

REVIEW ANSWERS

1. **B** The VPN is able to encrypt your communications while providing authentication to an authentication server. This is especially important for users connecting remotely over the Internet from insecure locations.

2. **A** For high-security installations, biometrics is an extremely secure method to authenticate users based on unique physical characteristics.

3. **C** When you use LDAPS (which uses TCP port 689), the authentication takes place over an encrypted channel to prevent the capture of authentication credentials.

4. **D** The VPN method provides a secure, encrypted channel over the Internet to your organization's private network.

5. **B** By using a VPN to a RADIUS server, you ensure that your communications are encrypted, and that secure authentication takes place to the RADIUS server.

6. **D** Using call-back verification, the server will call back the user after the initial connection to make sure she is calling from the designated user's home phone number. This prevents war-dialing attacks from hackers who dial random numbers looking for modems.

7. **C** For a three-factor authentication model, you need at least three different types of authentication. A biometric eye scan, while extremely secure, is still only a one-factor system, while the other methods are only two-factor, such as a smart card and a PIN.

8. **A** Although a user has been given access to log in to the network, he still needs to be authorized to use a particular resource based on access permissions.

9. **B** SSH creates an encrypted remote access session to prevent any communications from being intercepted. Telnet data is passed as clear text, making it very insecure.

10. **C** An LDAP server provides a centralized authentication database that can be used to securely authenticate a user to multiple services on the same network. This is the most efficient and secure method for a large network of 5000 users. Other methods would require tedious configuration and management of each individual user.

P A R T

IV

Network Security

Chapter 8   Securing Networks

Chapter 9   Secure Network Administration

Chapter 10   Securing Wireless Networks

Securing Networks

ITINERARY

○ **Objective 8.01** Explain the security function and purpose of network devices and technologies

○ **Objective 8.02** Distinguish and differentiate network design elements and compounds

	NEWBIE	SOME EXPERIENCE	EXPERT
ETA	3 hours	2 hours	1 hour

Network security devices and secure network design provide a first line of defense for detection and prevention of attacks at your network border. These security threats can be low-level, network-based threats such as TCP/IP protocol attacks, or they could high-level application threats such as application content downloaded from the Internet via a web browser. There are several network security tools available, such as firewalls, routers, switches, proxy servers, antispam filters, intrusion detection systems, web security gateways, and content filters, that not only detect network threats but take proactive steps to stop them from entering or leaving your network.

Setting up your network securely requires planning to make sure that your network is safely partitioned into network security zones. By splitting your network into public, private, and high-security zones, and regulating access between these zones with other types of networking techniques, you provide several lines of defense against incoming network attacks.

This chapter discusses the network security devices and secure network design principles that can maximize the ability to detect and prevent network security threats at your network's borders.

Objective 8.01
CompTIA Security+
Objective 1.1

Explain the Security Function and Purpose of Network Devices and Technologies

There are several types of network devices that make up your networking infrastructure. At the most basic level, you have routers and switches that form the backbone of your network to make sure that network information can properly flow from its source to its destination. More advanced devices, such as firewalls, proxy servers, web security, and content security servers, analyze the network information for its content to decide what can pass through to its destination and what must be blocked.

Firewalls

Firewalls are like physical security walls that are situated between an organization's internal network and any external public networks such as the Internet, as shown in Figure 8.1. The firewall protects an internal network from access by unauthorized users on an external network.

The external network can be located on the Internet or may even be another network within the same organization. A network firewall is a critical system in an organization's overall security architecture. The firewall controls and moni-

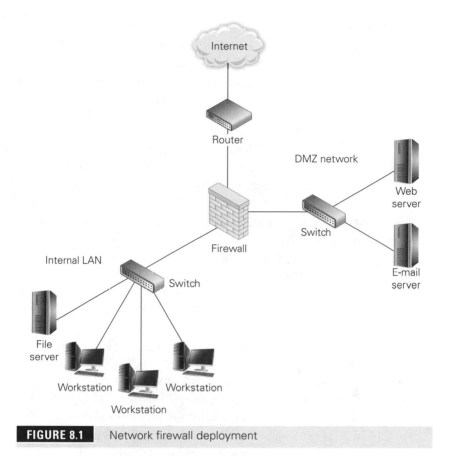

FIGURE 8.1   Network firewall deployment

tors access between different networks by filtering inbound and outbound traffic, manages access controls to requested locations, and typically blocks all services except those explicitly permitted by the administrator.

To configure the firewall, an administrator must set up a number of rules to use each time on incoming and outgoing network communications. These rules can be general or specific. For example, a firewall can be configured with a rule that states that any HTTP traffic can come and go on a specific network. It can also be much more detailed and state that an SMTP packet destined for a particular mail server can only come from a specific host. The best practice to use when configuring a firewall for the first time is to deny everything by default, and then create rules to allow the access you need. This ensures you're starting off with the most secure model and working backward to configure the firewall to accept certain types of communications.

Most firewalls log network traffic and activity, and activate alarms if anomalous situations are detected. The firewall implements security, authentication, and access controls at multiple levels while remaining completely transparent to internal users. Most firewalls provide the following services and security features:

- **Packet filtering**   The firewall server analyzes each network packet destined for inside or outside the network; it can filter out dangerous malformed packets, attacks, and spoofed IP addresses to prevent unauthorized access. Packets are also analyzed and acted upon depending on the rules enabled by the administrator.

- **Stateful inspection**   Stateful inspection of packets ensures that the firewall maintains a record of the connections that pass through, and monitors their state from when they are connected to when they close. This ensures the firewall is not only tracing packets but analyzing the state of the entire connection. Depending on the access rules configuration, certain actions can be taken when an anomalous change of state occurs (such as a connection hijack).

- **Access and authentication control**   The firewall can restrict access to networking services by source and destination IP address, type of service, time/day of the week, and also through authenticated access. Most firewalls have very flexible access control policies that can be fine-tuned by the administrator to secure access for specific users and networks.

- **Application layer filtering**   Firewalls can be aware of specific applications and services such as DNS and SMTP e-mail. This allows a firewall to analyze network traffic and apply access rules that are specific to that application. For example, the firewall can act as an application gateway for e-mail servers to help secure the connections between external e-mail servers and your local e-mail servers and clients that send and receive messages. The firewall can detect if these services are trying to be accessed on unauthorized ports for that specific application.

- **Network address translation (NAT)**   Most firewalls utilize NAT to map source IP addresses of outbound connections so that the connection appears to have originated from the firewall's address. This allows internal networks to be hidden behind a single Internet IP address with no additional registered addresses required.

Routers

A *router* is a network device that connects several networks together and relays data between them, as shown in Figure 8.2. A router usually contains a number of network interfaces, where each represents a different network. Smaller companies generally only have one main router, while larger companies could have several routers to relay information from all their networks.

Router software contains a lot of the same protection found in firewalls, including packet filtering and access control lists. These enable you to control more carefully the protocols, services, ports, and source and destination of the information that flows through the router. For example, you can configure the router only to accept FTP communications to a certain network. Other security features of routers include the capability to protect against spoofing and denial-of-service (DoS) attacks.

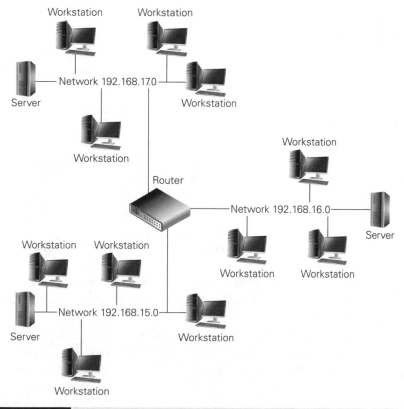

FIGURE 8.2   Router deployment

Switches

A *switch* is a network device used to segment networks into smaller, more manageable sections and relays packets between the segments. Switches can be used for security, load balancing, and performance improvements in a network.

A switch can work at multiple layers of the network and is more intelligent than a network hub, which is a simple device that is used to connect multiple computers to a network backbone. A switch is able to inspect network packets and determine the source and destination to provide more efficient network flow and prevent network packets from one segment, including broadcasts, from passing on to other network segments and causing network collisions.

You can configure the switch to accept only data from certain MAC address ranges to prevent MAC flooding attacks. In this type of attack, network packets are sent with multiple spoofed source MAC addresses, which flood the switch's MAC address tables and cause excessive network broadcasts.

Load Balancers

A *load balancer* is a network device that helps evenly distribute the flow of network traffic to other network devices. In larger networks that process thousands of network transactions per minute, the load balancer spreads the network load between each network device to ensure that network congestion and bottlenecks do not occur.

Your organization may have several routers on the network border to process incoming network connections and route them to their required destination. If a specific router receives too many network requests at one time, it can cause a bottleneck in processing requests and cause network delays. Other routers may not be receiving enough network traffic and are running at only partial capacity compared with what their resources are capable of.

Large organizations use load balancers with web services distributed among several web servers to service their customers with enough processing power and resources to respond to thousands of web requests per hour. The load balancer is required to analyze the incoming requests and route the requests evenly between these servers.

Load balancers perform their functions through round-robin techniques where each server in turn is sent a request, or else they can use intelligent load balancing methods (for example, current number of connections and response time) to detect which servers are overloaded and which servers have enough resource capacity to handle incoming requests. Many high-end load balancers work at the application layer to properly load-balance specific protocols and network application services.

Load balancers possess the network security awareness to help prevent DoS network attacks by detecting floods of network packets and preventing them from overloading the devices for which they are balancing network traffic.

Proxy Servers

A *proxy server* is a network server or device that accepts and forwards requests from clients to other servers. The proxy server performs this function on behalf of the client. The proxy is typically situated between the clients and the Internet, and it can be used to forward requests for many types of traffic and data transfers such as web and FTP. This protects the specific addresses of internal clients from being revealed to external servers and allows the proxy server to filter incoming and outgoing requests to prevent attacks and malware from reaching the client systems.

The most commonly used type of proxy server is for web browsing. A web client requests a specific URL in their web browser that is sent to the proxy server. The web proxy server forwards the request to the destination web site using its own IP addresses as the source of the request. When the data is retrieved, the proxy server may cache or content-filter the data and then return the data to the requesting client. Web proxy servers are used primarily for their caching capability, which boosts web browsing performance by storing content retrieved from an external web server. The next time a client retrieves the same web data, the web proxy can serve the information to the client without sending another request to the external web server. This greatly reduces the amount of bandwidth required to retrieve numerous web requests from an organization and provides significant cost savings.

Antimalware and Content Security Appliances

With the surge in malware (for example, viruses, spyware, Trojan horses, and back-door programs) directed at user desktops, not only from traditional e-mail spam but also from malicious web sites, peer-to-peer file sharing, and social media networks, there is a greater need for all-in-one network security appliances that can offer several layers of security protection against incoming messages from a wide scope of communications mediums.

You can run each type of security service, such as e-mail scanning or web scanning, on a separate network device, or you can integrate these security services to scan multiple network protocols (e-mail, web, social media, VoIP) from the same device. Integrated security appliances are very popular and cost efficient for small to medium-sized organizations, enabling them to scan all their network traffic with a single device.

Antispam Filter

An *antispam filter* is a type of network security service primarily targeted for e-mail communications. Antispam filters reside between your internal mail servers and your firewall; they process any incoming and outgoing mail messages before they deliver the messages to their destination.

Antispam filters use a variety of techniques to determine if an incoming message is spam or legitimate mail. If the message is determined to be spam, the message can be immediately deleted or quarantined by the antispam filter before it reaches the client user's mail inbox. Most antispam filters have a very high rate of effectiveness against most types of spam, and if configured correctly, they prevent users from ever having to see a spam message in their e-mail.

No antispam filter is perfect, and most use a variety of techniques to identify spam messages and prevent legitimate mail from being classified as spam (a false positive).

These techniques include

- **Databases of known spam**   The antispam filter usually comes with a default database of known spam messages. This is useful for catching the most obvious forms of historical spam, but it cannot identify new types of spam. The default database provides a good base configuration but requires additional antispam techniques and training to detect new spam.

- **Blacklists (or Block lists)**   There are several types of public blacklists (also called block lists) that contain a list of mail server IP addresses that are known to send spam messages. By comparing a connecting mail server to the blacklist, the antispam filter can determine whether to block or allow the connection from the mail server if it appears on the list. The list is checked as the mail connection begins, typically using a DNS-based lookup to a blacklist server. Blacklists are not perfect, and very often, perfectly legitimate mail servers are accidentally added to blacklists. That is why a variety of methods must be used during the antispam message processing to accurately determine if the message is spam or legitimate mail.

- **URL block lists**   Spam messages often contain URLs that, when clicked, take you to a web page that could be malicious in behavior and may contain spyware or malware, or else try to trick you into using your login credentials or credit card information for a phishing scam. Much as in the case of blacklists and DNS block lists, the antispam filter compares the URLs extracted from a message with a list of known spam URLs.

- **Bayesian filtering** This is an antispam technique that extracts tokens from spam messages and legitimate mail. These tokens are keywords and phrases that are statistically evaluated to determine the likelihood that a message is spam or legitimate mail. Bayesian techniques require scanning of inbound and outbound mail over a period of time to create a valid number of tokens that properly train the antispam filter to distinguish spam and legitimate messages.

- **Reputation services** The next generation of third-party block lists, reputation services track mail servers and score them with a good or bad reputation, depending on the amount of spam and viruses sent from those mail server addresses. An antispam filter queries the reputation service when it receives a mail connection, and if the sending mail server has a bad reputation, the filter can drop the connection before any transfer of mail occurs. This improves performance for the antispam filter, as it does not have to process any mail because the connection is rejected before any transfer of messages takes place.

Content Filtering

To address privacy concerns and data loss prevention, certain types of organizations (such as financial or medical companies) must now adhere to specific government regulations regarding the release of private data. This means that organizations must take greater control over the outbound content that is transmitted outside their organization's networks.

There are several types of rules in place that must be adhered to by financial organizations to protect the security and privacy of data, such as PCI (payment card industry) compliance. PCI is a compliance policy that defines the minimum amount of security that is required for credit card, debit card, ATM system, and other financial transactions. Most major credit card and banking companies are PCI-compliant. These compliance rules are primarily based on the storage and transmission of sensitive financial information. For example, a bank must ensure that a private customer's credit card or banking details are not transmitted outside of its networks, or if they must be transmitted, that they are encrypted.

Medical and health providers must adhere to strict rules, such as HIPAA (the Health Insurance Portability and Accountability Act). These rules ensure that these organizations are accountable for the privacy and security of their patient's medical records. Outbound content filtering can ensure that messages with specific identifying information can be blocked from being sent outside of the organization.

An outbound content filter on a proxy server can monitor outgoing e-mails (including deep content scanning of e-mail attachments and web file uploads) to scan the content for patterns of credit card or account numbers. If they are encountered in the message, they can be blocked or quarantined, or policies can be set in place to automatically encrypt the message before it leaves the organization.

Web Security Gateway

A *web security gateway* is a more complex device than a simple web proxy caching server. Beyond performing the basic tasks of a web proxy, it provides content filtering and application-level security to protect end users from accessing dangerous web sites and downloading files that are infected with worms, spyware, or malware, or else from connecting to servers that host phishing and fraud sites.

These types of application-level security devices provide specialized protection beyond that of a network firewall, which is designed to provide more basic access controls and filtering of all types of network traffic. Web security gateway devices can perform deep inspection of web HTTP traffic to prevent end users from accessing dangerous content and protect them from HTTP-specific script attacks such as cross-site scripting (XSS).

When a user accesses a web site, the request is filtered through the web security gateway. The web security gateway contacts the destination web site as a proxy for the client and analyzes the files and requests returned from the web site. It scans the network traffic for known types of web attacks and analyzes file downloads for malware, such as viruses, spyware, and Trojan horse software. These types of gateways can also scan text content of web sites to search for prohibited words and phrases that indicate offensive content.

For a web security gateway to be effective, all end-user web browser clients must be configured to use the gateway as their web proxy. This ensures that all web traffic is filtered through the gateway and processed for security issues before the client can continue their web session. Some web security gateways enforce authentication to allow only clients with authenticated access to traverse the web proxy and access content outside of the private network. The user's web surfing habits can then be tracked to monitor content and bandwidth usage

URL Filtering

Organizations can filter specific URLs or file types to prevent them from being accessed. Examples are adult sites and other types of content that should not be viewed or used on a corporate or public network such as at a library. URL filtering software uses a predefined list of sites that are allowed or blocked as required via policies. If a client tries to access a blocked web site or file, that client will receive a warning message and will not be allowed access to that particular web site.

There are also third-party public URL filtering products that contain a list of categorized web sites that are most commonly blocked because of their content. These are configurable by the administrator to block specific types of content, such as offensive sites, gambling, or even sites that reduce productivity such as shopping sites and social media.

Intrusion Detection and Prevention

As a first line of defense for your network security, the implementation of an *intrusion detection system* greatly enhances the security of your network. An intrusion detection system can monitor your network activity for suspicious behavior that can indicate if someone is trying to break in or damage your network. By proactively monitoring the network border, the detection system can immediately notify an administrator of the intrusion. Some detection systems (also called *intrusion prevention systems*) can self-repair the problem and either disconnect suspicious network connections or turn off network services that are being attacked.

Intrusion detection systems can also be either active or passive. In an *active detection system,* intrusion attempts are dealt with immediately by shutting down network connections or services that are being attacked. A *passive detection system* relies on notification to alert administrators of an intrusion.

A network-based intrusion detection system examines network patterns, such as an unusual number of requests destined for a particular server or service, such as an FTP server. The headers of network packets can be analyzed for possible spoofing attempts or suspicious code that indicates a malformed packet. Corrupted packets and malformed data can bring down a web server that's vulnerable to such attacks.

A network intrusion detection system typically consists of the following components, as shown in Figure 8.3.

- **Detection agent** The *detection* agents of an intrusion detection system usually are physically installed in a network and are attached to core network devices, such as routers, firewalls, and switches. Detection agents can also be software agents that use network management protocols, such as the Simple Network Management Protocol (SNMP). They simply collect the data passing through the network and send it on to the network monitor for analysis.

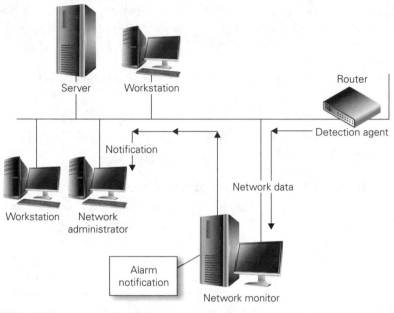

FIGURE 8.3 Network Intrusion Detection System (NIDS)

- **Monitor** The *network monitor* is fed information from the detection units and analyzes the network activity for suspicious behavior. This is the heart of the intrusion detection system, which collects information from the network, analyzes it, and then uses the notification system to warn of any problems. The monitor can utilize several methods, including heuristic-, behavior/anomaly-, rule-, and signature-based scanning to detect network threats. These are discussed in more detail in the next section.

- **Notification system** The *notification system* is used for notification and alarms, which are sent to the administrator. Once the network monitor recognizes a threat, it writes to a log file and uses the notification system to send an alert, such as an e-mail or an SMS message, to an administrator. The notification system is usually configurable, to allow for a variety of methods of communication.

To protect the entire network, the intrusion detection system is usually located at a central point, such as a main router, switch, or firewall system. A detection system can only monitor what it sees, so placing it further down in the system lessens the chance of finding intrusions, especially because your firewall and routers are the entry points to the network. This characteristic makes a network-based system much more important than a host-based system because of its capability to detect intrusions at the entrance to the network. The disadvantage of a network-based system is it can rarely detect intrusions originating from the internal network. This is where also using host-based intrusion detection systems in your overall security model is important.

Travel Advisory
Network-based intrusion systems also are not effective in monitoring encrypted communications, such as over a VPN.

When an intrusion is detected, the system works in either an active or a passive way to alert an administrator of the problem. A passive system will only send warnings and alarms through log files, e-mail, instant message, or SMS message. An active system tries to fix the problem through shutting off certain services or preventing connections from a suspicious host.

Active Detection

A network-based intrusion detection system that uses active detection methods can take immediate steps to halt an intrusion. These types of systems are also called *network intrusion prevention systems (NIPSs)* because they actively attempt to prevent intrusions rather than just detect them. The advantage of this method is that it can attempt to prevent the intrusion from continuing. Active detection prevents the suspicious activity from expanding into actual damage or data loss. This is a great advantage over passive detection systems, which merely log the incident or send an e-mail to the administrator, who might not see the message for many hours before she can perform any preventive actions. By then, it could be too late.

Exam Tip
A network intrusion prevention system (NIPS) tries to prevent an intrusion from occurring after detecting the intrusion.

Network-based active detection systems can automatically reconfigure logical network topologies to reroute network traffic in case of some form of network attack, such as a denial-of-service (DoS) attack. They can also detect suspicious activity on a network connection and terminate it, logging the IP address to prevent any further connections from that origin. The detection system can also sense attacks on certain ports or services, such as an SNMP port on a router, and shut the port down to prevent any more attacks on it.

The disadvantage of active detection systems is that the occurrence of false alarms can cause the system to shut down services or network connections for legitimate requests.

Passive Detection

Passive detection by network-based intrusion detection systems involves alerting an administrator of the intrusion, so that he can take the necessary actions to stop it. The system will not take any active steps to prevent the detected intrusion from continuing. The disadvantage of a passive system is that the administrator might not get the alert immediately, especially if he is offsite and not carrying a smart phone or other mobile device. By the time he gets to the system, the damage of the intrusion could have already been done.

Passive methods of detection usually consist of some form of logging utility that logs events as they happen and stores them for later examination or notifies the administrator of high-level warnings and errors. If no type of messaging alert function is configured, the administrator must scan the log files regularly for suspicious behavior.

> ### Exam Tip
>
> Make sure you know the difference between network- and host-based intrusion detection systems, as well as the difference between active and passive versions of these systems and how they mitigate threats.

Monitoring Methodologies

Network monitoring applications such as a NIDS/NIPS are used to monitor and analyze network traffic to detect security threats such as network-based attacks (DoS attacks, ping sweeps, and port scans). When a security threat is detected, the monitoring system logs the event and notifies the administrator or takes immediate steps to mitigate the incoming threat. Different types of monitoring methodologies can be used to detect intrusions and malicious behavior. The following sections describe these monitoring methodologies and their benefits and weaknesses.

> ### Exam Tip
>
> Understand the differences between signature-, behavioral/anomaly-, heuristic-, and rule-based monitoring methodologies, including their strengths and weaknesses.

Signature-Based Monitoring   *Signature-based* monitoring systems are similar to antivirus programs and contain predefined signature databases of known attacks that have appeared previously. Each type of attack can be recognized by its unique characteristics, and a signature is created for that type of attack. For example, signature-based systems can detect popular types of denial-of-service attacks. The signature (if available) can detect this exact information in the network packet and generate an alert to the administrator. These databases are dynamic, and the monitoring program must be continually updated to ensure it has the latest signatures to identity the latest types of threats.

Signature-based systems are powerful and efficient because they rely on the collective knowledge of security vendors, who analyze and collect information on Internet security threats and trends and who update their databases quickly when new threats arise. However, signature-based systems are unable to detect very new attacks whose signatures are not yet available. In this respect, signature-based systems are often used in conjunction with behavior-based systems.

Behavior/Anomaly-Based Monitoring   *Behavior-based* (also referred to as anomaly-based) monitoring systems do not use a predefined database of signatures but start from a baseline of normal behavior and then monitor network traffic based on these performance profiles to recognize behavioral anomalies that exceed the thresholds of the normal baseline. Such a monitoring system becomes more effective over time as baseline activity is recorded, allowing the system to detect aberrations to these baselines more efficiently. For example, a sudden burst of incoming connections that is out of character for the network will trigger the monitoring system to generate alerts of the activity and in some cases to take proactive steps to mitigate the anomalous behavior (which could be a DoS attack) by blocking the attempted connections.

The primary benefit of behavior-based systems is that they easily and quickly adapt to the current environment and can detect new variants of attacks that a signature- or rule-based monitoring system might not recognize. The monitoring system is actively looking for behavior that is inconsistent with the current system baseline profile; therefore, even new types of attacks will be recognized immediately and action can be taken. New attacks are often referred to as *zero-day* attacks, and signature-based monitoring systems might not recognize them as threats.

Local Lingo

zero-day threat   A type of attack that has rarely or never been encountered, such as an unknown virus or a malicious program that takes advantage of previously unknown weaknesses and vulnerabilities in a software program or operating system. As the attack is new, no existing defense or signature has been created to detect it.

The disadvantage of a behavior-based system is that it takes some time to build the baseline profile, and until the system learns enough information about the current system, it cannot accurately detect anomalies to that profile; efficiency is built over time. False positives can occur, in which normal behavior is flagged as anomalous, because the system has not had time to build its baseline profile to recognize it as normal behavior. Also, the anomalous behavior detected can generate an alert, but the monitoring system can only warn the administrator that the thresholds have been exceeded; the administrator must determine whether an actual attack is taking place and what steps to take to mitigate it. The behavior-based monitoring system doesn't always recognize the type of specific attack, only its symptoms.

Heuristic-Based Monitoring   Heuristic-based security monitoring continuously trains on network behavior; it is similar to how heuristic training occurs for antispam filters as discussed in a previous section. Heuristics uses an initial database of known attack types but dynamically alters their signatures based on learned behavior of inbound and outbound network traffic. These types of systems are powerful for detecting suspicious behavior that might not be detected by other methods, but they require constant tuning to prevent false positives.

Rule-Based Monitoring   Rule-based security monitoring takes more work to match the efficiency and effectiveness of other types of monitoring methods such as signature- and behavior-based systems. Similar to firewall access control rules, a rule-based security monitoring system relies on the administrator to create rules and determine the actions to take when those rules are transgressed. For example, a rule can be created that will block connections from an IP address if more than 100 connections are attempted from the same IP address within a certain time period, such as 30 seconds. This could indicate a DoS attack, and when the rule thresholds are exceeded, the offending connection will be blocked to contain the threat.

Rule-based systems require significant manual initial setup and constant maintenance to keep the rules current and up-to-date with the latest threats. These factors are handled automatically by a signature-based system, which already contains an up-to-date database of the latest security threats and compares these threats with the behaviors the system is experiencing. The system will then take action as appropriate.

Protocol Analyzers

Beyond basic network-level and content filtering, protocol analyzers have also become another defense in the security arsenal of organizations that want to prevent attacks and exploits from reaching their server and client systems.

Protocol analyzers (also known as network sniffers) can be stand-alone applications or used in conjunction with other network monitoring and intrusion detection applications to monitor and capture network data right down to the packet and frame level. This allows the network administrator to analyze each frame of network data to look for abnormalities and inconsistencies in network requests and responses that may indicate an intrusion or other malicious application running on the network. Due to the enormous volume of data that floods through a network, it would be impossible for a network administrator to examine each and every frame passing through the primary network router. Stand-alone analyzers are most useful for detecting isolated problems with specific systems or on a small subnet of clients.

Protocol analyzers can also be used in conjunction with intrusion detection and prevention systems to analyze large blocks of the network and analyze network protocols such as web HTTP and FTP data. This deep-level scanning of network data can detect specific behaviors of known exploits or network attacks, such as by detecting anomalous data in an HTTP request. This information can be communicated to the intrusion detection system, which will block those network packets from reaching the client. This technique is very similar to how antivirus or antispyware applications detect malicious programs by comparing them to known behaviors based on a signature file. To ensure efficiency, this signature file must be kept up to date with the latest known network and application exploits.

Objective 8.02
CompTIA Security+
Objective 1.3

Distinguish and Differentiate Network Design Elements and Compounds

Security of your network can be a daunting task for a network administrator. Depending on the size and complexity of the network, the administrator must examine the security implications of several interconnected communication systems, from the internal networking equipment of an organization, such as routers, firewalls, and switches, to users who access the organization's network remotely with VPN access.

Compounding the problem are the several types of Internet services that most companies and organizations need to run their business: web services, e-mail, and file transfer servers. These types of applications require special attention regarding security. At the same time, you need to protect your internal network hosts and servers from unauthorized access from the public Internet.

To provide maximum security with the least amount of administrative overhead, the use of security zones is recommended. *Security zones* are created when parts of your network are divided into special separated areas where similar systems and servers reside. By putting all your Internet servers in one zone and your internal network in another zone, you create a protective wall to regulate access between them. This type of topology is created through the use of a firewall, which controls access to the various zones through a rules-based access system.

Other network protection schemes, including the use of network address translation (NAT), network access control (NAC), virtual local area networks (VLANs), VPNs and remote access, virtualization, and cloud computing, can help you divide the network into more manageable zones to secure access.

Security Zones

Dividing your network into separate security zones lets you create physical and logical barriers between the different areas of your network. These zones enable you to allocate different types of security, depending on the sensitivity of the data and network equipment within that zone. This is the equivalent of setting up fences or walls between different buildings in a facility, which prevent users of one building from entering another building for which they are not authorized. A *firewall* is used to set up these zones on the network. A firewall is a special server or network device used to regulate network traffic and to prevent access to the private network from a public network, such as the Internet. The firewall uses a special set of rules to admit or deny network access, as appropriate, such as only allowing FTP traffic to a specific server. By setting up the firewall to split the network into different zones, you can more easily create firewall rules to allow access to servers in those zones.

The three main zones into which networks are commonly divided are the external public network, the internal private network, and a demilitarized zone (DMZ), as shown in Figure 8.4.

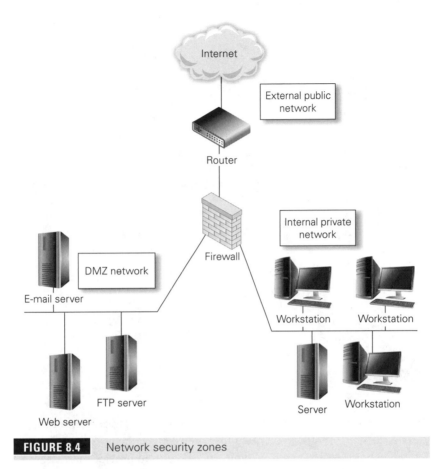

FIGURE 8.4   Network security zones

DMZ

The *DMZ* (demilitarized zone) is an area of the network where a high number of publicly accessed Internet systems should be located. The DMZ, in an overall network security topology, is situated between the public and protected zones (private network), as shown in Figure 8.5.

The DMZ provides a buffer zone between your external network devices, such as a router, and the internal network that comprises your servers and user workstations. The DMZ usually contains popular Internet services—web servers, mail servers, and FTP servers. These services may need to be accessed by those on the public network, the Internet. Your company might use a web site that hosts certain services and information for current clients and potential

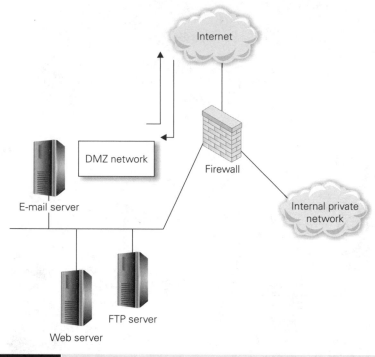

FIGURE 8.5 The DMZ

clients. A public FTP server on the DMZ might serve files to all users or only to certain clients. Your mail server needs to allow a connection from the Internet to let e-mail be relayed to and from your site, and also to provide mail access for your own users who might be using the system remotely.

Exam Tip

Know the purpose of the DMZ and how a firewall can be configured to separate these Internet servers from the internal network.

These Internet services, however, should be separated from your internal LAN. If you were to host a web server on your internal LAN that is accessible from the Internet, you would create vulnerabilities in your network because an unauthorized user might be able to compromise the web server and then have full access to your local LAN. If the web server is on your DMZ and it is some-how compromised, the hacker could only get as far as the DMZ because the in-ternal LAN is on another network, protected by the firewall.

Travel Advisory

Many web servers act as a front end for access to database servers, which need to be located on the internal LAN. Care must be taken to make sure that only those ports needed for access to the database are opened by the firewall and that access can only be granted from that web server. If a hacker were to compromise the security of the web server, he might be able to use that as a jumping point to get to the database server on the internal LAN.

Intranet

An *intranet,* or internal network, is a locally available web network that is not accessible from the public Internet. The prefix "intra" specifies this is an internal network. Many companies provide web services that are only relevant to their internal employees and not to the public or the company's customers. These web pages usually contain such services as a directory of contact information for everyone in the company, web pages dedicated to specific departments (for example, Human Resources or Engineering), or finance web pages dealing with the company's stock and financial plans. Web-enabled applications for internal use give employees access to internal services via a web browser.

The intranet only lets internal employees have access to these web pages because the information they provide can be confidential and shouldn't be accessed by the public, especially rival companies. The web servers that host intranet services are located on the private internal LAN in the overall security zone model to prevent access from both the public and DMZ zones.

Extranet

An *extranet* is an extension of your private network or intranet. An extranet extends outside the body of your local network to enable other companies or networks to share information. For example, an automobile manufacturing company could have an extranet that connects selected business partners, so they can access and share specific information on availability and inventories between the networks. These are often referred to as business-to-business (B2B) communications or networks because one company uses the internal resources and services of another.

Extranets can open security vulnerabilities in your network unless they are configured properly. Older types of extranets used dedicated communications links between the companies, which are much more difficult for an unauthorized user to penetrate. Now, most extranets use virtual private network (VPN) tunnels over the Internet to communicate, which makes them more susceptible to intrusion. To ensure extranet communications are secure, your VPN, encryption, and firewall configuration must be carefully planned to limit the access of an intruder.

Networking Security Techniques

Beyond physically dividing the network into zones to secure network communications, several software-based network configuration techniques can aid in securing your network from unauthorized intruders. These enable you to reconfigure the network logically instead of physically, which reduces administrative overhead and removes the need to purchase additional expensive networking equipment.

NAC (Network Access Control)

Any network is often at its most vulnerable from internal attacks from hosts on its own network rather than malicious entities attacking from outside the network. *NAC (network access control)* allows your network devices to allow or deny access to clients based on predefined access policies. These policies set out rules for what clients can access on the network and define a minimum set of parameters that clients must adhere to and ensure they are properly configured. This helps prevent viruses and worms that have infected a client on your network from infecting other systems by denying the client access to the network based on its current status.

NAC policies can assess a connecting host and examines several factors, for example, the computer's operating system and applications patch update level, the existence of antivirus software and the date of its signature files, the existence of network vulnerabilities, and the access rights of the user that is logged in; it then decides whether to limit access to network resources based on these factors. Any clients that do not meet the minimum policy guidelines can be denied access or have severe restrictions on their access, such as the inability to see and use network resources such as file servers.

NAC-aware appliances are typically inserted into the network before major access switches and routers. Ideally, NAC-aware routers and switches can be deployed on your network that remove the need for having separate devices on your network and allow your routers and switches to control access policies for your network. With multiple vendors each with its own NAC support, successful implementations of NAC on your network require that all network infrastructure devices such as routers and switches be from the same vendor, as interoperability with other types of NAC systems may result in incompatibility and blocked access for major portions of your network.

Most NAC methods require an agent to be running on the client. This agent can either be permanently installed as a service on the client system, or in some cases, temporary agents can be installed over the network using ActiveX or Java web plug-ins. If someone brings an unauthorized client into your network, the temporary software agent can enforce your network policies, even though the client does not have permanent NAC client software installed.

These methods require some administrative overhead, especially in regard to access for other devices (such as printers, smart phones, and other network-aware devices) that do not have operating systems or antivirus software running. Most NAC systems allow you to whitelist (allow full access without scanning the device) based on the system IP address or hardware MAC address.

NAT (Network Address Translation)

NAT (network address translation) is a networking technique that allows private IP addresses on your internal network to be translated into a routable address for communication on the Internet. NAT was initially created to solve the problem of the lack of IP addresses available for private networks to use on the Internet. The number of remaining IP address ranges is scarce, so an alternate method of using already existing addresses was needed. Private networks can make use of special private IP address ranges internally, and when they communicate with the Internet, they can use an external address. Most companies have only a certain number of external Internet IP addresses to use. To work around the problem, a NAT service can be installed, so when an internal client wants to communicate with the outside world, it is assigned an external IP address for that communication. From the outside world, any communications from that internal network seem to come from one external IP address. The NAT service takes care of handling what requests go back to which clients on the internal network, as shown in Figure 8.6.

NAT is also important for security because the internal address of the client cannot be accessed from anyone in the outside world on the Internet. If an unauthorized user tries to see what is in that network, that user can only get as far as the external router or firewall. Most routers and firewalls have the NAT service built in to provide this functionality.

One hacking method that's been used to try to compromise a network using a firewall is to "spoof" the IP address to make it look as if the request is coming from the internal network. The NAT service helps prevent these attacks because the addresses of the internal private network are hidden.

Internal Network Addressing

As part of the internal network security zone, the network is typically configured to use private Internet Protocol (IP) address ranges. These standard private addresses can be used by any internal network and cannot be routed

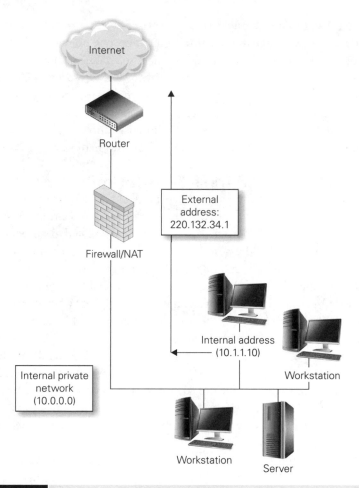

FIGURE 8.6   NAT (network address translation)

externally on the Internet. The following are the private address ranges that can be used.

- **Class A network**   10.0.0.0–10.255.255.255
- **Class B network**   172.16.0.0–172.31.255.255
- **Class C network**   192.168.0.0–192.168.255.255

Exam Tip

Know the standard nonroutable private address ranges for different classes of networks.

Using these private internal network addresses ensures that any internal network communications cannot be communicated externally unless granted access by the organization's network firewall, which uses NAT to convert the internal IP addresses to external addresses that can routed on the Internet.

Subnetting

Administrators can use *subnetting* to break larger networks down into more manageable subnetworks. Subnetting greatly reduces the amount of network "chatter" and broadcasts that are sent to all systems on a network, by isolating this networking activity to specific segments.

Subnetting logically divides the network regardless of the actual physical layout of a network. The router is the device that creates and controls the border between different subnetworks. The router facilitates communication between the subnets, while keeping inter-subnet traffic isolated on its originating network. These subnetworks can be physical Ethernet segments, or VLANs (virtual LANs) where the segmentation is not physical but logical.

Subnetting provides network security by hiding network details from external networks, and it makes sure that networking data for each subnet, especially potentially dangerous traffic such as excessive broadcasting, is isolated on its own segment.

VLAN

A *VLAN (virtual LAN)* is a type of logical network that exists as a subset of a larger physical network. In smaller networks, the network can be divided into segments fairly easily, with little administrative overhead. Splitting the network into segments allows network data and broadcast traffic to stay on the local segment, without broadcasting data to the entire network as a whole. Segmentation of LANs also provides extra security because a user on one LAN will not have access to another one without special permission.

Unfortunately, segmenting a larger network into smaller networks can be tedious and might involve the purchase of extra networking equipment, such as switches and routers, and extra cabling to separate them. This is where VLANs can help because the network segmentation is performed through software, rather than hardware. VLANs have the capability to isolate network traffic on specific segments, and even provide crossover functionality to enable certain VLANs to overlap and allow access between them.

> **Exam Tip**
>
> Know how VLANs can increase security and performance in a network, as well as the different ways they can be implemented.

The capability to create VLANs is dependent on the capabilities of your network equipment. Most modern switches and routers support the use of VLANs, which can be enabled simply through changing the configuration of the network device. There are three basic types of VLANs:

- **Port-based VLAN** The *port-based VLAN* uses the specific port of a network switch to configure VLANs. Each port is configured as part of a particular VLAN. To assign a client workstation to that VLAN, it needs to be plugged into that port.

- **MAC address–based VLAN** The *MAC address–based VLAN* tracks clients and their respective VLAN memberships through the MAC address of their network card. The switches maintain a list of MAC addresses and VLAN memberships, and they route the network packets to their destination, as appropriate. The advantage of MAC address–based VLANs is if clients' VLAN membership changes, they needn't be physically moved to another port. One drawback of this method is that being part of multiple VLANs can cause confusion with the switch's MAC address tables. This model is recommended for single VLAN memberships.

- **Protocol-based VLAN** A *protocol-based VLAN* is the most flexible and logical type of VLAN. It uses the addresses of the IP layer to assign VLAN settings, and an entire IP subnet can be assigned a certain VLAN membership.

Figure 8.7 shows an example of a typical VLAN configuration. This network is divided by network subnets, configured as part of a certain VLAN. The switches are using a port-based VLAN configuration across two floors of a building.

Remote Access

In today's corporate environments, employees need to access the resources of the organization's networks when they are not physically in the building. In the beginning, this was accomplished through the use of modems to connect to a network using a phone line. Modern remote access methods are primarily dominated by encrypted virtual private network (VPN) access over the Internet. Remote access offers opportunities for hackers to compromise computer networks that do not install proper security mechanisms for their remote users. By using remote access, an unauthorized user need not physically be at a console inside the organization's physical building. The unauthorized user can be halfway across the world in another country, merely using a simple dial-up Internet connection. To protect these communications from unauthorized access, a security policy must be put in place to provide authentication measures and data encryption for all remote access users. In addition, the use of network monitoring

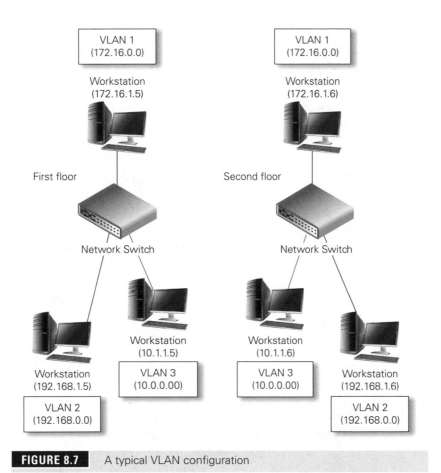

FIGURE 8.7	A typical VLAN configuration

and intrusion detection tools can aid in proactively monitoring the network for suspicious and unauthorized activity originating from remote access.

Modems

The modem was, and still is, an important tool for remote communications. A *modem* allows two computer systems to communicate over an analog phone line. While this is a much slower method than modern VPN and remote access solutions that use broadband Internet access, modems are still in use today as secondary methods of contact, especially for "back door" access for technical support and administration to critical systems for remote IT staff.

At minimum, any type of modem access to a network should require authentication before the session can begin, and the session should use encryption protocols. Additional types of authentication, for example, security tokens, are important, especially if the remote access device is stolen.

VPN

A virtual private network is a special, encrypted communications tunnel between one system and another. VPNs are used to secure remote access in most modern networks, as shown in Figure 8.8.

A VPN makes use of encrypted tunneling protocols (such as IPsec and SSL) to connect networks together. A tunneling protocol allows an existing internal protocol, such as private IP addressing, to be encapsulated and relayed over the Internet to its destination. This VPN link is encrypted to provide secure access to a private network over the public Internet. The VPN link should be protected with strong encryption and authentication mechanisms to ensure its security. VPNs can be integrated with a wide variety of authentication systems such as LDAP, RADIUS, Kerberos, and digital certificates. Another way to protect VPN communications is to allow the VPN to assign IP addresses as the user connects and to allow only these blocks of IP addresses to access the network.

Travel Assistance

For detailed information on VPN encryption methods, see Chapter 4. For detailed information on VPN and authentication integration, see Chapter 7.

After connecting to the VPN server, users have a secure channel between them and the network to which the VPN server is attached, enabling them access to network resources. VPN endpoints are typically secured by a VPN concentrator device or server that is responsible for managing the encrypted VPN tunnel between a client computer and the main network, or between two branch office networks in different geographical locations. A VPN server consists of a typical network server running VPN software services that manage the encrypted communications tunnel. The VPN server may run other services (such as authentication), but it may connect to other external servers for these

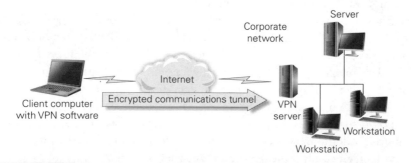

FIGURE 8.8   VPN (virtual private network)

services. A VPN concentrator is a specific hardware device dedicated to VPN connectivity. The VPN concentrator is an integrated device that manages all aspects of the connection, including the encryption tunnels and authentication of the VPN client. Authentication can be integrated within the concentrator, but it can also connect to external services, such as an organization's LDAP server, to authenticate clients.

Telephony

In most organizations, *telephony* services also come under the Information Technology (IT) banner because they are just as much a part of the everyday communications of the company as the computer network.

Instead of assigning a direct line for each user, which can be expensive, most large companies prefer to use a phone switch system, such as a private branch exchange (PBX). The PBX allows the company to maintain a certain number of internal and external lines. For example, a company of 200 people could only have 50 incoming lines and 20 outgoing lines. Internal users also have the capability to call each other using only three- or four-digit extensions. A centralized voice mail system is also usually a part of the entire phone network. This can generally be accessed from an outside line, in case someone wants to check her voice mail while at home or traveling.

Security for phone systems, however, has traditionally been lax compared to that for computer networks. If an unauthorized user were to gain access to the PBX, that user might be able to make expensive long-distance phone calls, all charged to the company. Unauthorized voice mail access can invade the privacy of your individual users and can also be used to glean information for corporate espionage. Important to note is that most phone PBX systems are equipped with a modem to allow remote access for the service technicians from the system vendor. If this modem is not secured with proper authentication systems, anyone might be able to call that number and access the phone system. A good practice is to unplug this modem when it is not in use and plug it in when a technician needs access to the system.

The voice mail system should be configured to allow only secure passwords for user voice mail boxes, with a minimum of six to eight characters, composed of uppercase and lowercase letters, numbers, and symbols. The same rules should also be applied to the PBX administrator account.

VoIP (Voice over IP)

The last several years have seen an exponential growth in VoIP (Voice over IP) communications where clients use the TCP/IP protocol to communicate over traditional computer networks. VoIP clients include basic phone services, but also include video conferencing and other types of multimedia applications that are communicated over a network.

The advantage for VoIP services is that the long-distance costs associated with traditional phone networks practically disappear, as phone services can be deployed globally and communicate over existing Internet communication lines. A user in an office in New York can call an office associate located in Tokyo using a VoIP phone that communicates over existing Internet and VPN connections between their offices, completely bypassing the traditional phone system network.

Security concerns over VoIP have also grown because it uses the same computer networks as other Internet traffic and is open to the same types of computer vulnerabilities, such as denial-of-service attacks, spoofing, eavesdropping, call interception, man-in-the-middle attacks, and even voice mail spam.

VoIP also offers less availability in the event that your Internet connection may fail, as none of your VoIP phones will work with no IP communications available. Most organizations utilize VoIP for specific applications such as video conferencing but continue to use traditional phone networks for the majority of their users because of their inherent security and high availability.

Telephony communications over a computer network require the same types of security safeguards that are used on your traditional networks and must be part of your overall network security infrastructure plan.

Virtualization

Virtualization technology allows computer desktops or servers to host and run additional "virtual computers." Using virtualization technology, a computer can host multiple instances of an operating system environment all running from the same computer on the same hardware. These virtualized environments run as if they were a separate system and can run applications, be networked, run remotely, and perform almost any type of function that a single computer running a single operating system can perform. Virtualized systems are very popular for cross–operating system and application testing that allows software to be run and tested on several different types of operating systems all on the same server.

High-powered servers can run several virtualized systems simultaneously, thus helping to reduce the cost of additional hardware and power resources. In addition, virtual systems provide improved security, high availability, and disaster recovery by running as separate processes on the same hardware.

Virtualization works by emulating a complete computer system environment by sharing a single system's processors, memory, and hard disks for several individualized operating system environments. These virtual machines run their own separate operating system and run their own separate applications like a real system. Several different operating system types, such as Linux, Windows, Mac, and Unix, can all run together on one computer in separate virtualized environments, while sharing the same hardware resources. Any software crashes or security issues in one virtual machine will not affect another virtual machine running on the same computer.

The advantages of virtualization are that the number of physical systems running in your environment can be consolidated on several high-end servers, allowing several virtualized environments to be running on each server. In large-scale data centers, this can greatly reduce the amount of hardware required and thus the space taken up by the hardware; it can likewise reduce the amount of infrastructure resources required such as power and environment controls, significantly reducing overall operating costs. In terms of desktop computing environments, administrators can deploy several secure desktop environments that can be accessed remotely without the need for separate keyboards, monitors, and input devices, greatly reducing the number of access points that create security risks.

Cloud Computing

Cloud computing is a technique for allowing network services to be distributed from a central web-based "cloud" that can be updated from any device connected to the cloud. Cloud computing provides a distributed service-based model where all aspects of the cloud, from the platform, to the software, to the entire infrastructure, are based on a distributed web service. This differs from the traditional client/server network model where there are specific servers that host network services and data, and client device applications that connect to the servers for the application to work properly.

Most people now use multiple devices to access and manage their applications and data, including computer desktops, laptops, and smart phones or tablet devices. Before cloud computing, each device would have to have its own copy of the data the user wanted to work on. For example, the latest version of a spreadsheet file that the user was working on with his desktop computer had to be transferred to a laptop so that he could work on it as he commuted home. When he returned to the office, the file would have to be transferred back to the work desktop again.

Cloud computing allows the user to save the file to his cloud web service, and the file is automatically synced to all other devices that are connected to the same cloud. With this model, the user always has access to the latest version of the file no matter which device he uses to access, and the file is stored in a safe location that is also backed up by the cloud service provider.

Cloud computing also allows applications to be run from the web-based cloud, with no need for additional software to be run on the client. For example, word processing and spreadsheet software can now be run as a web-based application instead of a client-based application. The web-based cloud service hosts both the application and the data without the need to store anything local to the client. This allows the user to use any client she wants to access her cloud-based services.

Security and authentication services for cloud-based services are centralized, and each device must authenticate and be authorized before allowed access to the cloud. Device security is critical for protecting access to the cloud. For example, if you lose your smart phone or laptop, and you do not have adequate security for accessing the device and its applications and data such as a password, you risk providing access to your cloud data to the person who finds the device and is able to launch the cloud application.

CHECKPOINT

✔**Objective 8.01: Explain the security function and purpose of network devices and technologies.** Network device security is your first line of defense against network attacks. Use firewalls, routers, and switches to control and secure network traffic. Use proxy servers, application firewalls, and content filters to prevent malicious content from entering your organization's networks. Use content filtering to control outbound content and facilitate data loss prevention. Use intrusion detection and prevention systems to proactively monitor and respond to network security attacks.

✔**Objective 8.02: Distinguish and differentiate network design elements and compounds.** Appropriate network design is critical to securing your network infrastructure. Differentiate your network into security zones to create logical and physical barriers between your different networks. Put high-security servers such as web servers and e-servers in the DMZ (demilitarized zone) to protect the private network. Use network security techniques such as private addressing, NAT, subnetting, and VLANs to separate networks. Secure remote access with authentication and encrypted VPNs (virtual private networks). Use virtualization and cloud computing to simplify and centralize network security administration.

REVIEW QUESTIONS

1. You have been tasked by your manager to perform an evaluation of the benefits of using virtualization in your QA testing environment. Which of the following is an advantage of using virtual machines in terms of security and cost efficiency?

   A. It reduces the need to install OS software updates.

   B. Multiple operating systems can be installed and run in their own separate, secure area on a single hardware device.

   C. It helps secure the hardware from unauthorized access.

   D. Antivirus and other security software only have to be installed once.

2. After a security review, it is recommended that your organization install a network intrusion prevention system (NIPS). Based on the current budget, your manager recommends that you install a less-costly network detection system (NIDS). What is the primary security difference between a network intrusion detection system (NIDS) and a network intrusion prevention system (NIPS) that you can use to justify the additional costs?

   A. A NIDS system only detects TCP/IP attacks.

   B. The NIPS system actively tries to mitigate an incoming intrusion rather than just detect it.

   C. The NIDS system can raise alarms when it detects an intrusion.

   D. A NIPS system is only host based, not network based.

3. You must install and secure your organization's Internet services, including web, FTP, and e-mail servers, within your current network topology, which uses a network firewall to protect your internal networks. In which security zone of your network should these servers be installed to isolate them from the Internet and your internal networks?

   A. DMZ

   B. VLAN

   C. Internal network

   D. Intranet

4. You are configuring your network to ensure that all details of internal IP addresses in your network are hidden from outside networks. You must also allow several internal hosts to be able to use an external IP address when communicating outside the network. Which of the following network security methods should you use?

   A. NAT

   B. VPN

    C. VLAN

    D. IP spoofing

5. Your organization is growing fast, and the number of clients and devices on your network has doubled in size over the last year. To help better partition and secure your network, which networking technology could you use?

    A. NAT

    B. NAC

    C. VPN

    D. VLAN

6. Your organization has a large remote user base, and it is becoming difficult to enable them to access a legacy local application server and share and collaborate on project documents. Which of the following technologies could you use to provide secure, centralized access to these resources?

    A. VLAN

    B. Web-based cloud computing application

    C. Virtualization

    D. VPN

7. Many of your users are downloading MP3 music files from the Internet and using up the company's valuable bandwidth resources. Which technology could you implement to help block the transfer of these files from the Internet?

    A. Content filter

    B. Antispam filter

    C. Protocol analyzer

    D. Intrusion detection system

8. You need to implement a solution that allows your users to browse web content safely, and also protect the company from legal liabilities in regard to the downloading of inappropriate and offensive content. Which of the following security devices would you install?

    A. Antispam filter

    B. Firewall

    C. Web proxy

    D. Web security gateway

9. Your users are complaining that web browsing is very slow, but your small office cannot afford a faster Internet connection. Which of the following technologies would help improve web browsing performance?

   A. Web proxy

   B. Firewall

   C. Authentication proxy

   D. Intrusion detection system

10. You have discovered there may be a networking security issue between your network firewall and e-mail server, which is accepting connections from an unauthorized external e-mail server. Which of the following network security tools would be best used for examining network traffic between your firewall and your e-mail server?

   A. Intrusion detection system

   B. Proxy server

   C. Protocol analyzer

   D. Firewall server

REVIEW ANSWERS

1. **B** Virtual machines all run in their own separate and isolated area on the system as if they were on a separate physical machine. This greatly increases security, as any issues arising in one virtual machine will not affect another virtual system. This also allows multiple operating systems to be installed on the same physical hardware, which saves money by avoiding the need to buy multiple hardware systems.

2. **B** The NIPS system actively tries to mitigate an incoming intrusion rather than just detect it. A network intrusion detection system actively monitors for intrusions and will alert the administrator when one is detected. A network intrusion prevention system goes a step further and tries to actively prevent the intrusion as it is occurring.

3. **A** The demilitarized zone (DMZ) is a network that typically contains Internet servers and services that are accessible from the outside world but should be isolated from your internal network. The DMZ ensures incoming connections for these services are routed to the DMZ and never reach the internal LAN.

4. **A** Network address translation (NAT) allows internal hosts with nonroutable Internet addresses to access the Internet using an external address. NAT also hides the IP information of the internal network from the outside world.

5. **D** A virtual LAN (VLAN) is used to segment a network into smaller logical units to aid in security and performance. The virtual LANs are logically isolated from each other to prevent network traffic and unauthorized access.

6. **B** You could convert your legacy application to a secure, cloud-based web resource that allows clients to remotely access the application and its data from any Internet connection. The data can be easily shared, and multiple users can collaborate on projects.

7. **A** A content filtering server can analyze network traffic and block specific file types, such as MP3 music files, from being downloaded. The end users will receive an error when they try to access blocked files.

8. **D** A web security gateway device is specifically engineered to content-filter HTTP web traffic and prevent attacks on web clients via the HTTP protocol. A network firewall, web proxy, or antispam filter would not prevent security issues specifically for HTTP applications.

9. **A** Web proxy servers are used primarily for their caching capability, which boosts web browsing performance by storing content retrieved from an external web server.

10. **C** A protocol analyzer is best suited for examining and capturing network packets and frames between the two devices. You would be able to examine the network traffic to determine the details of the unauthorized connection and use firewall rules to block it.

Secure Network Administration

ITINERARY

- **Objective 9.01** Implement and use common protocols
- **Objective 9.02** Identify commonly used default network ports
- **Objective 9.03** Analyze and differentiate among types of attacks
- **Objective 9.04** Apply and implement secure network administration principles

	NEWBIE	SOME EXPERIENCE	EXPERT
ETA	3 hours	2 hours	1 hour

Securing a network and its systems requires protection against a variety of attacks. These attacks might affect only certain areas of operations, such as an application attack on a specific FTP server, or they can disrupt your entire network, such as a denial-of-service (DoS) attack. Some attacks are attempts to gain unauthorized access to a system or to damage one particular user account or one server. Other attacks try to disrupt the entire network infrastructure itself or prevent customers from accessing an organization's public web site.

The purpose of the attack is not the main concern, however: The main concern is how the attacks occurred and how to prevent attacks from succeeding. By being aware of the various types of protocols, attacks, tools, and resources used by malicious users, you can protect yourself and your systems with knowledge. By knowing where and how to expect attacks, you can enact preventive measures to protect your systems.

Security must also include the network devices, protocols, and communications technologies that enable users to access the network's resources. Network devices such as routers, switches, and firewalls can be compromised, causing potentially much more damage than the simple theft of a laptop computer. Secure network administration means knowing how data flows in your network, and how to properly configure your communications devices for maximum security.

This chapter discusses the various types of networking threats and vulnerabilities and describes the procedures necessary to mitigate them.

Objective 9.01
CompTIA Security+
Objective 1.4

Implement and Use Common Protocols

To understand the types of attacks that can occur against a network, it is useful to know the basic underlying protocols of Internet-based computer networks and the application protocols that use them.

TCP/IP

The *Transmission Control Protocol/Internet Protocol (TCP/IP)* is the most basic communications protocol of the Internet. TCP/IP communications are point-to-point, and together the two aspects of the protocol, TCP and IP, manage and route network messages. TCP/IP is a request/connection type of protocol, where a client requests a service from a server, for example, a web browser that sends a request to a web server to retrieve a web page for viewing. These requests use application-layer protocols, such as HTTP in this case, that utilize TCP/IP to work properly. TCP manages how to partition communications and send network messages from source to destination. TCP is responsible for breaking network messages into smaller packages and frames, and then reassembling the messages as they are received at the destination. TCP uses error checking and flow control to ensure network messages get to their destination.

A related protocol in the TCP/IP suite of technologies is the *User Datagram Protocol (UDP)*. UDP is connectionless and is used to transport less important data that does not require the error correction or flow control that TCP provides. UDP is fast and is often used for streaming media to allow content to be transported quickly. The *Internet Protocol (IP)* is used primarily for addressing and routing the network packets from the source to the destination device. Internet Protocol version 4 (IPv4) is the standard for all IP communications today and has been in use since the early 1980s. IPv4 is a connectionless protocol where delivery is not guaranteed; it only concerns itself with getting to the next network point between the source and destination network hosts. IPv4 uses 32-bit addressing, which allows for 4,294,967,296 unique IP addresses. These are separated into the different class types (A, B, C, and D), which make use of subnetting and subnet masks to help subdivide networks and facilitate private internal IP addressing.

Travel Assistance

For more detailed information on IP address classes and subnetting, see Chapter 8.

The primary issue affecting IPv4 today is that with the exponential increase in public networks and devices, the number of available IP addresses is running out. IPv6 is the next generation of the IP protocol that seeks to solve the address space issue and also provide additional network enhancements. IPv6 uses 128-bit addressing, allowing for up to 2^{128} available addresses. Although IPv6 and IPv4 are not interoperable, most modern operating systems, such as Windows 7, now support both IPv6 and IPv4 running concurrently.

With the exhaustion of IPv4 addresses imminent, the push to support IPv6 has resulted in rapid implementation by ISPs and large companies.

There are several technologies available to aid in the transition from IPv4 to IPv6. For example, you can use the IPsec protocol to tunnel IPv6 traffic. Other technologies such as the Intrasite Automatic Tunnel Addressing Protocol (ISATAP) and Teredo also allow IPv4 and IPv6 clients to communicate with each other over an IPv4 network by tunneling IPv6 packets within IPv4 traffic.

ICMP

The *Internet Control Message Protocol (ICMP)* is utilized by the TCP/IP protocol for network diagnostics and troubleshooting. ICMP for the Internet Protocol version 4 (IPv4) is called ICMPv4. IPv6 also has its own version of ICMP, called ICMPv6.

ICMP is used primarily to determine if a network host is able to receive network messages. The *Ping (Packet Internet Groper)* utility uses ICMP for this purpose. ICMP is also used by the *Traceroute* utility to check if network packets can be routed from a source to its destination.

ICMP's diagnostic nature means that it is often susceptible to denial-of-service attacks. The messages returned from ICMP can abort a connection if the diagnostic message returned indicates the connection can't be completed. ICMP responses can be crafted to indicate a network issue, even if no issue exists, causing network communications failure. Rate limiting features of ICMP can also be abused by hackers who craft ICMP messages that indicate network congestion, resulting in the host limiting its data rate even though there are no network congestion issues.

HTTP and HTTPS

The Hypertext Transfer Protocol (HTTP) is the primary communications protocol that allows web browsers to connect to and retrieve content from web servers. When a user clicks a web hyperlink, HTTP tries to connect with the associated Uniform Resource Locator (URL). The browser sends an HTTP request to the corresponding web server hosting that URL. The web server returns the content of the web site to the browser through HTTP. HTTP is a stateless protocol, meaning that with each communication, the link between the browser and the server is created, and then it's broken when the communication is finished. All HTTP communications are sent in clear text, so no messages are secure, and they can be easily viewed using a protocol analyzer. This makes HTTP unusable for communications requiring security and privacy, such as web-based banking and other online financial transactions.

Internet web servers accept HTTP port 80 requests from client web browsers, and they send back the requested information to the client. Web servers are the most common forms of servers on the Internet, and as a result, they are the most often attacked. An attack can occur in a variety of ways. Some attacks disrupt users from accessing the information on a web site. Other attacks spread worms and viruses over the Internet. Some attacks vandalize web sites and deface information on web pages or replace it with false information. Most of these attacks take advantage of security vulnerabilities in the web server. The most popular types of exploits include malformed requests, buffer overflow attacks, worms, and denial-of-service (DoS) attacks.

The Hypertext Transfer Protocol over Secure Sockets Layer (HTTPS) is a secure means of communicating HTTP data between a web browser and a web server. HTTPS protects the communication channel by using SSL and certificates to provide encrypted and protected communications. HTTPS uses TCP port 443 for communications.

Exam Tip	
HTTP uses TCP port 80, and HTTPS uses TCP port 443.	

Telnet

Telnet is a text-based terminal emulation utility that's part of the TCP/IP suite of protocols. It allows a system to connect to a remote host to perform commands as if you were on the console of the remote machine. For Telnet to work properly, the remote machine must be running a Telnet server service, which listens for Telnet requests from other hosts. When the client connects, it must authenticate to the remote system using a user name and password specific to that system. Once authenticated, the user can run commands on the remote system as if he were directly on the command console.

Exam Tip	
Telnet uses TCP port 23.	

Unfortunately, Telnet provides little security other than basic authentication. This means transmissions, including the user name and password, are sent in clear text and can be easily discovered by someone monitoring and capturing the communication. To ensure no one can use Telnet to connect to a certain host, the Telnet service should be disabled.

Although Telnet is a basic utility of TCP/IP communications, its use has been discouraged in favor of more secure methods of remote access, such as SSH.

SSH (Secure Shell)

Just like the Telnet utility, SSH enables a user to log in to a remote machine and execute commands as if they were on the console of that system. Telnet, however, is insecure because its data isn't encrypted when communicated. SSH provides a secure, encrypted tunnel to access another system remotely. When a client connects to a system using SSH, an initial handshaking process begins and a special session key is exchanged. This begins the session, and an encrypted secure channel is created to allow the access. SSH can also be used in conjunction with other protocols such as FTP to encrypt file transfer communications.

Exam Tip	
SSH uses TCP port 22.	

FTP

The *File Transfer Protocol (FTP)* is used to upload files from a workstation to an FTP server or to download files from an FTP server to a workstation. By using an FTP application, you can transfer files from one Internet system to another.

A server hosting files runs an FTP server service that awaits file transfer requests originating from clients using FTP client software. Many FTP server sites on the Internet are public in nature and allow anonymous users to log in and download or upload files to their system. Other companies use authenticated FTP servers to enable clients to download engineering or technical support files. To access the server, the client needs to authenticate using a login and password. FTP servers are a widely used resource on the Internet and one of the most popular servers for hacking attempts and abuse.

The main security vulnerability of FTP is that any information passed is in clear, unencrypted text, including the logon information. This means a hacker monitoring the system with some type of packet sniffer can clearly read your login user name and password. Secure FTP (SFTP) is a program that uses Secure Shell (SSH) to transfer files. Unlike the original FTP, it can encrypt both commands and data, so it can't be captured by a packet sniffer.

Exam Tip	
FTP uses TCP port 20 for data transfer and port 21 for connection control information.	

TFTP

The Trivial File Transfer Protocol is a very basic FTP protocol. TFTP is connectionless and uses UDP port 69. Its use is limited to basic network file transfer operations, and it is often utilized for simple purposes such as a boot loader for booting a device over a network.

TFTP transmits in clear text and also has no encryption or authentication features. This limits its use to basic, low-security applications.

FTPS and SFTP

Basic types of FTP communications are not encrypted, so any login and password information is sent over the network in clear text and can be easily intercepted by a malicious hacker. FTPS (FTP Secure or FTP-SSL) software uses encrypted TLS/SSL communications to prevent interception by unauthorized users. You can also utilize SFTP, which is used to encrypt FTP sessions with SSH (Secure Shell).

> **Exam Tip**
>
> Remember that basic FTP communications, including login and password authentication, are transmitted in clear text. FTPS (TCP ports 989 and 990) or SFTP (TCP port 22) should be used to encrypt the session.

> **Travel Advisory**
>
> Do not confuse FTPS (which uses TSL/SSL) with SFTP, which uses the Secure Shell (SSH) to create an FTP tunnel through an SSH connection.

SCP

A related protocol for file transfers is Secure Copy (SCP), a utility that secures file copy operations (RCP) over SSH. SCP is often used as an alternative to SFTP when copying files from one system to another; however, SFTP is preferred because it has more comprehensive features and options than just a simple file copy operation.

> **Exam Tip**
>
> SCP uses SSH TCP port 22.

DNS

The Domain Name Service (DNS) provides a way to translate Internet domain names into IP addresses. For example, the web site www.example.com can be translated to an IP address of 192.168.1.12. This allows network applications and services to refer to Internet domains by their fully qualified domain name (FQDN) rather than their IP address, which can be difficult to remember and can often change. If a company changes its system's IP address, it can simply update the DNS tables to reflect this. External users will not see a difference because they will still be connecting to it by name.

DNS servers perform an extremely valuable function on the Internet, and wide-scale communication interruptions can occur if a network DNS server is disabled. Most client machines use DNS each time they try to connect to a network host. The client's DNS server is configured using its network settings, which can be set manually or automatically through services such as DHCP. Each time a client tries to access a host, such as a web site, the local DNS server is queried for the IP address of the domain name. The DNS server translates the name into an IP address, which the client uses to initiate its connection.

DNS servers can suffer from denial-of-service and malformed request attacks. In a DoS attack, the DNS server is inundated with DNS or ping requests. The load becomes so much that the DNS server cannot respond to legitimate DNS queries. DNS queries to servers can also be manipulated to include malformed input that could crash the server. Ensure that your DNS software is the latest version, with the most recent security patches installed, to prevent these types of attacks.

Exam Tip	
DNS uses TCP and UDP port 53.	

SNMP

The *Simple Network Management Protocol (SNMP)* allows you to use network monitoring programs to analyze diagnostic information on network devices. An SNMP agent service runs on the network device, which is accessed by a network monitoring tool. The SNMP agent provides real-time statistics on the device, such as device status, CPU, memory usage, and network activity.

The information available from the SNMP agent is organized into objects that are described by a MIB (management information base) file. Each hardware vendor typically provides its own MIB file unique to the device, which can then be imported into the network monitoring tool.

SNMP has very basic security that makes use of a type of password system called *community strings,* which are simple passphrases for SNMP to access each device. Most administrators leave the default community string *public* as is, but this opens up a vulnerability because anyone knowing the community string can connect to the SNMP-enabled device. SNMP passwords should be immediately changed from the default if set up on the switch.

You can also use an access control list to limit SNMP access to the specific IP address of your network monitoring system.

Exam Tip
SNMP uses UDP port 161. SNMP traps use UDP port 162.

IPsec

IPsec (IP Security) is a standards-based method of providing privacy, integrity, and authenticity to information transferred across IP networks. IPsec works on the IP layer to encrypt communications between the sender and the receiver. It is most often used to secure VPN communications over an open network, such as the Internet.

Travel Assistance
IPsec and its encryption methods are described in more detail in Chapter 4.

NetBIOS

NetBIOS (Network Basic Input/Output System) is a local area network (LAN) protocol originally created by IBM but widely adopted by the Microsoft Windows platform. NetBIOS is not routable outside of a local area network and must be used with NetBIOS over TCP/IP name mappings to allow Windows-based LAN computers to communicate with TCP/IP-based networks.

NetBIOS is considered a very insecure protocol and is usually blocked from transmitting beyond the local area network to limit its services to local Microsoft Windows clients.

Exam Tip
NetBIOS uses TCP ports 137, 138, and 139.

Identify Commonly Used Default Network Ports

One of the most overlooked problems with securing network activity is that of unknown ports, services, and protocols running on a system. For example, a simple file server might be set up for file sharing, but the server might also be running software such as a web service, the File Transfer Protocol (FTP) service, and the Simple Mail Transfer Protocol (SMTP) service. Although these running services might not be used on your system, they could create security vulnerabilities because unauthorized users can still connect to the file server using their protocols and ports. By compromising the vulnerabilities inherent in those services, malicious hackers might be able to gain access to the files on that system, bypassing any authentication or access control.

Unfortunately, many operating systems install some of these services by default. For example, someone setting up a Microsoft Windows server might want to use it only for file sharing, but installing the OS using the standard default configuration could lead to the system also installing a web server or other Internet services by default. When installing server OS software, you must ensure that you install only the services and protocols you need for the purposes of that system. Deselect or disable any other services that would be installed by default during the installation process.

> **Travel Advisory**
>
> When installing OS and application software, use a custom installation method that enables you to pick and choose which services you want to run. Running the default installation could install a number of programs and services you do not need. The bottom line is, the more software running on your systems, the more vulnerabilities that exist.

Before pinpointing a system or network for attack, malicious users often perform *ping sweeps* in which the ICMP Ping utility is used to find a valid range of IP addresses to attack on the network. A ping sweep performs a quick ping of all the devices in a certain IP address range, and if those devices respond to the ping request, the utility logs the address so that the user can then perform more detailed scanning on that address. After the valid IP addresses are found, an unauthorized user can try to find open security holes in a specific system or network using special types of software called *port scanners* that will analyze a system for every service and protocol it is currently using. This is accomplished by looking for open service ports listening for requests.

TCP/IP Network Ports

A TCP/IP port is a special numerical port used by a particular service. For example, HTTP web servers use port 80 by default for web surfing. Other services, such as the Domain Name System (DNS) and Post Office Protocol 3 (POP3), use ports 53 and 110, respectively. These services are usually waiting for a request, such as a Dynamic Host Configuration Protocol (DHCP) server waiting for a client request for a new IP address. By scanning these ports, a malicious hacker can determine what types of software and services are running on the server. From there, he can use that information to employ other methods for compromising the security of those services because of software bugs or security vulnerabilities that have not been fixed.

> **Exam Tip**
>
> A port scanner can be used to analyze a system for open TCP/IP ports. For example, a web server that also runs SMTP might show port 80 and port 25 as open and waiting for connections. The port scanner can run through an entire port range looking for common open services.

To protect your systems, the administrator should examine each server carefully and ensure it is running only services and protocols required for its specific function. Any other services should be disabled or uninstalled. In addition, any current services that are required should be examined to ensure that all systems are using the latest versions of the software with the most recent security patches installed. On a Windows system, for example, the administrator can run the *netstat* command to view any ports on the system listening for requests.

> **Exam Tip**
>
> Know the port numbers of some of the most common protocols and services.

The administrator can run a port scanner on her own system to discover whether any open ports and services are listening for requests. Table 9-1 lists the most common, well-known protocols and services and their corresponding TCP/IP ports.

Travel Assistance

See www.iana.org/assignments/port-numbers for a full list of network ports assigned by the Internet Assigned Numbers Authority (IANA).

Travel Advisory

Many service ports also listen on the User Datagram Protocol (UDP) as well as TCP. For example, DNS uses TCP port 53 for zone transfers and UDP port 53 for DNS queries.

TABLE 9.1   Well-Known TCP/IP Services and Port Numbers

Service	TCP/IP Port Number
DNS	53
FTP (Data)	20
FTP (Control)	21
HTTP	80
HTTPS	443
IMAP (Internet Message Access Protocol)	143
LDAP (Lightweight Directory Access Protocol)	389
NetBIOS	137–139
NTP (Network Time Protocol)	123
POP3	110
SMTP	25
SNMP (Simple Network Management Protocol)	161, 162
SSH (Secure Shell)	22
Telnet	23

Objective 9.03
CompTIA Security+
Objective 3.2

Analyze and Differentiate among Types of Network Attacks

Many of the types of attacks that can assault a network and computer system are geared toward specific system accounts, system services, or applications. The most damaging and, obviously, the most popular attacks by hackers involve disrupting the network itself. Because the network is the infrastructure that allows all systems and devices to communicate, disrupting those communication lines can be the most damaging attack a network can suffer.

The following sections outline some popular types of network-based attacks that have been used to intercept or disrupt communications and describe how to prevent them.

Exam Tip

Know these different types of network-based attacks and how to prevent them.

Denial of Service

Denial-of-service (DoS) attacks are well known for their ability to deny access to a particular web or Internet site, but DoS attacks can be launched against any type of network or system. In a DoS attack, a hacker overloads a specific server with so much data that the server is too busy to service valid requests coming from real clients on the network. System performance slows to a crawl. This affects a web site's ability to service legitimate requests because the client will not receive responses to queries. This type of attack can also be performed on entire networks, as the DoS is targeted at the central router or firewall where all data passes through. The network traffic becomes so high that nothing can get in or out of the network. The DoS attack is more serious than a single-server attack because network bandwidth is being compromised, which effectively denies access to all systems on that network rather than just one.

Distributed Denial of Service

In a more organized and devastating attack, a *distributed denial of service (DDoS)*, the flood of data originates from multiple hosts simultaneously. The combined effects quickly overload any server or network device. As opposed to a

DoS attack with a single origin, with a DDoS, a network administrator cannot pinpoint and deny access by one host because the attacks come from multiple hosts distributed throughout the Internet. Usually, these originating hosts are not willfully engaged in the attack. Malicious hackers can secretly install software on an insecure server somewhere else on the Internet and use that remotely to flood another host with data. This effectively hides the true origin of the attack, especially when the IP addresses are spoofed to show different originating addresses than those actually used in the attack.

Ping Attack

The most common form of attack uses simple TCP/IP utilities, such as *ping,* the command used to determine whether a certain host (classified as the destination host) is functioning and communicating with the network. A user sends a ping or query packet to the destination host. The destination host sends back a reply that it is indeed working and on the network. In a DoS attack, a malicious user can send a continuous stream of rapid ping attempts, called a "ping of death." The host is then overloaded by having to reply to every ping, rendering it unable to process legitimate requests.

SYN Flood

Another type of DoS attack is the *synchronous (SYN) flood.* SYN is an aspect of TCP/IP that allows systems to synchronize with each other while communicating. One system sends a SYN packet that is acknowledged by another system. The target system then waits for another acknowledgment from the sender.

This process can be abused by a malicious hacker by sending forged SYN packets to a host that is unable to reply to the request because the return address is incorrect. This causes the host to halt communications while waiting for the other system to reply. If the host is flooded with a high number of forged SYN packets, it will be overloaded and unable to respond to legitimate requests.

DoS attacks can be difficult to stop and prevent, but some simple configuration changes on the local routers and firewalls can help prevent them. The simplest way of protecting against ping flood types of attacks is to disable ICMP at the firewall or router level, so the host will not acknowledge any ping attempts from outside the network.

Travel Advisory

Turning off ICMP can deprive you of important feedback from network troubleshooting tools, because commands such as ping and traceroute use ICMP to function and can provide important network diagnostics information.

Other types of attacks, including SYN floods, are caused by vulnerabilities in the network protocols themselves. Make sure your OS is updated to the latest version by installing any recent service packs and security patches. This ensures that your underlying network protocols do not have any unresolved security issues.

Flood Protection

Some firewalls and other security products can also actively detect network flood attacks, actively block them and reclaim TCP resources used by the attack, and even try to trace them back to a source. Flood guard defenses can also prevent attacks based on multiple attempts to log in to a network device that can use up valuable networking resources.

Back Door

A *back door* is traditionally defined as a way for a software programmer to access a program while bypassing its authentication schemes. The back door is coded in by the programmer during development so that at a later time she can break into her own program without having to authenticate to the system through normal access methods. This is helpful to programmers because they need not access the program as they normally would in a typical user mode (where they would be forced to enter authentication information, such as a user name and password).

In hacking terms, a back door is a program secretly installed on an unsuspecting user's computer so that the hacker can later access the user's computer, bypassing any security authentication systems. This can also be an unauthorized account that is created on the system that the unauthorized user can access at a later time. The back-door program runs as a service on the user's computer and listens on specific network ports not typically used by traditional network services. The hacker runs the client portion of the program on his computer, which then connects to the service on the target computer. Once the connection is established, the hacker can gain full access, including remotely controlling the system. Hackers usually do not know what specific systems are running the back door, but their programs can scan a network's IP addresses to see which ones are listening to the specific port for that back door.

Back-door software is typically installed as a Trojan horse as part of some other software package. A user might download a program from the Internet that contains the hidden back-door software. Antivirus programs can detect the presence of back-door programs. Personal firewalls can also detect suspicious incoming and outgoing network traffic from a computer. Port-scanning software can also be used to identify any open ports on the system, including those you do not recognize. These open ports can be cross-referenced with lists of ports used by known back-door programs.

NULL Sessions

NULL sessions are a type of attack on Windows-based servers in which weaknesses in the NetBIOS networking protocol are exploited to allow a user to create an unauthenticated connection with a Windows server. NetBIOS allows these unauthenticated connections to permit users and devices to browse the Windows network. To the Windows system, the user appears as an anonymous user; however, a malicious user can use a low-level remote procedure call (RPC) and other probing utilities in an attempt to glean information on services running on the system, attempt privilege escalation, or access user account and passwords information. Worms have also been known to spread via RPCs in NULL sessions.

Simple registry and access permissions settings allow administrators to prevent anonymous NULL session connections and enforce authenticated access for non–system service–related access. Newer versions of Windows are not generally vulnerable to the risk of NULL session exploitation via default configuration parameters, but older versions of Windows such as Windows 2000 and NT still have these vulnerabilities.

Spoofing

One of the more popular methods for hacking a system is *spoofing* network addresses, which involves modifying the header of a network packet to use the source address of an external or internal host that differs from the original address. By spoofing the IP address, the hacker can fool the destination host into thinking the message is from a trusted source. The cause of this problem is that the architecture of TCP/IP has no built-in mechanism to verify the source and destination IP addresses of its network packets. A hacker can spoof the IP address to make it look as though it is coming from a different location—in fact, it can even be made to look like the IP address of an internal system.

IP spoofing is mainly used by malicious hackers to hide their identity when attacking a network system, especially in a DoS-type attack. By spoofing the IP addresses of the incoming packets, hackers may make it difficult for network administrators to determine the real source of the attacks before they can set up a filter to block out that IP address.

Another use for spoofing is to emulate a trusted internal system on the network. For example, if a local server has an IP address of 192.168.17.5, and it accepts only connections from that network, a malicious hacker can modify the source address of the packet to mimic an internal address, such as 192.168.17.12. This way, the server thinks the packets are coming from an internal trusted host, not a system external to the network, as shown in Figure 9.1.

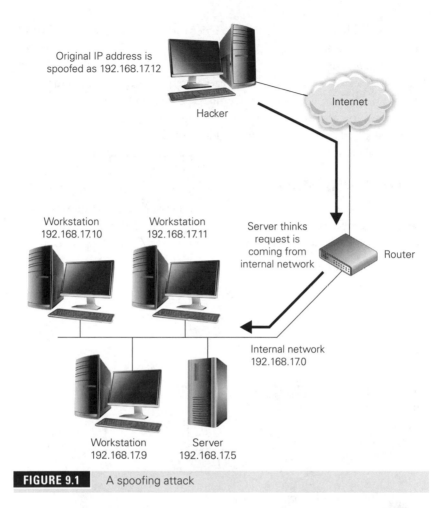

Original IP address is
spoofed as 192.168.17.12

Hacker

Internet

Workstation
192.168.17.10

Workstation
192.168.17.11

Server thinks
request is
coming from
internal network

Router

Internal network
192.168.17.0

Workstation
192.168.17.9

Server
192.168.17.5

FIGURE 9.1   A spoofing attack

To help prevent spoofing attacks, your router or firewall might be able to filter incoming traffic to restrict network traffic coming into the external interface. By configuring the filter to prevent external packets originating from internal addresses, you prevent spoofed addresses from entering the network.

Smurf Attack

A *smurf* attack uses a spoof attack combined with a DDoS attack to exploit the use of IP broadcast addressing and ICMP. ICMP is used by networks and through administrative utilities to exchange information about the state of the network. It is used by the Ping utility to contact other systems to determine whether they are operational. The destination system returns an echo message in response to a ping message.

A hacker uses a smurf utility to build a network packet with a spoofed IP address that contains an ICMP ping message addressed to an IP broadcast address. A *broadcast address* includes all nodes of a certain network, and messages to that address will be seen by all of them. The ping echo responses are sent back to the target address. The amount of pings and echo responses can flood the network with traffic, causing systems on the network to be unresponsive, as shown in Figure 9.2. To prevent smurf attacks, IP broadcast addressing should be disabled on the network router, because this broadcast addressing is used only rarely.

TCP/IP Hijacking

An unauthorized user can effectively *hijack* a network connection of another user. For example, by monitoring a network transmission, an attacker can analyze the source and destination IP addresses of the two computers. When the at-

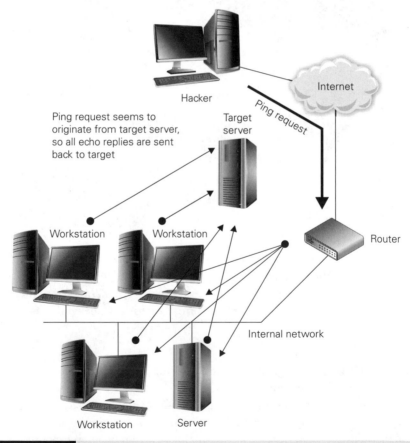

FIGURE 9.2 A smurf attack

tacker discovers the IP address of one of the participants, she can knock him off his connections using a DoS or other type of attack, and then resume communications by spoofing the IP address of the disconnected user. The other user is tricked into thinking he is still communicating with the original sender. The only real way to prevent this sort of attack from occurring is installing some sort of encryption mechanism, such as IPsec.

Man-in-the-Middle

A *man-in-the-middle* attack occurs when a person uses a packet sniffer between the sender and the receiver of a communication on the network and intercepts or listens in on the information being transferred, modifying its contents before resending the data to its destination. These types of attacks usually occur when a network communications line is compromised through the installation of a network packet sniffer, which can analyze network communications packet by packet. Many types of communications use plain, clear text, and this can be easily read by someone using a packet sniffer. During an encrypted communication, a hacker can intercept the authentication phase of a transmission and obtain the public encryption keys of the participants, as shown in Figure 9.3.

To prevent man-in-the-middle attacks, a unique server host key can be used to prove its identity to a client as a known host. This has been implemented in newer versions of the SSH protocol, which was vulnerable to man-in-the-middle attacks in the past.

Replay

A *replay* attack occurs when an unauthorized user captures network traffic and then sends the communication to its original destination, acting as the original sender, as shown in Figure 9.4.

Hacker intercepts SSH
encryption host keys and
impersonates the client
and server, or just listens in

Fake
server

Fake
client

SSH

SSH

Hacker
man-in-the-middle

Client

Server

FIGURE 9.3   A man-in-the-middle attack

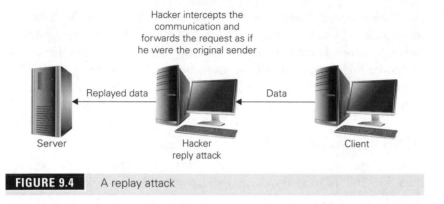

Hacker intercepts the
communication and
forwards the request as if
he were the original sender

Replayed data   Data

Server   Hacker   Client
                 reply attack

FIGURE 9.4   A replay attack

To prevent replay attacks from succeeding, timestamps or sequence numbers can be implemented. This allows the authentication system to accept only network packets that contain the appropriate stamp or sequence number. If the timestamp is beyond a certain threshold, the packet is discarded.

Xmas Attack

An *Xmas* network port scan sends a network request to a system with many nonstandard TCP options enabled to look for active and listening TCP ports. This type of network scan sometimes evades detection by a firewall or network intrusion detection system (NIDS) because it uses nonstandard scanning options. It can also identify operating systems based on their response to these nonstandard options. It is referred to as a Christmas (Xmas) attack because all the enabled options in the network frame are like the lights of a Christmas tree to the scanned device, which responds to these requests (or does not reply, which can also indicate certain characteristics of the device).

DNS Poisoning

The *DNS poisoning* technique takes advantage of a DNS server's tables of IP addresses and host names by replacing the IP address of a host with another IP address that resolves to an attacker's system. For example, a malicious user can masquerade her own web server by poisoning the DNS server into thinking that the host name of the legitimate web server resolves to the IP address of the rogue web server. The attacker can then spread spyware, worms, and other types of malware to clients connecting to her web server. This type of attack has a great potential for damage, as several thousand clients can be using the DNS server or its cache of IP addresses and host names, and all of them will be redirected to the poisoned address in the DNS cache tables.

The malicious attacker can perform this attack by exploiting vulnerabilities in a DNS server that does not perform authentication or any type of checks to ensure the DNS information is coming from an authentic source. This information can be passed from one DNS server to another, almost like a worm, and the rogue address can be quickly spread.

DNS poisoning attacks can be mitigated by ensuring that your DNS server updates its information only from authoritative sources by proper authentication or the use of secure communications. Most DNS software has been updated to prevent these types of attacks, and typically only out-of-date DNS software is vulnerable to DNS poisoning.

ARP Poisoning

ARP (Address Resolution Protocol) poisoning is a type of network attack technique in which the ARP cache of systems on the network is modified to point to an IP address with the Media Access Control (MAC) address of an unauthorized user. ARP is used by systems on a network to associate an IP address of a system with its hardware MAC address. The attacker sends spoofed ARP messages to the network and masquerades as another system so that returned network packets will go to the attacker's system and not its original destination. The malicious user can then modify the data in transit or modify the routing information to use the data as a DoS attack against a router.

ARP poisoning and spoofing can be mitigated by using DHCP or other network services that help network clients keep track of the MAC address of connecting systems to detect receipt of an ARP that does not resolve properly. Physical access to the network should also be controlled by disabling unused ports on network switches and hubs and using port security to limit who can connect to the enabled ports.

Domain Kiting

Domain kiting refers to the practice of registering a domain name, then deleting the registration after the five-day grace period, and then re-registering it to start another five-day grace period. This results in the domain being registered to the user without his having to pay for the registered domain.

The central authority for domain registrations, the Internet Corporation for Assigned Names and Numbers (ICANN), allows a five-day grace period before the registrar has to pay for a new domain registration. This helps prevent mistaken domain registrations, typos, copyright infringements, and other issues related to domain name registration.

Some unscrupulous domain *registrars,* the organizations that register domains on a user's behalf, take advantage of the five-day grace period by deleting the registration before the end of the grace period. The domain is then immediately re-registered to allow the registrar to register a domain name indefinitely without actually having to pay for it.

Malicious users or registrars have also been known to do this with recently released domains that have not been renewed (either purposely or accidentally) and effectively own the domain with no chance for the previous owner or a new owner interested in the domain name to officially register it.

A similar practice, called *domain tasting,* utilizes this five-day grace period to test certain domains to track the amount of traffic they receive. These domains' names often use common misspellings or popular web site domain names. The domains that receive the most traffic are re-registered every five days to take advantage of the grace period and continue to generate advertising revenue for a domain that has never been paid for. These practices are often performed using fraudulent user names and addresses of domain registrars, and a single registrar can perform this with hundreds of thousands of domain names.

Legal domain registrars and other Internet advocacy groups have been working with ICANN to try to find a way to curb this activity by forcing fees for every registration and have obtained the support of Internet advertising companies who have started blocking kited domains.

Network administrators with several domains under their control must be wary of their domains and their expiry dates to ensure they are properly registered and renewed each time they are close to expiry to prevent the domains from being stolen by another individual or registrar. Many legitimate registrars offer several security features to prevent domain names from being transferred or renewed by a third party.

Objective 9.04
CompTIA Security+
Objective 1.2

Apply and Implement Secure Network Administration Principles

Securing your network not only requires the use of specific network devices, but also their proper deployment and configuration. The ability of your network devices to provide network border security and prevent inbound threats is greatly diminished if they are not properly set up in a secure manner. The following sections describe how to implement basic secure network administration principles.

Networking Device Configuration

Several key devices within your network can be configured to increase security against attacks and unauthorized intrusion. These devices are your first line of defense, and it is vital that they be secured through proper configuration and management. Your primary networking equipment includes the firewall, routers, and switches.

> **Travel Assistance**
>
> See Chapter 8 for a detailed description of these network security devices and their secure deployment.

The firewall is a barrier on your network border that protects your internal networks from external networks such as the Internet. In its default configuration, a firewall will block any and all network traffic. This is the best practice of *implicit deny,* meaning that anything that is not explicitly defined in an access rule is denied. This denies all access by default until you apply access rules for only the specific services required. This way, you start off with the strongest base security policy for your firewall configuration, and slowly add rules to allow access as required.

To configure the firewall, you must set up a number of rules to allow incoming and outgoing network communications for specific ports and protocols. These rules can be general or specific. For example, a firewall can be configured with a rule that states that any HTTP traffic can come and go on a specific network. It can also be much more detailed and state that an SMTP packet destined for a particular mail server can come only from a specific host IP address.

> **Travel Advisory**
>
> Documenting the rules applied to the firewall and why you are implementing them is important. When auditing these at a later date, you might find you are allowing access to services that do not exist anymore and the rules can be removed.

A firewall can be an independent hardware device or a software application running on a computer or server. In either case, the firewall software should always be kept current with the latest versions and patches. This will ensure you are using the most recent software that does not contain known software bugs and security vulnerabilities.

A router connects several networks together and relays data between them, while a switch segments these networks into smaller, more manageable sections and relays packets between these segments. These devices help prevent network traffic from bridging over unnecessarily to another network by separating the networks physically and also logically with software (such as with VLANs) to prevent insecure cross-network access or broadcast chatter.

After the network firewall, these devices form the backbone of your network, and their security is critical to make sure your entire network is secure from intrusion and is not vulnerable to network attacks that can slow down or completely stop network communications.

ACL Rules

Most network device software contains includes packet filtering and ACLs (access control lists) that let you carefully control the protocols, services, ports, and source and destination of the information that flows through the device. For example, you can configure a device to accept only FTP communications to a certain network.

ACLs are used by network devices to control traffic in and out of your network. They can be general in nature or specific to certain types of communications. *Access lists* are typically used in firewalls to control communications between public and private networks, but they can also be used on internal routers and switches to regulate traffic within the network. An access list entry that is contained inside the ACL usually includes the origin of the network packet, the destination, the protocol used (TCP or UDP), the TCP/IP port used, and whether access is allowed or denied.

The following types of parameters can be controlled using an access list:

- **Source address** Specifies the originating source IP address of a packet, whether an internal or external machine or an internal address that it proxies to an external address.
- **Destination address** Specifies the IP address where the packet is going, which can be internal or external to the network.
- **Port numbers** Specifies the TCP/IP port number the communication is using. Each type of TCP/IP service uses a standard port.
- **Protocol** Identifies the protocol being used in the transmission, such as FTP, HTTP, or DHCP, and is usually used in conjunction with a port number that's standard to that protocol or service. This parameter can also be used to define whether the protocol is using TCP or UDP.
- **Permit or deny** Permits or denies the communication specified in the access list entry.

The following is an example of code for an ACL entry for a router:

```
permit source 192.168.13.2 destination 10.1.5.25 tcp port 80
```

The syntax used by your network device will be similar to this entry but varies from vendor to vendor. In this example, the ACL entry permits TCP traffic on port 80 (the default port for HTTP) from a host 192.168.13.2 to a host on network 10.1.5.25. The destination might be some type of secured web server that needs to be accessed from a web browser client on the source host. This prevents any other system—internal or external—from connecting to that web server, as shown in Figure 9.5.

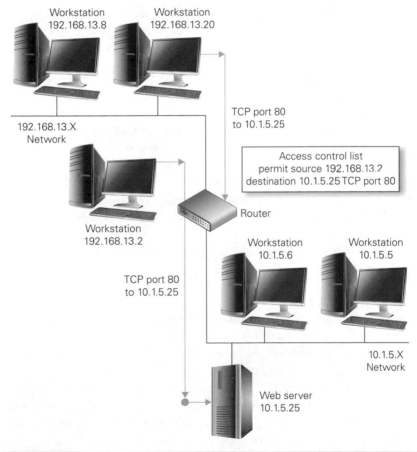

Access control lists prevent other systems from connecting to a web server.

Port and MAC Address Security   Most network devices allow you to secure the device right down to the port level. For example, a network switch might have 24 port connections that connect your client workstations. You can configure the switch to only allow certain devices to use specific ports, and even disable ports that aren't in use to prevent an unauthorized user from simply plugging his device into the port.

You can also configure network devices to accept only data from specific MAC address ranges, which limits access to the switch or port based on the hardware address of the connecting client.

Network Device Threats and Risks

Several weaknesses can be exploited and threats can compromise devices on your network, including weak passwords and account security, software and firmware vulnerabilities that lead to unauthorized access, and direct network attacks on the device itself.

Weak Passwords

Like servers and workstations, network devices control access via login credentials, and it is critical that the accounts and passwords used are secure. Passwords to critical network devices must be very strong to prevent unauthorized users from connecting to the device and attempting to log in and guess the password or use some other brute-force method. Select a "strong" password that is at minimum eight characters in length and that includes both uppercase and lowercase characters, numbers, and special characters such as the @ symbol. Passwords should never be written down. If necessary, password and account information can be stored on an encrypted USB key and stored in a locked safe only accessible to authorized users.

Default Accounts

Most network devices have a preinstalled default administrative account, usually called *admin* or *administrator*. Because an unauthorized user can easily guess this account name and use it to try to log in to the device, you should disable this account and create another account with administrative rights and with an account name that does not represent its function. If your team consists of several administrators, you might use their names or other identifying information to help audit access and configuration changes to the device. Any Guest accounts or other accounts with diminished access rights should also be disabled.

Transitive Access and Privilege Escalation

Transitive access refers to elevated access permissions that have been passed on to another user. It is possible that through misconfiguration of your network device access rules, you inadvertently allow access to users based on access rules that are too wide in scope and so allow transitive access. For example, you may create an access rule that allows network access to a specific web server, but because the rule is general and not well defined, you've allowed access to all TCP/IP ports and protocols for that host, when all that was required was HTTP port 80. Make sure that when you create access rules and permissions, they only allow what is required for the specific service, right down to the TCP/IP port and protocol, and between specific source and destination IP addresses.

Another aspect of unauthorized access is privilege escalation. *Privilege escalation* refers to the practice of exploiting coding bugs that exist within software. In certain situations, it can be possible for an unauthorized user to gain more privileged access to a network device by taking advantage of the bug exploit to bypass the device security and perform commands with higher-privileged access than expected.

Vulnerabilities that typically lead to privilege escalation scenarios are most often found as buffer overflow attacks, where conditions and boundaries are not properly checked on user-entered fields in a network device's firmware or operating system and allow highly privileged command execution. In the event that a documented exploit is found in a network device firmware or OS, a patch must be installed (if available) to fix the bug to prevent proof-of-concept exploits from turning into real security threats. You must be diligent in making sure the network device software is running the latest patch level so that all known bug fixes are deployed.

Network Loops

A *network loop* occurs when there is more than one network path between two network hosts. For example, a user might accidentally connect two ports on a network switch together, or improperly connect two network switches together. The confused switch starts broadcasting on all ports and eventually floods the network because the broadcasts are constantly looping.

Many network devices now come with loop protection to detect these scenarios and take active measures to isolate the looped ports and prevent the broadcasts from bringing down the network.

Network Device Hardening

One of the most important steps in securing your network and systems is to make sure that the devices that form the infrastructure of your network are examined for security vulnerabilities. Several aspects of networking devices can create a number of security holes if not properly examined or configured, including firmware, configuration, and log files.

Secure Remote Access

Most network devices can be configured remotely over the network. However, this creates a security vulnerability if the method used to remotely configure the device is not properly authenticated or secure. If possible, insecure remote access methods, such as the use of Telnet or basic HTTP to connect to device, should be disabled. This will prevent users from accessing the device, unless they use secure methods such as SSH or HTTPS, or are physically attached to the device with a network cable. For deeper security, enable access only for the IP address of the client from which you are connecting.

Disable Unused Services

The administrator must examine the configuration settings of a network device after installation to make sure that the default configuration is suitable for the network's security needs. The administrator should enable secure settings and disable any options or services that are not required by the current deployment.

Optional services can create security vulnerabilities. For example, in many network devices, SNMP is enabled by default to allow the device to be examined by network monitoring equipment. But SNMP has been known to contain a number of security vulnerabilities and sends its data in clear text, so disabling its use is best. SNMP also makes use of a type of password system called *community strings,* which are used as simple passphrases for SNMP to access each device. Most administrators leave the default community string *public* as is, but this opens up a vulnerability because anyone knowing the community string can connect to the SNMP-enabled device. SNMP passwords should be immediately changed from the default if set up on the device.

> ### Exam Tip
>
> Remember that SNMP has been known to contain many security vulnerabilities and should be disabled if it is not required, as it is often enabled by default on network devices. The default public community name string should be changed when SNMP is installed.

Another protocol used for network diagnostics, ICMP, is used by utilities such as Ping and Traceroute. Enabling ICMP leaves the network device open to DoS attacks that can quickly disable a router and cut off the communications flow for your network. ICMP can also be used for identification of systems that are live and accepting connections, which can lead to them being attacked. If you do not require the ICMP service, it should be disabled.

Firmware/OS Updates

Firmware is software that controls the functions of the network device—like a device OS. Firmware is typically encoded in flash memory and can be updated just like any other software application by obtaining a newer version of the release and then installing it into the device's flash memory.

Like any other OS or application software, the system should be running the most recent versions with the latest security and bug-fix patches installed. Some firmware updates also include additional security functionality that was not in previous versions. For network devices such as firewalls and routers that form the first line of defense in network security, you should regularly update the firmware or operating system to maintain maximum security.

Log Files

You should examine the log files from your network devices on a periodic basis to check for any system or security issues. The logs for your network devices will be very large, as they log all activity of connections that are passed into your network or blocked. It is useful to filter the logs to blocked connections to see if there is any pattern to known network attacks that you can see. Examine the logs to look for any anomalies that can indicate a security issue such as a hacking attempt or unauthorized configuration change.

CHECKPOINT

✔**Objective 9.01: Implement and use common protocols.** Understand the basic protocols such as TCP/IP, ICMP, HTTP/S, Telnet, SSH, FTP/SFTP/ FTPS, SCP, DNS, SNMP, IPsec, and NetBIOS to understand how they communicate and their security vulnerabilities.

✔**Objective 9.02: Identify commonly used default network ports.** To protect your systems, the administrator should examine each server carefully and ensure it is running only services and protocols required for its specific function. Well-known protocols and ports include HTTP (80), HTTPS (443), Telnet (23), SSH (22), FTP (20,21), DNS (53), SNMP (161, 162), NetBIOS (137–139), SMTP (25), POP3 (110), IMAP (143), LDAP (389), and NTP (123).

✔**Objective 9.03: Analyze and differentiate among types of attacks.** Understand and know how to prevent the different types of network attacks such as denial-of-service attacks, ping and SYN floods, back door, null sessions, spoofing, Smurf attacks, hijacking, man-in-the-middle, replay, Xmas attacks, DNS and ARP poisoning, and domain kiting.

✔**Objective 9.04: Apply and implement secure network administration principles.**   Several weaknesses and threats can compromise the devices on your network, such as firewalls, routers, and switches. These threats include weak password and account security, software and firmware vulnerabilities that lead to unauthorized access and direct network attacks, such as denial-of-service attacks, on the device itself. Use access control lists to control traffic into and out of your devices.

REVIEW QUESTIONS

1. You need to set up a secure FTP server to allow your company's clients to upload their files. Which of the following FTP protocols would you use?

   A. SFTP

   B. FTP

   C. TFTP

   D. FTP over HTTP

2. You want to secure one of your network switch segments to only allow access from specific clients on the development network. Which of the following should you implement?

   A. Use a VPN for the development network.

   B. Create a firewall rule to restrict access to the switch ports.

   C. Create a VLAN for the entire development network.

   D. Restrict the switch port access to the MAC addresses of the clients.

3. You need to secure one of your routers (IP address 10.1.5.25) to prevent access to the SNMP port. On your firewall, which of the following access rules will block SNMP access to the router?

   A. permit 10.1.5.25 udp port 53

   B. deny 10.1.5.25 tcp port 143

   C. deny 10.1.5.25 udp port 161

   D. permit 10.1.5.25 udp port 389

4. It is discovered that your primary router has a serious software vulnerability that makes it susceptible to denial-of-service attacks. What should you do to resolve the issue?

   A. Disable SNMP.

   B. Disable ICMP.

   C. Enable flood protection.

   D. Update the firmware.

5. Your web server is being flooded by a denial-of-service attack. Using a network analyzer, you see that there are IP broadcast replies being sent back to the address of your server from multiple addresses. Which type of network attack is this?

A. Man-in-the-middle

B. Back door

C. Smurf

D. DNS poisoning

6. When creating firewall rules, which of the following principles should be applied to maximize security by blocking all traffic and only allowing access as required?

A. Implicit deny

B. Explicit deny

C. Unauthenticated deny

D. Denial of service

7. During a denial-of-service attack, a network administrator blocks the source IP with the firewall, but the attack continues. What is the most likely cause of the problem?

A. The denial-of-service worm has already infected the firewall locally.

B. The attack is coming from multiple, distributed hosts.

C. A firewall can't block denial-of-service attacks.

D. Antivirus software needs to be installed.

8. You have just performed a security port scan on your e-mail server. Which of the following services and ports that appeared in the test as open and accepting connections should be disabled?

A. TCP port 21

B. TCP port 25

C. TCP port 110

D. TCP port 143

9. Your network router has the ability to be remotely configured through a web browser. Which of the following would be the most secure method for remote access?

A. FTP over HTTP connection

B. HTTP connection

C. Telnet

D. HTTPS connection

10. You have just installed a new SNMP monitoring system for all your network devices. Which of the following should you do to enhance security for the implementation?

    A. Change the password of the network monitor.

    B. Disable SNMP access on all inbound network ports.

    C. Change the default SMTP community string.

    D. Enable ICMP.

REVIEW ANSWERS

1. **A** SFTP is used to encrypt FTP sessions with SSH (Secure Shell). The other methods such as FTP, TFTP, or FTP over HTTP are not secure and communicate in clear text.

2. **D** You should enable MAC address security on your switch ports to only allow the hardware addresses of the specific clients on the development network to access those ports.

3. **C** The access rule should be set to deny the SNMP UDP port 161 for the specified IP address.

4. **D** In the event that a documented vulnerability is found in a network device firmware or operating system, it should be updated or a patch applied to fix the bug to prevent the device from being compromised.

5. **C** A smurf attack uses a spoof attack combined with a DDoS attack to exploit the use of IP broadcast addressing and ICMP. By spoofing the address of the web server in an IP broadcast, the attacker causes the replies from other systems on the network to the broadcast all to be sent back to the web server, causing a denial of service.

6. **A** Implicit deny means that anything that is not explicitly defined in an access rule is denied. This denies all access by default until you apply access rules for only the specific services required.

7. **B** A distributed denial-of-service (DDoS) attack comes from multiple, geographically distributed hosts, making it difficult for the network administrator to block it.

8. **A** TCP port 21 (FTP) is not required on your e-mail server, and it should be disabled to prevent hackers from connecting to the e-mail server on this port.

9. **D**   To securely administer your router remotely with a web browser, you should make sure you are using an HTTPS connection that is encrypted via SSL. Other methods send their communications in clear text.

10. **C**   The default SNMP community string is "public." This is a basic type of password used between all systems being monitored by SNMP. This should be changed to a more secure value.

Securing Wireless Networks

ITINERARY

- **Objective 10.01** Implement wireless networks in a secure manner
- **Objective 10.02** Analyze and differentiate among types of wireless attacks

	NEWBIE	SOME EXPERIENCE	EXPERT
ETA	2 hours	1.5 hours	1 hour

An aspect of network security that is often ignored but provides a direct threat to your organization's networks is the use of wireless communications. Without proper security procedures, any person with a wireless device can connect to your network and eavesdrop or access private data by bypassing the traditional security defenses used in wired LAN networks. A firewall or router with maximum security configured for your wired LAN will not stop a hacker who is able to access your network from an unencrypted and insecure wireless access point.

From the end-user perspective, the popularity of wireless devices and the wide availability of free and open public wireless access means that you can access the Internet anywhere at any time. To be able to check your e-mail, manage your finances, perform your work, or just browse the Web is an incredible boost to personal and business productivity, but this easy access to the Internet also creates the potential for deep security and privacy threats. Using your wireless device, such as a laptop, on an open, unencrypted network could mean your passwords and private data are being transmitted in clear text and could be captured by hackers monitoring these networks.

Wireless security is an integral part of your overall network security strategy and design. Strong wireless security not only protects your networks from unauthorized intrusion but also protects your users from having their authentication credentials and sensitive data intercepted when they use wireless devices.

This chapter provides an overview of wireless networks and their function and design, describes the different wireless and encryption protocols, and provides detailed information on wireless threats and the security techniques to mitigate them.

Implement Wireless Networks in a Secure Manner

Objective 10.01

CompTIA Security+
Objective 1.6

One of the greatest changes in networking technology is the phenomenal growth and penetration of wireless communications. Wireless networks use radio frequency technology to transmit data through the air, effectively bridging the gap between data connectivity and user mobility. Wireless networks allow the mobile world to reach the Internet, not only with laptop computers, but also with other telecommunication devices, such as wireless-enabled smart phones, tablets, and many other devices.

Wireless connectivity lets a user perform their daily computing functions, such as checking e-mail, calendar scheduling, and browsing the Internet, without physically plugging into a network. Wireless applications also extend into the business world, where inventories are taken by hand-held devices and entire floors of a building are set up with wireless networks to enable mobile users to move their laptops and other wireless devices from room to room without the encumbrance of wires.

The popularity and explosive growth of wireless networks, however, have also introduced increased concerns for the security of wireless data. More so than traditional wired networks, wireless security heavily involves the use of encryption technologies, coupled with traditional security mechanisms such as access control and authentication.

Wireless security depends on the different types of wireless network configurations available and the types of devices that will connect to them. The following sections discuss the various wireless network technologies and their topology, and the protocols, hardware, and software that make them work.

Wireless LAN Technologies

Wireless LANs (WLANs) use electromagnetic airwaves to transfer information from one point to another without the need for a physical connection. To communicate these signals, the sender and receiver need to be tuned to the same radio frequency. The receiver tunes in one radio frequency, rejecting all others. WLANs can comprise a range of technologies, each with its own set of strengths and limitations.

Narrowband Technology

A *narrowband* system transmits and receives data only on a specific radio frequency. The signal frequency is kept as narrow as possible—large enough to communicate only the required information. Crossover between communications streams is prevented through the use of separate channel frequencies. The radio receiver filters out other radio signals, accepting only those on its designated frequency. The disadvantage of narrowband technology is that a Federal Communications Commission (FCC) license must be issued for each site where it is employed.

Spread-Spectrum Technology

Most WLAN systems use spread-spectrum technology to transmit their information. *Spread-spectrum* technology is a wideband radio-frequency technique used to ensure reliable and basic security for communications systems. More bandwidth is consumed than in a narrowband transmission, but spread-spectrum technology produces a stronger signal. Two types of spread-spectrum radio exist—frequency hopping (FHSS) and direct sequence (DSSS):

- FHSS   *Frequency-hopping spread-spectrum* uses a narrowband carrier that changes frequency in a pattern known to both the transmitter and the receiver. When synchronized, a single logical channel is maintained. FHSS uses a lower data rate (3 Mbps) than DSSS systems but can be installed into virtually any location without fear of interference interrupting its operation. FHSS is used by the Bluetooth standard.

- **DSSS**   *Direct-sequence spread-spectrum* generates a redundant bit pattern for each bit to be transmitted. Through the use of these bit patterns, transmissions can be easily recovered if interfered with or damaged, without the need for retransmission. DSSS delivers higher speeds than FHSS and is used by the 802.11 wireless standards.

- **OFDM**   *Orthogonal frequency-division multiplexing* transmits large amounts of data by breaking up the main signal into smaller sub-signals sent at the same time over different frequencies. This prevents transmission interference and cross-talk between signals while maintaining a high data rate. OFDM is used by the 802.11a, 802.11g, and 802.11n standards.

Infrared Technology

Infrared (IR) systems use high frequencies, just below visible light in the electromagnetic spectrum, to carry data. Like light, IR transmissions can't go through solid objects, and IR is mostly used for short, line-of-sight communications between devices. Infrared technology is rarely used in wireless network applications. Instead, it is geared more toward implementing fixed networks for allowing devices to communicate with each other when in line of sight of their IR ports.

Wireless Access

In a typical WLAN setup, a device called an *access point* is connected to a wired network from a fixed location using standard LAN cabling. The access point acts as a gateway, connecting the wireless and the wired LANs together. A single access point can support a small group of users and can function within a range up to several hundred feet. The access point is usually mounted at the top of a wall or ceiling to provide maximum coverage for the wireless area. The access point and any wireless device usually contain an antenna that can be extended to aid in signal reception.

To access the WLAN, the user can use a regular PC with a special WLAN adapter, a laptop computer with a wireless PC card, or even a hand-held device, such as a smart phone. The wireless adapter appears to the operating system of the computer or device as a typical network adapter.

Site Surveys

The *site survey* is a physical examination and review of your current network environment. An initial site survey should be performed before installation of a wireless network to ensure the environment will be conducive to wireless communications. The survey can also help determine the best placement and coverage for your wireless access points. When your wireless network is in place, you can use site survey software to scan and test your wireless network to examine its power and range. The following sections outline several important issues to examine for the site survey.

Physical Environment   Your physical environment can greatly affect the performance of your wireless network:

- Clear or open areas provide better radio range than closed or filled areas.
- Metal physical obstruction can hinder the performance of wireless devices. Avoid placing these devices in a location where a metal barrier is situated between the sending and receiving antennas.
- Radio penetration is affected by the building materials used in construction. Drywall construction allows greater range than concrete blocks, while metal construction can hinder and block radio signals.

Antenna Type and Placement   Access points are limited by range—ranging from 100 meters indoors to 500 meters outdoors—depending on the physical environment. In large wireless environments, multiple access points are needed to provide a wide coverage area for the clients. The access point ranges must overlap, so network connectivity will not be lost roaming from one access point to another.

Antenna and access point placement are important to make sure they are not close to any other electrical wires or device (especially those that broadcast on a similar frequency) where interference can cause a loss of wireless signal. Access points should be positioned at a high, central point of the area that they are servicing to ensure the widest, unobstructed coverage.

In smaller LAN-based access points, the antenna is attached directly to the device and cannot be moved away from the device. Extend the antenna to its maximum length to ensure a strong signal. Antennas that can be attached to access points with a cable should still be located as close as possible to the access point. The longer the cable, the more chance that signal attenuation or electromagnetic interference (EMI) can occur.

Local Lingo

Attenuation   Describes how an electronic signal becomes weaker over greater cable distances.

Many wireless access points use *dipole* antennas that split the signal wire into two wires that provide omnidirectional coverage with the wireless signal radiating outward in all directions. With 802.11n networks, you can use *MIMO (Multiple In Multiple Out)* technology that uses multiple sending and receiving antennas to boost the power and range of the network. All devices on the network must support MIMO to use its multipath benefits. Older hardware uses only a single in/out path.

Exam Tip

Antenna placement is a key factor in ensuring maximum range and power for your wireless Network. Be aware of the different issues that affect antenna placement and how to improve wireless network reception.

Power Level Controls   Wireless devices have the capability to limit their power level to control the range and speed of wireless access. This is useful for security purposes if you know you can limit the range of your access point coverage to just the needed areas of your location. This prevents casual, unauthorized access from a longer distance (such as a hacker outside your building).

Exam Tip

War driving is a technique used by hackers to access unsecured wireless networks. By driving around in close proximity to a company's physical premises, they can scan for unprotected networks.

You may also need to boost the transmit power of specific access points if their range is not reaching difficult points in your physical location where wireless clients experience issues communicating with the network.

The problem with adjusting your power settings is that this also affects your effective data speed on the wireless network because less power and range means a greater signal-to-noise ratio, which can lower speeds. For example, setting your power output setting on your access point to 50 percent from 100 percent will decrease the range of your wireless network, but it may also affect data speeds and connection strength for those connected to the network. In many cases, setting your transmit power too high can increase signal noise and data loss, and it may even contravene local rules and standards for signal broadcasting.

Site Survey Software   You can use specialized software for your access points that can scan your wireless network and record signal strength and interference levels, depending on your location on your premises. You can run the software on a laptop and walk around your building to look for zones with a low signal strength or high interference. Using this information, you can rearrange your access point and antenna placement, as well as modify your wireless network settings to increase range and power to these low signal zones.

WLAN Topologies

WLANs can be as small and simple as two PCs or laptops networked together through their wireless interfaces. This type of peer-to-peer (P2P) network requires little configuration and administration, and the wireless devices would only have to be within range of each other to communicate. No intermediary access points or servers are on this *ad hoc* network. Each client would have access only to the resources of the other client.

More complex networks can encompass a large number of access points, connected with many different wireless PCs, laptops, or hand-held devices. Installing an access point can extend the range of a small wireless network, effectively doubling the area in which the devices can communicate. The access point is directly connected to a wired network, so any wireless clients accessing that access point can communicate with the resources of the wired LAN through the access point. Resources on the wired network that wireless clients might access include file servers, mail servers, and the Internet. Figure 10.1 shows an example of a typical WLAN access-point configuration.

An access point can accommodate many clients, depending on the number and the type of bandwidth transmission required. Typical access points can handle up to approximately 50 client devices. The disadvantage is that the more users connected to the access point, the less bandwidth there is available to each client.

Wireless Protocols

Just like regular networked LANs, WLANs run on specific networking protocols optimized for use with wireless communications. As wireless networks began to proliferate, a number of competing wireless protocols were released that weren't always compatible with each other. A wireless device using one type of protocol might be unable to access a WLAN using an entirely different protocol. The

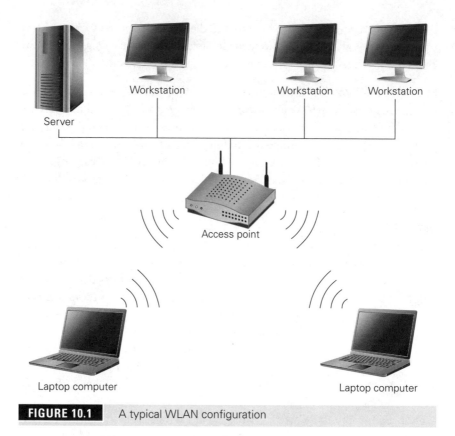

FIGURE 10.1   A typical WLAN configuration

most popular protocol for wireless devices currently in use is the Institute of Electrical and Electronics Engineers (IEEE) standard, 802.11n, and also the older standard 802.11g. The following sections outline some of the most common wireless protocols.

Wireless Access Protocol

The *Wireless Access Protocol (WAP)* is a specification that provides the delivery mechanisms for transmitting information to wireless devices. WAP supports the use of Wireless Markup Language (WML) instead of HTML to send web data to wireless devices, such as hand-helds and cell phones. Through the use of WML, web site content can be tailored so that it can be handled by WAP browsers embedded into wireless devices. Wireless devices typically have small amounts of memory and slow processors, so the web content must be stripped down to work on these types of devices.

Security for WAP is handled through the use of Wireless Transaction Layer Security (WTLS), which provides authentication and encryption functionality similar to the Secure Sockets Layer (SSL) in typical web networking. The wireless client and the server must be authenticated for wireless transactions to remain secure and to provide encryption. WTLS resembles SSL in that both rely on certificates on the client and server to verify the identities of the participants involved.

Exam Tip

Know that WAP security for wireless networks is performed via Wireless Transaction Layer Security (WTLS).

Unfortunately, WAP hasn't caught on as strongly as other wireless protocols and architectures because it's limited to smaller hand-held devices, a fact that restricts its usefulness with higher-bandwidth wireless solutions.

Bluetooth

Bluetooth wireless technology is designed to enable and simplify wireless communication between small, mobile devices. In an effort to implement wireless methods that eliminate the need for proprietary cables, Bluetooth attempts to allow connectivity between any devices, including peripherals such as cameras and scanners. For example, no cables are needed to transfer digital photographs between a camera and a PC, or to transfer data between an address book program on your PC and your smart phone, because the communications can be performed using Bluetooth wireless. Bluetooth has low power consumption and transmits via common radio frequencies (2.4 GHz). Configuration is usually performed dynamically in the background, allowing seamless communications between Bluetooth wireless devices.

Bluetooth also enables devices to form small wireless networks called *piconets,* which are established using a radio transceiver embedded within each Bluetooth device. This is designed to operate in a noisy radio environment and to provide a fast, robust, and secure connection between devices. The range for Bluetooth, however, is much smaller than typical wireless networks, allowing for a link range between 10 cm (about 4 inches) and 10 meters (about 33 feet), because typical Bluetooth connectivity is used between one device and another. Figure 10.2 illustrates how a Bluetooth network works.

FIGURE 10.2	Bluetooth network

802.11

IEEE 802.11 refers to a family of specifications developed for WLAN technology. 802.11 specifies an over-the-air interface between a wireless client and a base station, or between two wireless clients. The IEEE accepted the specification in 1997.

Several specifications are included in the 802.11 family:

- **802.11**   Applies to WLANs and provides 1 or 2 Mbps transmission in the 2.4 GHz band using either frequency-hopping spread-spectrum (FHSS) or direct-sequence spread-spectrum (DSSS).

- **802.11a**   An extension to 802.11 that applies to WLANs and provides up to 54 Mbps in the 5 GHz band. 802.11a uses an orthogonal frequency-division multiplexing (OFDM) encoding scheme, rather than FHSS or DSSS.

- **802.11b**   Also referred to as 802.11 High Rate or Wi-Fi, this extension to 802.11 applies to WLANs and provides 11 Mbps transmission (with a fallback to 5.5, 2, and 1 Mbps) in the 2.4 GHz band. 802.11b uses only DSSS. 802.11b was a 1999 ratification to the original 802.11 standard, allowing wireless functionality to provide performance comparable to the Ethernet 10BaseT standard, which runs at 10 Mbps.

- **802.11g**   Applies to WLANs and provides 54+ Mbps in the 2.4 GHz band.

- **802.11n**   Applies to WLANs and operates on both the 2.4 GHz band and the 5 GHz band. It can provide from 54 Mbps to 600 Mbps with the use of four spatial streams at a channel width of 40 MHz. 802.11n uses OFDM and can also utilize MIMO antenna technologies to boost power and range.

Travel Assistance

For detailed information on the IEEE wireless standards, see http://standards.ieee.org/wireless/.

Currently, the 802.11n standard is the most recent and popular for home and business wireless users. However, many 802.11g wireless devices and access points still exist and interoperate with 801.11n networks. The popularity of wireless networks, however, has created the need for even better security for WLANs at home and in the workplace. Without any type of security mechanisms, WLANs can be easily compromised; with no mechanisms for authentication or encryption configured, an unauthorized user can simply bring her own wireless laptop or wireless device into the range of the WLAN for instant access.

Travel Advisory

With the proliferation of home networks with high-speed Internet connections, many users have also added wireless systems to their home networks. When proper wireless security measures are not implemented, unauthorized users nearby can access a neighbor's network without subscribing to the service and perform illegal activities, using someone else's home network so that it cannot be traced back to the hacker.

Securing Wireless Networks

Securing a WLAN with as many layers of security as possible is extremely important. The following methods can collectively be used to secure access to 802.11 networks:

- Access point security
- An SSID
- MAC address filtering
- Encryption—Wired Equivalent Privacy (WEP) and Wi-Fi Protected Access (WPA and WPA2)
- A secure virtual private network (VPN)
- A personal firewall

Access Point Security

Security for a WLAN begins at its primary points of access, and the wireless access point security configuration is of critical importance to the network administrator. Most access points allow administrative configuration to be performed wirelessly; however, this creates a security risk because any user with wireless access can attempt to access the configuration via brute-force or other account cracking methods. If possible, configuration should be limited to a wired connection, and the administrator's machine must be physically cabled to the access point to perform these tasks. Remote configuration should be disabled if wired access can be performed on the access points. If wireless configuration must be used, network administrators should be sure that these occur over encrypted channels such as Hypertext Transfer Protocol over Secure Socket Layer (HTTPS) and SSL.

The administrator user name and password must be secure, like any user name and password used on an important server or router on the network. This includes modifying the default *admin* account name (if possible) to something less recognizable and using a secure password of at least eight alphanumeric characters, including uppercase, lowercase, and special characters.

From this point, several security features can be enabled for the entire WLAN that are discussed in the following sections. Ensure that all access points have the same configuration, or you may leave one of your access points with security weaknesses and vulnerabilities that can be exploited. For example, you may forget to disable SSID broadcast on one of your access points, which allows unauthorized users to attempt to access the network using the SSID name.

Service Set Identifier (SSID)

The most simple wireless network access control is the use of a network identifier or name. This SSID can be set up on one or a group of wireless access points. It provides a way to segment a wireless network into multiple networks serviced by one or more access points. This is helpful in companies that are separated by departments or physical floor locations.

To access a particular network, client computers must be configured with the correct identifier. For roaming users, multiple identifiers can be enabled on their wireless devices, enabling them access to different networks as required. This type of security is minimal, however, because it simply employs a network password, which could easily be compromised by word of mouth or through access points that broadcast the network name.

Travel Advisory

Many access points advertise their SSID by default. For security reasons, check the settings of all your access points to disable this feature. The disadvantage of disabling broadcasts, however, is that new clients cannot see and connect to the network if they do not know the SSID name. It is a best practice to disable SSID broadcasting, but at the same time, anyone who wants to crack a wireless network knows that even with SSID broadcasting disabled, the network is detectable with advanced hacking tools.

MAC Address Filtering

Access points can be identified with network names and passwords, but a client computer can be identified by the unique MAC address of its wireless network card. Access points can be configured with a list of MAC addresses associated with the client computers allowed to access the wireless network. If a wireless client's MAC address isn't included in this list, the wireless client isn't allowed to connect with the access point and the network. This is a much better solution than using network identifiers alone, but maintaining the list of client MAC addresses can quickly become a daunting task with larger networks. In addition, each access point must be configured individually, so each node contains the same list of addresses. This type of security is best suited to small networks because the administrative overhead quickly limits its scalability.

Exam Tip

Enable MAC address filtering on access points to control which clients can access the network.

WEP Security

The *Wired Equivalent Privacy (WEP)* security protocol is an IEEE 802.11 standard for encrypted communication between wireless clients and access points. WEP uses the RC4 key encryption algorithm to encrypt communications before they are transmitted over the wireless network. Each client or access point on the WLAN must use the same encryption key. The key is manually configured on each access point and each client before they can access the network. Basic WEP encryption has been proven to be vulnerable to attack because of the weak 40-bit RC4 cipher, and even 128-bit WEP encryption has been cracked. Most devices now support up to 256-bit encryption. If your devices do not support WPA (described in the next section), they should use 256-bit WEP encryption in conjunction with the MAC address filtering and network identifier methods described previously.

Exam Tip
Know that the highest level of encryption available, such as WPA or WPA2, is best to use. Older levels of encryption, such as WEP, have proven to be vulnerable.

WPA and WPA2 Security

Wi-Fi Protected Access (WPA) is the most recent and secure form of encryption for wireless networks and was created to fix several weaknesses in the WEP standard. WPA is the 802.11i standard, an amendment to the 802.11 standard to improve encryption security. WPA can be used in two ways: using a preshared key or using an authentication server that distributes the keys. The preshared key method (also called Personal WPA or WPA-PSK) means that all devices on the WLAN must use the same passphrase key to access the network. The authentication server method (also called Enterprise WPA) is more suited for environments with hundreds of clients, where using a single passphrase key for each device is not scalable, and the authentication server takes care of key management between the wireless devices on the network.

Using WPA, data is encrypted using a 128-bit key that is actually routinely changed during sessions using the *Temporal Key Integrity Protocol (TKIP)*. This ensures that a single session key cannot be hacked by the time the protocol changes keys. WPA also provides for improved integrity checking of data traversing the wireless network to ensure it cannot be intercepted and changed on the way to its destination. This provides much more protection than the original WEP protocol.

A WPA network, however, is only as strong as the passphrase used. A WPA passphrase can be from 8 to 63 characters, and it is recommended that this passphrase be as strong as possible and not based on known dictionary words. It should include numbers, uppercase and lowercase letters, and special characters such as the @ symbol. All devices on the WPA network must share the same passphrase, including all access points.

WPA2 is the most recent version that replaces WPA with a stronger 256-bit encryption, and adds Robust Security Network (RSN) support that includes added protection for ad hoc networks, key caching, preroaming authentication, and the Counter Mode with Cipher Block Chaining Message Authentication Code Protocol (CCMP). CCMP utilizes the Advanced Encryption Standard (AES) cipher to replace TKIP. All currently manufactured devices support WPA2 in addition to WPA.

If your network devices support WPA2, they should use this type of encryption. However, many older devices do not support WPA2, and you will have to use WPA or some other common encryption method that can be supported by all your clients.

Wireless Authentication Protocols

While encryption protocols such as WEP, WPA, and WPA2 focus on the encryption of the communications link and data for wireless networks, there is still the need to provide a secure authentication function for accessing wireless networks. The protocols in the following sections are popular methods for the transmission and security of authentication data within standard wireless encryption protocols.

EAP

The *Extensible Authentication Protocol (EAP)* is used primarily in WEP-, WPA-, and WPA2-based wireless networks for securely transporting authentication data, but it has also been used previously for remote access authentication to local area networks.

EAP separates the message exchange from the authentication process through the use of a different exchange layer, and it provides a module-based infrastructure that supports several different types of authentication methods. Microsoft Windows uses EAP to authenticate remote access, VPN, and site-to-site connections over PPP (Point-to-Point Protocol). With this method, you can use most standard authentication servers, such as RADIUS or Kerberos, to authenticate connections.

Although EAP provides a very flexible authentication infrastructure, one of the major issues with EAP is that part of the initial exchange, including authentication credentials and results, are transmitted in clear text. For WEP, WPA, and WPA2 wireless networks, EAP authentication occurs before any wireless transmissions are encrypted.

EAP has been extended with other protocols to help improve security, such as EAP-TLS, which utilizes Transport Layer Security, and to support the use of authentication with client certificates. This means that even if a hacker were able to obtain a user's authentication credentials, he still would not be able to access the wireless network with the client's private key, which establishes the encrypted session.

LEAP

The *Lightweight Extensible Authentication Protocol (LEAP)* is a protocol created specifically by Cisco Systems, Inc. LEAP was developed to address some of the security issues of EAP, while still providing its flexibility of authentication methods. LEAP provides its authentication using its own version of MS-CHAP (the Microsoft version of the Client Handshake Authentication Protocol, which in itself is insecure) to a RADIUS server. LEAP uses frequent changes to a WEP encryption key and client reauthentication to prevent the current key from being in use too long. Due to general weaknesses in the WEP key itself, LEAP has been largely replaced by PEAP and extended versions of EAP such as EAP-TLS.

PEAP

The *Protected Extensible Authentication Protocol (PEAP)* is a protocol that uses TLS to transport EAP within an encrypted communications tunnel over the wireless connection. This has advantages over the similar protocol EAP-TLS, as there is no need for a client certificate.

When using PEAP, the encrypted tunnel is formed to a server using TLS and a server-side certificate. This provides for secure key exchange between the client and the server, which then allows normal EAP authentication methods for the client authentication stage.

VPN Wireless Access

For larger networks with high security requirements, a VPN wireless access solution is a preferable alternative or addition to the other solutions discussed. VPN solutions are already widely deployed to provide remote workers with secure access to the network via the Internet. The VPN provides a secure, dedicated tunnel through a public network such as the Internet. Various tunneling protocols are used in conjunction with standard, centralized authentication solutions using a login and password.

The same VPN technology can also be used for secure wireless access. In this application, the public network is the wireless network itself. Wireless access is isolated from the rest of the network by a VPN server and, for extra security, an intermediary firewall. Authentication and full encryption over the wireless network are provided through the VPN server. The VPN-based solution is scalable to a large number of users. Figure 10.3 illustrates the architecture of a VPN-based wireless network.

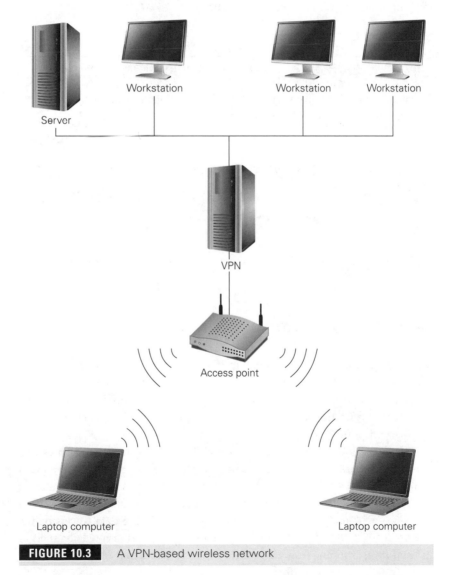

Server

Workstation

Workstation

Workstation

VPN

Access point

Laptop computer

Laptop computer

FIGURE 10.3   A VPN-based wireless network

Personal Firewall

In addition to the overall wireless network security, all wireless PCs and mobile devices should be equipped with personal firewall software protection. Similar to home computers with permanent cable modem or DSL Internet access connections, wireless clients can be vulnerable to attacks by unauthorized users accessing the same network. The personal firewall software can be used to protect the roaming user's confidential local data against many types of possible attacks for both incoming and outgoing connections.

> **Exam Tip**
>
> Be aware of the advantages and disadvantages of the wireless access security solutions discussed in this chapter. Depending on the type of network and the scope of security required, some of these solutions won't be acceptable, or they'll need to be augmented by other methods.

Objective 10.02
CompTIA Security+
Objective 3.4

Analyze and Differentiate among Types of Wireless Attacks

The following sections describe some common security issues with wireless networks.

Data Emanation

In its most basic form, *data emanation* occurs when any sort of data is transmitted over an electromagnetic medium. For example, when electricity passes through a cable, it creates an electromagnetic field that can be detected and measured. In communications, you could capture data emanation from an electronic communication and use it to rearrange the electronic signal to reveal the original communication.

This is a serious issue in wireless networking, as unprotected and unsecured wireless communications can be easily intercepted and an unauthorized user can steal user names and passwords and sensitive private data. All information on an unencrypted WLAN is transmitted in clear text, and any wireless user can use a protocol analyzer or sniffer application to view the data traversing the WLAN. All WLANs should communicate using secure encrypted channels to prevent eavesdropping from unauthorized users. The actual equipment for the wireless LAN, such as access points and other wireless devices, must also be physically secure.

Bluetooth Vulnerabilities

Several vulnerabilities in vendor implementations of Bluetooth have allowed unauthorized access to personal data on cell phones and computer devices. Bluetooth can also be susceptible to unauthorized messages, a practice called *bluejacking*. An unauthorized user can send unwanted messages to another Bluetooth device in range of the originating device. This has most often been used for Bluetooth spam advertising, in which a Bluetooth device such as a smart phone suddenly receives a text message containing the spam message. Bluejacking is relatively harmless and a nuisance much like spam e-mails, but there is the potential for harmful media to be transferred from one device to another.

A more serious Bluetooth vulnerability is called *bluesnarfing*. Many Bluetooth phones and devices use a discovery mode that allows a hacker to detect and connect automatically to other Bluetooth devices, much like a WLAN. Without proper authentication, an unauthorized user can connect to unprotected Bluetooth devices and access any data stored on the device. If an unsuspecting user leaves his device in discovery mode, it is not protected from access by other Bluetooth devices in the vicinity.

Bluetooth defines three security modes:

- **Nonsecure mode**   No security features are enabled.
- **Service-level security mode**   Application security policies are used, in which the actual applications on the wireless device are responsible for security.
- **Link-level security mode**   The most secure of the three modes authenticates the actual communications link before data transmission can begin. Data encryption can also be performed in this mode, once the link is authenticated. Authentication allows the devices to decide whether a connection will be formed based on available identification at the hardware level. Once the link is established, additional security might be applied to the data transmission using encryption. Stronger encryption can also be enabled at the software level, if needed.

Exam Tip

Remember that bluesnarfing is a serious Bluetooth security threat, and link-level security is recommended to secure the communications link and transfer of data. Bluetooth should be disabled if you are not using it.

War Driving

Many corporate WLANs and home-based wireless networks are set up and configured with no encryption or access control. Hackers have been known to roam neighborhoods with a large corporate presence and use simple laptops with wireless connectivity to connect to unprotected WLANs and access their resources. This is called *war driving*. Several programs are available that allow unauthorized users to scan an area for open and unprotected wireless networks. After accessing the network, the user can attempt several types of attacks, such as eavesdropping and sniffing the wireless data, or accessing and capturing the data on other wireless devices on the network.

Administrators can lower the susceptibility of their wireless networks to war driving attacks by encrypting their networks and disabling the broadcast of their service set identifiers (SSIDs). These and other techniques are discussed in the section "Securing Wireless Networks."

Rogue Access Points (Evil Twin)

With wireless networks, much of the typical physical security that prevents someone from plugging into a network is unavailable. Anyone within the vicinity of a WLAN can connect to it easily with the use of a laptop or other wireless-equipped device. Unauthorized users can also set up their own wireless access points to which unsuspecting users connect and transmit sensitive and private data, including user name and password credentials, directly on the hacker's network. Sometimes called *evil twins*, often these access points are set up with legitimate names, for example, as a Wi-Fi hot spot for a popular network carrier. The wireless access is typically set up as password-free and unencrypted, and an unsuspecting user could connect and use her banking or credit card details, which are then stolen by the hacker for identity theft and fraud.

You can prevent rogue devices and access points from connecting to your wireless network by setting a unique SSID name and encrypting the network, since any rogue access points and devices will require the SSID name and encryption passphrase to connect to the network. In certain cases, Media Access Control (MAC) address filtering can also be used to allow only certain hardware addresses access to the network; however, this is not practical for networks with hundreds of wireless clients. Your networks should be routinely scanned for evidence of rogue access points or devices.

> ### Local Lingo
>
> **MAC address**   Stands for Media Access Control address, a unique hardware address assigned to network interface cards. This address is expressed in hexadecimal format.

As an end user accessing a free rogue access point, your only protection is to always use secure, encrypted web sites via SSL when using an open wireless access point you are unfamiliar with, or use a VPN connection when you are connected to the access point. This way, if you happen to be connected to a rogue evil twin access point, your information remains encrypted and undecipherable to the hacker. Be careful when connecting to wireless access points advertised as a popular wireless provider and make sure that the page is legitimate before entering any type of authentication or payment card details.

War Chalking

War chalking is the act of marking a physical area, such as the wall of a building or sidewalk, with symbols that indicate a free and open wireless access point is active in that location. War chalking was more popular in the earlier days of wireless access when local Wi-Fi access points (hot spots) were few and far between. It indicated to a mobile user that she could connect her wireless device to an open access point in that area if she needed to quickly access the Internet.

This is an outdated practice in an era of almost full wireless or mobile data access coverage, but it can still present a security risk, primarily if the indicated access point is a rogue evil twin where the network traffic will be monitored by a hacker looking for authentication credentials and credit card numbers.

Packet Sniffing and Eavesdropping

On an unencrypted open wireless network, any hacker can use a packet sniffer or network eavesdropping tool to analyze wireless network data as it passes through the network. The hacker can use this information to obtain authentication credentials of a user, including user names and passwords, and also sensitive financial information such as credit cards and bank account numbers. The hacker could also initiate a man-in-the-middle attack, where data is actually modified en route to its destination. For example, the hacker could spoof the sender or destination address, or even a network MAC address to emulate another host.

To prevent packet sniffing and eavesdropping, the wireless network must be encrypted with a strong encryption technique. While security measures such as SSID names, disabled broadcasting, authentication, and MAC address access control can prohibit unauthorized access, only by encrypting the data can you make it indecipherable to those who are monitoring network traffic.

WEP IV Attack

On wireless networks encrypted with WEP, the WEP encryption technique uses a special 24-bit *initialization vector (IV)* that is combined with its 40-bit WEP key to encrypt each network packet. This extends the life of the WEP key, as the IV changes with each transmission. WEP in itself has proved to be an insecure protocol, and coupled with a short 24-bit IV factor that is sent in clear text, it could enable a hacker to discover the IV through repetition. In very large and busy wireless networks, the IV itself can be repeated in a space of hours. The hacker can then use various utilities to decrypt subsequent packets that were encrypted with the same IV key stream. This makes it possible to not even need to decrypt the WEP key to decrypt packets.

This type of attack has become less common as WEP is replaced by stronger encryption methods such as WPA2.

CHECKPOINT

✔**Objective 10.01: Implement wireless networks in a secure manner.**
More so than security for traditional wired networks, wireless security heavily involves the use of encryption technologies, coupled with traditional security mechanisms such as access control and authentication. Wireless networks should use WPA or WPA2 encryption with a strong passphrase, should disable SSID broadcasts and use a unique SSID name, should use MAC address filtering if possible, and should have access points that are properly secured with a strong password for administrative configuration, with remote configuration disabled.

✔**Objective 10.02: Analyze and differentiate among types of wireless attacks.**
Data emanation causes unauthorized access to authentication credentials and unencrypted sensitive data. Hackers use war driving techniques to drive around looking for open, unencrypted Wi-Fi networks. A rogue "evil twin" access point masquerades as a legitimate wireless access point to trick users into communicating sensitive information over a network completely under

the control of a hacker. War chalking identifies open Wi-Fi hot spot locations by marking physical locations with symbols. Hackers can use packet sniffers to eavesdrop on unencrypted wireless networks to discover authentication credentials and sensitive data being passed in clear text. IV attacks focus on the weak 24-bit initialization vector that is used to help strengthen WEP keys, and which can then be used to break the WEP key.

REVIEW QUESTIONS

1. You have connected to a free, open Wi-Fi hotspot at your local coffee shop. Which of the following security measures should you use to secure your session?

   A. Only use HTTPS sites secured with SSL.

   B. Set up MAC address filtering.

   C. Use a packet sniffer.

   D. Reconnect at regular intervals to refresh the encryption key.

2. You have set up a wireless network for your small office of 50 users. Which of the following encryption protocols would you implement to ensure the highest level of encryption security?

   A. WAP

   B. WPA

   C. WEP-128 bit

   D. WPA2

3. You are connecting to a secure, encrypted wireless network. During the initial connection phase, you are asked to enter a passphrase. Which WPA encryption method is in use on the network?

   A. WPA-EAP

   B. WPA-TKIP

   C. WPA-PSK

   D. WPA-Enterprise

4. You are setting up new Bluetooth-enabled mobile phones for your executive team. Which of the following security features do you enable to prevent Bluesnarfing?

   A. Enable link-level security.

   B. Disable the IR port.

   C. Disable wireless access.

   D. Set an SSID.

5. You are setting up a new wireless security network for your small office. You have set the SSID of the network to a secure value. Which other feature can you enable to enhance SSID security?

   A. Enable SSID broadcast.

   B. Enable SSID tunneling.

   C. Disable SSID snarfing.

   D. Disable SSID broadcast.

6. Which of the following types of wireless attacks utilizes a weakness in WEP key generation and encryption to decrypt WEP encrypted data?

   A. IV attack

   B. War driving

   C. PSK attack

   D. Eavesdropping

7. To further secure your wireless network, you implement MAC address filtering. Which of the following statements describes the wireless network behavior after you enable MAC address filtering?

   A. It allows wireless access only for specified MAC addresses.

   B. It prevents wireless access only from specified MAC addresses.

   C. It encrypts only specified wireless device MAC addresses.

   D. It encrypts only MAC addresses not specified.

8. After checking the signal strength of a specific floor of your building, you realize that two of the farthest offices on the floor have very poor signal strength. Which of the following actions can you perform to provide a cost-effective solution to increase signal strength to that part of the building?

   A. Disable encryption to speed up the network.

   B. Add an additional access point.

   C. Use a cable to extend the antenna range of the closest access point.

   D. Switch to the 5 GHz band instead of 2.4 GHz.

9. You are installing a wireless network in a manufacturing facility. Which of the following aspects of the wireless network do you concentrate on to prevent security issues with EMI?

   A. Use of WPA2 encryption

   B. Use of 802.11g or 802.11n

   C. SSID network name

   D. Access point and antenna placement

10. Your company is moving to a new facility, and you are responsible for installing a wireless network for the new office building. Which of the following should you perform to prepare for a secure implementation?

   A. Back up the current wireless configuration.

   B. Check for war chalking at the new site.

   C. Perform a site survey.

   D. Perform a radio frequency sweep.

REVIEW ANSWERS

1. **A**   When using an open wireless access point and browsing personal web sites such as your e-mail and banking sites, make sure you use secure, encrypted websites via SSL, or use a VPN connection. This ensures that your session with the web server is encrypted. Any hacker on the same open network can use a packet sniffer to view unencrypted communications.

2. **D**   WPA2 is currently the strongest level of encryption security available for a wireless network. WPA2 replaces the weaker WPA and adds Robust Security Network (RSN) support that includes added protection for ad hoc networks, key caching, preroaming authentication, and CCMP, which utilizes the AES cipher to replace TKIP.

3. **C**   WPA-PSK uses a preshared key passphrase that requires all devices on the wireless network to use the same passphrase to access the network. WPA-Enterprise uses an authentication server to perform key management and exchange for all wireless clients.

4. **A**   Bluesnarfing is a hacking method in which an unauthorized user can connect to unprotected Bluetooth devices and access any data stored on the device. Link-level security authenticates the actual communications link before data transmission begins. Data encryption can also be performed when the link is authenticated.

5. **D**   By disabling SSID broadcast, you assure your access points will not advertise the SSID they are using for wireless clients to connect. A user would require prior knowledge of the SSID before he could access the network.

6. **A**   The IV (initialization vector) attack uses the weakness in the 24-bit generated IV that is paired with the WEP encryption key. The IV can be discovered over time on busy networks that use repeat IV values, and used to decrypt the cipher stream without knowing the WEP key.

7. **A**   A list of authorized client MAC addresses must be configured on each access point for the network. If any client tries to communicate with the access point and its MAC address isn't in the list, it will be denied access.

8. **B**   You can use a cable and an external antenna to extend the range of your closest access point to the office with the low signal. This is an easy and inexpensive solution rather than purchasing and installing a new access point.

9. **D**   Antenna and access point placement is important to make sure that it is not close to any other electrical wires or devices (especially those that broadcast on a similar frequency) where electrical interference can cause a loss of wireless signal.

10. **C**   An initial site survey should be performed before installation of a wireless network to ensure the environment will be conducive to wireless communications. The survey can also help determine the best placement and coverage for your wireless access points.

Application, Data, and Host Security

Chapter 11   Securing Host Systems

Chapter 12   Securing Applications and Data

Securing Host Systems

ITINERARY

○ **Objective 11.01** Analyze and differentiate among types of malware

○ **Objective 11.02** Carry out appropriate procedures to establish host security

	NEWBIE	SOME EXPERIENCE	EXPERT
ETA	3 hours	2 hours	1 hour

While your communications networks are the primary origins for external threats to your internal systems, you must also dedicate resources to the security of your organization's host systems on the network. System administrators must be aware of the numerous threats and risks to their server and client systems that originate within your networks.

Malicious software such as viruses, worms, Trojan horse programs, and logic bombs can wreak havoc on an unsecured server or client system. Host security includes using a strong security baseline and making sure all operating system and application software is up to date, and that all user accounts and passwords are as secure as possible. Specialized host security software is also required to scan and monitor the system for dangerous malware and attempts at intrusion.

Mobile devices are also a cause for additional concern for system security. Due to their portable nature, mobile devices are a prime risk for theft, and mobile devices must be secure to prevent unauthorized access and loss of confidential data. In addition, malware can be transmitted by a USB key or external hard drive to the system, just as easily as malware can be spread via e-mail or the Web.

This chapter explores various security threats and risks for host systems, including software threats such as malicious programs (viruses, worms, Trojan horses, and so on), system peripherals and removable storage, and account and password threats. It also describes host security hardening techniques.

Analyze and Differentiate among Types of Malware

Objective 11.01
CompTIA Security+
Objective 3.1

Systems security means not only securing sensitive data against unauthorized access, but also protecting the integrity and existence of that data from malicious users and software. Most companies use security resources, such as security guards and cameras, to prevent unauthorized physical access to their equipment and facilities. Organizations must also protect themselves from threats originating from the numerous technological pathways that can potentially provide unauthorized system access.

Damage from virus attacks or unauthorized access gained via back-door or Trojan horse types of programs can be catastrophic. A simple worm attached to an e-mail message can cause mail and network systems to grind to a halt. Other viruses contain payloads that destroy or damage information that might never be recovered if a backup plan is not in place.

System administrators must be aware of the numerous types of system software attacks, know how these attacks gain entry into the system, and what can be done to rectify the issue if they infect a system. First and foremost, proactive protection in the form of knowledge and user education is critical in dealing with these types of threats.

Viruses

Viruses are probably the most common and prevalent type of system attack. A *virus* is a computer program that replicates itself within the affected system, even if the virus program does not harm the system. Most computer viruses self-replicate without the knowledge of the computer user.

Like a human virus, computer viruses can be passed along from one system to another—via e-mail messages, instant messaging, web site downloads, removable media, and network connections. An enormous amount of expense and time can be required to clean up and restore operations after a virus attack. Some companies take many days, or even weeks, to get back to full operations after their systems have been infected with a virus. For certain time-sensitive businesses, a virus infection can be fatal to the entire computer system and company work.

Types of Viruses

Viruses come in a variety of forms, with different locations and methods of infection and severity of payload. The following sections outline some common virus types.

Boot Sector Viruses   *Boot sector* viruses infect the boot sector or partition table of a disk. The *boot sector* is used by the computer to determine what operating systems (OSs) are present on the system to boot. The most common way a boot sector virus finds its way into a system is through an infected disk or removable media device that is inserted into the computer. After infecting the boot sector, the virus will not allow the system to boot into the operating system, rendering the computer useless until the boot sector is repaired.

The best way to remove a boot-sector virus from a system is to boot the system using an antivirus or similar emergency recovery media. This lets you start up the computer with basic start-up files, bypassing the boot sector, and then run the antivirus program on the recovery media.

Companion Viruses   A *companion* virus disguises itself as a legitimate program, using the name of a legitimate program but with a different extension. For example, a virus might name itself *program.com* to emulate a file called *program.exe*. A .com file is a higher priority than a standard .exe file with the same name, so the virus file program.com would run first. Typically, the virus runs the legitimate program immediately after installing the virus code, so it appears the system is performing normally. Some viruses replace the original legitimate file with their own version that performs the same tasks and includes new, malicious code to run with it.

File Infector Viruses   *File-infector* viruses generally infect files that have the extensions .com or .exe. These viruses can be extremely destructive because they try to replicate and spread further by infecting other executable programs on the system with the same extensions. Sometimes, a file-infector virus destroys the program it infects by overwriting the original code.

Travel Advisory

If your computer is afflicted with a file-infector virus, do not attach it to a network or it could start infecting files on other workstations and file servers.

Macro Viruses   A macro is an instruction that carries out program commands automatically within an application. Macros are typically used in popular office applications such as Microsoft Word and Excel. A *macro virus* uses the internal workings of the application to perform malicious operations when a file containing the macro is opened, such as deleting files or opening other virus-executable programs. Sometimes these viruses also infect program templates that are loaded automatically by the applications. Each time the user creates a file using the default template, the macro virus is copied to the new file.

Memory-Resident Viruses   When a system is infected by a virus that stays resident in the system memory, the *memory-resident* virus will continue to stay in memory and infect other files that are run at the same time. For a memory-resident virus to spread, the user has to run an infected program that, once activated, inserts the virus into system memory, where the virus examines each new program as it is run and, if the program is not already infected, infects it.

Polymorphic Viruses   *Polymorphic* viruses change themselves with each infection. These types of viruses were created to confuse virus-scanning programs. These viruses are difficult to detect by scanning because each copy of the virus looks different from the previous copies.

Metamorphic Viruses   A *metamorphic* virus is capable of recompiling itself into a new form, and the code keeps changing from generation to generation. A metamorphic virus is similar to a polymorphic virus because both can modify their forms. A metamorphic virus does not decrypt itself to a single constant virus body in memory, though, as a polymorphic virus does. A metamorphic virus can also change its virus body code.

Stealth Viruses   A *stealth* virus hides itself from virus protection software by encrypting its code. Stealth viruses attempt to cover their trail as they infect their way through a computer. When a stealth virus infects, it takes over the system function that reads files or system sectors. When something or someone attempts to access the corrupted file, the stealth virus reports that the original file is there. In reality, however, the original information is gone and the stealth virus has taken its place.

File Types That Commonly Carry Viruses

Some types of files are susceptible to virus infections because they are common to certain types of computer systems and applications. The following are a few of the most popular types of program files targeted by viruses:

- **.bat**   An MS-DOS batch file contains a series of commands for the OS that are executed automatically in sequence.

- **.com**   MS-DOS command files usually execute within a command shell interface, or they can be by executed from a user interface such as Windows. Most early computer viruses were created as .com files because the main DOS program files were in this form.

- **.doc/.docx**   These file extensions are associated with Microsoft Word. Along with Microsoft Access and Excel files, .doc and .docx file extensions are susceptible to macro virus infection.

- **.dll**   A dynamic-link library (DLL) is a library of executable functions or data that can be used by a Windows application. Typically, a DLL provides one or more particular functions and a program accesses these functions.

- **.exe**   An executable file is most commonly found on MS-DOS and Windows OSs.

- **.html**   The .html or .htm extension is used for a document written in HTML coding that can be opened by web browsers.

- **.mdb**   This file extension is associated with a Microsoft Access database. As with Word and Excel files, the .mdb file is susceptible to macro virus infection.

- **.scr**   This is the default file extension for Microsoft Windows screensavers. As screensavers are popular items to copy to other users, .scr files are typically easy targets for viruses.
- **.vbs**   Files with the .vbs extension are for Microsoft Visual Basic Scripting, a subset of the Visual Basic programming language. This powerful language can create scripts that can perform a wide variety of functions such as control applications and manipulate the file system. VB Script is powerful and can be used to create malicious code.
- **.xls/.xlsx**   These file extensions are associated with a Microsoft Excel spreadsheet. As with Word and Access files, .xls and .xlsx files are susceptible to macro virus infection.
- **.zip**   This extension is used for a compressed file that contains one or more other files. Zip files are compressed to save space and to make grouping files for transport and copying faster and easier. Zip files must also be checked by antivirus software to ensure that the files in the archive are not infected.

Exam Tip
Recognize which types of files are most likely to carry a virus.

Trojan Horses

Trojan horse programs are named from the ancient myth in which Greek warriors invaded the gated city of Troy by hiding inside a gigantic wooden horse. Once inside the city gates, the warriors leapt from inside the horse and attacked the surprised inhabitants, winning a decisive battle.

A Trojan horse program hides on your computer system until called upon to perform a certain task. A Trojan is usually downloaded through e-mail attachments, web sites, and instant messages. Trojans are usually disguised as popular programs such as games, pictures, or music. When the program is run, it usually appears to the victim user as if nothing has happened, but the Trojan has secretly installed itself on the user's computer.

Popular Trojan horse programs used by attackers include NetBus, Sub7, and Back Orifice, which enable the attacker to take control of a user's computer once the Trojan horse file is installed.

Back-door software is typically installed by a Trojan horse. This allows a hacker access to the client computer that bypasses any authentication. The Trojan horse runs a service on the victim's computer and opens a port (such as TCP/IP port 12345 in the case of the NetBus Trojan software) on the system to which the attacker can be connected when he runs the control application from a remote location. When connected, the attacker has full access to the infected system.

Antivirus programs can detect the presence of Trojan horse and back-door programs. Personal firewalls can also detect suspicious incoming and outgoing network traffic from a computer. Port-scanning software can also be used to identify any open ports on the system, including those you do not recognize. These open ports can be cross-referenced with lists of ports used by known back-door programs.

> **Travel Advisory**
>
> A firewall can detect suspicious incoming and outgoing network traffic from your computer. If you do not recognize a program, it could be a Trojan horse communicating out to the network.

Logic Bombs

Although it can be running on a system for a long time, a *logic bomb* program will not activate until a specific trigger, such as reaching a specific date or starting a program a specific number of times, is set off. Logic bombs can be highly destructive, depending on their payload. The damage done by a logic bomb can range from changing bytes of data on the victim's hard disk to rendering the user's entire hard drive unreadable.

Logic bombs are distributed primarily via worms and viruses; however, cases of malicious programmers inserting code into a trusted application that will trigger at a later time have been documented. Logic bombs can be difficult to detect because after the initial installation, there may be no indication for hours, days, months, and even years that the logic bomb is present before it is scheduled to release its malicious payload.

Most antivirus software is able to detect the most common types of logic bombs; however, if a logic bomb is hidden within a trusted application, it may be difficult to detect its presence until it is too late.

For software development companies, all code must be peer-reviewed before the application is released to ensure that a single malicious programmer cannot insert hidden logic bomb code.

Worms

A computer *worm* is a self-contained program or set of programs that can spread full copies or smaller segments of itself to other computer systems via network connections, e-mail attachments, and instant messages. Worms are most common in various types of networking application servers such as e-mail servers, web servers, and database servers.

The explosive increase in worms within e-mail attachments and instant messages has caused antivirus companies and messaging software companies to reevaluate the functionality of their applications to prevent the spread of messaging-based worms. A user receives an attachment to an e-mail or an instant message that contains a malicious worm. When the attachment is opened, the worm infects the user's computer and then replicates itself by sending copies of the same e-mail or instant message to everyone in the user's address book. Each user, in turn, sees a message arrive from someone familiar and automatically opens the attachment, thinking it is safe. These types of worm infections can spread quickly and can bring down an e-mail server in a matter of minutes.

Application server vendors have taken steps to prevent these types of worms from spreading by patching their applications to prevent malicious attachment code from executing.

Adware and Spyware

Adware (advertising software) and *spyware* are potential software threats that are not always considered security risks. Many free or low-cost software programs are often supported financially by embedding advertising content within the applications themselves. Although this provides a modest revenue stream for the software developers, it also opens the door to potential security threats such as compromised private and personal data. Even software as simple as a downloadable screensaver may contain adware or spyware that installs code to deliver advertising to the user and/or collect personal information for use in targeted advertising.

In addition to the nuisance of the advertising (which is not easily disabled) is the threat that the program itself is sending the user's personal information back to the advertiser. This information can include web surfing habits, key logging, online purchases, and personal contact information such as e-mail address, home address, and credit card details. This personal information can be used directly by the advertiser or sold to other companies that will also use or distribute the personal information.

Spyware is not necessarily involved with advertising, and it can be installed by any type of software application, even trusted, popular application and entertainment software. Spyware typically tracks the user's habits while using an application such as a music player that relays the user's musical preferences back to the application vendor. This information can then be compiled by the vendor and sold to third parties such as record companies.

Many types of antivirus and personal firewall software can detect and clean software designated as adware and spyware. It is critical that end users run some type of security software on their computers and regularly scan their hard drives for evidence of adware and spyware programs that are secretly sending personal data from the computers to advertisers. User education is also important to advise users not to download non-work-oriented software that may contain adware or spyware, such as games, screensavers, entertainment, or social media software, to a networked company computer.

Rootkits

A *rootkit* is a type of back-door program that is inserted into application software and allows a remote user *root* access (administrator access) to the system on which the software is installed, without the permission or knowledge of the user. This access potentially results in full control over the target system. Although rootkits are usually related to malware and Trojan horse types of malicious software, they are also becoming more common in trusted applications that are potentially used by millions of users.

For example, a well-known entertainment company was found to be distributing rootkits on its music CDs. This software was installed on a user's computer while the music CD was played on the system. This software installation was not disclosed to the user, and the software (primarily used for digital rights management of music copyright) allowed root access and control of the computer system for anyone aware that the software was installed. After the issue was widely publicized on the Internet, the company quickly intervened to ensure that this software was no longer distributed with its music CDs.

Rootkits are not always installed by application software. They can be distributed via firmware updates for a hardware device, embedded into the primary operating system kernel (kernel rootkits), and included on application software libraries such as DLL files. Rootkits do not spread like a worm or virus; they typically infect one system only. However, rootkits themselves are typically spread as the payload of replicating worms and viruses.

Several types of rootkits exist, including the following:

- **Firmware rootkits**   The rootkit is embedded within the firmware of a device, such as a computer peripheral or network device. The rootkit is always available, as it is embedded within the firmware of the system and is always activated when the device is running.
- **Kernel rootkits**   The rootkit is embedded within the operating system core itself. This effectively hides the rootkit, as it runs as a hidden process and can rarely be spotted by checking active processes on the system.

- **Persistent rootkits**   The rootkit is enabled when the system starts and will not turn off unless the system is shut down. This type of rootkit is often installed and activated within the Windows Registry and is run each time the system boots.
- **Application rootkits**   The rootkit is activated and run in current system memory only when a specific application is launched and is not persisted when the system is shut down and restarted.
- **Library rootkits**   In software applications that use code library files, such as Windows DLLs, the rootkit can intercept specific system and API calls and replace them with its own code.

Most antivirus software applications are able to detect the presence of rootkits; however, they may be difficult to clean from a system, especially if they are embedded in the kernel or boot sectors of an OS. In such cases, it is often the safest and most secure practice to reinstall the system to ensure that any rootkit code is deleted.

Botnets

Botnet is short for *robot network*. A *bot* is typically any type of computer system that is attached to a network whose security has been compromised and that runs malicious software completely unknown to the system users. Botnets (often called "zombie" computers) are typically used for *distributed denial-of-service (DDoS)* attacks in which hundreds or even tens of thousands of computers are overtaken and programmed to send network attacks to a single target site. Botnets can also be used to send out large amounts of spam, adware, spyware, and malware.

An infected computer (which is typically infected by a worm, virus, or Trojan horse) that is made part of the botnet might not show any initial effects. It is only after the computer is remotely "turned on" to start its attack on another computer that the compromise becomes apparent. Typical symptoms include slow responsiveness and large amounts of network packets being sent from the infected system.

Because compromised servers are controlled by the botnets and are typically not under local control, and because of servers' distributed nature, which means the affected servers could be located anywhere in the world, it can be difficult to mitigate the effects of these types of coordinated attacks. It is also very difficult to plan for future attacks. Although the originating addresses of the systems in the botnet can be blocked, other compromised systems can be easily added to the botnet to continue the attack from different addresses. Nevertheless, regular investigations of system activity and frequent antivirus scans can help prevent a system from becoming infected with a virus or worm and becoming a bot within a larger botnet.

Carry Out Appropriate Procedures to Establish Host Security

Objective 11.02

CompTIA Security+
Objective 4.2

The following sections describe the procedures an administrator should take when securing server and workstation operating systems and applications and creating and deploying a security policy across all systems in the network.

Host Software Security Baseline

A *security baseline* is a minimum standard that each system and application must meet to supply the absolute minimum standard of protection against security vulnerabilities and to mitigate threats and risks. Security baselines are created to provide assurance that all aspects of operating system and software applications are running at a specified base level of security.

To establish initial baselines, specific security requirements of your environment and a history of past security vulnerabilities in your systems and applications should be compiled. You can also gather information from industry security standards, associations, and organizations of systems administrators. This information helps ensure that your operating systems and applications are all running the latest software updates, patches, and hot fixes that minimize the risks of known software exploits. After these baselines have been compiled and configured specifically for your environment, they must be implemented across the network and updated regularly to ensure maximum security efficiency for all systems in your organization.

Security templates and *policies* provide a documented minimum configuration baseline for all of your server and workstation operating systems and applications. When a server or workstation is first installed, the template must be applied so that the system meets the minimal version and security update policies as outlined by the organization.

Organizations typically have separate security *group policies* that cover different organizational groups such as development, sales, human resources, IT, and so on. This ensures that the security issues that are specific to a certain organizational department are treated in separate policies. For example, a server in a human resources department may have much stricter security policies and baselines than a server in the sales department. The human resources server contains confidential data about employees and therefore causes greater security concerns for the privacy and security of the data than a file server containing sales and marketing information.

Operating System Hardening

The operating system (OS) is the primary software that controls how your system works and how it interoperates with your hardware. The OS is the most critical part of your computer system. *Operating system hardening* refers to keeping the OS and any software patches up to date and removing unnecessary software services from the system.

Despite having been tested before being released, every OS experiences some software bugs and security vulnerabilities that crop up after release. New versions of the software or bug fixes and patches are released to correct these issues, and you should make sure that these are installed on the system as soon as possible. You must also be aware of any types of operating system vulnerabilities in virtual machines installed in your environment that run multiple types of operating systems on the same hardware platform.

In addition to software updates, many other areas of your OS need to be examined for security vulnerabilities, including setting configuration options, examining available running services, and securing file systems.

Operating System Updates

Your OS software should be operating at the latest release version with the most recent security patches applied. OS vendors regularly release software updates, which are often rolled into larger software packages called *service packs* or *updates*. Smaller bug fixes or patches that fix critical security vulnerabilities (often called *hot fixes*) are usually released quickly, so administrators can patch their systems before hackers can take advantage of the vulnerability. Vendors usually provide these patches and service packs as downloads from their web sites. Some OSs have automatic system update functions that can periodically connect to the vendor's web site and download the latest versions of software components. Some vendors release an update DVD or Internet download every few months that contain all the latest patches and bug fixes since the last version.

It is especially important that you perform this software update procedure just after a new system has been installed. The OS installed on a computer is often the original version that shipped with the hardware; since that time, a number of service packs and patches have probably been released.

Travel Advisory

Even if you just installed a service pack for your OS, you need to install any security patches released after that service pack to be fully protected and current.

Server and Workstation Patch Management

In organizations with hundreds and often thousands of workstations, it can be a logistical nightmare to keep all the operating systems and application software up-to-date. In most cases, automatic operating system updates can be enabled on workstations that allow them to be automatically updated via the network. However, administrators must have a clear security policy and baseline plan to ensure that all workstations are running a certain minimum level of software versions.

Before installing any update or patch onto networked systems, it should first be installed on a server in a lab environment. In some cases, software updates have been known to fix one problem but cause another. If no lab system is available, you can patch a server after business hours, constantly monitoring that server and having a backout plan in place to remove the update if something should go wrong.

BIOS Security

The basic input and output system (BIOS) of a host system contains the program code and instructions for starting a computer and loading the OS. BIOS software can be updated when new hardware support and device drivers are required. BIOS software updates may also contain bug fixes and security enhancements that prevent problems in the BIOS code from being exploited and causing a system to be compromised; the BIOS of servers and clients should be updated to the latest version.

Most BIOS programs also contain a basic password feature that allows the network administrator to assign a password to the BIOS system that must be entered before any BIOS changes or updates can occur. This provides an additional layer of security to prevent unauthorized access to the BIOS software or the primary system settings.

Administrators should be aware that unauthorized users can also boot a system (if they have physical access to it) using CD or DVD media that can boot their own OS and bypass the actual BIOS and OS of the computer. The disc contains a minimal OS software environment and does not boot any code from the system hard disk. From the disc's OS, an attacker can access the host system and its hard disk.

Services and OS Configuration

After you've installed an OS, configuring a number of administrative and security-related options can increase your system security. Other options might make your system more vulnerable to attack—that's why installing or enabling only the necessary options for a particular system is critical. By enabling unnecessary options, you create potential vulnerabilities for unauthorized users to exploit.

The system should also be investigated for services installed by default that are not required, and this is especially important when you are enabling services to be run on your system. Examples of services that might not be needed, but could be running, are file- and print-sharing services and Internet services such as the Hypertext Transfer Protocol (HTTP), the File Transfer Protocol (FTP), the Simple Mail Transfer Protocol (SMTP), the Domain Name System (DNS), and the Dynamic Host Configuration Protocol (DHCP). If the system you are configuring does not need to share files, the server service should be disabled so that no one on the network can connect to a network share on that system. Enabled Internet services can cause a variety of security vulnerabilities by opening network ports on your system to which unauthorized users can connect. For example, enabling web server services on your system enables hackers to connect to your system by issuing HTTP requests to the server, where they can attempt a variety of attacks to gain access or to disrupt communications.

Exam Tip
Services that are not required by the system should be disabled or removed, while existing services should be configured to provide maximum security.

File System Security

For file servers that share files with other users and computer systems, the file system in use must properly address security concerns for locking down file sharing. Older types of disk file systems, such as file allocation table (FAT), do not provide the same security as NTFS on Microsoft systems or ext3 or later on Linux. Newer file system formats allow for greater access controls, such as specific security permissions for files and directories. Some file systems also provide encryption capabilities, so no one can read the contents of a system without the proper encryption key.

Another aspect of file system security is how access permissions are configured for files on the server. Without proper access control, users can read or modify files that could be confidential in nature. Protection is critical for OS files that contain administrative programs and sensitive configuration programs. Access to system files should be granted only to system administrators, and user files should be stored on a separate disk or partition to ensure these system files are not accidentally accessed or removed.

Users should each have a separate home directory, to which only that user has access. Group or department directories should be set up for files that must be shared among groups.

System User Accounts and Password Threats

Although the most common form of system authentication is a login and password procedure, this is also considered one of the weakest security mechanisms available. Users' passwords tend to be weak because users use common dictionary words or personal information that can be easily guessed by an unauthorized user. Often a user's password is the name of a spouse or a pet, or a birth date. Or the user may reveal passwords to others or write them down in conspicuous locations, such as a note taped to the computer monitor.

Most operating systems come with a default administrative account called *admin, administrator,* or another obvious name that points to this account as being necessary to manage and administer the system. For Unix-based systems, the *root* account is still the primary account that's been used for decades for full access to a Unix system. Most malicious users and attackers look for the admin or root account of a system or device as the first account to be compromised.

It is a best practice for network administrators either to disable or rename the admin account, or, if that is not possible, to create an alternative administrative account with equal access rights and name it something inconspicuous. This ensures that a malicious user cannot automatically try to log in using the well-known account names for the admin user. It is a regular practice to use separate logins for each administrator to ensure that any admin account actions can be properly logged and audited. Generally, network administrators should never name accounts after their job function, such as *admin, backup, databaseadmin,* and so on.

Enforcing the use of strong passwords, which are not based on dictionary words or personal information but include the use of alphanumeric characters and uppercase and lowercase letters, greatly diminishes an unauthorized user's ability to guess a password. To ensure the usefulness and efficiency of a login and password procedure, account and password policies, such as enforced password expiry and rotation after a specific period of time, must be created and strictly followed.

Travel Assistance
For detailed information on user account and password security, see Chapter 6.

Management Interface Security

Access to servers should be restricted to authorized individuals, such as the network administrator. Servers should be stored in a locked room with controlled access, and locked in some type of cage or rack to prevent passersby from being able to access the console or the server equipment itself. The server console should be password-protected, so only authenticated users can physically access the server or attempt access through a network connection. Any cables, including network, keyboard, and mouse connections, should be secured and be as short as possible to prevent devices (such as a keystroke logger or network sniffer) from being introduced in the connection.

Remote management access over the network to a host must be secure so that only the network administrator can access the remote management console through a special management application or a web browser. Most management programs allow you to restrict remote access to specific workstations using an IP address or MAC hardware address. Authentication must also be enabled to force a user to authenticate as an administrative user before he can access the management console. Web connections should always use HTTPS (HTTP over SSL) to encrypt management access communications.

When a host management console is left unattended, the user should log off and lock the computer with a password. This prevents passersby from being able to access the systems of others and gaining access to restricted network resources. Many operating systems include the ability to auto-lock the host, or time-out a web session after a certain period of inactivity.

Host Internet Access

Most users have access to the Internet to send and receive e-mail and instant messages, and to access information they need to do their work. Although most networks are secured from outside intrusion through the use of routers and firewalls, several security vulnerabilities can be created by users inside the network.

At the office, users often download and install applications that should not be operating on the company network, such as chat, file and music-sharing programs. Unfortunately, these applications can contain security vulnerabilities that allow access to unauthorized users outside the company via unique service ports that the company firewall might not be blocking. Beyond the security vulnerabilities, user interaction with external Internet users can result in viruses or

Trojan horse programs being downloaded, which allow back-door access to the user's computer. To protect against the use of these programs, the network administrator should block the service ports accessed by these programs on the main network firewall so that they cannot communicate with the Internet. The administrator can also assign access rights to users on their computers that deny them the ability to install any type of software that is not already loaded on their system.

Some users also download questionable content from the Internet, such as pornographic materials or other objectionable content, onto their office computer. This presents a legal problem for the company, as many companies have been sued for allowing such access. To prevent this activity, network administrators can install special web filter programs that block access to these sites. These filters use a list of known objectionable sites that is compared to the web sites users try to access through their web browsers. These lists can also contain web sites of well-known phishing, spyware, and malware sites, which can also be blocked accordingly.

Travel Assistance
For detailed information on firewalls, content filters, and web security gateways, see Chapter 8.

Software Access and Privileges

All software on the workstation should be kept current with the most recent patches and upgrades to remove security vulnerabilities from previous versions. The administrator should ensure that users have only the access privileges they need to perform their job functions. For example, any system functions that enable changes to be made to the network address of a computer—or any other type of system change—should be off limits to a regular user and accessible only to the administrator. Regular users should not be able to access any application or configuration programs other than what are required for their jobs. The most efficient way of preventing certain system functions from user abuse is to enact network-wide security policies that are automatically set for each workstation on the network. This can save considerable time over an administrator having to visit each workstation and block out items one by one.

Host Security Applications

A wide variety of security software can be installed on your system to protect it against various types of security threats such as viruses, spyware, malware, e-mail spam, access intrusion, network attacks, and web browsing threats. The following sections describe some of the types of system security software that can be installed to protect your system.

Antivirus and Antispyware Software

To protect your systems from being infected by viruses, spyware, and other types of malicious code, antivirus systems should be installed in all aspects of the network—from desktop computers to servers and firewalls. Because viruses and spyware can enter a company network in a variety of ways, such as from a user bringing in a USB key from home, from e-mail attachments, and from Internet downloads, antivirus protection should be set up for all these different types of access points.

Antivirus protection should be set up on every server, desktop, and laptop in the system and should include scheduled updates of virus signature files (discussed in more detail later in this section) from a central antivirus update server. This can protect both the computers and the networks to which they connect, as well as provide a first level of defense from the user level to prevent viruses from spreading to the network.

Protecting just the end-user systems is not enough, however. All servers should be protected to prevent viruses transmitted from a desktop system from spreading to any of the server systems. The reverse situation is also a great concern: If a common file on a server is used by all company systems, they can also be infected simply by accessing the infected server file.

Most viruses and spyware enter a system from e-mail attachments and Internet downloads that come from outside the company. E-mail servers that send and receive mail should be protected with special antivirus software that can scan incoming e-mail for attachments with viruses. The virus is either cleaned or quarantined, or the message is deleted, and notification e-mails are sent to the source and recipient to warn about the existence of the virus.

Travel Advisory

When installing antivirus software on an e-mail server, be certain you install the version of the software that examines incoming mail and attachments. Normal antivirus protection only prevents viruses in normal program files outside the e-mail system.

Many types of network firewalls or other types of network-perimeter devices can be set up with virus-protection software that can scan files being downloaded from the Internet. With the amount of traffic that goes through a firewall, this type of protection can slow down the network considerably, so be aware and evaluate your system needs carefully.

Virus Signature Files   Antivirus software companies update their software regularly to add code that protects against new virus and spyware threats that are created every day. Having to update the entire software package on every user's computer in a company would be extremely expensive and impractical. Antivirus software companies use a virus pattern or signature file to patch users' systems conveniently and quickly.

Each computer virus contains or creates a specific binary code that can be used as a unique identifier. From these binary signatures produced by the virus, the antivirus engineers create a signature file that can be used to identify the viruses when scanning with the antivirus scan engine program. These signature files can contain thousands of known virus types. They can even include special algorithms for detecting common virus-like behavior that can indicate a new virus. When the virus is identified, the antivirus software can use that information to quarantine the file or attempt to remove the virus from the file.

To make use of these signature files, you must be diligent in regularly updating the system with the latest virus definition file. This usually involves connecting to the antivirus vendor's web site and downloading and installing the latest signature file. Some antivirus programs can be set up to automate this process, checking for a new signature file on a schedule and automatically updating the file without user intervention. When you first install an antivirus program, you should immediately check for updated signatures to make sure you are scanning with the most recent signature files.

Antispam Software

One of the most annoying e-mail problems, *spam,* is a deliberate attempt by an advertiser or business to mass e-mail a large number of users with unsolicited advertisements. Any time you enter your e-mail address on a public web site or a newsgroup, you open yourself to the possibility of having your e-mail address added to spam mailing lists. These mailing lists are shared among Internet spam advertisers, and sometimes, you can receive multiple junk e-mails every day. This annoys not only users, but also network administrators because of the amount of space and bandwidth these mass mailings can consume. Many ISPs and corporate networks use antispam mail filters that block incoming spam e-mail from reaching users' inboxes.

Spam has evolved from the early years of simple text adverts to full HTML messages with clickable links, images, and even spam messages hidden in attached images and document files. The links in spam messages are often redirected to malicious sites containing spyware, malware, and phishing activities.

Travel Assistance
For detailed information on antispam solutions that reside between your e-mail server and your e-mail client host, see Chapter 8.

Antispam software is widely available for host systems. Most e-mail clients now include spam-blocking applications that filter e-mail as it is downloaded from the mail server. Utilizing spam training identification, mail clients can automatically detect spam messages and move them to a special junk or spam e-mail folder. This keeps the spam and junk mail distinct from regular e-mail messages that are passed directly to the mail client inbox.

These types of spam blockers are normally not as efficient as dedicated antispam devices at the network border; however, they do provide an additional layer of protection for any spam messages that happen to make it to the client from the server. Users can typically add friends and co-workers to a trusted list that will bypass the spam scanner to ensure that these e-mails are never blocked.

Host-Based Firewalls

Most organizations have firewall servers or appliances that protect the perimeters of their network from Internet attacks and hide the details of the internal network. Computer users who connect directly to an Internet connection rarely have any type of hardware-based firewall. Software-based firewall applications, however, have become an absolute necessity for a user connecting directly to the Internet from home or work directly using a cable modem, digital subscriber line (DSL), or dial-up methods. A software firewall application performs several critical functions to protect a user's host computer:

- **Blocks incoming network connections**   The primary purpose of the personal firewall is to block incoming network connections from the Internet. It can hide your system from port-scanning attacks whereby malicious hackers probe network-connected computers for open network ports and vulnerabilities. The firewall software effectively makes your computer invisible to those on the Internet, and it will not reply to any network probes or diagnostic utilities such as Ping or Traceroute. Worms and other malware threats that are spread through the Internet will be stopped in their tracks by the firewall software, as they will not be able to see your system to connect to it.

- **Watches for suspicious outbound activity**   A personal firewall application monitors outbound activity and allows the user complete control over what applications are allowed or blocked access to the Internet. For example, when your antivirus software periodically retrieves the latest virus signature file from an Internet site, your personal firewall will alert you that the application is trying to access the Internet. In this case, the activity is acceptable, and you can allow the software to pass through the firewall and to do so automatically on subsequent accesses so you will not receive an alert each time. This type of protection is extremely important to protect against Trojan horse and spyware applications that may be running on your computer and sending private information back to a malicious user. The personal firewall will detect the suspicious outbound activity and alert you. You can block the application if you do not recognize it and then attempt to remove it with your antivirus or antispyware software.

- **Provides ability to block/allow programs** All applications that potentially try to communicate out to the Internet can have their access controlled by the personal firewall. The personal firewall allows you to control which applications can send data to the Internet and which cannot. Some applications need to communicate to other servers to work properly, and care must be taken not to block critical system or application services. In addition, trusted applications can occasionally visit an Internet site to check for new updates to the software, and this can be considered acceptable activity. Other applications, however, may be secretly sending information out to the Internet, such as personal identification information or data about your activities on your computer, such as lists of web sites you have visited.

- **Warns of unpatched software and outdated antivirus files** Many personal firewalls can scan your computer to make sure that your OS and application software are running the latest versions, and they will alert you if your software seems to be out of date. Most personal firewalls will alert you if your antivirus signature files are out of date and will prompt you to run the updated software to get the latest files.

- **Provides web browser security** Personal firewall software can also strengthen the security and privacy of your web browsing sessions. The software can block pop-up and banner ads to prevent you from accessing known phishing or spyware sites and to ensure that your web browsing cookies and web cache are not causing security and privacy issues. Many firewalls will also block web sites that run scripting, which is a primary source for browser exploits and security risks. However, scripting and cookies are often necessary for certain web sites such as online banking, and it will be necessary to adjust your firewall settings as appropriate to protect your web browsing sessions without impacting functionality.

- **Provides e-mail security**   Some personal firewalls monitor your inbound and outbound e-mail and can quarantine suspicious attachments to help prevent the spread of viruses, worms, and Trojan horse software. In some cases, if you are infected by a worm and your e-mail application is attempting to mail the worm to everyone in your address book, the personal firewall can detect this activity and block outbound mail from being sent out from your computer and prevent you from accidentally infecting other computers.

Web Browser Security

As web browsers are the most widely used Internet applications, security is of the utmost importance. Web browser vulnerabilities and misuse can open a computer system to a vast array of security risks and threats, including viruses, worms, malware, spyware, and identity theft.

Security Modes and Trusted Sites   Many popular web browsers such as Internet Explorer, Firefox, and Safari come with enhanced security settings that allow users to run their web browser in specific security modes such as high, medium, or low. Each security mode offers a level of security that is contrasted with ease of use. For example, high security modes typically disable many web site features that cause security concerns such as scripting, ActiveX and JavaScript controls, and installation of third-party software and other potentially malicious software. Unfortunately, many legitimate web sites use these technologies, and users can be frustrated with the number of warnings that occur when accessing these web sites. Many popular web sites also require scripting and pop-up windows and will not work properly if they are disabled. Lower security modes tend to allow certain levels of scripting, while disabling the most obvious web site security risks. Administrators can use security policies to force the use of a security mode that offers the highest security possible for all users. It is much safer to start with a strong security mode and to add exceptions to that mode rather than start with a weak security mode.

Exam Tip

Administrators must lock down operating systems and applications with a strong security mode, and then add exceptions to that mode rather than starting with a weak security mode and strengthening as they go.

Users can add lists of trusted sites to ensure that these legitimate sites bypass any high-security controls. For example, a user may add an online banking web site to the list of trusted sites to allow cookies, scripting, and pop-up windows to be used, while blocking all other web sites with these functions.

Pop-up Blockers   Several popular add-ons and extensions to web browsers allow certain types of *pop-up advertising* to be blocked before it appears on the user's monitor. These pop-up ads, typically generated by JavaScript or some other type of web scripting language, can be a nuisance when web browsing, as the ad will open up a new browser window in front of the one you are currently viewing. The ad will link to another site for advertising purposes and will direct you to a new web site if clicked. In many cases, closing the pop-up ad may cause another ad to pop up in its place. The web site may also open up several pop-up windows, and often it may be difficult to close them without having to shut down and restart the web browser.

Pop-up ads can be a security issue if they link back to spyware and malware sites or download malicious scripts and applications to the browser. Many pop-up ads contain a link or control to close the window, but the control is actually a link to another web site or a control to download malicious software. For the user, it is sometimes difficult knowing how to close the pop-up ad properly to prevent others from appearing.

Most modern web browsers contain some type of pop-up ad-blocking capabilities, ensuring that when you visit a web site containing pop-up ads, the primary web site will appear, but all pop-up ads will be blocked and will not appear on your monitor. Some third-party ad-blocking software goes further by blocking banners ads within the primary web site itself.

In some cases, pop-up windows are used for legitimate purposes, such as help windows with additional information or the installation of legitimate software. Most web browsers give you control on whether to block or allow pop-up ads and windows, and you can allow certain trusted sites to display pop-ups if you are aware of their content.

Cookies   *Cookies* are small files that are saved on your computer and store data for a specific web site you have visited. Cookies can contain all types of data specific to that web site, such as information to track unique visitors to the web site, login information for the user, and information on other web sites you have visited. Some cookies are cleared after your session on a specific web site ends, other cookies expire over a certain period or time, and still other cookies do not expire at all but stay on your system (until you delete them).

Due to the often sensitive information they contain, cookies can often be a security and privacy risk in the event a cookie with your credentials for a specific web site is accessed by a malicious user. Many web users also have privacy concerns with web site cookies that track previous web sites they have visited.

Most web browsers have a configuration option that lets you examine each cookie on your system. You can keep or delete cookies, or clear all the current cookies off of your system. Cookies can also be expired after a certain amount of time has passed. When you start web surfing again, new cookies will appear in your cookie directory. You also have the option of blocking third-party cookies, which are typically cookies from advertising sites not related to the current site you are browsing. Blocking third-party cookies can greatly reduce the change of your private web browsing history from being leaked to third-party sites.

> ## Travel Advisory
>
> To protect your privacy even more and to avoid sending demographic information to web sites, most web browsers allow you to disable cookies and to delete any existing ones on exiting the program. Unfortunately, many web sites require cookies to be enabled to function properly.

Private Web Browsing Data   As you use your web browser, it collects data on the web sites you visit, the site addresses, and any downloads you make from the web site; caches certain types of content such as frequently loaded images; and stores cookies with personal identifying data for a specific web site. Most of this data is helpful to store—for example, your browsing history will contain all the sites you have visited, and you may need to access the history to remember a specific web site if you want to return there. Cookies remember information about a specific web site, such as login credentials, and fill them in for you the next time you visit that web site.

Privacy concerns for your personally identifiable information and web surfing habits will increase as this data collects over time, and is important to clear this data periodically. All web browsers offer some type of functionality to clear the information manually or automatically after a certain period of time. Most web browsers also offer antiphishing protection to prevent your personal data from being revealed to phishing fraud sites. Some web browsers like Firefox also offer a "private" browsing mode that does not save any browse history or cache any data or images while you are web browsing.

Host-Based Intrusion Detection System

A *host-based intrusion detection system (HIDS)* monitors a specific host for suspicious behavior that could indicate someone is trying to break into the system. An HIDS monitors inbound and outbound network activity, networking service ports, system log files, and time stamps and content of data and configuration files to ensure they have not been changed. The host-based system can only monitor the system on which it is installed and is typically used for critical server systems rather than user workstations.

A host-based system can detect attacks that occur from a malicious user who is physically accessing the system console. The unauthorized user may be trying to access an administrator account or trying to copy files to or from the system, for example. The intrusion detection system is able to alert the administrator if someone has tried to log in to an account unsuccessfully too many times.

A HIDS using active methods of detection can take immediate steps to halt an intrusion. This is the preferable method, because it prevents the suspicious activity from continuing. Passive methods merely log the incident or send an e-mail to the administrator, who might not see the message for many hours before she can take action. If the intrusion is detected as originating at the system console, the system can shut down and disable that user account or automatically log out the user. Locking accounts is a form of detection used by most network operating systems that disable accounts if a predefined number of unsuccessful logins occurs. The disadvantage of active detection is the case of a false positive detection, in which the system automatically shuts down services when no attack is occurring; this can cause unnecessary and often costly downtime.

Passive detection methods do not take active steps to prevent an intrusion from continuing if it is detected. Passive methods typically include logging events to a system log that can be viewed by an administrator at a later time, or if configured to do so, to forward the log entries through e-mail, instant messaging, or a text message. This enables the administrator to be notified as the intrusion is happening. This gives the administrator a chance to catch the unauthorized user in the act and to prevent damage or data theft. If the administrator is not immediately notified, they must be sure to audit system log files regularly for critical warnings and errors that indicate suspicious activity.

Exam Tip
Remember that active intrusion detection takes steps to mitigate an intrusion, while a passive system typically logs the event or generates alarms.

Mobile Device Security

Mobile computing devices include laptops as well as mobile phones, personal organizers, personal digital assistants (PDAs), tablets, netbooks, and other types of wireless devices. Security concerns for mobile devices derive from the nature of their portability, which makes them susceptible to theft, vandalism, and unauthorized access to data. The following describes additional security precautions to consider with mobile devices.

Protection from Theft

A mobile phone lying on a desk can be tucked into a coat pocket in seconds, but even unattended laptops can disappear quickly off a user's desk, even during office hours. Mobile devices should never be left unattended, and small items, such as mobile phones and PDAs, should be safely secured in a pocket, purse, or belt holster. Larger items, such as laptops, can be secured to a desk or workstation by using a special lockable cable.

Password/Screen Lock

If a mobile device is stolen, a simple authentication scheme can deter the unauthorized user from accessing any sensitive information on the device. The thief may simply want the hardware rather than the data that resides within, but any device that contains confidential information can be stolen for its valuable content, such as company data or personal identity information. A simple screen lock password can block access to the device until the password is properly entered. On laptops, you can enable a BIOS password that is required at boot time before the operating system loads to prevent anyone from starting up the laptop unless the password is entered.

GPS Tracking

Many mobile devices, primarily phones, contain GPS (Global Positioning System) chips so that they can be tracked by and use the services of GPS satellites. If your device is ever lost or stolen, you can track the location of the device via its GPS coordinates and attempt to recover it.

Remote Wipe

If your device is lost or stolen, an unauthorized person may be able to access your data if there are no authentication or encryption mechanisms in use. Many mobile devices have the ability to remotely delete their contents. Your mobile device can be tracked by its hardware address, and you can use a management application or a web browser application to initiate a remote wipe of the device so that all your data is deleted. You may have lost the hardware, but your private data is removed from the device.

Device Encryption

Beyond authentication, devices can be protected through the use of encryption. By encrypting the contents of a mobile device, the corresponding encryption key is required before any user can read any data. If the user does not have the key, no access is granted. This is useful for password files that users sometimes keep on their PDAs, flash memory cards, and other mobile devices. Many OSs now come with encrypted file systems, such as BitLocker for Windows and

FileVault for Apple MAC OS. Users can selectively encrypt partitions or entire hard drives that require a password key for access. The files are encrypted and decrypted "on the fly" as the authorized user accesses them. The drive encryption typically employs Advanced Encryption Standard (AES) 128- or 256-bit encryption technology. This encryption slows down performance but provides excellent security for laptops and prevents an unauthorized user from accessing any contents of the hard drive.

Voice Encryption

Voice communications over mobile phones can be intercepted and captured just like any other network communication. For high-security environments and for personal confidentiality, you can encrypt voice communications between users. Software encryption programs are available that run on your mobile device and, when activated, encrypt the voice communication between two users. The other user requires the same software to decrypt and encrypt the communication.

Mobile Camera Security

Almost everyone owns a personal and/or company mobile phone. Mobile phones are now used for more than telephone conversations and often offer a combination of features—such as a web browser, e-mail reader, music player, PDA, data storage, and a camera. In high-security environments, mobile phones with cameras are often banned because they can be concealed and used to take high-resolution images that can be instantly transferred offsite via the cell phone network. In unprotected environments, it can be easy for an unauthorized user to connect a mobile phone or other type of mobile device to a computer and copy data to the device for later use. Mobile phones are considered vital communications devices, and it can be difficult to justify the temporary confiscation of a camera mobile phone. But in high-security environments, doing so protects the confidentiality and security of data.

CHECKPOINT

✔ **Objective 11.01: Analyze and differentiate among types of malware.**
Slow responsiveness and high network activity can indicate malware activity on a system. Keep antivirus software up to date to be able to detect new types of viruses and spyware. Don't connect malware-infected host systems to a network until they are cleaned.

✔**Objective 11.02: Carry out appropriate procedures to establish host security.**   Use antivirus software to protect yourself against a wide variety of malware programs. Host-based firewalls can monitor the inbound and outbound network activity of your system and notify you of abnormal behavior provide the ability to block or allow access. Use passwords and encryption to protect the data of mobile devices. Use security baselines and policies to establish a strong, secure foundation for your OS, applications, and web browsers for all your systems.

REVIEW QUESTIONS

1. You suspect that your server has been compromised because it has been running slow and is unresponsive. Using a network analyzer, you also notice that large amounts of network data are being sent out from the server. Which of the following is the most likely cause?

   A. The server has a rootkit installed.

   B. The server requires an operating system update.

   C. The server is infected with spyware.

   D. The server is part of a botnet.

2. As part of your security baselining and operating system hardening, you want to make sure you protect yourself from vulnerabilities in your operating system software. Which of the following tasks should you perform?

   A. Update antivirus signature files.

   B. Install any patches or OS updates.

   C. Use an encrypted file system.

   D. Use a host-based intrusion detection system.

3. You suspect that your server has been infected with a rootkit malware program. Which of the following actions would be most effective at removing the rootkit software?

   A. Install antispyware software.

   B. Disable the BIOS of the computer system and reboot.

   C. Install the latest operating system update patch.

   D. Reinstall the operating system.

4. A user has brought a virus-infected laptop into the facility. It contains no antivirus protection software and hasn't been hooked up to the network yet. What's the best way to fix the laptop?

   A. Get the laptop on the network and download antivirus software from a server.

   B. Boot the laptop with an antivirus boot CD.

   C. Get the laptop on the network and download antivirus software from the Internet.

   D. Connect the laptop to another computer and clean it up from there.

5. You are creating a standard security baseline for all users who use company mobile phones. Which of the following is the most effective security measure to protect against unauthorized access to the mobile device?

   A. Enforce the use of a screen lock password.

   B. Enable the GPS chip.

   C. Install personal firewall software.

   D. Automatically perform a daily remote wipe.

6. Your network has had a history of problems with users downloading software from the Internet that contains Trojan horse software with back-door access. Which of the following security mechanisms will help detect Trojan horse software activity?

   A. Antispam software

   B. Pop-up blocker

   C. Host firewall software

   D. Adware detection

7. A security patch for your OS was released about a week after you applied the latest operating system service pack. What should you do?

   A. Wait until the release of the next full service pack.

   B. Download the patch only if you experience problems with the OS.

   C. Do nothing—the security patch was probably included with the service pack.

   D. Download and install the security patch.

8. Your application firewall is indicating that some type of HTTP worm is trying to infect one of your database servers, which also seems to be running an HTTP web server on port 80. This server does not need any type of web services. What should be done?

   A. Install antivirus software.

   B. Change the web server to use a different port.

   C. Disable the web server.

   D. Update your firewall software to the latest version.

9. To protect the confidentiality of web user browsing history and web site credentials, which of the following security baseline policies should you enable for all user web browsers?

    A. Block third-party cookies.

    B. Periodically delete the browser cache.

    C. Enforce SSL.

    D. Disable JavaScript.

10. You have recently installed antivirus software on several client workstations and performed a full scan of the systems. One of the systems was infected with a virus less than an hour after the installation of the software. Which of the following is the most likely issue?

    A. The virus was already pre-existing on the system.

    B. Antivirus signatures need to be updated.

    C. The virus could only be blocked by a pop-up blocker.

    D. Operating system software was out of date.

REVIEW ANSWERS

1. **D**   If your system has been infected with a worm or virus and has become part of a botnet, at certain times it may take part in distributed denial-of-service attacks on another system on the Internet and may exhibit slow responsiveness and a large amount of network data being sent out of the system.

2. **B**   The most recent software updates and patches for your operating system will contain the latest bug and exploit fixes. This prevents known bugs and weakness in the operating system from being exploited.

3. **D**   The most effective way to remove a rootkit is to reinstall the operating system. Simply running antivirus or antispyware software might not remove embedded rootkit files that can be hidden from security software.

4. **B**   If a computer is infected with a virus, do not connect it to a network or you run the risk of the virus infecting other computers and servers. Use an antivirus program on a boot CD to clean the virus off the laptop before connecting it to the network.

5. **A**   To prevent unauthorized access to the device in the event it is lost or stolen, you can enable a screen lock password. The user will not be able to access the device until he enters the password.

6. **C** A host-based firewall software program can detect abnormal network activity and alert the user that network connections are trying to send data outbound from your system.

7. **D** Even though you just installed the latest service pack, a security vulnerability might have recently been discovered, requiring that you install a new security patch. You will not be protected from the vulnerability if you do not install the security patch, and it might be too dangerous to wait for it to be included in the next service pack.

8. **C** Any application or service that is not needed by the server should be disabled or uninstalled. Leaving services enabled, such as a web server, could make the server vulnerable to web server attacks, including HTTP-based worms.

9. **A** Third-party cookies are typically from advertising sites not related to the specific site you are browsing. By blocking these cookies, you will protect any identifying information in your web browsing history from being leaked to third-party companies.

10. **B** Your antivirus software is installed with a default database of virus signatures. It may be several months out of date, and it is a best practice to immediately run the signature file update to make sure you are running with the latest signatures, or else it may miss detecting a newly identified virus.

Securing Applications and Data

ITINERARY

- ○ **Objective 12.01** Analyze and differentiate among types of application attacks
- ○ **Objective 12.02** Explain the importance of application security
- ○ **Objective 12.03** Explain the importance of data security

	NEWBIE	SOME EXPERIENCE	EXPERT
ETA	3 hours	2 hours	1 hour

As part of a layered security model, your network perimeter is the first layer of defense for preventing network attacks and unauthorized intrusion. If a hacker were to penetrate the network perimeter, the next layer of defense is security for your host systems that provide protection against attacks and intrusions directed at specific host servers and clients in your network.

Application security is another layer of defense that provides protection for the applications that run on your hosts. These include Internet servers such as web, e-mail, FTP, and database servers. Internet web servers are the most common types of servers that come under attack, and extra care must be taken when deploying web applications because their public nature provides the opportunity for hackers to take advantage of vulnerabilities unique to web services, such as buffer overflows, input validation, cross-site scripting, and command insertion. A hacker can send malformed input to a web application, causing it to crash, provide unauthorized access, or result in data theft and loss. Clients who connect to malicious web sites from their web browser can have their login credentials and session information stolen, and allow a hacker unauthorized access to perform actions with the credentials of the target client.

Application security also requires careful consideration of how the application was designed and developed. Secure coding concepts must be closely adhered to. This ensures that when the application is created and deployed, it uses a secure baseline to prevent the most common types of vulnerabilities.

The final layer of security protection is for the actual data on your host systems. Stored data must be secured from unauthorized access, theft, loss, and manipulation.

This chapter explores various security threats and risks for applications, and describes securing coding concepts and application hardening. Protection for stored data is also discussed, including data loss prevention, encryption techniques, and security concerns for removable media.

Analyze and Differentiate among Types of Application Attacks

Objective 12.01
CompTIA Security+
Objective 3.5

Due to the wide variety of operating systems, programming languages, and application platforms, the chances of security vulnerabilities are greatly increased with the interaction of these different levels of software that host and provide application services. For example, a hacker may be able to insert operating system commands into a web application query input form that are run as if the hacker were the administrative user. Attacks on database servers and data queries can result in a hacker obtaining unauthorized access to confidential data stored by the database if the application is not secure and the stored data not encrypted.

Server administrators must be aware of the various types of application vulnerabilities that can exist within different types of Internet servers such as web, e-mail, and database servers, and know how to mitigate them and prevent the vulnerabilities from being exploited.

Web Application Vulnerabilities

Internet web servers accept HTTP requests from client web browsers, and they send back responses and the requested information to the client. Web servers are the most common forms of servers on the Internet, and as a result, they are the most often attacked. An attack can occur in a variety of ways. Some attacks disrupt users from accessing the information on a web site. Other attacks spread worms and viruses over the Internet. Some attacks vandalize web sites and deface information on web pages or replace it with false information. Most of these attacks take advantage of security vulnerabilities in the web server. The following sections outline some of the more prevalent web application security vulnerabilities.

JavaScript

JavaScript is a scripting language created by Netscape, but it is unrelated to the Java programming language. JavaScript's code is not compiled; instead, it is *interpreted* by the web browser. JavaScript can interact with HTML source code, enabling web authors to create web sites with dynamic content.

Since the introduction of JavaScript, the language has been plagued with security issues. The problems originate from the nature of JavaScript, which allows executable content to be embedded into web pages. These vulnerabilities include the ability for hackers to read files on a user's hard drive and to monitor and intercept a user's web activities. Security precautions are required to prevent malicious code from entering, executing, and retrieving data from the underlying system.

The insecurities of web browsers that implement JavaScript, rather than the JavaScript language itself, are the source of the vulnerabilities. Most security problems discovered in JavaScript implementations require the installation of software patches from the web browser vendor. JavaScript can also be disabled on your web browser. Check the browser's options to disable or enable the use of JavaScript for web sites accessed by users.

ActiveX

ActiveX is a technology created by Microsoft to create reusable components across Windows and web applications. This includes increasing the functionality of Internet applications. ActiveX components can be downloaded to the computer through the web browser. ActiveX functions are controlled by the users themselves. This requires the need for greater security controls because a malicious ActiveX component can be downloaded that could compromise the security of your system. Users must be careful when configuring their web browsers to control ActiveX programs.

> ### Exam Tip
> Know that ActiveX controls run with the same permissions as those used by the user currently logged in.

For web browsing security, ActiveX uses a form of authentication control based on security levels. The user's web browser can be configured to set a certain security level at which ActiveX controls can operate. The lowest level allows all ActiveX components to be downloaded automatically. Increased levels provide warning dialog boxes to alert the user of an ActiveX element and enable the user to download it or not do so. ActiveX relies on digital certificates and trusting certificate authorities to authenticate the origin of ActiveX controls. You should never download ActiveX controls that are unsigned as they will not have an identified and authenticated origin and are most likely malicious in nature.

Make sure your web browser is running the latest version so that the most recent security controls are in place and any previous security vulnerabilities are removed.

> ### Travel Advisory
> Many people, in the interest of higher security, disable some of the advanced web browser functions, such as downloading ActiveX components. Unfortunately, many web sites require these to perform even the most basic functions, and if you disable these functions, you might be unable to access the site. Try to maintain a balance between convenience and security.

Buffer Overflows

Buffer overflow is a programming term used to describe when input data exceeds the limits recognized by a program. For example, a program might be expecting only a certain number of characters in an input dialog box. If the number of characters exceeds this limit, the added information might also be processed.

This extra code could be malicious in nature and cause the program or even the entire system to crash. Buffer overflow attacks typically result in command shell access in which the attacker has administrative privileges.

Travel Advisory
A number of Denial of Service (DoS) attacks are in the form of buffer overflows.

For Internet web applications, the buffer overflow vulnerability is a common security concern for web servers and web browsers. A malicious web server set up by a hacker can crash the systems of the users connecting to that web site by sending various HTTP buffer overflow data streams to the client. Similarly, a malicious hacker using a simple web browser can send certain HTTP data to a web server that overflows its software buffers and crashes the web site.

Buffer overflows are caused primarily by poor input validation that allows illegal data to be entered into the application, which causes processing limits to be exceeded. Buffer overflows have been a thorn in the side of companies that create web server and web browser software. These vulnerabilities are easy to exploit and can significantly affect the performance of a system or cause it to crash.

Privilege Escalation

Many software applications contain bugs that create security vulnerabilities. In a *privilege escalation,* an unauthorized user exploits these bugs within the software to gain more privileged access to a computer system by taking advantage of the bug exploit to bypass the application and perform commands with escalated privileged access.

Vulnerabilities that typically lead to privilege escalation scenarios are most often found in web site code, where scripting and other types of running programs can potentially reveal exploits for malicious users to take control of a system. These are often buffer overflow attacks, in which conditions and boundaries are not properly set on user-entered fields in an application or web site and allow malicious users to crash the program or allow highly privileged command execution.

Protection against privilege escalation requires that programmers use input validation and test their code for bugs and exploits before releasing software. In the event that a documented exploit is found after software is released, it is critical that a patch be quickly made available to fix the bug to prevent proof-of-concept exploits from turning into real security threats. Systems administrators must be diligent in ensuring that any software they run is using the latest patch level to ensure that all known bug fixes are currently deployed.

Local Lingo

proof-of-concept exploit A situation when a potential threat due to a vulnerability in an application or operating system has become known to the general public, enabling malicious hackers to create code to exploit the vulnerability.

Cookies and Session Hijacking

Cookies are a necessary part of most web site application interaction, but they also provide a wide variety of security issues. Cookies contain session data for each web site you have visited that uses cookies. The data are usually innocuous items such as site preferences that are reloaded when a user revisits a site, but often they also contain session data, including some authentication and web form information, along with referral information on web sites you have already visited.

Cookies are easily abused by web site vulnerabilities and malicious code contained on web sites. Cookies are sent in clear text and can be easily captured by an unauthorized user using a network packet sniffer. An unsuspecting user might also click a web link that downloads a malicious script, which collects data on the user's web browser cookies and transmits it back to the hacker's web site.

Session hijacking can occur when a user's cookie for a web site, which can contain session authentication credentials for a remote server, is hijacked by another user who then uses that cookie to gain unauthorized access. The cookie might be transferred from the user's computer to that of that attacker, or it can be captured via a packet sniffer and man-in-the-middle network attacks.

To protect against session hijacking, web applications should regenerate session keys and IDs after a successful login so that a secondary attempt to use the same session credentials from a hijacked cookie will not work. Applications can also check other aspects of a session, such as the IP address, so if the address is different from the original cookie, a new session must be created and authenticated. High-security applications like web banking can use SSL to encrypt sessions, including the transfer of information in user cookies.

HTML Attachments

File attachments received from e-mail messages, IM messages, and download sites can often contain .htm and .html documents. These document types are the default files for web browsers. These HTML attachments, if opened, can automatically open your web browser and immediately connect to a malicious web site. When you are connected to the malicious web site, it may transfer files such as malware and Trojan horse software to your computer. Many e-mail readers automatically open HTML attachments, which can contain malicious dynamic content and automatically load other web data, images, or even hidden code that executes on the client.

If you receive an HTML attachment, make sure it is from a trusted source. Before opening it in a web browser, you should open the HTML file in a text editor to view its contents and check for any abnormal code. Most e-mail clients have security settings that prevent the loading of images in HTML messages unless you explicitly allow them. You can add known sites to a trusted sites list, which configures the e-mail client to automatically display images because you know they come from a trusted source.

Malicious Add-ons

Most web browsers enable all the functionality of add-ons, which are installable modules that provide useful functionality to a user's web browsing experience. These add-ons can be anything from decorative themes, to real-time alerts for weather and stocks, to web utilities. There is the possibility that these add-ons, if not from a trusted source, can contain malicious code that can do anything from installing a Trojan horse program that allows remote access to a user's computer, to stealing confidential personal information.

Make sure that when you install add-ons to your web browser, they originate from a trusted source, such as the web browser's official site. As developers upload their add-ons for public use, they are analyzed and scanned for evidence of malicious code. If you download an add-on from an untrusted source, you have no verification that the code has been tested. Personal firewalls can also alert you to abnormal network connection behavior after you have installed an add-on.

CGI Scripts

Common Gateway Interface (CGI) scripts are programs designed to accept and return data that conforms to the CGI specification. CGI programs are typically written in scripting languages, such as Perl, and are the most common way for web servers to interact dynamically with users. Web pages that contain forms typically use a CGI program to process the form's data once it's submitted.

Each time a CGI script is executed, a new process is started. For some web sites, multiple CGI requests can noticeably slow the server. CGI scripts also are vulnerable to programming bugs, so they should be written with the same care and attention as any software application. Poorly programmed CGI scripts can intentionally or unintentionally provide information about the host system that can aid malicious hackers in accessing the web server. Scripts that utilize user input from web forms can be used against the client machine. For example, on a server system, a subverted CGI script can be used to run malicious code as a privileged user and provide unauthorized access to any part of the system, including sensitive user data as well as logins and passwords. Another concern of CGI scripting is the ability of the user to input data that can be used to attack the web server through buffer overflows and malformed requests.

Cross-Site Scripting

Cross-site scripting (XSS) is a type of web site application vulnerability that allows malicious users to inject malicious code into dynamic web sites that rely on user input. An example of this would be a search engine web site or user message forum that utilizes user input. The malicious user can input a script or series of commands, such as JavaScript, within a legitimate input request that can provide the attacker with additional administrative access to hack user accounts and embed malicious code with cookies and other web-site code that can be downloaded by end users. An unsuspecting user can click a link that downloads a malicious script that collects data on the user's web browser cookies and transmits it back to the web site.

Cross-site scripting can be prevented by careful web programming and strong input validation that does not permit additional code to be included in dynamic input and is effectively ignored by the application. To prevent command insertion, any special characters that could be interpreted as a command are "escaped" as harmless data strings.

Cross-Site Request Forgery (XSRF)

Cross-site request forgery (XSRF or CSRF) is a type of attack that relies on the ability to use a user's current web browsing state, including session cookie data and login identity credentials, and trick that user into navigating to a web site that contains malicious code. At that point the hacker's code can use the session information to make unauthorized requests as the target user, change the user's account information, or steal his credentials. XSRF vulnerabilities have been found on many major web sites, including high-security banking sites.

To prevent XSRF attacks, a web application must verify that a request came from an authorized user, not just the browser of an authorized user. Web applications can require a second identifying value saved in a cookie that is compared with each and every request to the web site. This ensures that the request is coming not only from the same user and browser, but the same authenticated session. A hacker who manages to get a user to go to his malicious web site and steals her session cookie still requires the temporary session request value to take any action as the target user.

Header Manipulation

Header manipulation is a type of web application vulnerability where invalid or malicious data is inserted into HTTP headers. HTTP request and response messages have headers that include various HTTP commands, directives, site referral information, and address data. This data is simple text that can be modified by a malicious user. By manipulating this header information, a hacker can then perform a variety of attacks such as cross-site scripting, session and web page hijacking, and cookie modification.

In general, most web applications process server-side headers, which are generally safe and cannot be manipulated, while ignoring client-side headers in HTTP requests because of the security concern that they are easily manipulated.

XML Injection

XML (Extensible Markup Language) is similar to HTML in that it is a markup language that uses tags to define data. XML differs from HTML in that while HTML is designed to process and display data, XML is used to structure, store, and transport data. In fact, XML carries no data at all but is designed to structure and carry it. XML is used in a wide variety of web applications.

XML injection attacks are able to modify how an XML application processes its data. By injecting XML content into the XML application, the attack results in the application processing data according to the malicious injected XML code. Web applications that process XML documents require input and document schema validation to prevent XML injection attacks from occurring.

Command Injection

Sometimes web applications without proper input validation can allow OS-level commands to be inserted into URLs or input forms that are executed on the server. This can allow an unauthorized user to perform commands on the server with escalated privileges, or gain access to sensitive data without authentication or authorization. Each type of *command injection* attack is specific to an operating system, such as Unix or Windows, or the programming language of the web application.

For example, a malicious user might be able to specify a URL with an escape character, such as *?*, where they can type additional commands that are executed after the main URL. Unix systems can also make use of the pipe (|) command to allow you to enter additional commands that are run as part of the primary command execution.

You can prevent command injection by input validation techniques that allow the user to input only limited data in web application fields, and that filter out escape characters like the pipe (|) character that a user might enter to try to enter additional commands. Additional hardening techniques can be used to disable advanced functions in web applications that provide deep-level system access.

Directory Traversal

Directory traversal is a type of access vulnerability where a hacker can get unauthorized access to files on a web server other than the public files that are served on the web site. For example, a hacker might be able to learn the directory URL structure of a site by studying the naming conventions of the links. The hacker can input a manual URL to try to guess the link of a specific file, or actually navigate the web site directory tree through these URLs, such as ../ on a Unix system or ..\ on a Windows system, to go to the parent directory. If permissions are not properly set on the directory tree, the hacker may actually be able to read and copy important system files, including user login and password databases, such as /etc/passwd on Unix systems.

You can prevent directory traversal attacks by ensuring input validation on all web site input forms prevents changing directories, setting permissions on directories to prevent viewing the contents of a directory, preventing debugging information (such as error messages with full URL paths) from being displayed, or using back-end databases to store any information that needs to be viewed on a web site so that any important data files are not stored on the web server.

Zero-Day Attacks

A *zero-day* threat is a type of attack that has rarely or never been encountered, such as an attack technique that takes advantage of previously unknown weaknesses and vulnerabilities in an application or operating system software. As the attack is brand new, no existing defense has been created to detect it.

Zero-day attacks are very difficult to defend against, but in most cases, OS and software application vendors are very responsive in patching their software in the event a new vulnerability is discovered. You must always make sure your software is running the latest version with all security patches available installed.

You can also use specialized security software such as intrusion detection to be able to detect anomalous events that could indicate a zero-day exploit.

Internet Server Vulnerabilities

Beyond web services, other types of Internet-based servers provide additional services such as file transfer, e-mail, domain and address translation, and database transactions. The nature of the Internet means these servers are wide open to abuse from external users. Although network firewalls provide excellent protection against most types of attacks on your public-facing Internet servers, each type of server has its own way of providing information and services and could contain a number of security vulnerabilities that might allow it to be compromised by unauthorized users. The following sections outline popular Internet servers and identify their unique security vulnerabilities.

Exam Tip
Be aware of the different types of security vulnerabilities inherent with each type of Internet server and know how to prevent servers of that type from being exploited.

FTP Servers

FTP servers are used to transfer files from one system to another across the Internet. A server hosting the files will be running an FTP server service that awaits file transfer requests originating from clients using FTP client software. Many FTP server sites on the Internet are public in nature and allow anonymous users to log in and download or upload files to their system. Other companies use authenticated FTP servers to enable clients to download engineering or technical support files. To access the server, the client needs to authenticate using a login and password. Basic types of FTP communications are not encrypted, so any login and password information is sent over the network in clear text and can be easily intercepted by a malicious hacker. Secure FTP (SFTP) software uses encrypted communications to prevent interception by unauthorized users.

Exam Tip
Remember that basic FTP communications, including login and password authentication, are transmitted in clear text. SFTP should be used to encrypt the session utilizing SSH.

FTP servers are a widely used resource on the Internet and one of the most popular servers for hacking attempts and abuse. FTP server software can be vulnerable to attacks because of inherent bugs in its programming. Software bugs in FTP programs allow unauthorized individuals to gain administrative access to the machine on which the FTP service resides. The malicious hacker can then use that machine as a starting point for other activities, such as performing DoS attacks or hacking attempts on other machines. Because of bugs, any FTP server software you use should be the latest version, with the most recent security patches installed.

Another problem with FTP servers is they are usually installed by default with some kind of anonymous account. This account enables users to access the FTP server without having to authenticate. If the FTP server is a private server containing confidential data that should be accessed only by authorized users, this anonymous account and any anonymous access should be disabled.

DNS Servers

Domain Name System (DNS) servers provide a way to translate Internet domain names into IP addresses. For example, the web site *www.server.net* can be translated to an IP address of *192.168.1.12*. This allows network applications and services to refer to Internet domains by their fully qualified domain name (FQDN) rather than their IP address, which can be difficult to remember and can often change. If a company changes its system's IP address, it can simply update the DNS tables to reflect this. External users will not see a difference because they will still be connecting to it by name.

DNS servers perform an extremely valuable function on the Internet, and wide-scale communication interruptions can occur if a network DNS server is disabled. Most client machines use DNS each time they try to connect to a network host. The client's DNS server is configured using its network settings, which can be set manually or automatically through services such as DHCP. Each time a client tries to access a host, such as a web site, the local DNS server is queried for the IP address of the domain name. The DNS server translates the name into an IP address, which the client uses to initiate its connection.

DNS servers can suffer from DoS and malformed request attacks. In a DoS attack, the DNS server is inundated with DNS or ping requests. The load becomes so much that the DNS server cannot respond to legitimate DNS queries. DNS queries to servers can also be manipulated to include malformed input that could crash the server.

DNS servers are also susceptible to cache poisoning, where false DNS records are planted using spoofed addresses that result in your name server providing the IP address of a hacker's web site instead of the intended destination.

DNS servers use zone transfers, which send DNS information to other name servers. An attacker could perform an unauthorized zone transfer that allows them to list the contents of the DNS records that can reveal the addresses of critical servers and networking equipment. These zone transfers should be restricted to only allow transfers from designated and trusted DNS servers under your control.

To provide a strong base level of security for your DNS server, make sure that you are running the latest version of your DNS software with the most recent security patches installed. Software vulnerabilities are quickly identified and patched by DNS software vendors, and this will prevent attacks on any known exploits within your DNS software.

DHCP Servers

A *DHCP server* is used to allocate IP addresses and other network information on a network automatically, such as DNS and Windows Internet Naming Service (WINS) information, to clients as they access the network. DHCP servers can be configured instead of having to configure each client on the network manually with specific information. This greatly reduces administrative overhead—the use of static manual addressing means if something changes on the network, such as the address of a DNS server, you'd have to change the information manually on every client.

The main vulnerability with DHCP servers is the lack of an authentication mechanism to allow or disallow clients. Any client system that accesses the network and is configured for DHCP is allocated network information so that it can communicate with the network. This means any unauthorized user can plug his system into a network and be automatically configured for access. A malicious user can also attack a DHCP server using DoS methods to overload it or by trying to use up all the available IP addresses in the DHCP address pool. Then, no new clients can be assigned an address to communicate with the network.

Local Lingo	
DHCP address pool A range of IP addresses that have been set aside by the DHCP server to assign to new clients as they access the network.	

As a countermeasure to some attacks, DHCP servers can be configured to communicate only with clients with specific Media Access Control (MAC) addresses. The list of MAC addresses should contain only computers and devices on your internal network. This way, when a DHCP server sees a configuration request from an unknown host, it will ignore the request. You should also keep the DHCP server up to date with service packs and security hot fixes.

Another security concern is the ability for an unauthorized user to set up a rogue DHCP server on the network. If the server manages to answer a client's request for configuration information before the real DHCP server does so, the client might be configured with bogus information that could cause the user's communications to be redirected to other servers under the control of the attacker. The only way to prevent this type of scenario is to scan your network regularly for rogue servers running these services and to control physical access to the facility.

Database Servers

Database servers typically contain relational data used as a back-end repository of information for front-end applications and web services. The most popular forms of database software are Oracle, Microsoft SQL, and MySQL.

The front-end application that accesses the database usually sends commands as a set of procedures for the database to run on the data and so that it can return the required results. A malicious user can insert his own code into these procedures to run some query on the database that can reveal or damage confidential data. This is called a *SQL injection* attack and is similar to buffer overflow and invalid data types of attacks that can be performed from a web browser by passing certain parameters of input that transcend the boundaries of the software's thresholds. If the database software or query function is not configured or programmed correctly, the parameters could bypass built-in security to reveal confidential data or destroy thousands of data records. By keeping your database and application software current, and properly validating input, these security vulnerabilities can be avoided.

Exam Tip

Remember that SQL injection attacks harm database servers by inserting SQL commands into input fields of the application that provides the front end to the database. The commands are then run against the database, providing the unauthorized user with escalated privileges to harm the data stored there.

To protect data privacy and integrity, the use of authentication and access permissions should be configured for a database server. This creates a layered security model that first authenticates the user before he can use the database, and then restricts the user's access through the use of permissions and access control lists (ACLs). For example, for certain types of data, you might want most users to have read-only access. Other users who need more access can be granted permission to add, delete, and modify records.

LDAP and Directory Services

Directory services are a repository of information regarding the users and resources of a network. Directory service software applications and protocols are often left open and unprotected because the information they contain sometimes isn't considered important, compared to file server or database server information. Depending on the level of information they provide, however, directory services can be an excellent resource for unauthorized users and attackers to gain knowledge of the workings of the network and the resources and user accounts they contain.

A simple Lightweight Directory Access Protocol (LDAP) service that contains user names, e-mail addresses, phone numbers, and locations can be a resource for unauthorized users looking for an accounting user or an engineering user, if a malicious hacker is performing corporate espionage. Other types of directory services, such as Microsoft Active Directory, can contain more critical network and user information, such as network addresses, user account logins and passwords, and access information for servers.

At the bare minimum, users who query directory services should be authenticated via a login ID and password. This will at least prevent casual unauthorized users from accessing the data on the network's directory services through queries. This is especially important when protecting more critical network-wide directory services, such as Microsoft Active Directory. Only the administrators of the network should have access to read and change the highest levels of the directory hierarchy, while common users should be allowed only to look up basic information, such as the e-mail address of another user. To increase security, directory services should be used in conjunction with secured, encrypted communications protocols, such as Secure Sockets Layer (SSL) or Transport Layer Security (TLS).

Applications that perform lookups to LDAP directories are also susceptible to injection attacks. *LDAP injection,* which is similar to SQL injection attacks, inserts code into user-based input that is utilized in a query to an LDAP server. If the application does not properly validate user input, commands can be inserted into the LDAP queries to perform malicious actions against the LDAP directory, including unauthorized queries and data modification.

E-Mail Servers

E-mail servers store incoming mail for users and are responsible for sending outbound mail from local users to their destination. Most e-mail servers are configured to protect user inboxes by requiring users to authenticate to the account. If the user login or password is not valid, the user won't be able to access the contents of the inbox.

The *Post Office Protocol version 3 (POP3)* is an Internet protocol that provides a way for users to retrieve mail from their inboxes using a POP-enabled e-mail client. The e-mail messages are stored on the server until the user connects to it and downloads messages to the e-mail client. Most POP accounts are set to delete the messages from the server after they've been retrieved.

The *Internet Message Access Protocol (IMAP)* is similar to POP in that it's used to provide a mechanism for receiving messages from a user's inbox. IMAP has more functionality than POP, however, because it gives the user more control over what messages they download and how it stores them online.

Both basic POP3 and IMAP send credentials in clear text when authenticating. To protect the transfer of credentials from packet sniffers, you should use Secure POP or the Secure IMAP services that utilize the Secure Sockets Layer (SSL) to encrypt the login and passwords.

Exam Tip

POP uses TCP port 110, and IMAP uses TCP port 143. Secure POP uses TCP port 995, and Secure IMAP uses TCP port 993.

The *Simple Mail Transport Protocol (SMTP)* is the e-mail message-exchange standard of the Internet. While POP and IMAP are the Internet protocols used to read e-mail, SMTP is the Internet protocol for delivering e-mail. SMTP is used to navigate an e-mail to its destination server. Mail servers that run SMTP have a relay agent that sends a message from one mail server to another. Because mail servers, as per their function, need to accept and send data through an organization's routers and firewalls, this relay agent can be abused by unauthorized users who relay mail through the server. These e-mails are usually sent by spammers sending out unsolicited e-mails while hiding the original sending location of the e-mails through spoofed addresses. The need for e-mail server security becomes even more important when these users send malicious e-mails with attachments that contain viruses, malware, and phishing attempts.

To protect the mail server from this type of abuse, the SMTP relay agent should be configured to send only mail originating from its own network domain. SMTP authentication should also be enabled to allow only authenticated clients to relay through the SMTP server to send mail.

Exam Tip

SMTP uses TCP port 25 for communication, although many ISPs have started to use alternative ports to prevent connections from spammers' relays. It is a security best practice to disable SMTP relay on your SMTP server.

Objective 12.02
CompTIA Security+
Objective 4.1

Explain the Importance of Application Security

Ith a wide variety of attack vectors, applications are extremely vulnerable to security issues. Poor input validation, weak error and exception handling, and misconfiguration can create vulnerabilities in your applications that can lead to crashes, unauthorized access, and loss of data. Application security begins in the design and development phase to create a secure architecture, while application hardening, configuration baselines, and software update maintenance provide continued security when the application is deployed and in use. The following sections describe important concepts and best practices for application security.

Secure Coding Concepts

For applications, security begins in the design and development phase of creating a software application. Developers must build their application from a secure base and use secure coding concepts to make sure that when the application is deployed, it does not contain security issues but is designed to be resistant to application errors and crashes that can create a condition of vulnerability within the application. The following sections describe some basic secure development concepts that should be applied when creating application software.

Input Validation

Input validation refers to the process of coding applications to accept only certain valid input for user-entered fields. For example, many web sites allow users to fill in a web form with their name, address, comments, and other information. If proper input validation code has not been included in these types of web forms, in certain cases a malicious user can enter invalid input into a field that may cause the application to crash, corrupt data, or provide the user additional unauthorized system access. Invalid input often leads to buffer overflow types of errors that can be easily exploited. Encoding proper input validation within an application reduces the risk of a user inadvertently or intentionally entering input that can crash the system or cause some other type of security concern.

Escaping

Another concept related to input validation is *escaping*. Without proper validation, hackers can input actual commands into input fields that are run by the operating system. Escaping recognizes specific types of command characters and parses them as simple data rather than executing the text as a command.

Fuzzing

Fuzzing is a testing technique that can help test input validation and error/exception handling by entering random, unexpected data into application fields to see how the software program reacts. Many application vulnerabilities originate from input validation issues, buffer overflows, and error handling, and fuzzing helps make sure that the software does not crash, lose or manipulate data, or provide unauthorized access based on input validation defects.

Error and Exception Handling

Developers must be careful when coding applications that they design how the software program should react to error conditions and exceptions. In many cases, an unexpected error condition can reveal security vulnerabilities that can be exploited. For example, a software program may crash and drop to a command line that can be used by a hacker, or error messages may indicate full file and directory paths that the hacker can use as knowledge to further penetrate the system.

Error and exception handling is largely determined by the operating system and the programming language environment in use, as they can offer varying levels of tools to deal with software exceptions. Generally, developers must make sure that a program should still be able to retain its state and continue to function in the event of an error condition. The program should be able to roll back to its previous state without interrupting the flow of the application.

Error messages must be informative to the user, but system details should never be revealed unless the software is running in a special debugging mode only available to the developer where verbose error logging will help them trace a problem to fix a programming issue.

Transitive Access

Transitive access occurs when you have access permissions or trusts between different components of a software application that allow user access to pass through unexpectedly and without proper authorization to access another software component.

For example, consider an application or operating system that establishes a trust relationship between two software components, A and B, which allows full access for data passing between these components. Another separate trust relationship is set up between components B and C that allows similar full access between these components. If there is no explicit nontransitive access specified, any user who is authenticated and authorized for component A is allowed access through component B, and then by the separate trust relationship, unauthorized access to component C.

You must be careful when coding software that no software components allow pass-through transitive access by ensuring that trusts between components are nontransitive and require explicit authorization before access is granted.

Application Hardening

Application software, just like any other software such as a host operating system or device firmware, is vulnerable to security issues originating from existing bugs, out-of-date software, and misconfiguration.

For all the applications and services used in your environment, you must use application hardening techniques to prevent application vulnerabilities from being exploited. By using a secure baseline of application configuration, hardening techniques, and patch management, you ensure that your application software is at a default level of high security that lessens the probability of issues originating from the application software.

Application Configuration Baseline

Depending on the type of application, the configuration can be very simple or very complex. What is most important is that the actual configuration of your application is by default set to a secure baseline. Only the most basic default options should be enabled on an application to provide a majority of users with the functionality they require. Enabling additional options and services means the additional possibility of security issues. If they are not required, additional options and services should be disabled. For example, for word processing or spreadsheet applications, you may have a company-wide security baseline that prevents the running of external macros within the applications. This prevents users from being infected by macro viruses in documents they receive from external sources. To still allow macro functionality from trusted sources, you can enable access only for macros that were created internal to your organization.

Applications should also have proper authentication and authorization configured so that users are only allowed to use the services they require from the application, and do not have access to any other, additional functionality. For example, another company-wide application is the web browser. For maximum security, you can install the web browser application with heightened security settings that cannot be modified by users. This ensures that when users browse the web, they have a default application configuration that prevents connections to untrusted sites that could contain malware. Users will not have proper authorization to make any changes to the web browser configuration.

Application Patch Management

Application software can contain a variety of bugs and security vulnerabilities that can be exploited by malicious users. For internal application software, such as word processing, spreadsheets, or custom-built applications, bugs are usually annoying at most and might not provide real security threats. The usual effect of software bugs is simply interruption or corruption of services that affect performance, productivity, and data integrity. Software applications specifically made for the Internet, however, can provide more than simple annoyances, because security vulnerabilities created in the software can allow an unauthorized user to access your internal network through the faulty application or service.

To protect you from inherent bug or security vulnerabilities, all application software should be upgraded to the latest versions and the latest service and security patches installed. In the most recent version of the software, known problems have been corrected. This does not, however, protect you from any problems that might have arisen since the most recent version was distributed. Continuing product research and testing, and the proliferation of compromised security incidents, might require the software vendor to release an interim update or patch (typically called a *security patch* or *hot fix*) for the affected program.

Vendor web sites should be checked regularly for software updates for any applications running on your systems. Many vendors can automatically notify you through e-mail updates if you registered the software for technical support, or the software itself could contain a procedure that checks for the latest versions of its components automatically.

Objective 12.03
CompTIA Security+
Objective 4.3

Explain the Importance of Data Security

Beyond network, host, and application security, data security is your last line of defense in your security infrastructure. Stored data must be secured from unauthorized access, theft, loss, and manipulation. The following sections describe security issues and solutions in regard to data security.

Data Loss Prevention (DLP)

A majority of security concerns are centered on preventing inbound threats such as network attacks, malware, and viruses, from entering your organization's network. For organizations that operate in a 24/7 digital world where there is a constant flow of data being passed in and out of their networks via e-mail, instant messaging, web, and other communications channels, the concept of outbound security has quickly become of equal importance.

Data loss prevention (DLP) is the concept of using security and content control features to prevent confidential, private data from leaving your organization's networks. DLP has become so important that certain types of organizations, including financial or medical companies, must adhere to strict guidelines and regulations regarding the storage and communications of private data. For example, banks and other financial companies must ensure that a customer's banking and credit card info are secure and never transmitted without being encrypted. Hospitals, doctor's offices, and other health-related organizations must ensure patient confidentiality in regard to their personal health records.

DLP requires that organization create compliance policies that detail which users can send types of documents and data outside of their networks, and the types of actions that should be applied to outbound messages that violate a policy. From a technical perspective, data loss prevention techniques use deep content scanning (such as with a content filter network device) on outbound network traffic to take action on messages or requests, depending on various criteria about their content. For example, a company can create content rules that automatically encrypt any outbound e-mail messages that contain patterns of credit card numbers or social security numbers. A high-security organization may block document attachments to e-mails, or even HTTP or FTP uploads of documents marked as "confidential" or "secret" to prevent them from leaving their network. DLP requires the ability to scan multiple network protocols and services (e-mail, web, IM, and so on) to ensure that there is no way that sensitive data can leave your network.

DLP becomes even more difficult when dealing with cloud computing, where data can be stored and transmitted within a distributed service cloud across public networks. Once the data is transmitted in the cloud, the concept of confidentiality disappears. Your DLP policies must ensure that specific confidential data is not transmitted out of your organization into the cloud.

Data Encryption

For data confidentiality, the ability to render data unreadable through encryption is a key component of data loss prevention. A majority of security resources are dedicated to protecting the confidentiality of data while in transit over a network. Of equal importance is the protection of data while it is stored on server hard disks, mobile devices, and USB flash drives. The following sections describe how data is encrypted using both hardware and software technologies to protect the confidentiality of stored data.

Travel Assistance
For details on cryptographic techniques for encryption, see Chapter 4.

Trusted Platform Module

A *trusted platform module (TPM)* is a special hardware chip that is typically installed within a computer system or device, such as on the system motherboard of a computer desktop or laptop. This module provides authentication by storing security mechanisms such as passwords, certificates, and encryption keys that are specific to that system hardware. The chip itself contains a built-in RSA key that is used for encryption and authentication. In the past, hardware-based passwords on desktops and laptops were typically stored in clear text and therefore vulnerable to unauthorized access. With the advent of TPM, any system passwords are now stored and encrypted on the TPM chip. The TPM provides greater security benefits over software-based solutions as it runs in a closed hardware subsystem that mitigates external threats. TPM-based systems are compatible with most popular operating systems.

Laptops are especially prone to physical theft because of their portability, and if the hard drive contents are not encrypted, an unauthorized user can easily access these files. TPM allows the contents of the hard drive to be encrypted; the user simply generates a key that is stored on the TPM chip. When the user needs to access the hard drive, she uses operating system software, such as Windows, to send the key to the TPM chip for authentication. This prevents an unauthorized user from accessing the hard drive contents of equipment.

Hardware Security Module (HSM)

A *hardware security module (HSM)* is a specialized hardware appliance used to provide on-board cryptographic functions and processing. These physical hardware devices can be a stand-alone device attached to a network or connected directly to a server as a plug-in card. HSMs are primarily used to host integrated cryptographic functions, such as a public key infrastructure server for encryption, decryption, and secure key generation and management, but they can also be used to provide onboard secure storage of encrypted data. With their processing speed and security, HSMs are often used for banking applications (such as ATMs) that require scalable, performance-based solutions for critical key management and security.

Whole Disk Encryption

In *whole disk encryption,* the entire contents of a computer system's hard drive are encrypted, typically by encrypting the disk volume that contains all the operating system data; this does not include the booting instructions located in a boot volume or master boot record (MBR). By encrypting all files, including temporary and swap space files, you ensure that no unauthorized user can access this data if the system is compromised or stolen.

Many operating systems come with their own proprietary whole disk encryption mechanisms that encrypt and decrypt data on the fly as the user is operating the computer. You can encrypt a system's operating system volume on the hard drive and provide authentication for the boot process (which cannot be encrypted). It is critical that disk encryption systems use some form of authentication for the boot process, such as a locked-down mini–operating system or a TPM mechanism whose only function is to authenticate the user before booting the system. Otherwise, an authorized user can still boot the system and access user files as if he were the original user. To authenticate the user, a combination of passwords, passphrases, PINs, or hardware tokens can be used before allowing access to the encrypted disk volumes.

Database Encryption

Company databases can consist of millions of records and terabytes of data. It is the heart of an organization, and if this data is damaged, lost, or stolen, it could mean the end of that company. While most security resources are spent on encryption of data in transit, you must also consider the confidentiality of data in storage.

Databases can be encrypted so that even if an attacker were able to gain unauthorized access to a database, they would not be able to read the data without the encryption key. You can encrypt the entire database itself, the actual physical database files (which also protects backups of the database), or for more granularity you can even encrypt individual cells/records in the database that are decrypted as authorized by the user.

As with other encryption methods, key management and authentication can create security issues, and it is a best practice that the encrypted key never be stored with the encrypted data. Encryption keys should be stored and managed by external devices such as an HSM.

Individual File Encryption

Data encryption can also be taken to a very granular level where only individual files and folders are encrypted by the file system itself, rather than the contents of entire partitions or a whole disk. This type of encryption has the benefit that each encrypted file or folder will have a different encryption key. This approach provides more strict access control; however, it requires efficient key management to properly manage different keys with different user authorizations.

Removable Media and Mobile Devices

The ability to transfer information easily from one computer device to another has been made easier with removable media and mobile devices. Technologies such as removable hard drives, USB keys, and flash memory in mobile devices give users flexibility in moving data from one system to another.

Removable media can contain critical and confidential data that must be protected from unauthorized access and physical damage or destruction. The portable nature of many types of computer media means more opportunities for an unauthorized user to obtain or damage the information they contain. Security must be a priority to protect the confidentially and integrity of data, especially when this information is being physically moved from one place to another. This involves the use of encryption and authentication to secure access to the data, as well as physical and environmental protection of the removable media itself.

While the data is protected by encryption, there are security concerns with the methods used to access and decrypt data. A user must authenticate using a password, passphrase, or some other identifier before he can decrypt the contents of the device. If the authentication process is weak, the strong encryption techniques can be easily subverted. More advanced USB flash drives are able to store the actual encryption key on a separate controller part of the USB device that is protected from the main flash drive where the data is encrypted.

CHECKPOINT

✔ **Objective 12.01: Analyze and differentiate among types of application attacks.** Popular web application attacks include cross-site scripting, cross-site request forgery, buffer overflows, poor input validation, scripting, directory traversal, and command injection. Disable anonymous accounts for FTP, and use SFTP or other secure alternatives. Secure DNS servers to prevent cache poisoning and unauthorized zone transfers. Database servers need to be secured from SQL injection attacks that result from SQL commands being run in input queries. LDAP is vulnerable to similar injection attacks from command insertion. Disable SMTP relay on e-mail servers to prevent spammers relaying mail through your server.

✔**Objective 12.02: Explain the importance of application security.** Applications must be designed and developed with security in place. Use input validation to make sure hackers cannot insert malformed input or command requests in application input forms. Escape out special characters and command characters so that they are processed as data, not actual commands. Use fuzzing to test input validation by entering random, unexpected characters into application input forms. Don't display file name and directory paths in error messages. Make sure your application handles exceptions without crashing or providing unauthorized access. Make sure applications have secure configuration baselines, and that all software is up-to-date with all security patches installed.

✔**Objective 12.03: Explain the importance of data security.** Use data loss prevention (DLP) concepts such as outbound content filtering and encryption to prevent confidential data loss and interception. Use TPMs for secure storage of encryption keys and certificates for hardware platforms. HSMs are used for high-end security applications that require secure key generation and management on a separate hardware appliance. Whole disk encryption encrypts an entire disk or volume while providing authenticated access for the boot partition of the disk. Database encryption can secure data in storage on a database server. You can encrypt the physical database files, or encrypt data cells/records within those files for granular protection that includes user authorization for accessing specific encrypted data.

REVIEW QUESTIONS

1. Your e-mail server has been listed on a spam black list because a large amount of spam is being relayed through it. Which of the following actions should you take?

   A. Enable SMTP relay.

   B. Use an antispam filter.

   C. Disable SMTP relay.

   D. Use SMTP relay authentication.

2. You are implementing input validation for a web application that connects to a back-end database. Which of the following techniques can you use to ensure your input validation is working properly?

   A. Testing input of known valid characters

   B. Fuzzing

   C. Escaping out command characters

   D. SQL injection

3. While testing exception handling with a web application, you encounter an error that displays a full URL path to critical data files for the application. Which of the following types of vulnerabilities would this application be susceptible to?

   A. Buffer overflow

   B. Session hijacking

   C. Cross-site scripting

   D. Directory traversal

4. Your web application currently checks authentication credentials from a user's web browser cookies before allowing a transaction to take place. However, you have had several complaints of identity theft and unauthorized purchases from users of your site. Which of the following is the mostly likely cause?

   A. Cross-site scripting

   B. Session hijacking

   C. Header manipulation

   D. Lack of encryption

5. To protect your users while web surfing, you create a web browser configuration baseline that will be applied to all of your users in your organization. Which of the following components should you block by default?

   A. Unsigned ActiveX controls

   B. JavaScript

   C. Search engines

   D. Web browsing history

6. As part of your application hardening process, which of the following activities helps to prevent existing vulnerabilities in applications from being exploited?

   A. Exception handling

   B. Fuzzing

   C. Updating to the latest software version or patch

   D. Escaping

7. An executive is traveling with his laptop computer to a conference. The contents of his laptop contain very confidential product information, including development specifications and product road maps. Which of the following techniques can be implemented to protect the confidentiality of the data on the laptop?

    A. Make sure all software is up to date.

    B. Password-protect the laptop BIOS.

    C. Move the confidential documents to a USB key.

    D. Encrypt the hard drive using a TPM.

8. You have had several instances of product development plans for your company being leaked to other, rival companies. Which data loss prevention technique can you use to prevent these documents from leaving your organization's networks?

    A. Use secure FTP for file transfers.

    B. Block access to file sharing web sites.

    C. Use a content filter to block development documents from being sent outbound.

    D. Use a network firewall to block outbound connections to rival companies.

9. You are implementing a web application that communicates to a back-end database server that stores data for the web site. Which of the following hardening techniques can you use to help protect against SQL injection attacks?

    A. Input validation

    B. Fuzzing

    C. Database encryption

    D. Configuration baseline

10. During testing of a web application, you discover that due to poor input validation, you can easily crash the server by entering values in the input forms much greater than the system can handle. What type of vulnerability is this?

    A. Session hijacking

    B. Buffer overflow

    C. Privilege escalation

    D. XML injection

REVIEW ANSWERS

1. **D**   By using authenticated SMTP relay, you allow only authorized mail servers and clients to connect to your e-mail server to send and relay messages.

2. **B**   Fuzzing is a testing technique that enters random, unexpected character sequences into application input forms to test how well they validate input. Fuzzing makes sure that all types of input data are tested to make sure they don't crash your application, or cause exceptions that lead to security vulnerabilities.

3. **D**   Directory traversal is a vulnerability that allows an attacker who knows the details of an application server's directory tree to manually traverse the directory using input commands in the URL location bar or input forms in the application. Error messages should never display the full paths of files to prevent hackers discovering the directory structure.

4. **B**   Session hijacking occurs when a malicious hacker is able to access your session cookie and then use the session information to make unauthorized requests as the target user.

5. **A**   Although ActiveX controls are required for many web sites to run correctly, you should never allow users to download unsigned ActiveX controls. If they are not properly signed and authenticated, they are most likely malicious.

6. **C**   Application vendors will release updated software versions of their product or provide a security patch to resolve any security vulnerabilities in previous versions of the software. It is a best practice to always keep your application software up-to-date.

7. **D**   A trusted platform module (TPM) allows the contents of the hard drive to be encrypted with encryption keys that are stored on the TPM chip, which can only be accessed by the end user. This prevents an unauthorized user from accessing the hard drive contents of equipment.

8. **C**   Using a content filter on your outbound traffic, you can detect and block development documents that are being sent outbound via e-mail attachments, IM file transfers, FTP, and web uploads.

9. **A**   To help prevent insertion of database commands into your web application input fields, you can require strong input validation to make sure that SQL commands cannot be passed on to the back-end database server.

10. **B**   Buffer overflows are caused primarily by poor input validation that allows illegal data to be entered into the application, causing processing limits to be exceeded.

Threats and Vulnerabilities

Chapter 13   Monitoring for Security Threats

Chapter 14   Vulnerability Assessments

Monitoring for
Security Threats

ITINERARY

o **Objective 13.01** Analyze and differentiate among types
of mitigation and deterrent techniques

	NEWBIE	SOME EXPERIENCE	EXPERT
ETA	2 hours	1 hour	0.5 hour

With massive amounts of access control, network, and system information be-ing collected every minute, every hour, and every day, administrators can find it difficult to stay abreast of current issues and find time to examine and analyze monitoring and logging information for anomalies that indicate possible secu-rity problems.

Small issues can quickly escalate into serious breaches and attacks against your systems. A denial-of-service (DoS) attack on an Internet web server might be noticed immediately on the network, but other security issues are not so easy to detect, such as unauthorized access of files, users with improperly assigned rights and permissions, unauthorized access to a locked area, and Trojan horse programs installed and running silently on a workstation.

To aid the administrator, there are a variety of monitoring, logging, auditing, and reporting tools available that can quickly identify possible security issues and notify the administrator through alerts and notifications. These monitor-ing utilities must be configured and customized specifically for your environ-ment to be able to detect behavior that is not consistent with your regular activities.

This chapter describes the various monitoring, logging, and auditing proce-dures, as well as monitoring methodologies and tools that aid the administrator in monitoring a network and systems for security-related issues.

Objective 13.01
CompTIA Security+
Objective 3.6

Analyze and Differentiate among Types of Mitigation and Deterrent Techniques

There are several security tools available to the administrator to detect suspi-cious behaviors that have passed the thresholds for normal system and net-work operation. From specialized network monitors and intrusion detection systems (IDSs), to general utilities such as system and performance monitors and logging applications, these tools must be customized by the administrator who must also employ proper procedures and methodologies to maximize their benefits. The following sections describe best practices for security monitoring and provide an overview of the tools and methodologies for efficient detection of security issues.

Security Posture

Your security posture is your organization's overall philosophy toward monitor-ing for security threats and anomalies. The following are the three main con-cepts that should be implemented in your overall security posture.

- **Initial baseline configuration**   With any type of monitoring or measurement over time, you must initially start with a baseline of current activity and then measure this against future activity. The initial baseline provides you with a level of activity that is considered "normal" for your environment. When you have your baseline and continue to monitor further activity, any anomalies that go beyond your measured baseline thresholds will be easily apparent.

- **Continuous security monitoring**   Security monitoring is not a one-time operation; it is a continuous process that requires constant vigilance. Whether it is watching security cameras, sorting through event logs, using network monitors, or reading and reacting to alarm notifications, security monitoring is a 24/7 operation that never ceases. Even though you may have automated security monitoring and notification methods in place, an administrator must still be aware of the result of that monitoring; be ready to react to security alerts, alarms, and notifications; and study reports of activity trends over periods of time.

- **Remediation**   The remediation aspect of security monitoring is being able to take swift action against immediate security events. This requires that you have recorded your initial baselines, have properly configured your monitoring and alert systems, and have set procedures in place to deal with immediate security issues. You must also be able to deal with issues that grow more apparent over time by studying trends in your security reports. Remediation requires the resolution of an issue, using proactive prevention methods to prevent or mitigate the issue when it recurs, and adjustment of your monitoring and alert procedures to more quickly and accurately detect the event in the future.

Detecting Security-Related Anomalies

Several monitoring tools can help administrators collect data on system and network performance and usage, and compare these statistics against measured baselines of typical system and network behavior. By analyzing performance trends over time, administrators can discover anomalies in the behavior of the system that differ greatly from the performance baselines; such anomalies can indicate a security issue such as a network attack or virus/worm infections. The following sections describe some of the common concepts and security tools for monitoring your systems and networks for security-related issues.

System and Performance Monitoring

System and performance monitors examine how much CPU, memory, disk input and output, and network bandwidth is being consumed at any particular time or during a specified time period. Administrators can examine the resulting data for trends that might indicate anomalous behavior.

For example, if a web server is infected with a virus or worm, it can be unresponsive to client requests or fail to respond in a timely manner. Several unrecognized processes might be running on the system and taking up most of the CPU processing time (with levels of 90 percent or more), memory usage might be unusually high, and network usage may have jumped as the worm tries to replicate itself to other servers. In other cases, excessive network usage (especially a large amount of network connections from external systems) often indicates a DoS attempt.

> **Exam Tip**
>
> Recognize what types of performance behaviors can indicate security issues when using system and performance monitors. High processor usage and network usage could indicate potential DoS attacks or virus and worm activity.

Performance Baselines   You can establish performance baselines and then track performance data to look for thresholds that surpass the baselines. This information allows you to recognize anomalous system behaviors and perform a closer examination to discover the source of the anomalies that affect system performance. To establish a good performance baseline, you must measure your system activity for 24 hours a day for at least 7 days. Data will be collected during working hours, nonworking hours, and weekends to provide an accurate view of your system performance at different times of day and days of the week. Simply sampling performance data for a few hours during the day will not provide an adequate overview of system performance trends. Likewise, measuring performance for only a few days during the week will not produce a sufficient baseline for activity during off-work hours and weekends.

The performance baseline should indicate that most primary activity occurs during normal working hours, with lighter activity during nonworking hours. Occasional spikes in activity in off-hours can also indicate normal behavior; system backup or archiving processes, for example, will increase CPU, memory, disk, and network activity during the times the processes are taking place. Your baseline will include this information as well, so that you can anticipate that performance spike. Performance spikes that you cannot account for can indicate unauthorized activities or other security-related issues.

After you have recorded a system baseline, many performance monitors allow you to set alarm thresholds for parts of the system. For example, the system can notify you when CPU or memory usage exceeds a specific threshold (such as 90 percent).

Take care when setting thresholds, however, to be sure that you don't receive alarm notifications for slightly above-average behaviors or for very short spikes in activity. For example, you might set your performance monitor to send an alert when CPU usage exceeds 90 percent for at least 30 minutes; this ensures that each momentary processing spike will not generate an alert, and that prolonged usage at a high rate will generate a notification.

Protocol Analyzers

A *protocol analyzer* is a device or application that can intercept, log, and analyze network traffic. Each individual network packet can be examined to decode its header information (which contains the packet's origin and destination) and its contents. Figure 13.1 shows a typical protocol analyzer display from a popular program called Wireshark, which shows each inbound and outbound network packet and the exact details of each packet's contents.

Travel Assistance
More information on Wireshark can be found at www.wireshark.org.

Protocol analyzers are not used continually to monitor every packet that passes through the network. Because of the huge amounts of data flowing across a network, this would be an impossible task. Instead, they are used to troubleshoot specific network segments or traffic to and from a specific host on the network. Administrators can use an analyzer to track specific network protocols as they send out queries and receive responses; this helps narrow down sources of communications issues.

In terms of monitoring for security issues, protocol analyzers are very useful for viewing within specific network packets the source, destination, and content of the packet. For example, a network administrator might suspect that a specific workstation on the network is infected with some kind of Trojan horse program that is communicating data from the workstation to an attacker's computer over the Internet. By using the protocol analyzer, the administrator can watch every single network packet that leaves the workstation and narrow down the search using the ports specifically used by Trojan horse programs. The examination of the workstation will show communications to and from these

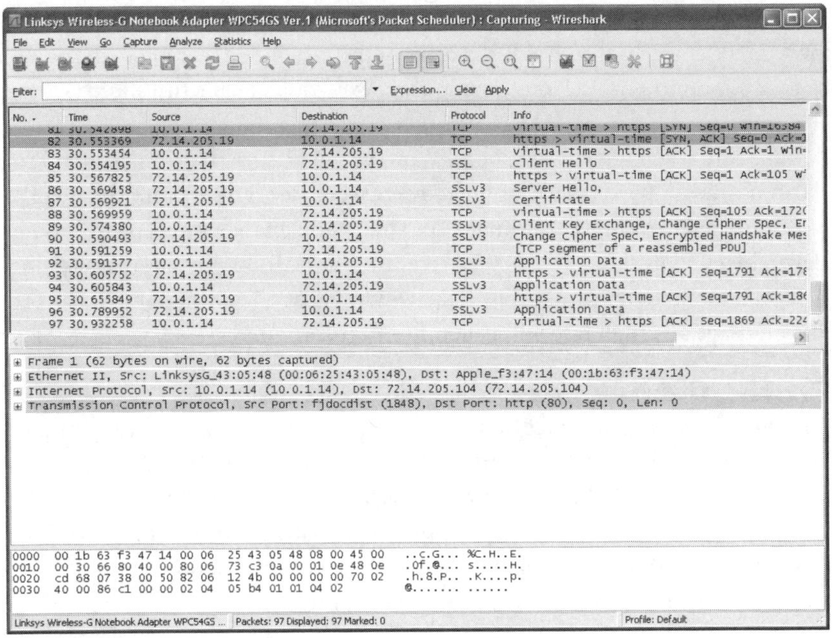

FIGURE 13.1 The Wireshark protocol analyzer

ports to a specific external IP address on the network. At this point, the administrator can confirm the type of Trojan horse program being used and attempt to clean it off the infected workstation. The external IP address to which the Trojan horse program is communicating can also be blocked at the firewall to prevent any future occurrences of data being transmitted to that address.

Protocol analyzers and similar network monitoring tools can also be used to track general trends in networking bandwidth. For example, suppose you hear complaints from users that a specific web server is too slow to respond. By enabling the protocol analyzer to analyze network packets going to and from the web server, you discover massive amounts of network traffic originating externally from the network. By analyzing the network packets, you discover ping messages from multiple IP addresses. This indicates that your web server could be suffering from a distributed denial-of-service (DDoS) attack in which multiple computers on the Internet are sending a flood of ping requests to the web server in an effort to slow it down or crash it. You can then take steps to mitigate the attack, such as disabling the ping service on the web server.

Network Monitor

Network monitoring applications allow the administrator to take a real-time view of current network activity on the entire network. Network monitors display a map of the network and indicate bandwidth usage and network trends, similar to how a traffic congestion map would depict a major expressway. Network monitors are usually located in full view of the administrator so that she can constantly monitor the health of the network with a quick glance.

Administrators can be alerted if a specific section of the network has lost connectivity due to a failed switch or network cable. The display will indicate that section of the network in a warning color (such as red) that can be noticed immediately by the monitoring administrator. Alerts can also be sent via e-mail, text message, and pager to notify the administrator of critical network errors.

Beyond general network troubleshooting issues, network monitors can be a valuable resource for alerting the administrator to network problems that result from security-related issues. For example, if one of the organization's Internet web servers is experiencing a DoS attack, the network monitor will indicate severe network congestion on the network between the primary router/firewall and the web server. In many cases, the network monitor can show the web server as completely unavailable, as it cannot respond to the diagnostic queries from the monitor due to the attack. Abnormal network activity can also be detected by the monitor on specific hosts on the network that could be infected with a worm, virus, or Trojan horse program that is trying to replicate itself to other systems on the network. This allows the administrator to pinpoint the source of the anomalous network activity quickly and take immediate steps to shut down the server or workstation and run diagnostics and antivirus scans to try to clean the infected host.

Intrusion Detection and Intrusion Prevention Systems

An *intrusion detection system (IDS)* can monitor networks, host systems, and physical locations for suspicious behavior that can indicate a malicious hacker is trying to break in to or damage a network or host system, or gain unauthorized physical access to an organization's building. The detection system can immediately notify an administrator or security guard on an intrusion through methods such as an e-mail, pager, and audible and visible alarms.

An *intrusion prevention system (IPS)* takes active steps to repair an intrusion situation, such as to disconnect suspicious network connections or turn off network services on a host that are under attack. A user who triggers an intrusion detection system while physically entering a facility without authorization could find himself trapped between two automatically locked doors such as in a man-trap.

Detection systems do just what their name implies; they detect a security intrusion and alert you to that intrusion. The disadvantage of security systems that merely detect security issues is that by the time you are able to react to the detection, the hacking attempt may have already performed its intended damage, or the perpetrator may have already stolen equipment and left the premises in the case of a physical intrusion.

The advantage of prevention systems is that they take active steps to mitigate the intrusion before it actually causes damage or loss. Consider the case of a security camera and a security guard. If your physical security involves only cameras and recorded video, an unauthorized person may break into a facility, triggering alarms and surveillance recordings, but he is still able to perform whatever malicious act was his intent. If the video monitoring and alarm system is not checked until the next day, the intruder is long gone and his intended security transgression has already been completed.

A physical security guard who, in conjunction with alarms and video surveillance, is able to patrol an organization's building would be able to confront, scare off, or apprehend the unauthorized intruder before he could do damage to your premises or its assets.

The advantages and disadvantages with detection versus prevention are also affected by budget concerns. Generally, any time of active prevention system will cost much more than a detection system. It will cost you much more money to hire a physical security guard to patrol and monitor your premises than it would be to install camera surveillance equipment. As part of your risk analysis, you must decide whether the assets and data you are protecting are worth the extended money required to use prevention systems in your organization.

Travel Assistance

Network intrusion detection systems (NIDSs) and network intrusion prevention systems (NIPSs) are discussed in more detail in Chapter 8. Host intrusion detection systems are discussed in Chapter 11.

Bypass of Security Equipment

As part of your security monitoring procedures, some thought and preparation must also be put into resolutions for situations where your monitoring and detection equipment is bypassed, either through manual bypassing of controls, loss of power, system failure, or some other sudden and unexpected event. For example, during a power outage, a physical intruder would be able to bypass security lighting, camera surveillance, and possibly even electronic access control equipment. To prevent alarms from being triggered, an intruder could cut phone, network, power, and video cables to prevent the operation of detection systems. Many security systems use phone or network lines to send alerts to central monitoring stations. If these lines are cut, the security system may not register any activity at all. Many systems use wireless network as a failback in the event physical communications lines are cut.

The following concepts describe different ways for security systems to react to these extraordinary events that can bypass their functionality.

Failsecure/Failsafe   The security system reacts to a failure in the most secure way possible. In a *failsecure* (also referred to as *failsafe*) scenario, the security system will lock down entirely, or even disable functions to prevent usage or entry. For example, in the event of a power outage, a door that is operated through an electronic key reader will remain locked until the power is restored. This ensures that the door cannot be opened if the power is shut down or the electronic reader suffers a malfunction. In the situation of a network server that reboots due to a crash or malfunction, it may only reboot to a nonprivileged state that requires administrative intervention before it is brought back to its full functionality. This prevents hackers from bypassing security controls due to system malfunction or failure and gaining command-line access to the system. Where possible, most security aspects of an application or security system should default to a failsecure mode. This makes sure that security is not compromised during exceptional events or system failures.

Failopen   In a system using *failopen* security, the system will default to a nonsecure and permissive state. In the previous example of the door with the electronic key reader, in the event that power is lost or the key reader malfunctions, the door will be unlocked for the duration of the outage. Depending on the facility, this may be the proper method to implement for employee safety in the event of a disaster such as a fire. The employees in that area of the building would not be able to escape if the door automatically locked in failsecure mode. In the example of a network device in a facility that requires connectivity at all times, it may be better policy to allow network traffic to flow through unprotected than to shut down the system entirely because of a failure. The monetary damage that could be caused by blocking all communications is considered worth the risk of allowing network traffic through without network security.

Monitoring Logs

Each aspect of a computer system or device, whether it is the operating system, an application, or a system service, generates log files. Log files are used to track informational notifications, warnings, and critical errors within each of these critical system components and services. These logs contain information vital to the system's health and security, and they must be analyzed by the security administrator on a regular basis to monitor for behaviors and anomalies that are inconsistent with regular system operation.

The following sections describe some of the most important log files to examine on a system or network and cover how to analyze their contents properly to identify security threats.

System Logs

System logs record information such as warnings, notifications, and critical error messages on a variety of system processes, such as kernel processes, application processes, memory and disk warnings (such as low disk space), and just about any service running as part of the core operating system. Many types of services and applications have their own logs outside the primary system log, but most of the critical information about the primary operating system is stored in the system log.

Although security issues are more likely to be discovered using an external log analyzer and IDS/IPS that can automatically detect anomalies, smaller organizations without an expensive security infrastructure can rely on manual examination of the system logs for any security issues.

In many cases, the log files are not in a format that is easily readable by the administrator, and an external log viewer is required. Due to the great amount of information that is stored in the system log, administrators must be able to parse and search the log files for pertinent information. For example, if you know the name of a specific process for troubleshooting, you can load the log file into a log analyzer program and search the file using the name of the process, such as *smtp*, to display only log entries specific to the Simple Mail Transfer Protocol (SMTP) e-mail server process. From here you can analyze each mail server connection and response and more easily troubleshoot the issue you are experiencing.

It is also important that you configure the system logs to record and display only the information you need; many logging subsystems can be configured to show only warning or critical error messages, while not logging each and every minor occurrence on the system. This will make logs easier to search and analyze and decrease the amount of resources (especially disk space) required to process and store the logs. However, certain logs, such as access logs, should display all information for tracking all system logins and logouts.

Performance Logs

Performance monitors examine how much CPU, memory, disk input and output, and network bandwidth is being consumed at any particular time or over a specified time period. From this information, administrators can examine the *performance log* data for trends indicating anomalous behaviors. The log tracks performance trends against a baseline of normal behavior. Several system characteristics can be tracked (such as CPU, memory, disk usage, network usage, and so on) and compared to the baseline over time. Figure 13.2 shows an example of the Windows Performance Monitor screen that is monitoring CPU, memory, and disk usage.

Performance logs provide data spanning over minutes, hours, days, and weeks, and performance trends can be mapped based on this data to indicate any anomalous trends or spikes in behavior. For example, the administrator might notice from the performance log data that CPU usage spikes for a few hours starting at midnight until 2 A.M. However, this is the time that the server runs its daily backup routines, so the CPU spike appears in the performance report every day at this time. This is a baseline behavior for this system. CPU spikes that occur for large periods of time at other times of the day, especially

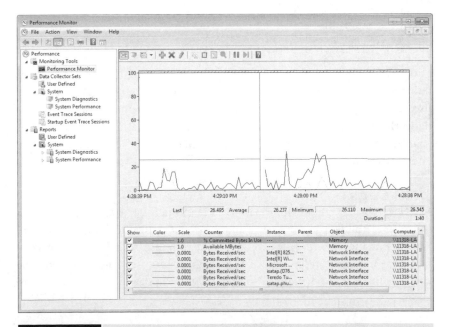

FIGURE 13.2 Windows Performance Monitor

during nonworking hours, could indicate that the server is under attack or that a Trojan horse program is sending out data at specific times.

Access Logs

Access logs provide information on user logins and logouts from specific servers and network resources. Access logs are a valuable audit tool, as they provide information on when a specific user has logged in or out of the network. If security anomalies occur during a certain time period, you might be able to narrow down what users were logged in at the time of the incident.

Access logs also record failed attempts at logging, and patterns of behavior can be detected by checking the access logs for numerous attempts at trying to access an account. For example, suppose the access logs show that someone has tried to access the administrator account over the network during nonworking hours. After several attempts at guessing the password, the account was locked out to prevent further brute-force attempts. The access logs will show the IP address from which the attempted logins originated, and the administrator can determine whose workstation is the source of the attempted unauthorized access.

A typical access log can display information similar to the following:

```
08:33 Login: admin 192.168.1.110 Success
08:52 Logout: admin 192.168.1.110
10:45 Login: admin 192.168.1.110 Success
11:50 Logout: admin 192.168.1.110
15:20 Login: admin 192.168.1.110 Success
17:10 Logout: admin 192.168.1.110
23:11 Login: admin 192.168.1.99 Failure
23:57 Login: admin 192.168.1.99 Failure
23:59 Login: admin 192.168.1.99 Failure
```

This indicates normal login and logout behavior for the admin user from his or her workstation during normal work hours. However, starting at 11:11 P.M., a user attempted to log in as the admin user from a different workstation on the network and failed three times. In most cases, if automatic account lockout is enabled, the admin user account can be locked out after the third unsuccessful attempt, depending on the configuration.

DNS Logs

DNS logs typically contain information on DNS queries to the server, including the source IP address of the request and the domain name of the destination IP address that the DNS server will return in the response. DNS logs can also contain error messages and notifications for regular processes such as failed zone transfers that occur when the DNS server cannot update zone information to another system.

This information can help administrators track the source of possible DNS poisoning attempts, in which the DNS tables of IP addresses and hostnames are compromised by replacing the IP address of a host with another IP address that resolves to an attacker's system. If authentication measures are in place to protect against DNS poisoning attacks, you might see a number of failed attempts to update the zone information on your DNS server in the DNS logs. These logs can help you track down the IP address of the attacker's server, which will be indicated in the DNS queries.

In a DoS attack, DNS logs will indicate that a specific host is sending large amounts of queries to your DNS server. If you determine the IP address source of the queries, you can take steps to block that address from connecting to your DNS server.

Travel Advisory

Typically, DNS logging is enabled only while you're trying to troubleshoot an issue. If the DNS server is logging every single query from clients, the massive amounts of DNS lookup queries that can occur in a large organization can cause performance issues.

Firewall Logs

As all inbound and outbound network traffic passes through the network firewall, the firewall logs are a critical resource when examining network trends and analyzing for anomalous behavior. A firewall is the first line of defense at the network's perimeter, and network attacks are often first detected and discovered in the *firewall logs*. For example, when new worms infect Internet servers and then try to spread to other Internet servers, the connections have to pass through an organization's firewall. The network administrator monitors the firewall and is first to notice and report these worm outbreaks. The administrator will notice hundreds of denied connections to servers on the network, as the firewall is blocking these connections from entering. DoS attacks are also detected in a similar manner.

The most common types of anomalous network behaviors that can be detected at the firewall are port scans. Hackers often use port scanning software to scan a specific network address to probe for open ports, or to perform a scan of all IP addresses on the network to see which systems respond. Hackers can then use this information to target systems they know are alive on the network and to listen for requests on specific ports. Firewalls (if they are implemented properly) will protect the details of the internal network and will not allow port and IP scanners to glean any information from the network.

Firewall logs can be scanned for patterns of port scanning behaviors, such as a single network address trying to connect to consecutive port numbers on the same system from port 1 to 65525, or an IP range scan in which a single network address is scanning banks of IP addresses such as 192.168.1.1 to 192.168.255.255. For example, the following log trace shows behavior of a port scan from a specific IP address:

```
Source: 172.16.1.12 Destination: 192.168.1.128 TCP Port 21
Source: 172.16.1.12 Destination: 192.168.1.128 TCP Port 22
Source: 172.16.1.12 Destination: 192.168.1.128 TCP Port 23
Source: 172.16.1.12 Destination: 192.168.1.128 TCP Port 24
Source: 172.16.1.12 Destination: 192.168.1.128 TCP Port 25
Source: 172.16.1.12 Destination: 192.168.1.128 TCP Port 26
Source: 172.16.1.12 Destination: 192.168.1.128 TCP Port 27
```

The port scan will continue until it reaches port 65525 in an effort to find open ports that can be accessed and potentially attacked.

Exam Tip

Recognize different types of attacks based on the details of firewall log messages.

Firewall logs (including personal software firewalls) are also an important tool for exposing Trojan horses or other types of malicious software installed on client computers that are trying to communicate through the firewall back to the hacker's computer. The administrator can see the source and destination IP addresses of the request and identify which computers might be infected on the network, and then take immediate steps to clean the Trojan horse program.

Antivirus Logs

Antivirus logs are generated by antivirus software running on server and client systems. They contain important information on the number and types of viruses that have been detected, quarantined, or cleaned on the system, and they also provide diagnostic information on the antivirus signature updates. In many cases, client logs can be coalesced on the central antivirus server for more efficient log monitoring and auditing.

Administrators can analyze antivirus logs to gather information about computers on the network that have been attacked by viruses, computer files that have been quarantined or cleaned, or, more important, computer files that are infected and cannot be cleaned. This information can alert the administrator to clients on the network that are continually infected or attacked, which can indicate that the user's antivirus program is not working properly or the user is involved in risky Internet behaviors, such as unauthorized downloading of files or receiving viruses via instant message chats.

Antivirus programs use signature files, databases of patterns of known viruses that are continually updated and downloaded by antivirus programs at scheduled intervals. If this update process breaks down and the antivirus program cannot communicate with the antivirus signature file server (after being blocked by a firewall of if the signature server is unavailable, for example), your system will not be protected from the newest virus threats. By regularly analyzing the antivirus logs, administrators can ensure that they are regularly updating their signature files, and that no communications issues exist between the antivirus program and the signature update server. If the update fails at each scheduled interval, the administrator can troubleshoot the network path to determine what is blocking the updates from being downloaded.

Security Logging Applications

Because a specific system or network device can contain log files for a variety of operating system processes, system services, and application programs, several different log files might need to be analyzed by the security administrator. Many of these logs are extremely large and can generate megabytes of data within a single day of operation. It would be very difficult for the administrator to be proactive and manually monitor and analyze each of these logs every single day.

For Unix-based systems, the *syslog* (system logger) functionality allows all systems on a network to forward their logs to a central syslog server. The syslog server stores these log entries in one large log file. The administrator can perform simple text and pattern searches on this log to pinpoint specific information required from all the server logs on the network.

Windows-based systems rely on the Event Viewer (shown in Figure 13.3), an application that provides a centralized location to view application, system, and security logs. Log entries are typically divided into different categories such as Error, Warning, and Information that allow the administrator to sort and scan the logs for critical errors and warnings, while ignoring more informational log entries. Security logs typically contain entries indicating "Success" or "Failure," such as when a user accesses a specific file or directory.

Reports and Trend Monitoring

Most security monitoring applications can coalesce information from several log sources into one database that can be easily searched and analyzed using the logging application, and they can generate reports on log entries for specific services or overall trends in the logging data. This is much easier and efficient than scanning through individual log files. Reports can scan the most important

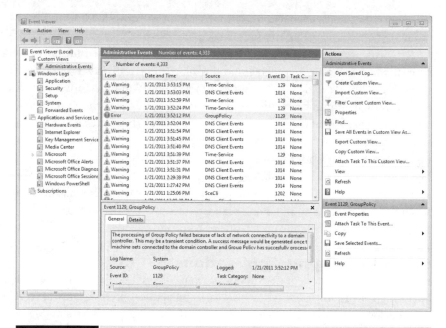

FIGURE 13.3 Windows Event Viewer

information for you to know and display them in an easy-to-read format with graphs and charts.

Important reporting information to generate includes:

- **Antivirus and malware reports** Shows how many inbound viruses and malware programs were blocked, and can also show how many virus or malware infected messages were sent outbound from systems internal to your network.

- **Firewall reports** Analyzes trends in the total amount of network activity inbound and outbound. This report can also highlight the top types of attacks that were blocked by the firewall.

- **Antispam and mail content filtering** Reports on the number of spam messages that were blocked by your antispam filter, and any specific content blocked inbound or outbound from deep content scanning of e-mail messages and their attachments.

- **System reports** Reports on the amount of disk space used, CPU, memory, network usage, and other hardware-related trends. These reports are important for capacity planning and identifying servers that need to be upgraded, or identifying where additional servers are required.

Reports should be created at minimum on a weekly basis. By comparing reports on a week-to-week basis, you can more spot short-term spikes and anomalous behavior that can indicate a security issue, while other trends, such as network usage, can be monitored longer-term for capacity planning. For the executive level, you can create monthly and yearly reports to analyze overall trends that have a longer-term impact on your systems for capacity planning and expansion.

Alarms and Notifications

Most security logging applications and monitors can scan current activity and the system log files, and generate alarms and notifications of specific critical errors to the administrator. Alarms notifications can be sent in a variety of ways, including an on-screen alert (from your monitoring application or personal computer), e-mail message, page, and text messaging.

Alarms should be triggered by any monitoring function that exceeds a threshold. For example, you want to receive an immediate alarm notification if one of your hard drives is running out of space, or if your network intrusion detection system has detected a critical security intrusion. You must be careful to fine-tune your threshold so that you are not receiving too many alarms for issues that are noncritical. If you receive too many, you will eventually stop paying attention to them and critical alarms may go ignored. Alarm notifications need to be flexible to allow you to fine-tune the results of your monitoring applications to view and report only on serious or critical errors. Informational data, such as general notifications or low-level warnings, are usually ignored.

System Auditing

No matter how many security procedures you have in place, an active community of hackers and crackers will invent new ways to circumvent them. Fully effective security policies and procedures must be audited on a regular basis to test and assess their efficiency. *Auditing* also ensures that both users and network administrators are conforming to security procedures. Auditing can be general in nature, where logs of the most common activities are analyzed for any suspicious behavior. More advanced and detailed techniques can involve proactive monitoring of as many systems as possible, even down to the desktop level. Auditing is, ultimately, a way of ensuring accountability and preventing small problems from escalating into large security breaches.

System Baselines

The goal of any type of auditing is to create a baseline of current activity and then measure future activity against this baseline for changes from preexisting thresholds. Creating a security baseline involves analyzing user activity, such as physical entrance and exit from the facility, recording logins to systems, and recording file and application access. The amount of information that can be collected is daunting, and the security administrator must balance the time needed to analyze all this activity versus the security risk levels they represent.

Auditing Event Logs

When monitoring the event log files on your system, you must check for the most common types of security-related events, and then compare them with your baseline to discover any anomalies that require investigation.

Information recorded from user activity can be organized into the following specific event areas.

System-Level Events   *System-level events* include events specific to a certain system or a network of systems, including the following:

- **Login and logout times**   The logs of users that entered and exited a system can be helpful in determining which user was accessing the system at the time a security event occurred.
- **Login attempts**   If a user seems to be trying to access an account too many times with the wrong password, this could indicate someone is trying to hack into that account. Many network operating systems can limit the login attempts by disabling the account if too many unsuccessful logins occur.
- **Password and account changes**   By analyzing account and password changes, you can monitor whether a user has suddenly gained privileges he or she never had before and that weren't entered by the network administrator.

User-Level Events   *User-level events* can be recorded to monitor activities performed by users. Like application-level events, a large list of activities can be recorded. The following are the most common user-level events that should be recorded:

- **Use of resources**   The administrator can record what resources the user accessed during a login session such as files, servers, printers, and any other network services. This will help indicate whether users are accessing information to which they should not have access or information that is inappropriate to their job and security level.

- **Command and keystrokes**   At a granular level, the keystrokes and commands used by a user while logged in can be recorded and analyzed for unusual activity. This sort of logging can be the most time-consuming to analyze.
- **Security violations**   Each time a user attempts to access a resource for which he doesn't have the necessary privileges, an entry can be written to a log. Too many attempts at inappropriately accessing resources can indicate attempted unauthorized activity.

Application-Level Events   These events happen at the *application level*, for example, when a user is using an application to view or manipulate data. The amount of information that can be collected with this type of monitoring can be overwhelming, so only certain key elements should be recorded:

- **File access**   The application logs can record which files were accessed and whether they were modified to monitor what time a certain file was modified from its original form. Monitoring critical system files for this type of activity is especially important.
- **Error messages**   By recording error messages that occur during the use of an application, you can analyze whether the user is intentionally trying to use the application in a manner for which it wasn't designed.
- **Security violations**   Any attempts at using an application to compromise access permissions should be recorded. Repeated security violations of the same resource can indicate improper behaviors.

Exam Tip

Know what types of networking and system activities beyond everyday use can be considered suspicious.

User Access Rights Review

Beyond monitoring and auditing system log information for security breaches and anomalous behavior, security administrators must also regularly review the access rights and permissions granted to users on the network. Evidence of a user having inappropriate access privileges can be gleaned from an audit log that identifies specific files being accessed by a user who should not be granted access. Realistically, many users can have access permissions they don't require.

Analyzing user security rights and policies on a regular basis is critical to ensuring that existing security holes in user policies can be repaired before a user accesses or damages data to which he or she should not be allowed access.

Group policies are often the most common source of users gaining inappropriate rights and privileges. Network administrators who lack knowledge about how to use these policies can assign inappropriate access rights to several users in a group. A specific user typically has access only to the files in her own private home directory. When group permissions and policies are applied to that user, she gains the additional rights allocated to the group. A user can belong to several groups, each with its own set of security rights. For example, suppose a user was transferred from one department to another (such as from sales to marketing). When analyzing the user's security rights, an administrator realizes that she still has access to the sales department's files, in addition to those granted to the marketing department. The administrator can remove the user from the sales group to remove her access rights to sales directories and files.

Group policy management software systems can aid the administrator in managing an organization's group policies to ensure that policies such as group policies, domain policies, and individual user policies do not give a user inappropriate access rights. Group policy management software can accurately determine the final policy applied to a user, which helps the administrator determine what access rights a user has when all policies are applied.

Reviewing Audit Information

Simply recording and collecting information isn't helpful unless the information is reviewed and analyzed. The auditing information can be viewed manually or forwarded by an automatic system, but you must construct meaningful information from the data before it can be useful.

Reviewing all this information can be a daunting task, but many tools and reporting applications can translate the raw data into something coherent and useful. To maximize the efficiency of your reporting procedure, only data perceived as beyond normal operating thresholds should be included. For example, unless a specific incident occurs, you'd have no need to analyze logs of which users logged in and out at certain times. Instead, you might choose to see only those users who logged in after normal working hours to look for suspicious activity.

Auditing the Administrator

In most corporate environments, the network administrator analyzes and audits network activity. In high-security environments, an independent auditor can be asked to analyze the log information. The network administrators have full access to all systems in the company, and their activities must also be recorded and monitored, along with that of regular users. High-level functions, such as user account creation, modification, and deletion, as well as changes to system configuration files, should be monitored and analyzed on a regular basis by a security professional.

Storage and Retention Policies

Security administrators have the task of regularly examining logging and audit data such as system and network intrusion logs. In most cases, this information is automatically collected and saved to a specific location to be retrieved and analyzed by the administrator. Data storage and retention policies that are applied to typical company information such as user data files and e-mail messages should also apply to logging information. This policy ensures that log data can be stored and retained for a sufficient amount of time so that it can be analyzed properly and preserved as legally required for evidence in investigations of security incidents.

CHECKPOINT

✔**Objective 13.01: Analyze and differentiate among types of mitigation and deterrent techniques.**   Anomalous behaviors can be detected by performing a baseline of normal system operation and then analyzing data that goes beyond the thresholds of the baseline. Failsafe or failsecure means that you implement maximum security in the event of a failure or malfunction, while failopen errs on the side of permissiveness during a failure scenario. Signature-based monitoring systems contain predefined signature databases of known attacks, but they are unable to detect the newest attacks that do not yet have signatures available. Behavior-based monitoring systems start from a baseline of normal system behavior and then learn from these system performance profiles to recognize behavioral anomalies that pass the thresholds of the normal system baseline. Rule-based security monitoring systems rely on the administrator to create rules and define the actions to take when those rules are transgressed. Configure your logs to display only the information you require to reduce resource usage and allow more efficient log searching. Performance logs can indicate security issues via behaviors that stray from the system baseline. Access and security logs provide an audit trail of who has logged in and out of the system.

REVIEW QUESTIONS

1. You are setting initial performance baselines for an important database server. Which of the following collected data is considered a good indication of a system performance baseline?

   A. Network bandwidth usage per hour for a 24-hour period

   B. CPU processing trends measured during typical working hours

   C. CPU, memory, and network usage data collected for an entire week

   D. Concurrent connections during the busiest server times

2. A signature-based monitoring system has failed to detect an attack on one of your web servers. Which of the following is the most likely cause?

   A. A firewall is misconfigured.

   B. Signature-based systems scan only outbound traffic.

   C. You did not properly implement an access rule for that type of attack.

   D. This a new type of attack that has no signature available yet.

3. Which of the following types of scanning methodologies checks for anomalous behavior on a system that differs from its routine baseline performance?

   A. Behavioral-based

   B. Rule-based

   C. Signature-based

   D. Role-based

4. Your building's physical security is very critical, and you need to implement procedures to deal with security issues in the event of a malfunction with the security card access control system or a power outage. For maximum security, which of the following concepts should you use in your implementation?

   A. Surveillance video

   B. Failopen security

   C. Security guards

   D. Failsafe security

5. Due to downsizing, your department of IT administrators has been drastically reduced, and the time available to monitor your security applications and logs is at a minimum. Which of the following logging procedures would reduce the amount of time examining and analyzing several different logs?

    A. Disabling logging

    B. Logging only minor errors

    C. Logging only warning and critical errors

    D. Enabling verbose logging of all errors

6. You are auditing a performance log for your web server. Which of the following performance statistics may indicate a security issue?

    A. Disk space free at 70 percent

    B. Memory usage at 45 percent on average

    C. CPU usage at 99 percent 75 percent of the time

    D. Network bandwidth usage at 50 percent on average

7. During routine examination of the firewall logs, you notice that a specific host is attempting to connect to the same internal IP address starting at port 1 and continuing to port 65525. Of which of the following issues could this be evidence of?

    A. A ping sweep of a server on your network

    B. Port scanning of a server on your network

    C. Normal behavior for network diagnostics

    D. DNS requests for name resolution

8. It has come to your attention that a confidential file was accessed without proper authorization. Which of the following logs would you examine to find out which users were logged in during the time the issue occurred?

    A. Access log

    B. DNS log

    C. Performance log

    D. Firewall log

9. After a security audit, which of the following items would *not* be considered anomalous behavior?

    A. Several unsuccessful attempts to log in as the administrator

    B. A ping sweep on the firewall for the IP range 10.10.0.0 to 10.10.255.255

    C. Error messages in the system's log that indicate excessive disk usage

    D. A member of the sales group accessing the sales shared file directory

10. You are performing an audit of a file server security log. Which of the following entries would be considered a possible security threat?

    A. Five failed login attempts for a user

    B. Two successful logins with the administrator account

    C. A 500K print job sent to a printer

    D. Three new files saved in the accounting folder by user finance

REVIEW ANSWERS

1. **C** To establish a performance baseline, you must measure your system activity for 24 hours per day for at least 7 continuous days. This ensures that you have data for an entire week's worth of activity, including working hours, nonworking hours, and weekends. Simply sampling performance data for a few hours during the day will not provide a sufficient indication of performance trends.

2. **D** Signature-based systems are powerful and efficient because they rely on the collective knowledge of security vendors who analyze and collect information on Internet security threats and trends and are able to update their databases very quickly when new threats arise. However, they are unable to detect very new attacks that do not have signatures available yet.

3. **A** Behavior-based monitoring systems start from a baseline of normal system behavior and then learn from these system performance profiles to recognize behavioral anomalies that pass the thresholds of the normal baseline of the system.

4. **D** Failsafe or failsecure means that you implement maximum security in the event of a failure or malfunction. In this example, making sure doors stay locked during an access card reader malfunction or power outage is an example of using failsafe concepts.

5. **C** To reduce that number of minor and informational types of messages in the logs, administrators should configure their logging systems to log only warning and critical error messages. This reduces the amount of resources required to store logs and reduces the time required to analyze them, as only the most important data is logged.

6. **C** A system running with its CPU usage at 99 percent for a long period of time can indicate that some anomalous process (such as a virus, Trojan horse, or worm) is causing CPU processing to spike beyond the normal system operating baseline.

7. **B**   A host system that is scanning a server for any open ports using the entire port range indicates that a port scanning program is being used to determine which services are running and which ports are open and available. A malicious hacker might be trying to find vulnerabilities and attack your system.

8. **A**   Access logs provide valuable audit tools because they provide information about when a specific user has logged in to or out of the network. If security anomalies occur during a certain time period, you might be able to narrow down which users were logged in at the time of the incident.

9. **D**   A member of a group accessing the shared files for the group to which she belongs does not constitute anomalous behavior; however, ping sweeps against the firewall, disk error messages in the system's log, and several attempts to access the administrator account are all security issues that should be carefully examined.

10. **A**   A large number of unsuccessful logins for a specific user is unusual. Either the user has forgotten his password, or someone is trying to guess the password to hack into the account.

Vulnerability Assessments

ITINERARY

○ **Objective 14.01** Implement assessment tools and techniques to discover security threats and vulnerabilities

○ **Objective 14.02** Within the realm of vulnerability assessments, explain the proper use of penetration testing versus vulnerability scanning

	NEWBIE	SOME EXPERIENCE	EXPERT
ETA	2 hours	1 hour	0.5 hours

The networks and systems in your organization are always under constant threat of attack from hackers, physical intruders, and malware. No matter how secure your network is, there will always be risks from known and unknown vulnerabilities that can be exploited.

A variety of tools are available to the network administrator and security professional to test networks and systems for vulnerabilities and weaknesses; unfortunately, these tools are also available to unethical hackers who use them to exploit specific vulnerabilities. By proactively monitoring your network for vulnerabilities and taking immediate steps to rectify them, you ensure that hackers using the same tools will not find vulnerabilities to exploit. You must routinely scan your network for vulnerabilities, whether they be unpatched operating systems and application software (such as web servers and database servers), or unused open ports and services that are actively listening for requests.

When coding your own software applications, you must also be wary of developing code that contains vulnerabilities, and right from the design stage, place security as a top concern in your application architecture. As you develop your software code, you must stay within your secure design to prevent vulnerabilities from being introduced in your software.

Finally, to test your countermeasures and solutions for existing vulnerabilities, there are several methods available to simulate attacks on your current systems to ensure that your security controls are properly implemented and cannot be bypassed.

This chapter describes how to conduct vulnerability and threat assessments, including an overview of vulnerability testing tools, such as port scanners, network mappers, and protocol analyzers, which can aid in identifying vulnerabilities in your network. As part of your prevention and mitigation techniques, the importance of penetration testing is also discussed, including how it differs from and complements vulnerability assessments.

Objective 14.01
CompTIA Security+
Objective 3.7

Implement Assessment Tools and Techniques to Discover Security Threats and Vulnerabilities

As part of your overall vulnerability and threat assessment procedures, you must perform an assessment for each asset in your organization to ascertain the risks and impact to that asset. All possibilities, both physical and nonphysical, should be assessed. For example, confidential data can be stolen from a file server by someone physically stealing the system, or by a hacker accessing the data through a network security vulnerability.

Identify the following when performing a vulnerability and threat assessment:

- **Vulnerability** A *vulnerability* is a security weakness that could be compromised by a particular threat. An operating system (OS) might be vulnerable to network attacks, for example, because it was not updated with security patches. A file server could be vulnerable to viruses because no antivirus software is installed. Web servers and database servers might have vulnerabilities that allow cross-site scripting and SQL injection attacks. *Physical vulnerabilities* affect the physical protection of the asset. Physical assets, such as network servers, should be protected from natural disasters and physical theft by storing the equipment in special rooms with protective mechanisms to prevent these threats. *Nonphysical vulnerabilities* usually involve software or data. Software security vulnerabilities can be created because of improper software configuration, unpatched or buggy software, lack of antivirus protection, weak access and authentication controls, unused open network ports, and misconfigured or nonexistent network security devices.

- **Threat** A *threat* creates the possibility of a vulnerability being compromised. A variety of threats can pose security risks, including the following:

  - **Natural disasters** A natural disaster is a fire, flood, or other phenomenon that causes physical damage to company assets—usually the facilities and the equipment within them.

  - **Equipment malfunction** Electronic equipment is vulnerable to normal wear and tear that can result in failed components—from a failed power supply fan to a failed hard drive.

  - **Employees** Assets face both malicious and benign threats from employees. The source of the threat could be human error, such as someone deleting a directory of files by mistake, or theft, vandalism, disgruntled employees, and corporate espionage.

  - **Intruders** An unauthorized person can compromise the access controls of a facility to gain access and perform theft, vandalism, or sabotage.

  - **Malicious hackers** A threat by malicious hackers is a nonphysical threat that involves a hacker's ability to compromise network security to access or damage assets on a company's network.

- **Risk** After threats and vulnerabilities have been identified, your next step is to assess the risk of a threat compromising a vulnerability—such as what can happen in a security breach. For example, a combination of the lack of antivirus software protection (a risk) and the introduction of a virus (a threat) would result in a virus-infected server, which could damage or delete sensitive data. Or an unused open network port could be a target for a denial-of-service (DoS) attack that renders the server unable to respond to legitimate network requests.

- **Impact** A *risk assessment* reflects the worst possible scenario of a security compromise and should be quantified with a direct financial value for losses and potential losses. A company should reflect on the amount of damage to reputation and financial security if a hacker were to launch a successful DoS attack on the company's web servers. A loss of service—even for a few hours—can severely damage a company; consider, for example, the case of a company that offers stock-trading services. On top of immediate costs for equipment or data loss, the potential loss of prolonged downtime must be factored into the equation. Hundreds of thousands of dollars of revenue can be lost while the site is unavailable to customers. Once the potential loss is calculated for each type of risk, the results can be used to create solutions and countermeasures that are cost-efficient, depending on the risk situation.

- **Likelihood** The final factor for the assessment is how likely it is that a particular vulnerability to a threat will occur. For example, the probability that a malicious hacker will attempt to attack the network is greater than the chances that a natural disaster will occur. Certain software vulnerabilities are more likely to be exploited than lesser-known ones. By assessing the likelihood of the threat, you can allocate solutions for mitigation according to its impact and probability of occurrence.

Vulnerability Assessment Tools

As part of your vulnerability and threat assessment, you need to be able to examine your network and systems for existing vulnerabilities.

Vulnerability assessment and network scanning programs are important tools for a network administrator who routinely runs preventive security scans on the network. These programs provide detailed information about which hosts on a network are running which services. They can also help identify servers that are running unnecessary network services that create security risks, such as a file server running FTP or HTTP services that could provide unauthorized access to data.

Common tools, such as network mappers, port scanners, vulnerability scanners, protocol analyzers, honeypots, and password crackers, are used by network administrators to identify and prevent such attacks. Unfortunately, these same tools are major weapons in the malicious hacker's arsenal. Attackers can use them to determine what systems are running on your network, what services and open ports they are running, what operating system and application software they are running, and what vulnerabilities can be exploited. Due to their simplicity, these tools are commonly used to probe and scan networks, even by amateur hackers who have no knowledge of networking protocols.

Network Mappers

A *network mapper* program scans a network and uses network IP packets to determine which hosts are available, what operating systems are running, and other types of information about a network host. Most network mappers use the Ping utility to perform Internet Control Message Protocol (ICMP) sweeps of entire ranges of IP addresses looking for hosts that respond. The response contains a lot of information about the host and its place on the network (such as whether it's behind a router or firewall on a subnetwork). Hackers who already know the address of a specific target can also use a network mapper to analyze the host for open ports, services, and OS specifics.

When used against an entire network, a network mapper program can determine how many hosts are running on the network, on which subnetworks they reside, and what services and ports are running. This information offers a virtual map of the entire network for a malicious hacker who can narrow his scope of attack to specific systems, or for the network administrator who needs to find and correct weaknesses on a network.

One of the most popular tools used for network mapping is an open-source and publicly available utility called *Nmap* that is used by hackers to scan and map networks and used by administrators to audit their networks for security weaknesses. The Nmap command-line utility uses simple text commands with switch options to perform tasks. For example, to perform a ping sweep on a system with Nmap, you'd enter the following:

```
nmap -sP 192.168.1.128
Host 192.168.1.128 appears to be up.
MAC Address: 00:B1:63:3F:74:41 (Apple)
Nmap done: 1 IP address (1 host up) scanned in 0.600 seconds
```

To perform a scan to identify the OS of a system, you'd enter this:

```
nmap -O 192.168.1.128
MAC Address: 00:B1:63:3F:74:41 (Apple)
Device type: general purpose
Running: NetBSD 4.X
OS details: NetBSD 4.99.4 (x86)
Network Distance: 1 hop
```

Travel Assistance

The Nmap tool can be downloaded from www.nmap.org.

Port Scanners

After an attacker has determined what systems are on a network and identified IP addresses that respond with acknowledgments of a live system at that address, the next step is to discover what network services and open ports are running on the system. By using a *port scanner,* an attacker can determine which ports on the system are listening for requests (such as TCP port 80), and then he can decide which service or vulnerability in the service can be exploited.

For example, if an attacker sees that SMTP port 25 is open and listening for requests, he knows that an e-mail server is operating and can launch more probes and tests to determine what mail server software is running and whether vulnerabilities can be exploited to relay spam through the server. The following example shows a listing of a port scan from the Nmap application:

```
nmap -sT 192.168.1.128
Interesting ports on 192.168.1.128:
Not shown: 1709 closed ports
PORT   STATE SERVICE
21/tcp   open   ftp
53/tcp   open   domain
554/tcp  open   rtsp
10000/tcp open  snet-sensor-mgmt
```

A standard set of ports, including 65,535 TCP ports and User Datagram Protocol (UDP) ports, are available for running network services on a computer system. The first 1024 ports are *well-known* ports, which means they make up the most common types of network ports, such as DNS (53), SMTP (25), HTTP (80), HTTPS (443), and FTP (21). Beyond these first 1024 ports are tens of thousands of port ranges that are used by third-party applications, services, and networking devices. Table 14-1 lists the most common well-known protocols and services and their corresponding TCP/IP ports.

Travel Advisory

Many of these ports also listen on UDP as well as TCP. For example, the Domain Name System (DNS) uses TCP port 53 for zone transfers and UDP port 53 for DNS queries.

A port scanner will send probing network packets (sometimes called a *port sweep*) to each of the 65,535 ports (both TCP and UDP) and listen for a response. If the system port does not respond, the attacker knows it is either dis-

---

TABLE 14.1	TCP/IP Services and Port Numbers

Service	TCP/IP Port Number
HTTP	80
FTP (Data)	20
FTP (Control)	21
DNS	53
DHCP	67
SMTP	25
SNMP	161
Telnet	23
POP3	110
IMAP	143
NTP	123
NNTP	119
SSH	22
LDAP	389

abled or protected (behind a network firewall or proxy server, for example). When it does respond, this service is running on the target system, and the attacker can then use more focused tools to assault that particular port and service. For example, a SQL server may be listening on port TCP/UDP 1433. If a port scanner receives a response from this port, the attacker knows that this system is running a SQL server, and he can then direct his attacks against specific SQL vulnerabilities.

The following are different types of port scanning methods that can be used to detect open ports on a system:

- **TCP scanning** A TCP scan uses the TCP protocol and its commands to connect to a port and open a full TCP connection before breaking off the communication. For example, when scanning a system for Telnet port 23, the port scanner will fully connect to that port on the destination host. If no response is received, the port is deemed closed or protected by a firewall.

- **SYN scanning** A SYN scan uses small, basic IP packets to scan a host and does not open a full TCP connection to the destination host. The SYN scan will break off the communication before the handshake process is complete. This is often called *stealth* scanning and is less intrusive than a TCP scan, which opens a full connection to receive its information.

- **UDP scanning** The UDP scan is not as effective as other scans, since UDP is a connectionless protocol. This scan gets its open port information by detecting which ports are not returning acknowledgments to requests, since a UDP request will receive a "host unreachable" message via ICMP in response. If no response is received, the port is open and listening for requests. However, this method is not foolproof, because if the port is blocked by a firewall, the user/attacker will receive no response and might assume the port is open.

Port scanners are often built into popular network mapping and vulnerability assessment tools, such as Nmap, because they provide the foundation for determining what services and open ports are on a system, which then leads to a specific vulnerability scan against those services and ports.

Vulnerability Scanners

When an attacker has ascertained which systems are available on the network, his next step is to probe these systems to see what vulnerabilities they might contain. At this point, he has an idea of what systems are alive and which network ports are open and listening for requests.

A *vulnerability scanner* is a software program specifically designed to scan a system via the network to determine what services the system is running and whether any unnecessary open network ports, unpatched operating systems and applications, or back doors can be exploited. Network administrators can use the same vulnerability scanner software to take preventive measures to close vulnerabilities that exist on their systems.

Travel Advisory

Nessus (available at www.nessus.org) is a popular, free, Unix-based vulnerability scanner that scans systems for thousands of vulnerabilities and provides an exhaustive report about the vulnerabilities that exist on your system. Another popular tool, GFI LANguard (www.gfi.com), is a commercial software network security scanner for Windows systems.

Vulnerability scanners can include a number of scanning and security assessment abilities, such as port scanning, network scanning and mapping, and OS and application server scanning. The vulnerability scanner contains a database of known OS weaknesses and application program vulnerabilities (such as web and database servers), and it scans the target system to determine whether any of the vulnerabilities listed in its database exist. For example, a database server and front-end web application can be scanned to determine whether they are vulnerable to specific database and web server attacks. By determining the OS of a system, such as Windows or Unix, and then using the database of known vulnerabilities and weaknesses for that OS, the attacker can target his attacks.

Protocol Analyzers

A *protocol analyzer* can intercept, record, and analyze network traffic. Network administrators use the analyzer to track specific network protocols as they send out queries and receive responses and to narrow down sources of communications issues; however, they are also used by hackers to intercept clear-text communications (such as user account and password information) that are transmitted over unsecured protocols. For example, HTTP web traffic is transmitted in clear text, and any information transmitted to a web site in clear text, such as a login ID and password, is not encrypted and can be easily viewed by a hacker using a protocol analyzer. Confidential information can also be captured from sensitive e-mail messages passed over the network.

To protect against unauthorized sniffers, network switches can keep network broadcast traffic isolated on its own network segment; hackers would need access to the specific network segment to get at the data stored there. In addition, any sensitive data should be transmitted over the network using secure protocols that encrypt their contents.

Exam Tip

To prevent network traffic from being intercepted by a protocol scanner, use secure protocols such as Hypertext Transfer Protocol over Secure Sockets Layer (HTTPS) instead of HTTP for web traffic, or Secure Shell (SSH) instead of Telnet for remote access.

OVAL

The *Open Vulnerability and Assessment Language (OVAL)* is a security standard that provides open access to security assessments using a special language to standardize system security configuration characteristics, current system analysis, and reporting. OVAL is not a vulnerability scanner, but it provides a language and templates that help administrators check their systems to determine whether vulnerabilities, such as unpatched software, exist.

OVAL uses Extensible Markup Language (XML) schemas as its framework, with three schemas geared toward specific parts of the security standard (system characteristics, current system definition, and reporting the assessment results). These XML files can be fed through an OVAL interpreter program that examines the system, compares it to public databases of known vulnerabilities, and generates the test results that indicate any open vulnerabilities on the system.

Local Lingo

XML Extensible Markup Language is a markup-language specification that allows structured data to be shared across different computers and platforms. XML uses custom property tags to ensure data is stored and communicated properly, but does not define how the data is displayed, which is typically a function performed by HTML.

This information relies on repositories of publicly available security content that contain a collection of security definitions provided by the security community, which continually adds to the collection and drives OVAL development and evolution. This process provides a comprehensive testing and reporting standard supported by the security community that creates a baseline and checks for known vulnerabilities on computer systems.

Travel Assistance

More information about OVAL can be found at http://oval.mitre.org.

Password Crackers

Password cracker programs (also referred to as *password auditing tools*) are used by hackers to attack a system's authentication structure (such as its password database) and attempt to retrieve passwords for user accounts. The programs are also used by security administrators to proactively audit their password database to look for weak passwords.

Passwords crackers use a variety of methods:

- **Dictionary attack** This type of attack relies on a dictionary of words that contain common passwords that are tried against the authentication database. Because users often use known dictionary words as passwords, this attack can succeed in cracking many passwords.

- **Brute-force attack** This attack uses a calculated combination of characters in an attempt to guess the password. The brute-force method will keep trying every single combination until it gets the password right.

- **Hybrid attack** Many programs use a combination of dictionary and brute-force attacks to add numbers and special characters (such as the @ symbol for *a*) on to the dictionary words in an attempt to crack more difficult passwords.

Travel Advisory

Examples of password cracking programs include LC4 and Cain & Abel.

After the attacker cracks a specific password, they will be able to access that user account. The administrator account for a system is most commonly attacked because it has full access privileges.

Many older computer authentication schemes stored the passwords in clear text, making it easy for a hacker who is able to access the password database file to crack an account. Most modern operating systems at the least provide some type of one-way hashing function to protect the password database. If the password database file is accessed by a hacker, it will be of no use because the contents are encrypted. However, many sophisticated password-cracking programs are able to analyze the database and attack weak encryption methods repeatedly to crack passwords over time. For example, the LANMAN hash used in older Windows-based systems to protect passwords was weak and could be cracked fairly easily if the hacker could gain access to the password database.

Protecting against password-cracking programs relies on a strong password policy, as discussed in previous chapters. Setting maximum login attempts will lock out an account if the password has been unsuccessfully entered a set number of times.

Exam Tip

Know what constitutes a strong password to protect against dictionary attacks. Remember that a lockout countermeasure allows only a specific number of login attempts before the account locks to protect against brute-force attacks.

Protecting the password database is also a primary concern. Although a maximum login attempt policy will prevent most online brute-force attempts from guessing a password, if a hacker manages to access the database itself, he can run a cracking program against it offline for many days and weeks to crack the passwords in the database. One method of protecting the password database (other than using traditional security methods such as access permissions) is called *salting,* which refers to adding a suffix of random characters (called a *salt*) to the password before it is encrypted. Each password has its own salt, which is different for every password in the database, even identical passwords. Salting makes it difficult for a hacker to use brute-force methods to crack the password database. The longer the salt added to the password, the less likely it is to be cracked. Early implementations used 12-bit salts; however, 32- to 128-bit salts are recommended.

Travel Advisory

Windows does not use salting in its password databases; however, modern versions of Unix and Mac OS (10.4 and greater) do use salting.

Unix-based systems also protect their hashed password databases by using a *shadow password database.* The normal password database (located in /etc/passwd) contains the hashed passwords, but the whole file itself is readable by users other than the root user. In password shadowing, the hashed passwords are removed from the main password database and stored in a file (/etc/shadow) that is not available to unprivileged users; hackers cannot access the shadow password database to take it offline and run cracking programs on it.

Honeypots and Honeynets

A *honeypot* is a device or server used to attract and lure attackers into trying to access it, thereby removing attention from actual critical systems. The name refers to using a pot of honey to attract bees, which in this case are malicious hackers. The honeypot server is usually situated in the network DMZ and runs popular Internet services that are vulnerable to attack, such as web or FTP services. The server does not have many basic security features enabled, and it freely advertises open Internet ports that can be picked up by malicious hackers' port scanners, as shown in Figure 14.1.

A slight security danger exists if the honeypot isn't configured correctly. If an unauthorized user hacks into the server, she might be able to attack other systems on the DMZ. To prevent this scenario, some honeypot systems can emulate services, instead of actually running them, or are installed as a stand-alone server with no existing connection to other critical servers.

Travel Advisory

To ensure your honeypot system does not allow an intruder to attack other machines, use service emulation rather than running the full services, or isolate the honeypot on its own network segment.

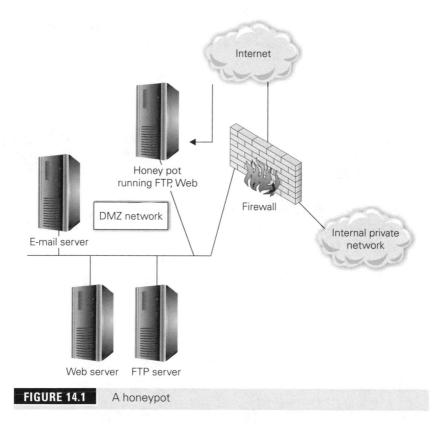

FIGURE 14.1 A honeypot

Honeypots can be used as decoy devices that attract attention away from real production servers, or they can be used by network administrators to learn the identity of malicious hackers through logging and auditing. By keeping accurate logs of the IP addresses being used by an attacker, the administrator might be able either to track down the source of the attack or to pass information to legal authorities. From a legal standpoint, however, doing this can be tricky, especially if the server advertises files for downloading or viewing, because this is considered entrapment and is illegal.

Honeypot systems are best suited for understanding the different types of attacks that can happen to your network. You can log when and what types of attacks are occurring in the system logs, and then use that information to secure your network even further by including protection against attacks that were overlooked in the original security plan.

A *honeynet* is a large-scale network of several honeypot servers to more accurately resemble a target network. Several different network services run on the honeynet to attract more types of attacks, while diverting these attacks from your production network. Virtualization services can also be used to emulate a honeynet network on a single system to provide enhanced security while using less hardware resources.

Exam Tip

A honeypot is the name given to a device or server used to attract and lure attackers into trying to access it, diverting their attention from actual critical systems. A honeynet is a network of honeypot servers to more accurately reflect a target network.

Application Code Assessments

The previous sections described tools and techniques to perform vulnerability assessments on existing network devices, servers, and applications. Another critical aspect of vulnerability assessment that occurs before an application even exists is that of the development cycle of an application. While vulnerability testing is vital for security of existing applications, you significantly lower the probability of existing vulnerabilities by assessing your application for security issues during its design, coding, and testing phases.

The following sections describe how to code applications from the ground up with a secure foundation, and maintain the security baseline throughout the application's development.

Baseline Reporting   A *baseline* is a report of the planned and approved architecture, design, and default configuration of your software application. Created during the design stage of your software, the baseline report is compared to your actual development progress to make sure you are on track with your original plan.

The baseline report includes all networking services and ports to be used, data storage techniques, linked modules, default access permissions, authentication mechanisms, user accounts, and default configuration and security settings. The baseline should represent the most secure design and configuration for your application that must be adhered to when coding.

Use the baseline to keep your development coding on track to prevent any additional items that may cause security issues from creeping into your code, such as new services and network ports that are not required, or unnecessary administrative privilege access for certain application processes. The development process is never perfect, and additional requirements and features may appear during coding. Make adjustments to your baseline if the services are required for the application, and new attack surfaces appear, but continue to focus on security as your top baseline priority and never add services that are unnecessary.

Determine Attack Surfaces   Using your baseline report, you can create a determination of your current level of attack surfaces. An *attack surface* is an aspect of your software application that is vulnerable for an attacker to exploit. The most obvious examples of attack surfaces include network ports and running services. Other attack surfaces include input boxes, authentication and authorization methods, and insecure third-party libraries and programs.

For example, your web application may listen for requests on HTTP port 80, use basic clear-text authentication credentials, and store data in an unencrypted third-party database on the same server. That makes three attack surfaces that leave your application open to attack from a hacker who can exploit these vulnerabilities. In reviewing your design, you can decide to use HTTPS instead of HTTP for SSL encryption, switch to secure authentication methods such as LDAPS, and use a third-party database program that offers greater security for storing your web application's data such as database encryption.

You must review your existing attack surfaces during the entire development cycle. From week to week, you may add functionality that creates a new attack surface that you did not think about during the architecture and design phase.

Attack surfaces cannot be eliminated entirely, or your application would not work at all, but they can be reduced to the bare minimum required for your application's features. From your baselines established at the beginning of the development process, you can determine the number of acceptable attack surfaces that are required, and keep to that framework throughout the entire development cycle of the product.

Architecture   When designing an application, software architects and developers must create the architecture with security first and foremost in mind. Coding should be defensive in nature and not aggressive in the amount of permissiveness provided to end users. This requires much theoretical work and also diligent experimentation and testing to provide the framework for an application that provides strong security as its foundation.

Any attack vectors such as running services and network ports must be kept to a minimum, secure network protocols must be used for communication, and authentication must be built into the application to provide proper authorization for specific tasks and operations. The goal is to create an application that runs on a secure foundation, runs efficiently, and provides all required features in a secure, authenticated environment.

Design Reviews   A *design review* takes the initial product design specification created by the software architects and developer, which is then reviewed by several cross-functional areas, including other developers, quality assurance, and other technical groups, to review the application design.

This provides a peer review of the original design and planned architecture to ensure that the software is built as per the feature specification and that it meets all secure design goals. The application must be coded with strong security in place by keeping the number of attack surfaces to a minimum.

Design reviews occur before coding of an application begins. When the basic architecture of an application is already functionally coded, it is very difficult to go back and rework it due to a critical security issue found in later stages of coding and testing. You may also break existing functionality when you try to rework your design. If specific design flaws are discovered during the review, the architect and developers can rework the design to resolve the flaw before any development begins.

Code Reviews   Just as a writer who is too familiar with their own written output requires an editor to review their work, *code reviews* are a detailed line-by-line review of a developer's code from another developer. Code reviews are a necessary part of the development life-cycle to prevent security issues arising from poor coding practices.

By allowing another developer to scan your code, you provide a fresh set of eyes to scan your work from an objective viewpoint for any issues, whether performance-, efficiency-, or security-related, and offer alternative solutions to provide a stronger, secure code base.

While quality assurance teams can test the final compiled code to make sure it works according to the official design specifications and test cases, development code reviews provide an additional layer of design testing before the code is compiled to eliminate security and performance issues before the code reaches the testing stage.

Within the Realm of Vulnerability Assessments, Explain the Proper Use of Penetration Testing Versus Vulnerability Scanning

Objective 14.02
CompTIA Security+
Objective 3.8

The preceding sections discussed the use of *vulnerability scanning* to examine your network systems for unnecessary running services and open ports, unpatched operating system and application software, or any other types of network vulnerabilities that can be exploited by a hacker.

Generally, vulnerability scanning comprises these characteristics:

- **Passively testing security controls** Vulnerability scanning is a passive test of your security controls and configuration using tools such as port scans, vulnerability scanners, network mappers, and protocol analyzers. Passive scanning means that the system is not being actively attacked, but you are making a step-by-step examination of your system to look for vulnerabilities that can lead to an attack.

- **Identify vulnerabilities** Vulnerability scanning is specifically used to identify certain vulnerabilities. A port scanner can instantly detect what unneeded running ports you have on your system. Operating system scans can identify if you are not running the latest patches and software. A vulnerability scan is simple, fact-oriented information gathering and will not be able to tell you the result from a security standpoint of the exploitation of a particular vulnerability or flaw.

- **Identify lack of security controls** Vulnerability assessments specifically identify areas with a lack of security controls. With their all-encompassing scope of scanning, vulnerability scanning examines all aspects of your system for issues, including the configuration of your operating system or application.

- **Identify common misconfiguration** Using vulnerability scanning techniques, you can also identify specific areas of your system's configuration that require tightening to prevent security issues deriving from a poor default or user-defined configuration.

Penetration testing evaluates the security of a network or computer system by actively simulating an attack. Attacks are performed using the same types of tools and exploits that malicious hackers use to compromise system security. These tools can be used to test network and system resilience to a real attack scenario and test the effectiveness of existing security measures implemented after a vulnerability assessment. While a vulnerability scan can identify security risks and vulnerabilities, it cannot simulate the effect of real attacks.

Exam Tip

A vulnerability scan is used to identify specific weaknesses in current systems and networks, but it cannot simulate real attacks. Penetration testing is used to simulate an actual attack on a system and can be used to test your security countermeasure and resilience to an attack.

Penetration testing provides the following additional benefits beyond vulnerability scanning:

- **Verify a threat exists**   Penetration testing can verify that a real threat exists if a specific identified vulnerability is exploited. The outcome of an exploit is never certain unless you take active steps to test the vulnerability and realize how deep a threat it represents.

- **Bypass security controls**   You can use penetration testing to find out what occurs when specific security controls are bypassed. For example, a simple vulnerability scan on weak passwords in your authentication system will not be able to detect any issues in the event a hacker is able to disable or bypass the authentication system. Penetration testing uses real-time attack scenarios that can't always be addressed through vulnerability scanning alone.

- **Actively test security controls**   Penetration testing actively tests security controls by simulating real attacks against the host system or application. This differs from the passive nature of vulnerability testing and can test the true depth of security controls, along with the level of weakness for specific vulnerabilities.

- **Exploit vulnerabilities**   Vulnerability scanners can detect a potential security issue, but only penetration testing can reveal whether that particular vulnerability could result in a specific security threat. Through active penetration testing, the vulnerability can be exploited, as the result will determine how deep the vulnerability is.

One of the drawbacks to penetration testing is that it can disrupt a live production system. To lessen the effects of the simulated attack, you should perform penetration testing after regular work hours at a time when any disruption to the network will not affect many users. Because of the disruptions tests can cause, many network administrators are able to perform only vulnerability assessments on their networks and systems; they cannot go a step further and perform actual penetration testing.

Travel Advisory

Check with your company's security policies to determine whether you are allowed to perform penetration testing before you start such a process.

Penetration tests are often performed by outside vendors who are allowed access to the network by upper management—in some cases, without the network administrator's knowledge. This ensures the testing scenario is as close to a real, unsuspected attack as possible, and it provides a detailed analysis of any weaknesses in network and system security that still remain, even after vulnerability assessments have been performed.

White, Black, and Gray Box Testing

When performing vulnerability and penetration testing, you can use any of several types of methods, each with its own advantages and disadvantages. What is important is that you use a variety of methods, from detailed internal testing of software code and internal processes to simulations of attacks from users who are completely unfamiliar with the inner workings of the system. By testing the software from different viewpoints and attack scopes, you can uncover vulnerabilities that may not have been apparent during other types of testing.

White Box Testing

A *white box* test refers to the testing scenario where the user testing the system has prior knowledge of the system coding and design and is not testing the system from the perspective of an end user who would have no access to the internal details of an application.

White box testing is usually performed by quality assurance and system integration specialists who can test every aspect of the application, including deep levels of the application programming interface (API), network services, the underlying operating system, and manipulation of the input to the system for the full range of input validation.

This type of detailed testing is usually conducted with direction from development using detailed test plans and test cases for the code. The goal of white box testing is to deeply test the internal code of the system in terms of every functional operation the application can perform. Through this vigorous testing, the most obvious and critical of internal architectural errors can be discovered and resolved.

Black Box Testing

Black box testing is another method of security vulnerability and penetration testing that assumes the tester does not have any prior knowledge of system she is trying to crack. The tester has no idea how the software was developed, languages used, or network services running.

Black box testing is an excellent way to test your system's security by simulating an attack. From the tester's perspective, she is seeing this system or application for the first time and therefore can be a very objective and unbiased evaluator. Without any prior knowledge of the underlying code or operating system, the tester can start off using the most simple penetration and vulnerability-seeking techniques, and then proceed to more advanced methods to try to break the system.

Black box testing is a complementary testing method to white box testing and can often find bugs that the original developer could not find. However, because the tester has only limited access to the system, and no access to back-end aspects of the software, a black box test is not a comprehensive full system test and cannot be solely relied on for accurate vulnerability and penetration testing.

Gray Box Testing

Gray box testing is a hybrid method that includes aspects of both white box and black box testing. Gray box testing uses some prior knowledge of how the software application is designed, as used in white box tests, but the testing is performed from the perspective of an end user, as in a black box test.

While combining the best of both methods, gray box testing can find security issues and bugs that may not have been discovered using one of the other primary testing methods.

CHECKPOINT

✔ **Objective 14.01: Implement assessment tools and techniques to discover security threats and vulnerabilities.** Vulnerability assessment tools can be used by network administrators to find and mitigate vulnerabilities, but malicious hackers have access to the same tools to find vulnerabilities to attack. Perform port scanning to determine what services and open ports are running on your systems, and disable those that are not required. Protocol analyzers can capture and analyze individual network packets, including any clear text data sent within them. Use vulnerability scanners to determine whether your operating system and application software is up to date with the latest updates and patches. Ensure that password databases are protected via limited access rights and encryption to prevent attacks from password-cracking programs. Use secure coding methods and perform early design reviews before coding actually starts to provide a secure foundation for a newly developed application.

✔**Objective 14.02: Within the realm of vulnerability assessments, explain the proper use of penetration testing versus vulnerability scanning.**
Penetration testing evaluates the security of a network or computer system by simulating an actual attack. Vulnerability testing and assessments are helpful in identifying existing vulnerabilities and weaknesses, but only penetration testing can determine the effectiveness of the countermeasures used by the network administrator to fix these vulnerabilities. White box testing is a detailed test by users who are familiar with the system design and code. Black box testing simulates an attack from a user who is not familiar with the inner workings of a system. Gray box testing is a combination of white and black box testing.

REVIEW QUESTIONS

1. Which of the following aspects of vulnerability and threat assessment has a greater bearing on the allocation and budgeting for solutions and countermeasures?

    A. The likelihood and impact of the threat

    B. The risk of a threat compromising a vulnerability

    C. Whether the vulnerability is physical or nonphysical

    D. The nature of the threat

2. Which of the following is the most dangerous threat to a fault-redundant file server located on the network administrator's desk and fully secured with an antivirus program, strict authentication, and access controls?

    A. Equipment failure

    B. Virus

    C. Hacking

    D. Theft

3. You are designing a new web application service for your company. After an initial design review, it is discovered that a number of attack surfaces have been revealed that go well beyond the initial baseline proposed for the application, including unneeded network services that are enabled. What should you do?

    A. Rework the initial baseline.

    B. Perform a black box test.

    C. Reduce attack surfaces by removing unneeded services from the design.

    D. Reduce the attack surfaces during actual coding.

4. You are testing a new software application developed by your company. After extensive internal vulnerability testing, you want to simulate the end user experience and test with someone who has never used the product before. Which method of testing do you use?

   A. Gray box

   B. Open box

   C. White box

   D. Black box

5. Your intrusion detection system has detected a number of attempts at brute-force password attacks against your authentication server. Which of the following would be the most effective countermeasure against future password attacks?

   A. Allowing dictionary words as passwords

   B. Minimum password lengths

   C. A login lockout policy

   D. Firewall rules

6. The systems on your network run primarily on Microsoft Windows operating systems, but you have a legacy Unix server that you use for authentication for your development group. Which of the following security controls provides access-control protection for a Unix password database?

   A. Salting

   B. LANMAN hash

   C. Shadow password file

   D. Minimum password lengths

7. A port scanner has reported that your web server running with a supporting SQL database is listening and responding on TCP ports 80, 443, 21, and 1433. Which of these ports is unnecessary and should be closed to prevent hacking attempts?

   A. 80

   B. 21

   C. 1433

   D. 443

8. You are performing a vulnerability assessment for a web server. Which of the following web server characteristics would be detected as a risk by a vulnerability scanner?

   A. Operating system not updated to latest patch level

   B. HTTPS server listening on port 443

   C. Network packets being sent in clear text

   D. HTTP server listening on port 80

9. After a security audit and vulnerability assessment, several servers required software patches, and unused open network ports needed to be disabled. Which of the following should be performed after these vulnerabilities are fixed to ensure that the countermeasures are secure against a real attack?

   A. Advertise the system's IP address publicly.

   B. Put systems back into live production.

   C. Perform additional port scanning.

   D. Perform penetration testing.

10. New management has decided to test the security of the existing network infrastructure implemented by the current network administrators. Which of the following should be performed to provide the most objective and useful test of your security controls?

   A. Hire a real hacker to attack the network.

   B. Perform third-party penetration testing.

   C. Perform penetration testing by the network administrators.

   D. Initiate an external denial-of-service attack.

REVIEW ANSWERS

1. **A** By assessing the likelihood and impact of a threat, you can allocate solutions for mitigation based on their impact and probability of occurrence. You will not spend money on countermeasures for a threat that is not likely to occur or has minimal impact.

2. **D** Because the file server isn't stored in a secure location, anyone walking by the area could steal it. All the other protections are for network-based threats.

3. **C** If you discover a number of additional attack surfaces in your software design, you should review them and, if they are not required by the application, remove the services from your initial design. If you wait until the coding stage, it may be too late to undo work that could break other parts of your application.

4. **D** Black box testing is used to simulate an attack from someone completely unfamiliar with the inner design and workings of a software product. The goal is to try to find security issues and vulnerabilities from an objective testing source.

5. **C** A brute-force attack tries multiple permutations of password characters to try to guess the password. By limiting the number of incorrect logins (such as three to five attempts), you have the system automatically lock out the account to prevent any further attempts at cracking the password.

6. **C** Unix-based systems protect their hashed password databases by using a shadow password file. In the shadow file, the hashed passwords are removed from the main password database and are stored in a location that is unavailable to unprivileged users.

7. **B** Port 21 is used by FTP, which is not required for your web/database server. This service and port should be disabled to prevent hackers from connecting to the server via FTP. Ports 80 and 443 are used by HTTP and HTTPS, respectively, and port 1433 is used by the SQL database.

8. **A** A vulnerability scanner is designed to scan a system and determine what services that system is running and whether any unnecessary open network ports or unpatched operating systems and applications exist. In this case, HTTP listening on port 80 and HTTPS listening on port 443 are normal operating parameters for a web server. Unless you are using HTTPS, web network packets are always sent in clear text. The vulnerability scanner will detect that the system is not running the latest operating system patches and advise you to update the system.

9. **D** Penetration testing evaluates the security of a network or computer system by simulating an actual attack. This helps test a network's and system's resilience to a real attack and to test the effectiveness of existing security measures implemented after vulnerability assessments.

10. **B** Penetration tests are often performed by third parties who are allowed access to the network by upper management—in some cases, without the network administrator's knowledge. This ensures the testing scenario is as close to a real, unsuspected attack as possible and provides a detailed analysis of existing vulnerabilities.

About the CD-ROM

The CD-ROM included with this book comes complete with MasterExam and the electronic version of the book. The software is easy to install on any Windows 2000/XP/Vista/Windows 7 computer and must be installed to access the MasterExam feature. You may, however, browse the electronic book directly from the CD without installation. To register for the bonus MasterExam, simply click the Bonus MasterExam link on the main launch page and follow the directions to the free online registration.

System Requirements

Software requires Windows 2000 or higher and Internet Explorer 6.0 or above and 20MB of hard disk space for full installation. The electronic book requires Adobe Reader.

Installing and Running MasterExam

If your computer CD-ROM drive is configured to autorun, the CD-ROM will automatically start up upon inserting the disk. From the opening screen you may install MasterExam by clicking the MasterExam link. This will begin the installation process and create a program group named LearnKey. To run MasterExam, use Start | All Programs | LearnKey | MasterExam. If the autorun feature did not launch your CD, browse to the CD and click the LaunchTraining.exe icon.

MasterExam

MasterExam provides you with a simulation of the actual exam. The number of questions, the type of questions, and the time allowed are intended to be an accurate representation of the exam environment. You have the option to take an open book exam, including hints, references, and answers; a closed book exam; or the timed MasterExam simulation.

When you launch MasterExam, a digital clock display will appear in the bottom right-hand corner of your screen. The clock will continue to count down to zero unless you choose to end the exam before the time expires.

Electronic Book

The entire contents of the Passport are provided in PDF. The Adobe Reader has been included on the CD.

Help

A help file is provided through the help button on the main page in the lower left-hand corner. An individual help feature is also available through MasterExam.

Removing Installation(s)

MasterExam is installed to your hard drive. For best results removing this program, use the Start | All Programs | LearnKey | Uninstall option.

Technical Support

For questions regarding the content of the electronic book or MasterExam, please visit http://www.mhprofessional.com/techsupport/. For customers outside the 50 United States, e-mail: international_cs@mcgraw-hill.com.

LearnKey Technical Support

For technical problems with the software (installation, operation, removing installation), please visit www.learnkey.com, e-mail techsupport@learnkey.com, or call toll free at 1-800-482-8244.

Career Flight Path

CompTIA's Security+ certification is an international, vendor-neutral certification that validates knowledge for industry-wide security principles and best practices. The recommendation is for the exam candidate to have at least two years of networking experience with an emphasis on security.

CompTIA Security+ certifications are valid for three years from the date the candidate is certified. After three years, the certification must be renewed by passing the most current exam, or by participating in CompTIA's new continuing education program, which allows individuals to keep their skills current and their certification up to date without retesting.

The CompTIA Security+ certification consists of one exam: Security+ Exam: SY0-301 (2011 Edition).

The Security+ exam is organized into six domain areas:

- **Network Security (21 percent)** Includes topics such as network security devices, secure administration and network design, network protocols, ports, and wireless security.

- **Compliance and Operational Security (18 percent)** Includes topics such as risk management and mitigation, security training and procedures, incident response, environmental controls, business continuity, and disaster recovery.

- **Threats and Vulnerabilities (21 percent)** Includes topics such as malware, network attacks, social engineering, wireless attacks, application attacks, monitoring, physical security, vulnerability assessment, and penetration testing.

- **Application, Data, and Host Security (16 percent)** Includes topics such as secure application coding and testing, host security and system hardening, mobile device security, and data security.

- **Access Control and Identity Management (13 percent)** Includes topics such as access control methods and models, security groups and roles, file and print permissions, logical access control, and authentication.

- **Cryptography (11 percent)** Includes topics such as general cryptography concepts, hashing, encryption algorithms and protocols, public key cryptography, Public Key Infrastructure (PKI), and certificate management.

Recommended Prerequisites

CompTIA recommends that the candidate have the knowledge and skills equivalent of those tested for in the CompTIA Network+ certification. The CompTIA Network+ exam is a vendor-neutral certification exam that is targeted at networking professionals with at least nine months of experience in network support or administration, and who also have a CompTIA A+ certification.

The CompTIA Network+ certification consists of one exam: Network+ Exam: N10-004 (2009 Edition).

Security+ and Beyond

Security+ is an excellent exam that lets you prove your knowledge about basic network security. Security+ is also a great stepping-stone for more advanced security certifications, such as the Certified Information System Security Professional (CISSP) certification. If you have at least five full years of experience in information security, CISSP certification is the logical next step for professionals who develop policies and procedures in information security.

The CISSP certification consists of ten domain areas:

- Access Control
- Application Development Security
- Business Continuity and Disaster Recovery Planning
- Cryptography
- Information Security Governance and Risk Management
- Legal, Regulations, Investigations, and Compliance
- Operations Security
- Physical (Environmental) Security
- Security Architecture and Design
- Telecommunications and Network Security

For more information on the CISSP certification, please visit www.isc2.org.

Getting the Latest Information on Security+

Security+ is a great place to start your network security professional career. To find out the latest information about the Security+ exam, please visit www.comptia.org.

Index

Numbers

3DES encryption, 117–118
802.11 standard, 292–293, 296
802.11a, 292
802.11b, 292–293
802.11g, 292–293
802.11n, 290, 292–293
802.1X standard, 204

A

acceptable use policy, in
  network security, 15–16
acceptance, dealing with risk,
  5, 11
access control
  auditing user access rights,
    391–392
  backup user account, 159
  to data, 106
  to files and printers,
    173–174
  firewall services for, 216
  grouping users and,
    160–162
  identification verification
    cards in, 179–180
  implicit deny, 164–165
  to Internet, 326–327
  job rotation, 164
  least privilege approach, 165
  levels of security, 160
  lighting systems, 176
  locks, 177–178
  logs, 179, 384
  man-traps, 178–179
  mandatory vacations, 164
  as mitigation and deterrent
    techniques, 175
  models, 165–167
  NAC (Network Access
    Control), 234–235
  overview of, 158
  password management,
    170–171
  physcial barriers, 175–176
  review Q&A, 181–185
  risk mitigation actions, 7

roles and privileges, 171–172
  security policies, 14–15
  separation of duties, 163
  to servers, 326
  to software, 327
  user account policies,
    167–169
  users and resources and, 159
  video surveillance, 176–177
access control lists. See ACLs
  (access control lists)
access logs, 384
access points
  antenna placement,
    287–288
  overview of, 286
  power levels, 288–289
  rogue (evil twin), 302–303
  securing, 294
  wireless networks and, 96
  WLAN topologies and, 289
accounts
  domain accounts, 171
  identification and, 160
  logging changes to, 390
  managing for data
    security, 26
  operating system security
    and, 325
  securing default, 274
  termination policy, 22
  user account policies,
    167–169
ACLs (access control lists)
  files and printers and,
    173–174
  protecting database
    servers, 356
  rule-based access
    control, 167
  setting up rules for network
    devices, 272–274
active/active clusters, 75–76
active detection, intrusion
  detection and prevention,
  225–226, 335
active/passive clusters, 75–76

ActiveX, 346
ad hoc networks, WLAN
  topologies, 289
adaptability, acceptable use
  policy governing, 16
add-ons, malicious, 349
Address Resolution Protocol
  (ARP), 269
administration, of secure
  networks
  analyzing/differentiating
    types of network
    attacks, 261
  ARP poisoning attacks, 269
  back door attacks, 263
  configuring network
    devices, 271–272
  DDoS (distributed denial
    of service) attacks,
    261–262
  disabling unused
    services, 276
  DNS, 255–256
  DNS poisoning attacks,
    268–269
  domain kiting attacks,
    269–270
  DoS (denial of service)
    attacks, 261
  examining log files, 277
  flood attacks, 263
  FTP, FTPS, TFTP, and
    SFTP, 254–255
  hardening network
    devices, 275
  HTTP and HTTPS,
    252–253
  ICMP, 252
  identifying commonly used
    ports, 258–260
  IPSec, 257
  man-in-the-middle
    attacks, 267
  NetBIOS, 257
  NULL session attacks, 264
  overview of, 250
  ping attacks, 262

administration, of secure
networks *(continued)*
   principles for, 270
   replay attacks, 267–268
   review Q&A, 278–281
   SCP, 255
   securing remote access, 276
   setting up ACL rules,
     272–274
   smurf attacks, 265–266
   SNMP, 256–257
   spoofing attacks, 264–265
   SSH (Secure Shell),
     253–254
   SYN flood attacks, 262–263
   TCP/IP, 250–251
   TCP/IP hijacking attacks,
     266–267
   Telnet, 253
   threats and risks to
     network devices, 274–275
   updating OS and
     firmware, 277
   Xmas attacks, 268
administrators
   auditing, 392–393
   operating system security
     and, 325
   restricting remote access
     to, 326
   role in managing access
     and authentication, 158
   role in preventing
     attacks, 313
   rootkits allowing remote
     administrator access,
     319–320
   securing access points, 294
   securing default
     accounts, 274
Advanced Encryption Standard
   (AES), 118, 337
adware, 318
AES (Advanced Encryption
   Standard), 118, 337
AH (authentication header), in
   IPSec, 126–127
alarms
   associated with monitoring
     logs, 389
   performance monitors
     and, 377

ALE (annual loss expectancy),
   9–10
algorithms. See also
   cryptography
   asymmetric key, 113
   for encryption, 108–110
   symmetric key, 117–119
annual loss expectancy (ALE),
   9–10
antenna, placing for wireless
   network, 287–288
antispam software
   in host-based security,
     329–330
   network security and,
     220–221
   reports, 388
antispyware software, 328–329
antivirus logs, 386–387
antivirus software
   detecting Trojan horses and
     back doors, 317
   in host-based security,
     328–329
   logs, 386–387
   preventing adware and
     spyware, 319
   preventing logic bombs, 317
   reports, 388
   risk mitigation actions, 7
application layer filtering, by
   firewall, 216
application rootkits, 319
application security
   ActiveX, 346
   best practices, 359–361
   buffer overflows,
     346–347
   CGI scripts, 349–350
   command injection,
     351–352
   configuration baseline, 361
   cookies and session
     hijacking, 348
   database servers, 356
   DHCP servers, 355–356
   directory traversal, 352
   DNS servers, 354–355
   e-mail servers, 357–358
   FTP servers, 353–354
   hardening applications, 361
   header manipulation, 351

   HTML attachments,
     348–349
   Internet server
     vulnerabilities, 352–353
   JavaScript, 345
   LDAP and directory
     services, 356–357
   malicious add-ons, 349
   overview of, 344
   patch management, 362
   privilege escalation, 347
   review Q&A, 367–370
   types of application attacks,
     344–345
   web application
     vulnerabilities, 345
   XML injection, 351
   XSRF (cross-site request
     forgery), 350
   XSS (cross-site
     scripting), 350
   zero-day attacks, 352
applications
   assessing code in, 412–414
   logging application-level
     events, 391
   role of logs in IT
     documentation, 40
   for security logging, 387
applications, for host security
   antispam software, 329–330
   antivirus and antispyware
     software, 328–329
   host-based firewalls,
     330–332
   overview of, 327–328
architecture, in application code
   assessment, 413
Argon fire suppressant, 98
ARO (annual rate of
   occurrence), measuring risk
   likelihood, 9–10
ARP (Address Resolution
   Protocol), 269
ARP poisoning attacks, 269
asset identification, in risk
   assessment, 7, 10
asymmetric key encryption
   applying, 119–120
   overview of, 111–113
   in PKI, 134–135
   types of algorithms, 113

attachments, e-mail
  antivirus software
    scanning, 328
  worms and, 318
attachments, HTML, 348–349
attack surface, determining, 413
attacks, network
  analyzing/differentiating
    types of, 261
  ARP poisoning attacks, 269
  back door attacks, 263
  DDoS (distributed denial
    of service) attacks,
    261–262
  DNS poisoning attacks,
    268–269
  domain kiting attacks,
    269–270
  DoS (denial of service)
    attacks, 261
  flood attacks, 263
  man-in-the-middle
    attacks, 267
  NULL session attacks, 264
  ping attacks, 262
  replay attacks, 267–268
  smurf attacks, 265–266
  spoofing attacks, 264–265
  SYN flood attacks, 262–263
  TCP/IP hijacking attacks,
    266–267
  Xmas attacks, 268
attacks, social engineering
  e-mail hoaxes, 49–50
  overview of, 44–45
  pharming attacks, 48
  phishing attacks, 45–46
  shoulder surfing attacks,
    46–47
  spam, 49
  spim and, 48
  tailgating attacks, 47–48
  vishing attacks, 48–49
  whaling attacks, 46
attacks, web application
  ActiveX, 346
  buffer overflows, 346–347
  CGI scripts, 349–350
  command injection,
    351–352
  cookies and session
    hijacking, 348

directory traversal, 352
header manipulation, 351
HTML attachments,
  348–349
JavaScript, 345
malicious add-ons, 349
privilege escalation, 347
types of, 344–345
web application
  vulnerabilities, 345
XML injection, 351
XSRF (cross-site request
  forgery), 350
XSS (cross-site
  scripting), 350
zero-day attacks, 352
attacks, wireless network
  Bluetooth
    vulnerabilities, 301
  data emanation attacks,
    300–301
  packet sniffing and
    eavesdropping attacks,
    303–304
  rogue access points (evil
    twin), 302–303
  war chalking attacks, 303
  war driving attacks, 302
  WEP IV attacks, 304
attenuation
  access points and, 287–288
  cable shielding and, 94
audits
  data security, 26
  event logs and, 390–391
  IT documentation in, 40
  overview of, 389
  performing routine, 24
  reviewing information
    gathered by, 392
  storage and retention
    policies, 393
  system baselines, 389–390
  use of independent
    auditors, 392–393
  of user access rights,
    391–392
authentication
  802.1X standard, 204
  access control and, 158
  ActiveX vulnerabilities
    and, 346

in asymmetric
  cryptography, 112
back door attacks
  bypassing, 263
biometrics in, 205
cable modems and, 194
certificates in mutual
  authentication, 205
CHAP
  (Challenge-Handshake
  Authentication Protocol),
  200–201
cryptography and, 106
dial-up access and, 191–193
DSL lines and, 195
EAP (Extensible
  Authentication Protocol),
  201–202, 297–298
encryption providing,
  107–108
firewall services, 216
ISDN lines and,
  193–194
Kerberos, 203–204
LANMAN (LAN
  Manager), 201
LDAP (Lightweight
  Directory Access
  Protocol), 202–203
LEAP (Lightweight
  Extensible Authentication
  Protocol), 298
man-traps, 178–179
methods, 190
models for, 188–190
NTLM (NT LAN
  Manager), 201
operating system security
  and, 325
overview of, 188
PAP (Password
  Authentication
  Protocol), 200
password policy and, 41
PEAP (Protected Extensible
  Authentication
  Protocol), 298
PPP (Point-to-Point
  Protocol), 197–198
RADIUS (Remote
  Authentication Dial-In
  User Service), 202

authentication *(continued)*
  remote access applications
    for, 195
  remote access methods
    for, 191
  remote access protocols
    and, 197
  review Q&A, 207–210
  securing modem access, 239
  security levels and, 160
  services, 200
  SLIP (Serial Line Internet
    Protocol), 197
  SSH (Secure Shell) and, 196
  TACAS (Terminal Access
    Controller Access Control
    System), 203
  Telnet and, 195
  uses of PKI keys, 145
  using USB keys as access
    token, 169
  VPN protocols, 198–199
  VPN wireless access,
    298–299
  VPNs (virtual private
    networks) and, 196–197
  wireless, 297
  WTLS (Wireless
    Transaction Layer
    Security), 291
authentication header (AH), in
  IPSec, 126–127
authorization
  physical access policies, 14
  security levels and, 160
availability
  categorization of
    resources, 159
  in CIA (confidentiality,
    integrity, and
    availability), 88
avoidance, dealing with risk, 5, 11
awareness training
  overview of, 34
  threat awareness, 34–35

B

B-channels, ISDN, 193
back door attacks
  overview of, 263
  rootkits, 319–320
  Trojan horses in, 316–317

backup user account, 159
backups
  for business continuity and
    disaster recovery, 81–82
  documenting backup and
    recovery plans, 70, 85–86
  hardware for, 83
  media rotation and
    retention, 85
  offsite storage of media,
    86–87
  online backups, 87–88
  planning, 82–83
  restoring from, 86
  as risk mitigation action, 7
  of system configuration, 76
  types of, 83–84
baselines
  application configuration
    baseline, 361
  creating for host system,
    321–322
  in determining security
    posture, 375
  performance baselines,
    376–377
  reports, 412
  security control thresholds
    based on, 13
  system baselines, 389–390
basic input and output system
  (BIOS), 323
Basic Rate Interface (BRI),
  ISDN, 193
.bat files, viruses targeting, 315
Bayesian filtering, as antispam
  application, 221
behavior/anomaly-based
  monitoring, in intrusion
  detection, 227–228
biometric authentication, 205
BIOS (basic input and output
  system), 323
black box tests, in vulnerability
  and threat assessment, 417–418
blacklists, antispam applications
  and, 220
blackouts, power consistency
  and, 93
block/allow functionality, in
  firewalls, 331
block ciphers, in symmetric key
  encryption, 111

Blowfish, 118
bluejacking attacks, 300
bluesnarfing attacks, 300
Bluetooth
  overview of, 291–293
  vulnerabilities of, 301
boot sector viruses, 313
botnets, 320–321
BRI (Basic Rate Interface),
  ISDN, 193
broadband, ISDN
  connections, 194
broadcast addresses, smurf
  attacks and, 266
brownouts, power consistency
  and, 93
brute-force attacks
  on passwords, 408
  passwords policy and, 41
  protecting PKI keys
    from, 142
buffer overflows, web
  application vulnerabilities,
  346–347
bugs, patches for, 275
business continuity and disaster
  recovery
  backup hardware, 83
  backup types, 83–84
  backups in, 76, 81–82
  business impact analysis, 67
  CIA (confidentiality,
    integrity, and
    availability), 88
  clustering technology, 75–76
  contingency planning, 69
  documenting backups,
    85–86
  documenting recovery
    plans, 70
  electrical power issues, 93–94
  environmental controls, 89
  environmental issues, 91–93
  facility-related issues, 89–91
  fault tolerance in, 78–81
  fire suppression, 96–98
  HA (high availability) and
    redundancy planning, 72
  media rotation and
    retention, 85
  network cabling and, 94–96
  offsite storage of backup
    media, 86–87

business continuity and disaster recovery *(continued)*
  online backups, 87–88
  overview of, 64–65
  planning backups, 82–83
  recovery planning, 65
  recovery team, 66
  redundancy of Internet lines, 76–77
  redundancy of servers, 75
  redundancy of sites, 77–78
  reliability factors, 73–74
  restoring from backups, 86
  review Q&A, 99–102
  risk analysis, 66–67
  service levels, 72–73
  spare equipment, 74–75
  testing recovery plans, 71
  types of disasters, 67–68
business impact analysis, in disaster recovery planning, 67

C

cable modems, remote access authentication, 194
cabling
  documenting recovery plans, 70
  shielding from electrical interference, 94
  types of, 95–96
cache poisoning, DNS server vulnerability to, 268–269, 354
call-back feature, in dial-up security, 193
cameras, mobile camera security, 337
CAs (certificate authorities)
  certificates in mutual authentication, 205
  issuing digital certificates, 135
  as key escrow entity, 143
  overview of, 136
  renewing digital certificates, 150
  requesting digital certificates from, 147
  suspending and revoking digital certificates, 147–148
centralized storage system, for PKI keys, 139–140

Certificate Revocation Lists (CRLs), 148
certificates. See digital certificates
CGI scripts, 349–350
chain of custody, in collection of forensic data evidence, 55
change management policy, 23
CHAP (Challenge-Handshake Authentication Protocol), 200–201, 298
CIA (confidentiality, integrity, and availability), 88
ciphers/cipher text. See also cryptography, 106, 108–110
Class A networks, 236
Class B networks, 236
Class C networks, 236
classification of data
  as data protection strategy, 35–36
  in MAC (mandatory access control) model, 166
clean desk policy, 41
clients. See also host system security, 312
cloud computing
  DLP (data loss prevention) and, 363
  risk analysis and, 8–9
  securing remote communication, 243–244
clustering technology, in redundancy planning, 75–76
coaxial cabling, 95
code
  assessing application code, 412–414
  reviewing, 414
  secure coding practices, 359
codes of conduct, HR (human resources) policies, 20–21
cold sites, in site redundancy, 78
collusion, separation of duties and, 163
.com files, viruses targeting, 315
command injection attacks, 351–352
commands, logging user events, 391
Common Access Card, 180

communication
  ACL rules
    permitting/denying, 272
  contingency planning and, 69
  redundancy of Internet lines and, 76–77
  TCP/IP protocol for, 250–251
community strings
  disabling unused services, 276
  SNMP protocol and, 256–257
companion viruses, 313–314
complexity, of passwords, 170
computer rooms
  construction of, 90–91
  locking up, 178
computers
  locking up, 178
  setting machines restrictions on network access, 169
confidentiality
  in CIA (confidentiality, integrity, and availability), 88
  data classification and, 36
  encryption providing, 107
  sensitivity of data and, 159
confidentiality, integrity, and availability (CIA), 88
configuration
  backing up system configuration, 76
  documenting system configuration, 70
  identifying common misconfigurations, 415
  of network devices, 271–272
construction, of facilities, 90–91
contact information, documenting in recovery plans, 70
content filtering
  controlling access to objectionable content, 327
  network security and, 221–222
  reports, 388

contingency planning, disaster recovery and, 69

cookies
session hijacking and, 348
web browser security, 333–334

copy permissions, controlling access to files and printers, 173

countermeasures, in risk assessment, 10–11

CPUs, fault tolerance of, 80

CRLs (Certificate Revocation Lists), 148

cross-site request forgery (XSRF), 350

cross-site scripting (XSS), 222, 350

crosstalk, cable shielding and, 94

CRYPTOCard, as access token, 169

cryptography. See also PKI (Public Key Infrastructure)
algorithms, 108–110
applying asymmetric encryption, 119–120
applying symmetric encryption, 117–119
asymmetric key, 111–113
digital signatures, 113
hashes, 114–116
HTTPS and, 125–126
IPSec and, 126–127
overview of, 106–108
review Q&A, 128–132
SSH (Secure Shell) and, 127
SSL and TLS and, 124–125
steganography, 113
symmetric key, 110–111
wireless encryption protocols, 121–124

cryptosystems, 108

D

D-channels, ISDN, 193

DAC (discretionary access control), 166

damage control, in incident response, 51–52

data
destruction policy, 38–39
DLP (data loss prevention), 362–363

documenting standards and guidelines, 35–37
encryption options, 363–366
integrity, 106–107
overview of, 362
planning backups based on type and quantity of, 82
policies, 35
removable media and mobile devices and, 366
retention policy, 38, 83, 393
review Q&A, 367–370
storage policy, 393

data emanation attacks, 300–301

Data Encryption Standard (DES), 117–118

data loss prevention. See DLP (data loss prevention)

database servers
high availability and high service levels required for, 73
vulnerablilities of, 356

databases
encryption of, 365
shadow password database, 410
of spam, 220

DDoS (distributed denial of service) attacks
botnets and, 320
overview of, 261–262
smurf attacks and, 265–266

decentralized key storage, 141

decryption, 106

delete permissions, controlling access to files and printers, 173

demilitarized zones (DMZs)
honeypots and honeynets in, 410
use of security zones in network security, 231–233

denial of service attacks. See DoS (denial of service) attacks

department, grouping users by, 161–162

DES (Data Encryption Standard), 117–118

design review, in application code assessment, 413–414

designing network security, 229–230

destination address, ACL rules controlling, 272

detection agents, in intrusion detection system. See also IDSs (intrusion detecion systems), 223

deterrence. See also mitigation and deterrent techniques, 5, 12

device encryption, for mobile devices, 336–337

DHCP (Dynamic Host Configuration Protocol)
ARP poisoning attacks and, 269
investigating system for services that are unneeded, 324
vulnerablilities of DHCP servers, 355–356
well known ports, 259, 405

diagnostics, SNMP protocol and, 256–257

dial-up connections, 191–193

dictionary attacks, 408

differential backup, 84

Diffie-Hellman encryption, 119

digital certificates
Common Access Card and, 180
destruction of, 149–150
expiration of, 149
life cycle of, 146
in mutual authentication, 205
in PKI, 135–136
renewing, 150
requesting, issuing, publishing, and receiving, 147
suspending and revoking, 147–148

digital handshakes, in SSL security, 124

Digital Signature Algorithm (DSA), 120

digital signatures, 113

Digital Subscriber Line (DSL), 195

dipole antennas, for access points, 288

direct marketing, privacy policy regulating, 19

direct-sequence spread-spectrum (DSSS), 286
directory services, vulnerabilities of, 356–357
directory traversal attacks, 352
disaster recovery. See also business continuity and disaster recovery
    business impact analysis, 67
    contingency planning, 69
    documenting plans for, 70
    planning, 65
    risk analysis in, 66–67
    team, 66
    testing plans for, 71
    types of disasters, 67–68
disclosure, 56–57
discretionary access control (DAC), 166
disposal
    of documents, 37
    of hardware, 38–39
distributed denial of service. See DDoS (distributed denial of service) attacks
.dll files, viruses targeting, 315
DLP (data loss prevention)
    content filtering applications, 221
    data security and, 362–363
    as risk mitigation strategy, 25–27
DMZs (demilitarized zones)
    honeypots and honeynets in, 410
    use of security zones in network security, 2 31–233
DNS (Domain Name Service)
    investigating system for services that are unneeded, 324
    logs, 384–385
    overview of, 255–256
    vulnerablilities of DNS servers, 354–355
    well known ports, 259–260, 405
DNS poisoning attacks, 268–269, 385
,doc/.docx files, viruses targeting, 315

documentation
    accessing policy documentation, 32–33
    of backups, 85–86
    of IT systems, 39–40
    policies for, 35, 38
    of recovery plans, 70
    of standards and guidelines, 35–37
    of system architecture, 39
documents
    disposal of, 37–38
    retention and storage policies, 37
domain accounts, single sign-on and, 171
domain kiting attacks, 269–270
Domain Name Service. See DNS (Domain Name Service)
domain names
    DNS protocol and, 255–256
    domain kiting attacks, 269–270
domain tasting, 270
DoS (denial of service) attacks
    active detection of, 225
    DNS logs and, 385
    DNS servers and, 256, 354
    ICMP and, 252, 276
    load balancers preventing, 219
    overview of, 261
    ping attacks, 262
    security features of routers protecting against, 217
    SYN flood attacks, 262–263
DSA (Digital Signature Algorithm), 120
DSL (Digital Subscriber Line), 195
DSSS (direct-sequence spread-spectrum), 286
due care, network security policies, 17
due diligence, network security policies, 17
due process, network security policies, 17
dumpster diving, document disposal and, 37

Dynamic Host Configuration Protocol. See DHCP (Dynamic Host Configuration Protocol)

E
e-mail
    acceptable use policy, 16
    firewalls securing, 332
    high availability and high service levels required for, 72
    hoaxes, 49–50
    host access security and, 326–327
    phishing attacks, 45–46
    scanning attachments for viruses, 328
    spam, 49
    vulnerablilities of e-mail servers, 357–358
    worms within attachments, 318
EAP (Extensible Authentication Protocol)
    as authentication service, 201–202
    for wireless authentication, 297–298
eavesdropping attacks
    attacking wireless networks, 303–304
    preventing, 300
    war driving, 302
ECC (Elliptic Curve Cryptosystems), 119
electrical power, maintaining clean and consistent power, 93–94
EMI (electromagnetic interference)
    access points and, 287
    cable shielding and, 94
employees
    acceptable use policy, 16
    HR (human resources) policies, 20–22
    physical access policies, 14
    as threat, 401
encapsulating security payload (ESP), 126–127

encryption. See also PKI (Public Key Infrastructure)
  algorithms, 108–110
  applying asymmetric, 119–120
  applying symmetric, 117–118
  applying wireless encryption protocols, 121–124
  asymmetric key, 111–113
  of data, 363–364
  databases, 365
  of files, 365–366
  HSM (hardware security module), 364
  HTTPS and, 125–126
  IPSec and, 126–127
  overview of, 106
  protecting mobile devices, 336–337
  in protection of forensic data evidence, 54
  removable media and mobile devices and, 366
  securing WLANs, 296
  SSH (Secure Shell) and, 127
  SSL and TLS and, 124–125
  symmetric key, 110–111
  TPM (trusted platform module), 364
  uses of PKI keys, 145
  VPNs and, 240–241
  whole disk encryption, 365
  wireless encryption protocols, 121–124
  WTLS (Wireless Transaction Layer Security), 291
environmental controls, for business continuity
  electrical power issues, 93–94
  environmental issues, 91–93
  facility-related issues, 89–91
  fire suppression, 96–98
  network cabling and, 94–96
  overview of, 89

environmental issues
  acceptable use policy governing, 16
  humidity controls, 92
  monitoring temperature and humidity, 92–93
  overview of, 91–93
  temperature controls, 91
  ventilation controls, 92
equipment
  inventories, 40
  locking up, 178
  redundancy planning, 74–75
  threat of malfunction, 401
errors
  handling in application security, 360
  logging error messages, 391
escalation policy, 56
escaping, best practices in application security, 359–360
ESP (encapsulating security payload), 126–127
ethics, HR (human resources) policies, 20–21
EUDPD (EU Data Protection Directive), 26
event logs, system auditing and, 390–391
Event Viewer, security logging in Windows-based systems, 387
evidence, collecting and preserving in incident response, 52–56
exception handling, in application security, 360
.exe files, viruses targeting, 315
execute permissions, controlling access to files and printers, 173
expiration, setting account expiration dates, 168
Extensible Authentication Protocol (EAP)
  as authentication service, 201–202
  for wireless authentication, 297–298
Extensible Markup Language (XML), 407–408
extranets, network security zones, 233

F
face scanners, for biometric authentication, 206
Facebook, best practices protecting risk related to, 43
facilities
  computer room in, 90–91
  construction of, 90
  location planning, 89
  overview of, 89–91
failopen approach, to failure of security system, 381
failsecure/failsafe approach, to failure of security system, 381
false alarms, disadvantages of active detection systems, 226
false negatives, security systems and, 12–13
false positives, security systems and, 12
FAT (file allocation table), 324
father-son backup method, media rotation and retention, 85
fault tolerance
  CPUs, 80
  hard-drives, 79–80
  NICs (network interface cards), 80
  overview of, 78–81
  power supplies, 80
  redundancy planning and, 41
  risk mitigation actions, 7
FCC (Federal Communications Commission), 285
fencing, as physical barrier, 175–176
FHSS (frequency-hopping spread-spectrum), 285–286
fiber-optic cabling, 96
file allocation table (FAT), 324
file-infector viruses, 314
file servers
  access controls, 172–173
  high availability and high service levels required for, 73
File Transfer Protocol. See FTP (File Transfer Protocol)
files
  controlling access to, 173–174

encrypting, 365–366
logging access to, 391
protecting risk related to
    file sharing, 43
security of file system,
    324–325
transferring with SCP, 255
types targeted by viruses,
    315–316
filters, security
antispam filters, 220–221
application layer
    filtering, 216
content filtering
    applications,
    221–222, 388
packet filtering, 216, 272
URL filtering, 222–223
web security gateways, 222
fingerprint readers, for
    biometric authentication, 205
fire suppression
chemical-based, 98
overview of, 96–97
water for, 97
firewalls
for adware and spyware, 319
cable modems and, 194
configuring, 271–272
for data security, 26
for flood attacks, 263
host-based, 330–332
logs, 385–386
in network security, 214–216
protecting Internet
    servers, 353
reports, 388
security zones and, 230
for Trojan horses, 317
for viruses, 328
for wireless security, 300
firmware rootkits, 319
firmware updates, 277
first responders, in incident
    response policy, 51
flame detectors, 97
flood attacks, 263
FM-200 fire suppressant, 98
forensics
collecting and preserving
    evidence, 52–56
overview of, 52

FQDN (fully qualified domain
    names), 256, 354
frequency-hopping
    spread-spectrum (FHSS),
    285–286
frequency, of backups, 82
FTP (File Transfer Protocol)
investigating system for
    services that are
    unneeded, 324
overview of, 254
protocol analyzers and, 229
vulnerablilities of FTP
    servers, 353–354
well known ports, 260, 405
FTPS (FTP Secure), 255
full backup, 84
fully qualified domain names
    (FQDN), 256, 354
fuzzing, best practices in
    application security, 360

G

gateways, web security, 222
Global Positioning System
    (GPS), tracking mobile
    devices, 336
GPG (GNU Privacy Guard), 123
GPS (Global Positioning
    System), tracking mobile
    devices, 336
grandfather-father-son backup
    method, 85
gray box tests, 418
group policies
in establishing security
    baseline, 321
monitoring inappropriate
    use of rights and
    privileges, 392
groups
in access control, 160–162
privileges by, 172
guest accounts, securing, 274
guidelines, documenting, 35–37

H

HA (high availability)
backups, 76
clustering technology,
    75–76
overview of, 72

redundancy planning
    and, 41
redundant Internet lines,
    76–77
redundant servers, 75
reliability factors, 73–74
service levels, 72–73
site redundancy, 77–78
spare equipment, 74–75
hackers
types of disasters, 68
types of threats, 401
Halon fire suppressant, 98
hand geometry scanners, for
    biometric authentication, 205
hard-drives
for backups, 83
fault tolerance and, 79–80
hardening applications, 361
hardening network devices, 275
hardening operating systems
BIOS security, 323
file system security, 324–325
installing/enabling only
    necessary services, 324
overview of, 322
server and workstation
    patch management, 323
updates, 322
user account and password
    threats, 325
hardware
for backups, 83
disposal of, 38–39
fault tolerance, 79
reliability factors for, 73–74
hardware locks, as access
    control, 177–178
hardware RAID, 79–80
hardware security module
    (HSM), 364
Hash-based Message
    Authentication Code
    (HMAC), 116
hashes
HMAC (Hash-based
    Message Authentication
    Code), 116
message hashes, 115
overview of, 114
in protection of forensic
    data evidence, 54

hashes *(continued)*
  RIPEMD (RACE Integrity
    Primitives Evaluation
    Message Digest), 116
  SHA (secure hash
    algorithm), 115–116
header manipulation, 351
Health Insurance Portability
  and Accountability Act
  (HIPAA), 26, 221
heat detectors, 97
heuristic-based monitoring,
  in intrusion detection
  system, 228
HIDS (host-based intrusion
  detection system), 334–335
hierarchical trust model,
  138–139
high availability. See HA (high
  availability)
hijacking attacks, on TCP/IP,
  266–267
HIPAA (Health Insurance
  Portability and Accountability
  Act), 26, 221
hiring, HR (human resources)
  policies, 20
HMAC (Hash-based Message
  Authentication Code), 116
honeynets, 411–412
honeypots, 410–411
host-based firewalls, 330–332
host-based intrusion detection
  system (HIDS), 334–335
host system security
  adware and spyware,
    318–319
  analyzing/differentiating
    types of malware,
    312–313
  antispam software,
    329–330
  antivirus and antispyware
    software, 328–329
  BIOS security, 323
  botnets, 320–321
  controlling access to
    Internet, 326–327
  controlling access to
    servers, 326
  controlling access to
    software, 327

file system security,
  324–325
file types targeted by
  viruses, 315–316
hardening operating
  systems, 322
HIDS (host-based
  intrusion detection
  system), 334–335
host-based firewalls,
  330–332
installing/enabling only
  necessary services, 324
logic bombs, 317
mobile device security,
  335–337
review Q&A, 338–341
rootkits, 319–320
security applications for,
  327–328
security baseline for,
  321–322
server and workstation
  patch management, 323
Trojan horse attacks,
  316–317
updating operating
  systems, 322
user account and password
  threats, 325
virus types, 313–315
web browser security,
  332–334
worms, 317–318
hot and cold aisles, temperature
  controls, 91–92
hot fixes
  application patch
    management, 362
  updating operating
    systems, 322
hot sites, site redundancy, 77
hot spare, fault tolerance, 79
hot swap, fault tolerance, 79
HR (human resources)
  codes of conduct and ethics
    policies, 20–21
  hiring policies, 20
  termination policy,
    21–22
HSM (hardware security
  module), 364

HTML attachments, 348–349
.html files, viruses targeting, 315
HTTP (Hypertext Transfer
  Protocol)
  header manipulation, 351
  identifying commonly used
    network ports, 260
  investigating system for
    services that are
    unneeded, 324
  overview of, 252–253
  protocol analyzers and, 229
  securing remote access
    and, 276
  well known ports, 405
HTTPS (Hypertext Transfer
  Protocol over Secure Socket
  Layer)
  identifying commonly used
    network ports, 260
  overview of, 125–126,
    252–253
  securing access points, 294
  securing remote access
    and, 276
  web connection
    security, 326
human error and sabotage,
  types of disasters, 68
human resources. See HR
  (human resources)
humidity, monitoring, 92–93
hybrid attacks, on
  passwords, 408
Hypertext Transfer Protocol.
  See HTTP (Hypertext
  Transfer Protocol)
Hypertext Transfer Protocol
  over Secure Socket Layer. See
  HTTPS (Hypertext Transfer
  Protocol over Secure Socket
  Layer)

I

ICANN (Internet Corporation
  for Assigned Names and
  Numbers), 269–270
ICMP (Internet Control
  Message Protocol)
  disabling unused
    services, 276
  network mappers
    utilizing, 403

ICMP (Internet Control
Message Protocol) *(continued)*
overview of, 252
ping sweeps, 258–259
smurf attacks and, 265–266
IDEA (International Data
Encryption Algorithm), 118
identification. See also
authentication
security levels and, 160
termination policy
regulating return of
badges, 21
verification cards as access
control, 179–180
identify spoofing, 160
IDSs (intrusion detection
systems). See also intrusion
detection and prevention,
379–380
IEEE (Institute of Electrical and
Electronics Engineers), 290
IKE (Internet Key Exchange),
126–127
IM (instant messaging)
acceptable use policy
governing use of, 16
best practices, 42–43
host access security and,
326–327
spim attacks, 48
IMAP (Internet Message Access
Protocol)
vulnerabilities of e-mail
servers, 358
well known ports, 260, 405
impacts
business impact analysis in
disaster recovery
planning, 67
risk assessment and, 402
in risk assessment and
mitigation, 9–10
implicit deny
access control best
practices, 164–165
network device
configuration and, 271
incident response procedures.
See also security training and
incident response
collecting and preserving
evidence, 52–56

damage and loss control,
51–52
escalation policy, 56
first responders, 51
forensics, 52
overview of, 50
reporting and disclosure,
56–57
risk mitigation, 23–24
incremental backup, 84
information accuracy, privacy
policy regulating, 19
information assurance, CIA
(confidentiality, integrity, and
availability) and, 107
information collection, privacy
policy regulating, 19
information security, privacy
policy regulating, 19
infrared detectors, for
surveillance, 177
infrared (IR), WLAN
technologies, 286
initialization vector (IV), WEP
IV attacks, 304
input validation, best practices
in application security, 359
instant messaging. See IM
(instant messaging)
Institute of Electrical and
Electronics Engineers
(IEEE), 290
Integrated Services Digital
Network (ISDN),
193–194
integrity
in categorization of
resources, 159
in CIA (confidentiality,
integrity, and
availability), 88
encryption providing, 107
internal network addressing,
235–237
International Data Encryption
Algorithm (IDEA), 118
Internet
acceptable use policy
governing use of, 16
controlling access to,
326–327
planning redundancy of
Internet lines, 76–77

server vulnerablilities. See
server vulnerablilities
Internet Control Message
Protocol. See ICMP (Internet
Control Message Protocol)
Internet Corporation for
Assigned Names and
Numbers (ICANN), 269–270
Internet Key Exchange (IKE),
126–127
Internet Message Access
Protocol (IMAP)
vulnerabilities of e-mail
servers, 358
well known ports, 260, 405
Internet Protocol (IP), 251
Internet Security Association
and Key Management
Protocol (ISAKMP), 127
Internet service providers
(ISPs), 76–77
interviews
in collection of forensic
data evidence, 56
hiring policies and, 20
intranets, network security
zones, 233
Intrasite Automatic Tunnel
Addressing Protocol
(ISATAP), 251
intruders, types of
threats, 401
intrusion detection and
prevention
active detection, 225–226
IDSs (intrusion detection
systems), 379–380
monitoring methodologies,
226–229
overview of, 223–225
passive detection, 226
protocol analyzers and, 229
surveillance options, 176
inventories, in IT
documentation, 40
IP addresses
DHCP server
vulnerabilities, 355
DNS logs, 384–385
DNS poisoning attacks,
268–269
DNS server
vulnerabilities, 354

IP addresses *(continued)*
    internal network
        addressing, 235–237
    IP protocols and, 251
    NAT (Network Address
        Translation), 235
    smurf attacks and, 265–266
    spoofing attacks, 264–265
    TCP/IP hijacking attacks,
        266–267
    translating into domain
        names, 255–256
IP (Internet Protocol), 251
IPSec (IP Security)
    overview of, 126–127, 257
    as remote access
        protocol, 199
IPSs (intrusion prevention
    systems). See also intrusion
    detection and prevention,
    379–380
IR (infrared), WLAN
    technologies, 286
iris scanners, for biometric
    authentication, 205
ISAKMP (Internet Security
    Association and Key
    Management Protocol), 127
ISATAP (Intrasite Automatic
    Tunnel Addressing
    Protocol), 251
ISDN (Integrated Services
    Digital Network), 193–194
ISPs (Internet service
    providers), 76–77
IT documentation
    logs and inventories, 40
    overview of, 39
    system architecture, 39
IV (initialization vector), WEP
    IV attacks, 304

J

JavaScript, vulnerabilities
    related to, 345
job function, grouping users
    by, 161
job rotation, access control
    policies, 14, 164

K

Kerberos, 203–204
kernel rootkits, 319

keys, cryptographic
    centralized vs.
        decentralized key storage,
        139–141
    key escrows, 112, 142–143
    key history, 145–146
    multiple key pairs, 144–145
    overview of, 108
    recovery, 143–144
    storage and protection,
        141–142
keys (physical), termination
    policy and, 21
keystrokes, logging user
    events, 391

L

L2TP Access Concentrator
    (LAC), 198
L2TP (Layer 2 Tunneling
    Protocol), 198–199
L2TP Network Server (LNS), 199
LAC (L2TP Access
    Concentrator), 198
LANMAN (LAN Manager), 201
LANs (local area networks), 237
laptop computers, data
    encryption and, 364
Layer 2 Tunneling Protocol
    (L2TP), 198–199
LDAP injection attacks, 357
LDAP (Lightweight Directory
    Access Protocol)
    as authentication service,
        202–203
    single sign-on, 190
    vulnerablilities of, 356–357
    well known ports, 260, 405
LEAP (Lightweight Extensible
    Authentication Protocol), 298
least privilege, access control
    policies, 14, 165
legality, acceptable use policy
    governing, 15
length of passwords, policy
    governing, 170
levels of security, in access
    control, 160
library rootkits, 319
lighting systems, as access
    control, 176
Lightweight Directory Access
    Protocol. See LDAP

(Lightweight Directory Access
    Protocol)
Lightweight Extensible
    Authentication Protocol
    (LEAP), 298
likelihood
    measuring, 9–10
    in vulnerability and threat
        assessment, 402
LinkedIn, 43
LNS (L2TP Network Server), 199
load balancers, security features
    of, 218–219
local area networks (LANs), 237
location
    grouping users by physical
        location, 161–162
    planning facilities, 89
locks
    as access control, 177–178
    host consoles, 326
    screen locks protecting
        mobile devices, 336
    workstation, 42
logic bombs, 317
login/logout
    host consoles, 326
    limiting logon
        attempts, 168
    logging times and
        attempts, 390
    operating system security
        and, 325
    passwords policy and, 41
    user names for, 160
logs
    access logs, 179, 384
    in administration of secure
        network, 277
    antivirus logs, 386–387
    applications for, 387
    in collection of forensic
        data evidence, 53–54
    in data security, 26
    DNS logs, 384–385
    event logs, 390–391
    firewall logs, 385–386
    IT documentation, 40
    passive detection based
        on, 226
    performance logs, 383–384
    system logs, 382–383

loop protection,
detecting/preventing network
loops, 275
loss control, in incident
response, 51–52

M

M of N control, key recovery
and, 144
MAC (mandatory access
control), 166
MAC (Media Access Control)
ARP poisoning attacks
and, 269
DHCP server
vulnerabilities and, 355
MAC address-based
VLANs, 238
MAC address filtering, 295,
302–303
securing MAC
addresses, 274
macro viruses, 314
maintenance logs, IT
documentation, 40
malicious hackers, 401
malware
adware and spyware,
318–319
analyzing/differentiating
types of, 312–313
antimalware and content
security, 219–220
botnets, 320–321
file types targeted by
viruses, 315–316
logic bombs, 317
reports, 388
rootkits, 319–320
Trojan horse attacks,
316–317
virus types, 313–315
worms, 317–318
man-in-the-middle attacks, 267
man-traps, as access control,
178–179
management interface
security, 326
management, risk control by, 5
mandatory access control
(MAC), 166
mandatory vacations, as access
control policy, 14–15, 164

MD4 (Message Digest 4), 115
MD5 (Message Digest 5), 54, 115
.mdb files, viruses targeting, 315
Mean Time Between Failures
(MTBF), 73
Mean Time to Restore
(MTTR), 73
Media Access Control. See MAC
(Media Access Control)
media, backup
offsite storage of, 86–87
rotation and retention
of, 85
memory resident viruses, 314
message digital hashes
in protection of forensic
data evidence, 54
types of, 115
metamorphic viruses, 314–315
MIME (Multipurpose Internet
Mail Extensions), 123
MIMO (Multiple In Multiple
Out), 288
mirroring, RAID, 80
mitigation
access control
techniques, 175
dealing with risk, 12
risk assessment and, 6–7
risk management options, 5
mitigation and deterrent
techniques
access logs, 384
alarms and notifications
associated with logs, 389
antivirus logs, 386–387
auditing user access rights,
391–392
detection of
security-related
anomalies, 375
DNS logs, 384–385
event logs, 390–391
firewall logs, 385–386
handling occasions when
security equipment is
bypassed, 380–381
IDS, 379–380
network monitors, 379
overview of, 393
performance logs, 383–384
protocol analyzers, 377–378

reports and trends based
on logs, 387–389
review Q&A, 394–397
reviewing audit
information, 392
security logging
applications, 387
security posture, 374–375
storage and retention
policies for information
collected, 393
system and performance
monitors, 375–377
system baselines, 389–390
system logs, 382–383
use of independent
auditors, 392–393
mobile cameras, security issues
related to, 337
mobile devices
encryption of, 366
securing, 335–337
threats to, 312
mobile phones, 335–337
models, access control
DAC (discretionary access
control), 166
MAC (mandatory access
control), 166
overview of, 165–166
RBAC (role-based access
control), 166–167
rule-based access
control, 167
models, authentication
overview of, 188–189
types of, 189–190
modems, securing remote
communication, 239
modify permissions, controlling
access to files and
printers, 173
monitoring
access logs, 384
alarms and notifications
associated with, 389
antivirus logs, 386–387
applications for security
logging, 387
detection of
security-related
anomalies, 375

monitoring *(continued)*
in determining security
posture, 375
DNS logs, 384–385
firewall logs, 385–386
handling occasions when
security equipment is
bypassed, 380–381
IDS, 379–380
methodologies for network
security, 226–229
network monitors, 379
overview of, 382
performance logs, 383–384
protocol analyzers, 377–378
reports and trends based
on, 387–389
system and performance
monitors, 375–377
system logs, 382–383
motion detectors, for
surveillance, 177
move permissions, controlling
access to files and
printers, 173
MS-CHAP, 298
MTBF (Mean Time Between
Failures), 73
MTTR (Mean Time to
Restore), 73
Multiple In Multiple Out
(MIMO), 288
multiple key pairs, PKI,
144–145
Multipurpose Internet Mail
Extensions (MIME), 123
mutual authentication, 205

N

NAC (Network Access Control),
234–235
naming conventions, user
account policies, 168
narrowband, WLAN
technologies, 285
NAS (network-attached
storage), 83
NAT (Network Address
Translation)
firewalls utilizing, 216
network security
techniques, 235
natural disasters, 68, 401

NetBIOS (Network Basic
Input/Output System)
identifying commonly used
network ports, 260
NULL session attacks, 264
overview of, 257
netbooks, mobile device
security and, 335–337
netstat command, for viewing
ports, 259
Network Access Control (NAC),
234–235
Network Address Translation
(NAT)
firewalls utilizing, 216
network security
techniques, 235
network-attached storage
(NAS), 83
network attacks, 68
Network Basic Input/Output
System. See NetBIOS
(Network Basic Input/Output
System)
network cabling
documentation of recovery
plans, 70
shielding from electrical
interference, 94
types of, 95–96
network devices
configuring, 271–272
hardening, 275
setting up ACL rules for
network devices, 272–274
threats and risks to, 274–275
network interface cards (NICs)
cable modems and, 194
fault tolerance, 80
network intrusion prevention
systems/network intrusion
detection systems
(NIPS/NIDS), 225–226, 268
network mappers, in
vulnerability assessment, 403
network monitors
as component of intrusion
detection system, 224
overview of, 379
network security
acceptable use policy,
15–16
active detection, 225–226

administering. See
administration, of secure
networks
antispam applications,
220–221
cloud computing, 243–244
content filtering
applications, 221–222
designing, 229–230
DMZs (demilitarized
zones), 231–233
due care, due diligence, and
due process, 17
extranets, 233
firewalls, 214–216
internal network
addressing, 235–237
intranets, 233
intrusion detection and
prevention, 223–225
load balancers, 218–219
modems and, 239
monitoring methodologies,
226–229
NAC (Network Access
Control), 234–235
NAT (Network Address
Translation), 235
overview of, 15, 214
passive detection, 226
privacy policy, 17–19
protocol analyzers, 229
proxy servers, 219
remote access and,
238–239
review Q&A, 245–248
routers, 217
security zones, 230–231
service level agreement
policy, 19
subnetting, 237
switches, 218
telephony and, 241
URL filtering, 222–223
virtualization and, 242–243
VLANs (virtual LANs),
237–238
VoIP (Voice over IP),
241–242
VPNs (virtual private
networks), 240–241
web security gateways, 222

network security *(continued)*
  wireless networks. See
    WLANs (wireless LANs)
Network Time Protocol (NTP)
  identifying commonly used
    network ports, 260
  well known ports, 405
networks/networking
  detecting/preventing
    network loops, 275
  diagramming in recovery
    plans, 70
  disabling unused network
    services in risk
    mitigation, 7
  firewalls blocking incoming
    connections, 330
  high availability and high
    service levels required
    for, 73
  protecting wireless
    networks, 96
  protocol analyzers for
    analysis of network
    traffic, 377–378
  time and machine
    restrictions on access
    to, 169
NICs (network interface cards)
  cable modems and, 194
  fault tolerance, 80
NIPS/NIDS (network intrusion
  prevention systems/network
  intrusion detection systems),
  225–226, 268
Nmap utility, 403–404
NNTP, well known ports, 405
nondiscretionary access
  control, 166
nonrepudiation
  cryptography and, 106
  encryption providing, 108
  uses of PKI keys, 145
notifications
  associated with monitoring
    logs, 389
  as component of intrusion
    detection system, 224
  notification lists in
    recovery plans, 70
NTFS, 324
NTLM (NT LAN Manager), 201

NTP (Network Time Protocol)
  identifying commonly used
    network ports, 260
  well known ports, 405
NULL session attacks, 264

O
objectionable content, 327
OFDM (orthogonal
  frequency-division
  multiplexing), 286
offsite storage, of backup media,
  86–87
one-time pads, 120
online backups, 87–88
Open Vulnerability and
  Assessment Language
  (OVAL), 407–408
operating systems. See OSs
  (operating systems)
operational risk controls, 6
order of volatility, in collection
  of forensic evidence, 52–53
organizational policies
  human resources policies,
    20–22
  network security policies,
    15–19
  overview of, 13
  for risk reduction, 5
  security policies, 13–15
organizational security and
  compliance
  asset identification, 7
  data loss prevention, 25–27
  false negatives, 12–13
  false positives, 12
  human resources policies,
    20–22
  incident management and
    response, 23–24
  network security policies,
    15–19
  options for dealing with
    risk, 11–12
  overview of, 4
  review Q&A, 27–30
  risk analysis, 8–9
  risk assessment, 6–7
  risk controls, 5–6
  risk likelihood and impact
    analysis, 9–10

risk mitigation strategies, 22
risk-related concepts, 5
routine auditing, 24
security policies, 13–15
solutions and
  countermeasures, 10–11
user rights and permissions
  reviews, 24–25
orthogonal frequency-division
  multiplexing (OFDM), 286
OSs (operating systems)
  BIOS security, 323
  file system security,
    324–325
  hardening, 322
  installing/enabling only
    necessary services, 324
  server and workstation
    patch management, 323
  updates, 277, 322
  user account and password
    threats, 325
OVAL (Open Vulnerability and
  Assessment Language),
  407–408

P
P2P (peer-to-peer)
  best practices protecting
    risk related to, 43
  WLAN topologies, 289
packet filtering
  firewall services, 216
  network devices and, 272
Packet Internet Groper. See Ping
  (Packet Internet Groper)
packet sniffers
  attacking wireless
    networks, 303–304
  man-in-the-middle
    attacks, 267
  vulnerability of FTP to, 254
palm readers, for biometric
  authentication, 205
PAP (Password Authentication
  Protocol), 200
pass cards, termination policy
  regulating return of, 21
passive detection, intrusion
  detection and prevention,
  226, 335
passphrase, WPA, 297

Password Authentication
  Protocol (PAP), 200
password cracker programs,
  408–410
passwords
  aging, 170
  BIOS security and, 323
  data security, 26
  identification, 160
  logging changes to, 390
  operating system security
    and, 325
  password cracker
    programs, 408–410
  policies, 40–41, 170
  protecing PKI keys, 142
  protecting host
    management console, 326
  protecting mobile
    devices, 336
  recovery, 170
  securing access points, 294
  single-factor authentication
    and, 189
  single sign-on, 171
  weakness of, 274
  workstation protection
    policies, 42
patches
  application security
    and, 362
  firewalls warning of
    unpatched software, 331
  managing for servers and
    workstations, 323
  running latest, 275
  virus signature files, 329
PCI (Payment Card Industry)
  content filtering
    applications for, 221
  data protection
    regulations, 26
PDAs (personal digital
  assistants), 335–337
PEAP (Protected Extensible
  Authentication Protocol), 298
peer-to-peer (P2P)
  best practices protecting
    risk related to, 43
  WLAN topologies, 289
penetration testing
  characteristics of, 415–417

white box, black box, and
  gray box tests, 417–418
performance baselines. See also
  baselines, 376–377
performance logs. See also logs,
  383–384
performance monitors
  alarm thresholds, 377
  overview of, 375–377
permissions
  access control and, 158
  for accessing files and
    printers, 173–174
  file system security,
    324–325
  granting on need-to-know
    basis, 162
  implicit deny approach to,
    164–165
  RBAC (role-based access
    control), 166–167
  reviewing as risk mitigation
    strategy, 24–25
  transitive access and,
    274–275
permit/deny communication,
  ACL rules controlling, 272
persistent rootkits, 319
personal digital assistants
  (PDAs), 335–337
personal identification numbers
  (PINs), 160, 189
personal identification
  verification cards, 179
PGP (Pretty Good Privacy),
  122–123
pharming attacks, 48
phishing attacks, 45–46
phone systems. See also
  telephony
  securing remote
    communication, 241
  vishing attacks, 48–49
photoelectric detectors, for
  surveillance, 177
physical access
  barriers to, 175–176
  security policies
    controlling, 14
physical environment, site
  surveys for wireless
  networks, 287
physical vulnerabilities, 401

piconets, Bluetooth, 291
ping attacks, 262
ping of death, 262
Ping (Packet Internet Groper)
  network mappers
    utilizing, 403
  ping sweeps with, 258–259
  smurf attacks and, 265–266
  use of ICMP by, 252
PINs (personal identification
  numbers), 160, 189
PKI (Public Key Infrastructure)
  CAs (certificate
    authorities), 136
  centralized vs.
    decentralized key storage,
    139–141
  certificate life cycle,
    146–150
  digital certificates,
    135–136
  key escrows, 142–143
  key history, 145–146
  key recovery, 143–144
  key storage and protection,
    141–142
  multiple key pairs in,
    144–145
  overview of, 134–135
  review Q&A, 151–154
  trust models, 137–139
plain text, 106
Point-to-Point Protocol (PPP),
  197–198
Point-to-Point Tunneling
  Protocol (PPTP), 198
policies
  access control, 164–165
  change management, 23
  clean desk, 41
  data security and, 363
  documentation of, 32–33
  escalation of security
    incidents, 56
  in establishing security
    baseline, 321
  password, 170
  storage and retention of
    security-related
    information, 393
  user account, 167–169
policies, organizational

acceptable use policy, 15–16
due care, due diligence, and due process, 17
human resources policies, 20–22
network security policies, 15
overview of, 13
privacy policy, 17–19
for risk reduction, 5
security policies, 13–15
service level agreement policy, 19
polymorphic viruses, 314
pop-up blockers, 333
POP3 (Post Office Protocol)
identifying commonly used network ports, 259–260
vulnerabilities of e-mail servers, 357–358
port-based VLANs, 238
port scanners
detecting anomalous network behavior, 385–386
firewalls protecting against, 194
protecting against Trojan horses, 317
viewing open services with, 259–260
in vulnerability assessment, 404–406
port sweeps, 404
ports
controlling access using ACL rules, 272
corresponding to TCP/IP services, 405
DNS, 259–260
HTTP, 252
HTTPS and, 253
identifying commonly used network ports, 258–260
POP3, 259–260
securing, 274
for web surfing, 259
well known, 404
Post Office Protocol. See POP3 (Post Office Protocol)
power generators, maintaining clean and consistent power, 93–94

power supplies, fault tolerance and, 80
PPP (Point-to-Point Protocol), 197–198
PPTP (Point-to-Point Tunneling Protocol), 198
Pretty Good Privacy (PGP), 122–123
PRI (Primary Rate Interface), ISDN, 193
printers
controlling access to, 173–174
controlling access to print servers, 172–173
privacy
content filtering applications, 221
network security policies, 17–19
of web browsing data, 334
private documents, data classification, 36
private keys, 142
privileges. See also permissions
controlling access to software, 327
escalation of, 274–275, 347
by groups, 172
least privilege approach to access rights, 165
monitoring user access, 391–392
security roles and, 171
probability, information collected during risk analysis, 10
proof-of-concept exploits, 347–348
Protected Extensible Authentication Protocol (PEAP), 298
protocol analyzers
intercepting, recording, analyzing network traffic, 407
overview of, 377–378
role in network security, 229
protocol-based VLANs, 238
protocols. See also by individual type
ACL rules identifying, 272

remote access. See remote access protocols
tunneling. See tunneling protocols
wireless, 289–291
wireless encryption protocols, 121–124
proximity detectors, in surveillance, 176
proxy servers, 219
public documents, in data classification, 36
public key encryption, 111–112
Public Key Infrastructure. See PKI (Public Key Infrastructure)

Q
qualitative risk analysis, 8–9
quantitative risk analysis, 8–9
quantum cryptography, 120

R
RACE Integrity Primitives Evaluation Message Digest (RIPEMD), 116
RADIUS (Remote Authentication Dial-In User Service), 192, 202
RAID (Redundant Array of Independent Disks)
hard-drive redundancy, 79–80
hot swap devices, 79
levels, 80
overview of, 78
RAs (registration authorities), for digital certificates, 136
RBAC (role-based access control), 166–167
RC4 (Rivest Cipher), 119
read permissions, controlling access to files and printers, 173
recovery agents, 144
recovery, of PKI keys, 143–144
recovery planning, 65
Recovery Point Objective (RPO), 74
recovery team, 66
Recovery Time Objective (RTO), 73–74

redundancy. See also fault
tolerance; HA (high
availability)
    clustering technology, 75–76
    hard-drives, 79–80
    Internet lines, 76–77
    overview of, 72
    servers, 75
    sites, 77–78
    spare equipment, 74–75
Redundant Array of
    Independent Disks. See RAID
    (Redundant Array of
    Independent Disks)
registrars, of domain names, 270
registration authorities (RAs),
    for digital certificates, 136
reliability factors, for services
    and hardware, 73–74
remediation, in determining
    security posture, 375
remote access
    administering secure
        networks, 276
    cloud computing, 243–244
    management interface
        security and, 326
    modems and, 239
    overview of, 238–239
    telephony and, 241
    virtualization and, 242–243
    VoIP (Voice over IP),
        241–242
    VPNs (virtual private
        networks), 240–241
remote access applications
    overview of, 195
    SSH (Secure Shell) and, 196
    Telnet and, 195
    VPN (virtual private
        networks) and, 196–197
remote access authentication
    methods
    cable modems and, 194
    dial-up access and, 191–193
    DSL lines and, 195
    ISDN lines and, 193–194
    overview of, 191
remote access protocols
    overview of, 197
    PPP (Point-to-Point
        Protocol), 197–198

SLIP (Serial Line Internet
    Protocol), 197
    VPN protocols, 198–199
Remote Authentication Dial-In
    User Service (RADIUS),
    192, 202
remote wipe, protecting mobile
    devices, 336
removable media, encryption
    of, 366
replay attacks, 267–268
reports
    based on logs, 387–389
    baseline reporting, 412
    disclosure and, 56–57
reputation services, as antispam
    application, 221
resources
    access control, 159
    logging use of, 390
    organizing on
        need-to-know basis, 162
restoring, from backups, 86
retention
    of backup data, 83
    data retention policy, 38
    document storage policy, 37
    of security-related
        information, 393
retina scanners, for biometric
    authentication, 205
rights and privileges,
    monitoring user access,
    391–392
RIPEMD (RACE Integrity
    Primitives Evaluation Message
    Digest), 116
risk analysis
    in disaster recovery
        planning, 66–67
    information collected
        during risk analysis, 10
    overview of, 8–9
risk assessment
    asset identification phase, 7
    calculating impacts of
        threats, 402
    defined, 5
    overview of, 6–7
    risk analysis phase, 8–9
    risk likelihood and impact
        analysis phase, 9–10

solutions and
    countermeasures, 10–11
risk controls, 5–6
risk likelihood and impact
    analysis, 9–10
risk management
    options for dealing with
        risk, 11–12
    overview of, 5
risk mitigation
    change management, 23
    data loss prevention and,
        25–27
    incident management and
        response, 23–24
    overview of, 22
    routine auditing, 24
    user rights and permissions
        reviews, 24–25
risks, types of, 401
Rivest Cipher (RC4), 119
robot networks (botnets),
    320–321
rogue access points (evil twin),
    302–303
role-based access control
    (RBAC), 166–167
roles
    privileges and, 171–172
    RBAC (role-based access
        control), 166
rootkits, 319–320
routers
    ACL rules controlling, 273
    configuring, 271
    security features of, 217
RPO (Recovery Point
    Objective), 74
RSA encryption, 364
RSA SecurID token, 169
RTO (Recovery Time
    Objective), 73–74
rule-based access control, 167
rule-based monitoring, in
    intrusion detection system,
    228–229

S
S/MIME (Secure MIME),
    123–124
sabotage, as natural disaster, 68
sags, maintaining clean and
    consistent power, 93

salting, in password protection, 409

Sarbanes-Oxley Act (SOX), 26

SAs (security associations), IPSec, 127

SCP (Secure Copy), 255

.scr files, viruses targeting, 315

screen locks, protecting mobile devices, 336

screenshots, in collection of forensic data evidence, 54–55

Secure Copy (SCP), 255

Secure FTP (SFTP)
    overview of, 254–255
    preventing interception of FTP communications, 353

secure hash algorithm (SHA), 115–116

Secure MIME (S/MIME), 123–124

Secure Shell. See SSH (Secure Shell)

Secure Sockets Layer. See SSL (Secure Sockets Layer)

security applications. See applications, for host security

security associations (SAs), IPSec, 127

security controls
    identifying lack of, 415
    penetration testing and, 416

security modes, web browsers and, 332–333

security patches. See also patches, 362

security policies. See also policies
    access controls, 14–15
    overview of, 13
    physical access, 14

security posture, 374–375

security-related anomalies, detection of, 375

security templates, in establishing security baseline, 321

security training and incident response
    accessing policy documentation, 33
    awareness training, 34
    clean desk policy, 41

collecting and preserving evidence, 52–56

damage and loss control, 51–52

data and documentation policies, 35

data retention policy, 38

documenting standards and guidelines, 35–37

e-mail hoaxes, 49–50

escalation policy, 56

first responders, 51

forensics in incident response, 52

hardware disposal and data destruction policy, 38–39

importance of, 32–33

incident response procedures, 50

instant messaging policies, 42–43

IT documentation, 39–40

overview of, 31–32

P2P and, 43

password policy, 40–41

personally owned devices, policy covering use of, 41–42

pharming attacks, 48

phishing attacks, 45–46

reporting and disclosure, 56–57

review Q&A, 58–62

shoulder surfing attacks, 46–47

social engineering attacks, 44–45

social media and, 43–44

spam, 49

spim and, 48

tailgating attacks, 47–48

threat awareness, 34–35

vishing attacks, 48–49

whaling attacks, 46

workstation protection policies, 42

security violations, logging, 391

security zones
    DMZs (demilitarized zones), 231–233

extranets, 233

intranets, 233

overview of, 230–231

sensitivity, in categorization of resources, 159

separation of duties, as access control policy, 14, 163

Serial Line Internet Protocol (SLIP), 197

server vulnerabilities
    database servers, 356
    DHCP servers, 355–356
    DNS servers, 354–355
    e-mail servers, 357–358
    FTP servers, 353–354
    LDAP and directory services, 356–357
    overview of, 352–353

servers. See also host system security
    antivirus and antispyware software protecting, 328
    controlling access to, 326
    high availability and high service levels for Internet servers, 72
    patch management, 323
    redundancy planning, 75–76
    threats to, 312

service level agreement (SLA), 19

service levels, HA (high availability) and, 72–73

service packs, for updating operating systems, 322

Service Set Identifiers (SSIDs), 295, 302

services
    disabling unused services, 276
    installing/enabling only necessary, 324
    reliability factors for, 73–74

session hijacking, 348

SFTP (Secure FTP)
    overview of, 254–255
    preventing interception of FTP communications, 353

SHA (secure hash algorithm), 115–116

shadow password database, 410

shielded twisted-pair (STP) cabling, 95
shoulder surfing attacks, 46–47
signature-based monitoring, in intrusion detection system, 227
signature files, viruses, 329, 387
signature scanners, for biometric authentication, 206
Simple Mail Transfer Protocol. See SMTP (Simple Mail Transfer Protocol)
Simple Network Management Protocol. See SNMP (Simple Network Management Protocol)
single-factor authentication, 189
single loss expectancy (SLE), 9–10
single sign-on
  authentication model, 190
  to domain accounts, 171
site surveys, wireless network, 287–289
SLA (service level agreement), 19
SLE (single loss expectancy), 9–10
SLIP (Serial Line Internet Protocol), 197
smart cards, as access control, 179–180
smoke detectors, 97
SMTP (Simple Mail Transfer Protocol)
  identifying commonly used network ports, 260
  investigating system for services that are unneeded, 324
  vulnerabilities of e-mail servers, 358
  well known ports, 405
smurf attacks, 265–266
SNMP (Simple Network Management Protocol)
  disabling unused services, 276
  identifying commonly used network ports, 260
  overview of, 256–257
  well known ports, 405
social engineering attacks
  e-mail hoaxes, 49–50

overview of, 44–45
pharming attacks, 48
phishing attacks, 45–46
shoulder surfing attacks, 46–47
spam, 49
spim and, 48
tailgating attacks, 47–48
vishing attacks, 48–49
whaling attacks, 46
social media, 43–44
software
  controlling access to, 327
  for site survey for wireless network, 289
software firewalls, 330–331
software RAID, 79–80
son backup method, 85
sound detectors, for surveillance, 177
source address, ACL rules controlling, 272
SOX (Sarbanes-Oxley Act), 26
spam
  antispam applications, 220–221
  antispam software, 329–330
  overview of, 49
  reports, 388
spear phishing, 45
spikes, maintaining clean and consistent power, 93
spim, 48
spoofing attacks
  NAT in prevention of, 235
  overview of, 264–265
  security features of routers protecting against, 217
spread-spectrum, WLAN technologies, 285
spyware, host system security and, 318–319
SQL injection attacks, 356
SSH (Secure Shell)
  identifying commonly used network ports, 260
  man-in-the-middle attacks and, 267
  overview of, 127, 253–254
  as remote access application, 196

securing remote access and, 276
  well known ports, 405
SSIDs (Service Set Identifiers), 295, 302
SSL (Secure Sockets Layer)
  FTPS (FTP Secure) and, 255
  overview of, 124–125
  protecting directory services, 357
  securing access points, 294
standards, documenting, 35–37
stateful inspection, firewall services, 216
stealth scanning, 405
stealth viruses, 315
steganography, 113
storage
  of backup media, 86–87
  of documents, 37
  of PKI keys, 141–142
  policies for security-related information, 393
STP (shielded twisted-pair) cabling, 95
stream ciphers, 111
striping, RAID, 80
subnetting, network security and, 237
substitution, types of cipher encryption, 109
succession planning, for key employees, 69
suppliers, SLA (service level agreement), 19
surges, maintaining clean and consistent power, 93
switches
  configuring, 271–272
  security features of, 218
symmetric key encryption
  applying, 117–119
  overview of, 110–111
  in PKI, 135
SYN scanning, 405
SYN (synchronous) flood attacks, 262–263
syslog, 387
system
  backing up
    configuration, 76
  baselines, 389–390

documenting
architecture, 39
documenting
configuration, 70
logs, 382–383, 390
monitors, 375–377
reports, 388
security, 312
system auditing
event logs and, 390–391
overview of, 389
reviewing information
gathered by, 392
storage and retention
policies for information
collected, 393
system baselines, 389–390
use of independent
auditors, 392–393
user access rights, 391–392
system images, in collection of
forensic data evidence, 53

T
tablets, mobile device security,
335–337
TACAS (Terminal Access
Controller Access Control
System), 192, 203
tailgating attacks, 47–48
TCP/IP (Transmission Control
Protocol/Internet Protocol)
hijacking attacks, 266–267
ICMP and, 252
identifying commonly used
network ports, 259–260
overview of, 250–251
ports corresponding to
TCP/IP services, 405
SYN flood attacks, 262–263
TCP scanning, 405
TCP (Transmission Control
Protocol), 250–251, 268
technical risk controls, 6
Telecom, high availability and
high service levels required
for, 73
telephony, securing remote
communication, 241
Telnet
identifying commonly used
network ports, 260

overview of, 253
as remote access
application, 195
securing remote access
and, 276
well known ports, 405
temperature
controlling facility
environment, 91
monitoring, 92–93
Temporal Key Integrity Protocol
(TKIP), 296
Teredo, 251
Terminal Access Controller
Access Control System
(TACAS), 192, 203
termination, HR (human
resources) policies, 21–22
tests
black box tests, 417–418
gray box tests, 418
passive testing of security
controls, 415
penetration testing vs.
vulnerability scanning,
414–417
recovery plans, 71
white box tests, 417
TFTP (Trivial File Transfer
Protocol), 254–255
theft, protecting mobile devices
from, 336
third-party (single authority)
trust, 137–138
threats. See also vulnerability
and threat assessment
awareness training, 34–35
defined, 401
to network devices,
274–275
penetration testing
verifying existence of, 416
profiling during risk
analysis, 10
training users in threat
awareness, 34–35
three-factor authentication, 189
time restrictions, on network
access, 169
time zones, time offsets in
collection of forensic data
evidence, 54

TKIP (Temporal Key Integrity
Protocol), 296
TLS (Transport Layer Security)
EAP extended by, 298
FTPS (FTP Secure) and, 255
overview of, 124–125
PEAP authentication
using, 298
protecting directory
services, 357
tokens
as authentication
factor, 189
controlling access via, 169
TPM (trusted platform
module), 142, 364
Traceroute, use of ICMP by, 252
training, awareness training, 34
transference, dealing with risk,
5, 11
transitive access
best practices in
application security,
360–361
overview of, 274–275
Transmission Control
Protocol/Internet Protocol.
See TCP/IP (Transmission
Control Protocol/Internet
Protocol)
Transmission Control Protocol
(TCP), 250–251, 268
Transport Layer Security. See
TLS (Transport Layer
Security)
transport mode security, in
IPSec, 126
transposition, types of cipher
encryption, 110
trend analysis, based on logs,
387–389
Trivial File Transfer Protocol
(TFTP), 254–255
Trojan horses
back doors and, 263
firewall logs exposing, 386
firewalls protecting against,
331
malicious add-ons, 349
overview of, 316–317
trust models
hierarchical model,
138–139

trust models *(continued)*
in MAC (mandatory access control), 166
third-party (single authority) trust, 137–138
web of trust, 137
trusted platform module (TPM), 142, 364
trusted sites, web browsers and, 332–333
tunnel mode security, in IPSec, 126
tunneling protocols
encrypting communication between networks, 240–241
remote access protocols, 198–199
wireless access and, 298–299
twisted-pair cabling, 95
Twitter, 43
two-factor authentication, 189
Twofish, asymmetric encryption algorithm, 118

U

UDP scanning, 406
UDP (User Datagram Protocol), 251
Uniform Resource Locators. See URLs (Uniform Resource Locators)
uninterruptible power supply (UPS)
fault tolerance, 80
maintaining clean and consistent power, 93
unshielded twisted-pair (UTP) cabling, 95
updates
firewalls warning of outdated antivirus files, 331
firmware, 277
operating systems, 277, 322
running latest patches, 275
UPS (uninterruptible power supply)
fault tolerance, 80
maintaining clean and consistent power, 93

URLs (Uniform Resource Locators)
block lists for spam prevention, 220
directory traversal attacks and, 352
HTTP and HTTPS and, 252
URL filtering for network security, 222–223
USB devices
storing PKI keys, 142
using USB keys as access token, 169
user accounts
logging changes to, 390
operating system security and, 325
policies, 167–169
securing default accounts, 274
User Datagram Protocol (UDP), 251
user-level events, logging, 390
user names
securing access points, 294
single-factor authentication and, 189
users
access control, 159
auditing access rights, 391–392
authentication. See authentication
awareness training, 34–35
educating in prevention of social engineering attacks, 32
identification, 160
reviewing rights as risk mitigation strategy, 24–25
rights and privileges, 171
user groups in access control, 160–162
UTP (unshielded twisted-pair) cabling, 95

V

vacations, mandatory vacations as access control policy, 14–15, 164
.vbs files, viruses targeting, 315

ventilation, controlling facility environment, 92
video
as access control, 176–177
in collection of forensic data evidence, 55
fire detection/prevention, 97
view permissions, controlling access to files and printers, 173
virtual LANs (VLANs)
network security, 237–238
subnetting, 237
virtual private networks. See VPNs (virtual private networks)
virtualization
risk analysis and, 8
securing remote communication, 242–243
virus signature files, 329
viruses
antivirus logs, 386–387
antivirus reports, 388
antivirus software, 328–329
as disaster, 68
file types targeted by, 315–316
logic bombs distributed via, 317
overview of, 313
personally owned devices, policy covering use of, 42
types of, 313–315
vishing attacks, 48–49
VLANs (virtual LANs)
network security, 237–238
subnetting, 237
voice encryption, protecting mobile devices, 337
Voice over IP (VoIP)
securing remote communication, 241–242
vishing attacks, 48–49
voice scanners, for biometric authentication, 205
VoIP (Voice over IP)
securing remote communication, 241–242
vishing attacks, 48–49
VPNs (virtual private networks)
encrypting communication between networks, 240–241

as remote access
application, 196–197
remote access protocols,
198–199
wireless access and,
298–299
vulnerabilities
Bluetooth, 301
defined, 401
DNS servers, 268–269
identifying, 415
penetration testing
exploiting, 416
privilege escalation due
to, 275
vulnerabilities, web application
ActiveX, 346
buffer overflows, 346–347
CGI scripts, 349–350
command injection,
351–352
cookies and session
hijacking, 348
directory traversal, 352
header manipulation, 351
HTML attachments,
348–349
JavaScript, 345
malicious add-ons, 349
overview of, 345
privilege escalation, 347
types of, 344–345
web application
vulnerabilities, 345
XML injection, 351
XSRF (cross-site request
forgery), 350
XSS (cross-site
scripting), 350
zero-day attacks, 352
vulnerability and threat
assessment
application code
assessment, 412–414
black box tests, 417–418
gray box tests, 418
honeypots and honeynets,
410–412
network mappers, 403
OVAL (Open Vulnerability
and Assessment
Language), 407–408

overview of, 400–402
password cracker
programs, 408–410
penetration testing vs.
vulnerability scanning,
414–417
port scanners, 404–406
protocol analyzers, 407
review Q&A, 419–422
tools for, 402–403
vulnerability scanners,
406–407
white box tests, 417
vulnerability scanners
characteristics of, 415
overview of, 406–407
white box, black box, and
gray box tests, 417–418

W
WANs (wide area networks),
196
WAP (Wireless Access
Protocol), 290–291
war chalking attacks, 303
war driving attacks, 302
warm sites, site redundancy,
77–78
warm swap, fault tolerance
and, 79
Web, acceptable use policy
governing use of, 16
web application vulnerabilities
ActiveX, 346
buffer overflows, 346–347
CGI scripts, 349–350
command injection,
351–352
cookies and session
hijacking, 348
directory traversal, 352
header manipulation, 351
HTML attachments,
348–349
JavaScript, 345
malicious add-ons, 349
overview of, 345
privilege escalation, 347
types of, 344–345
web application
vulnerabilities, 345
XML injection, 351

XSRF (cross-site request
forgery), 350
XSS (cross-site
scripting), 350
zero-day attacks, 352
web browsers
ActiveX vulnerabilities, 346
buffer overflows,
346–347
cookies, 333–334
firewalls securing, 331
HTML attachments,
348–349
JavaScript
vulnerabilities, 345
malicious add-ons, 349
pop-up blockers, 333
privacy of web browsing
data, 334
proxy servers for, 219
security modes and trusted
sites, 332–333
web connections, securing with
HTTPS, 326
web of trust model, 137
web security gateways, 222
web servers
buffer overflows,
346–347
web application
vulnerabilities, 345
web sites
controlling access to
objectionable sites, 327
redundancy planning,
77–78
trusted sites, 332–333
WEP (Wireless Encryption
Protocol)
applying wireless
encryption protocols, 121
EAP used by, 297–298
LEAP authentication
and, 298
securing WLANs, 296
WEP IV attacks, 304
whaling attacks, 46
white box tests, 417
whole disk encryption, 365
Wi-Fi Protected Access. See
WPA (Wi-Fi Protected Access)
wide area networks (WANs), 196

Wireless Access Protocol (WAP), 290–291
wireless cells, 96
wireless devices, mobile device security, 335–337
Wireless Encryption Protocol. See WEP (Wireless Encryption Protocol)
wireless encryption protocols, 121–124
Wireless Markup Language (WML), 290–291
Wireless Transaction Layer Security (WTLS), 291
WLANs (wireless LANs), 96
　access points, 286
　Bluetooth, 291–293
　Bluetooth vulnerabilities, 301
　data emanation attacks, 300–301
　EAP (Extensible Authentication Protocol), 297–298
　LEAP (Lightweight Extensible Authentication Protocol), 298
　MAC address filtering, 295
　overview of, 284
　packet sniffing and eavesdropping attacks, 303–304
　PEAP (Protected Extensible Authentication Protocol), 298
　personal firewalls, 300
　review Q&A, 305–308
　rogue access points (evil twin), 302–303
　secure implementation of, 284–285
　securing access points, 294
　site surveys, 287–289
　SSIDs (Service Set Identifiers), 295
　technologies, 285–286
　topologies, 289
　VPN wireless access, 298–299
　WAP (Wireless Access Protocol), 290–291
　war chalking attacks, 303
　war driving attacks, 302
　WEP IV attacks, 304
　WEP security, 296
　wireless authentication protocols, 297
　wireless protocols, 289–290
　WPA security, 296–297
WML (Wireless Markup Language), 290–291
work area, termination policy and, 21
workstations (desktops)
　antivirus and antispyware software protecting, 328
　patch management, 323
　protection policies, 42
　setting machines restrictions on network access, 169
worms
　logic bombs distributed via, 317
　overview of, 317–318

WPA (Wi-Fi Protected Access)
　applying wireless encryption protocols, 121–122
　EAP used by, 297–298
　securing WLANs, 296–297
　version 2 (WPA2), 297
write permission, controlling access to files and printers, 173
WTLS (Wireless Transaction Layer Security), 291

X

.xls/.xlsx files, viruses targeting, 315
Xmas attacks, 268
XML (Extensible Markup Language), 407–408
XML injection, 351
XSRF (cross-site request forgery), 350
XSS (cross-site scripting), 222, 350

Z

zero-day attacks
　defined, 228
　training users in threat awareness, 35
　web application vulnerabilities, 352
.zip files, viruses targeting, 315
zombie computers, 320

The Best in Security Certification Prep

Dedication

This book is dedicated to all my family and friends, who have always given me their tremendous support throughout my writing career.

—*T.J. Samuelle*

Acknowledgments

First, I want to thank everyone at McGraw-Hill Professional, especially: Meghan Riley, Stephanie Evans, Christopher Crayton, Rachel Gunn, and of course Mike Meyers. And a big thanks to all the people in the graphics and production departments!

I would also like to thank my good friends and colleagues: Joe Piotrowski, Steve Hutson, Jorge Alves, Sonia Kang, Charlie Carpenter, Jean Charles Dupuis, Michael Yousef, Yngwie Malmsteen, and N.P.K.